P9-AOR-558

ELA

SIGNS
& SYMBOLS

SIGNS
& SYMBOLS

LONDON, NEW YORK,
MUNICH, MELBOURNE, AND DELHI

Project Editor Kathryn Wilkinson
Senior Art Editor Vicky Short
Editors Kim Dennis-Bryan,
Nicola Hodgson, Neil Lockley
US Editor Chuck Wills
Designer Tim Lane
Jacket Designer Silke Spingies

Editoral Consultant Miranda Bruce-Mitford
Consultant Philip Wilkinson
Contributors Ian Harrison, James Harrison,
Sally Regan, Anna Southgate, Amber Tokeley
Illustrator Debajyoti Dutta

Picture Researchers Megan Jones,
Roland Smithies, Sarah Smithies
Production Editors Maria Elia,
Sharon McGoldrick
Production Controller Louise Minihane

Managing Editor Julie Oughton
Managing Art Editor Christine Keilty
Art Director Bryn Walls
Publisher Jonathan Metcalf

First American Edition, 2008

Published in the United States by
DK Publishing
375 Hudson Street
New York, New York 10014

08 09 10 11   10 9 8 7 6 5 4 3 2 1
SD280—06/08

Copyright © 2008 Dorling Kindersley Limited
All rights reserved.

Without limiting the rights under copyright reserved above,
no part of this publication may be reproduced, stored in or introduced
into a retrieval system, or transmitted, in any form, or by any means
(electronic, mechanical, photocopying, recording, or otherwise),
without the prior written permission of both the copyright owner
and the above publisher of this book.

Published in Great Britain by Dorling Kindersley Limited.

A catalog record for this book is available from the Library of Congress.

ISBN: 978-0-7566-3393-6

DK books are available at special discounts when purchased in bulk
for sales promotions, premiums, fund-raising, or educational use.
For details, contact
DK Publishing Special Markets, 375 Hudson Street, New York, New
York 10014 or SpecialSales@dk.com.

Printed and bound in China by Leo Paper Products Ltd.

CONTENTS

INTRODUCTION

One of our distinguishing features as *Homo sapiens* is our enquiring mind. We have always questioned things, not least our existence on Earth: why we are here, where we come from, what happens after death, and what is the meaning behind the natural phenomena around us. Over thousands of years we have created a framework of beliefs that allows us, to some extent, to answer these ancient questions.

DEFINITIONS AND ANALYSIS

As part of this framework of beliefs, we have developed an extensive vocabulary of signs and symbols that remind us of our unity with the cosmos. Both signs and symbols are widely recognized, but the difference between the two is sometimes unclear.

A sign is straightforward in its function: it may be a constituent part of a written or a visual language, a visual vocabulary of warnings about the road ahead, or a dramatic statement about a company's product. Signs give us a simple message that is of immediate momentary relevance.

A symbol, on the other hand, is a visual image or sign representing an idea—a deeper indicator of a universal truth. Fire, for example, symbolizes both the Sun and the masculine life-force that is all around us, while a Spring flower represents rebirth and new life. When viewed in the light of symbols, life becomes enriched and meaningful.

From earliest times, symbols have related to the cosmos, fertility, death, and renewal, but the advent of psychoanalytical theory has

> SIGNS GIVE US A SIMPLE MESSAGE THAT
> IS OF IMMEDIATE MOMENTARY RELEVANCE.
> A SYMBOL... IS A VISUAL IMAGE OR SIGN
> REPRESENTING AN IDEA

caused ideas and objects to be examined in the light of the psyche and psychological needs. A dark shadow, for instance, can be seen as symbolic of inner insecurities. Many fairy stories, when analyzed, relate to the process of growing up, encountering obstacles, and emerging as adults; for example *Little Red Riding Hood*. For the most part, however, the ancient and archetypal symbols relate to the Universe and our relationship with the cosmos.

Some symbols, such as the circle and the bird in flight, are universally recognized. The first symbolizes, among other things, birth, rebirth, and the turning of the seasons, while the bird can represent the soul's ascent to

Heaven. Fabulous beasts, too, have appeared in art for millennia. These symbolize the joint qualities of the creatures they represent; a satyr, for example, is part-goat, part-man, indicating a human's higher and lower self.

MIGRATION OF SYMBOLS

The fact that some symbols appear in widely scattered parts of the world gives rise to debate on their origin. Did they occur spontaneously as a natural part of human's unconscious urgings, or were they the result of a transfusion of ideas from one country to another?

We are increasingly aware of the amount of travel that took place in the ancient world.

Trade routes criss-cross the globe and religious ideas, art styles, and even artists themselves traveled with the traders. That is how Islam reached Southeast Asia, Buddhism extended to Japan, and Portuguese is spoken in the heart of South America. As goods and ideas were exchanged, so were symbols, which gained significance far from their place of origin.

The dragon, a Chinese creation, is one such symbol. In China it represents the glory of both the Emperor and the Sun, but in European Christian art its symbolism is negative, representing humankind's baser self.

The image of the bird battling the serpent is found from New Guinea to the Americas and symbolizes the eternal struggle of the sky, Earth, and waters. Finally, the *tao t'ieh*, or highly stylized face that appears on the bronze vessels of Ancient China, re-emerges in the gargoyles of European cathedrals and in the motifs of cultures around the Pacific Rim.

THE G⊕DDESS

A universal symbol that probably developed in many places simultaneously is that of the goddess. Often depicted with a large belly and breasts, she represents fertility and abundance, and her image appears in prehistoric art from Malta to the Russian Steppes. She represents birth and, as the Earth Mother, renewal. Sometimes shown as a simple triangle, symbolic of female genitalia, the goddess is also depicted as a circle, representing the continuous cycle of birth and rebirth.

Due to the passage of time and the development of Judaism, Christianity, and Islam the myth of the archetypal goddess has largely vanished from human consciousness; however, some still recognize her symbols, and the worship of the Virgin Mary remains a partial link with these beliefs. As people have become increasingly disengaged from the natural world, so the all-producing and all-nurturing goddess

A UNIVERSAL SYMBOL THAT
PROBABLY DEVELOPED
IN MANY PLACES
SIMULTANEOUSLY IS
THAT OF THE GODDESS

ONCE WE SEE OBJECTS AS REPRESENTING
TRUTHS OR DEEPER ISSUES, WE BEGIN TO
DEVELOP AN AWARENESS OF THE DUAL
NATURE OF EXISTENCE

has been replaced by creator gods, or by a transcendent god who appears detached from the creative process. Male gods, unlike the Mother Goddess, control nature.

SYMBOLS IN DAILY LIFE

The use and recognition of symbols enriches our lives. Once we see objects as representing truths or deeper issues, we begin to develop a realization of the dual nature of existence—the inner and outer life—all around us. A simple ladder, for example, serves both as a tool and a reminder of the spiritual climb toward self-awareness or a higher truth; a bowl can represent the receptive feminine principle

and creation; a lily rising from the mud can be a reminder of purity of spirit; while a lamp may signify the light of truth. Seeing objects in this symbolic way allows us to live more "harmoniously" by increasing our awareness, not only of day-to-day living but also of the universal truths of existence.

SYMBOLS IN ART, LITERATURE, AND DREAMS

When used in art, symbolism serves as a visual language for interpreting a scene; however, symbols once routinely used in Renaissance art are no longer widely recognized, making it harder to understand the hidden meaning of

...DREAM SYMBOLISM IS INTERPRETED AS REFLECTING THE WORKINGS OF THE UNCONSCIOUS MIND

a painting. In Christian art, for example, birds were a well known attribute of St. Francis, as was the wheel for St. Catherine. Early Buddhist art depicted the Buddha in aniconic form: his body was not shown, but his presence was symbolized by a throne or footprint.

More generally, the portrayal of water in art might symbolize the unconscious mind or the Primordial waters, while Classical goddesses often represent specific virtues such as wisdom. In more modern art, objects included do not necessarily mean anything to the viewer but have deep resonance for the artist, such as a connection with childhood. Similarly, in the Australian Aboriginal Dreaming, a person's life

and surroundings make up his or her own unique "thumbprint," often painted in the sand.

Symbolism occurs in some famous literary works. In *The Pilgrim's Progress*, a Christian allegory, Pilgrim represents everyman, striving to attain union with God. In C. S. Lewis's *Narnia* stories, Christian allegory also appears in the form of Aslan the lion, who represents Christ.

The symbolic nature of dreams has long been recognized. Being chased or falling are commonly interpreted as symbolic of an individual's fears of growing up and facing the responsibilities of adult life. However, it is not just in psychoanalysis that dream symbolism is interpreted as reflecting the

workings of the unconscious mind: many societies also recognize its importance. The Semai of Malaysia, for example, believed in the importance of dream symbolism and trained themselves to confront symbolic fears while dreaming, so that they could then resolve the underlying fears in their waking life.

SYMBOLS TODAY

While much symbolism has remained unchanged for millennia, a new form has developed. Today's culture heroes, such as Superman and Spider-man, are similar to the heroes in ancient creation myths who performed some heroic deed, such as stealing fire for humankind or recreating the world after a flood. However, other modern culture heroes include celebrities, who appeal to us because of their looks, because they are universally admired, or because their luxurious lifestyle represents an ideal to which many people aspire. This attraction is presumably a response to the deep seated insecurities that we face today.

Other symbols are doom-laden: for example, the mushroom cloud over Hiroshima that marked the advent of the atomic bomb, or the collapse of the Twin Towers of New York's World Trade Center, both of which represent our worst fears of annihilation.

A FRESH PERSPECTIVE

Wherever we live, we are surrounded by symbols—if we choose to see them. We can go through life ignorant of this rich imagery, or we can open our eyes to the deeper truths inherent in much that surrounds us. For those interested in exploring the philosophical and the metaphysical, a world filled with symbols is infinitely rich and rewarding, leading us to a greater understanding of ourselves and bringing a fresh perspective to our lives.

THE
COSMOS

By observing the movement of the Sun, the Moon, stars, and planets, and by noticing the changing seasons, humans have gradually developed a view of the natural rhythm of the Universe. Over milennia, we have constructed a cosmology that explained our observations and helped us fit into the natural order; we also assigned control of nature's forces to gods whom we worshiped.

This led to a widespread belief that in order to survive all the horrors that the gods could unleash, humans and deities needed to cooperate with one another. So, people made sacrifices and offerings to invoke cosmic harmony—gentle rain for the crops and fair winds for sailors—while natural disasters, such as devastating droughts, earthquakes, or floods, were invariably blamed on divine retribution.

As a result, cosmic symbolism is closely bound with religion. The Sun, for example, is a universal cosmic symbol for divine power, while Buddhists regard fire as the wisdom that burns away all ignorance. To Christians and Hindus water is often symbolic of purification, and to all the great world religions the heavens are home to the divine.

Indeed, the sky and everything in it, from the Moon and stars to thunder and lightning, is symbolically associated with the divine world. Mountains, too, have sacred status because of their proximity to the heavens. They each had their gods, goddesses, and supernatural representatives, which varied according to culture.

Creation myths and myths concerning a global flood are common to all cultures and make use of cosmic symbolism as well as themes of divine retribution in order to explain the mysteries of the Universe. Such

TO SURVIVE ALL THE HORRORS THAT THE GODS COULD UNLEASH, HUMANS AND DEITIES NEEDED TO COOPERATE WITH ONE ANOTHER

symbols were important to early societies because they helped people to live in a more harmonious way, and also to understand and strive toward their divine enlightenment.

Early science tried to establish symbolic links with the four main constituents of the cosmos, namely earth, fire, water, and air. Air and fire were regarded as symbolically masculine and active, while earth and water were feminine and passive; achieving a balance between the elements was seen as the foundation for cosmic harmony.

Signs and symbols have played a vital role in broadening our scientific understanding of the world in which we live: astronomy and astrology, for example, evolved from ancient times when people used cosmic symbolism to explain why planets moved across the sky, or why stars formed constellations. Seasonal and cosmic symbolism, too, are often intertwined, as measurements of time have always been based on the daily and seasonal movements of the Sun and the Moon.

Despite the many discoveries of modern science, cosmic symbolism remains relevant to many people throughout the world and continues to color our language. Celebrities are "stars"; many national flags bear cosmic symbols, such as the Sun and the Moon, indicating divine rule and power; precious stones, particularly birthstones, are still imbued with symbolic meaning; and astrology remains as popular as ever. Even today, we still try to find meaning in our world through signs and symbols.

THE SUN

Most cultures have at some time worshiped the Sun as the supreme cosmic power—the life-force that enables all things to thrive and grow. As the source of heat, the Sun symbolizes vitality, passion, and youth. As the source of light, it represents enlightenment. It is also an emblem of royalty and empire. In some traditions the Sun is the Universal Father. Its rising and setting symbolizes birth, death, and resurrection.

CIRCLING THE EARTH

The winter and summer solstices mark the shortest and longest days of the year and have inspired myths and festivals worldwide. The winter solstice symbolizes the victory of light over darkness, or the end of one cycle and the beginning of a new cycle of light and growth.

The summer solstice celebrates the Earth at its abundant peak, although it also marks the Sun's waning power; druids welcomed the summer solstice at dawn. Both solstices are marked with fire, representing the Sun's warmth and also fertility.

▲ Sun mask
This fearsome Sun mask represents the Sun's authority over the four compass points (north, south, east, and west) and was used ceremonially. It originates from the Bella Coola or Nuxalk tribe of British Columbia.

◄ The dawn
Dawn is a symbol of hope, joy, and youth. It represents birth, new beginnings, and freshness. In Christianity it is a symbol of resurrection. Often it is used to symbolize the dawn of the world or humankind, and is therefore also associated with many creation myths.

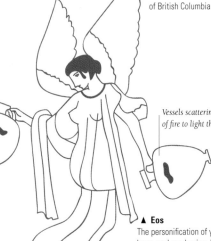

Vessels scattering sparks of fire to light the dawn

◄ Stonehenge solstice
Britain's most potent symbol of the summer solstice, Stonehenge in Wiltshire, has been a focus for pagan celebration for thousands of years. People gather there to greet the dawn as it rises over the Heel Stone on midsummer's day.

▲ Eos
The personification of youth, hope, and awakening, Eos, goddess of the dawn, was worshiped in Ancient Greece. Her fingers symbolized the pastel fingers of dawn stealing across the sky, and she was adorned with morning dew.

GODS AND LEGENDS

Much symbolism is associated with the Sun in cultures around the world. Usually personified as masculine, it was regarded as female in certain cultures, including Japan and some American Indian tribes. The most elaborate Sun cults were those of Egypt, Central America, and Peru. The Sun is seen as a benign, fertilizing force, as well as a fiery destroyer.

▲ Phaeton
In Greek mythology the journey of the Sun across the sky is represented as a chariot driven by the Sun god, Helios, traveling across the heavens. His son, Phaeton, drove the chariot recklessly and was only stopped when Helios threw a lightning bolt, killing Phaeton.

▲ Phoenix
A universal symbol of death, rebirth, and the Sun, the mythological phoenix is usually portrayed as an eagle-like bird rising from the flames.

► Apollo
The Greek god Apollo brought life-giving light to Earth. Portrayed as vigorously youthful and golden-haired, he was associated with Helios, the god who drove the Sun's chariot across the sky.

Dung ball

► Surya
A Vedic sun god, Surya, represents immortality, the flames of death and rebirth (sunset and sunrise); he crosses the heavens daily in a chariot drawn by seven fiery horses.

▲ Rahu
The Hindu demon, Rahu, had no body and was believed to swallow the Sun, causing eclipses. It would reappear again, as the demon had no body to contain it. A similar story is known in Chinese mythology.

▲ Icarus
In Greek mythology Daedalus made artificial wings for his son, Icarus. Despite his father's warning, Icarus flew too near the Sun, and his wings melted. Symbolically, his pride and lack of respect for the gods resulted in his downfall.

▲ Khepri
The Ancient Egyptian god of the rising Sun, Khepri, was associated with the scarab beetle, which rolls its balls of dung, symbolizing the Sun's journey across the sky. It is associated with new life and is a lucky charm.

POWER AND THE SUN

The Sun has been portrayed as the symbolic center of the cosmos. This most brilliant of the celestial bodies is a symbol of royalty and imperial splendor. The Chinese regard the Sun as an imperial Yang symbol. The Japanese use it as a national emblem, and believed their emperors were directly descended from the Sun goddess, Amaterasu.

▼ Sun King
Louis XIV of France claimed the solar symbol as his emblem, and became known as the Sun King. He was famous for the splendor of his lifestyle.

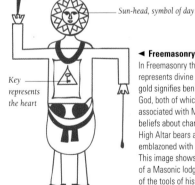

Compasses

Sun-head, symbol of day

Key represents the heart

◄ Freemasonry
In Freemasonry the Sun represents divine love, while gold signifies benificence of God, both of which are associated with Masonic beliefs about charity. The High Altar bears a red cloth emblazoned with solar symbols. This image shows a member of a Masonic lodge composed of the tools of his trade and is laden with symbolism, including the Sun-head.

▲ Japanese flag
The Sun has been used as a symbol of power on several flags. Japan's flag bears a red disc representing the rising Sun.

SEE ALSO
Gold pp.44–45
Egyptian deities pp.138–39
Greek & Roman deities pp.140–41
Hinduism pp.158–63
Taoism & Shinto pp.170–71
Christianity pp.176–79
Freemasonry pp.260–61
Colors pp.280–83
Flags pp.324–29

THE MOON

The mysterious Moon has always captured the human imagination. Its luminous presence in the night sky made it a symbol of hope and enlightenment. Like the Sun, it is often associated with birth, death, and resurrection, but it also controls the waters and is a fertility symbol. Presiding over dreams, the Moon is linked with bemusement; its dark side relates to the occult. Its feminine qualities bind it to the Mother Goddess.

▲ The Moon
The shadows created by craters on the surface of the Moon have fascinated people throughout history and have been the inspiration for myths and stories around the world.

LUNAR INFLUENCE

The Moon's cyclical journey through the heavens and its constantly evolving form provided early societies with a powerful symbol for the cycle of human life. From crescent to full Moon, its forms were each attributed a special significance, as were lunar eclipses. In addition to influencing the tides, weather, and life in general, the Moon was credited with ruling over human destiny.

▲ Lunar eclipse
Worldwide, cultures have developed myths about eclipses. Many believe they are omens of natural disasters or a ruler's death. Certain Asian cultures thought eclipses were caused by a demon or dragon swallowing the Moon.

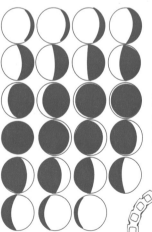

◄ Waxing and waning
The cyclical waxing and waning of the Moon is symbolic of birth, life, death, and rebirth. The crescent, waxing Moon represents growth, while the waning Moon is associated with death.

◄ Mayan calendars
The Maya had a system of interlocking calendars tracking and combining the cycles of the Moon, Sun, Venus, and the Pleiades. Other calendars, including the Roman, Chinese, Jewish, Celtic, and Islamic, are based on the lunar cycles.

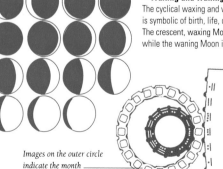

Images on the outer circle indicate the month

THE FULL MOON

The full Moon shares the symbolism of the circle as an image of wholeness and strength. The Chinese associate it with the essence of Yin and the feminine; to Buddhists it represents spiritual power. The Harvest Moon (a full Moon near the September equinox) symbolizes agricultural fertility. The word "lunatic" comes from the Latin for moon, *luna*, and originally meant "Moonstruck." The full Moon was thought to worsen lunacy and is associated with wild behavior in animals and humans.

WOLF HOWLING AT THE MOON

MOON GODS AND GODDESSES

Some cultures in Oceania and certain African tribes see the Moon as a fertilizing male god, but it is usually regarded as feminine. As the Queen of Heaven, the Virgin Mary is associated with the Moon, and lunar deities range from protective mother figures to fierce virgin goddesses, such as the Roman hunter goddess, Diana. All Moon goddesses are seen as weavers of destiny and are often portrayed as a spider.

◄ Bastet
The Egyptian goddess, Bastet, is sometimes referred to as a Moon goddess, possibly due to the fact that the Greeks identified her with Artemis, goddess of hunting and the Moon. She is associated with lunar fertility symbolism.

▲ Artemis
Twin sister of the Greek Sun god, Apollo, Artemis merged with Moon goddesses, Selene and Hecate. Artemis, virginal hunting goddess, is the New Moon, mature Selene is the full Moon, and mysterious Hecate the dark side of the Moon.

▲ Chang E
The Chinese goddess, Chang E, is the Eastern version of the "Man in the Moon." Offerings are made to her at the annual Moon Festival.

◄ Ixchel
Ixchel is the Maya Moon goddess. A mother goddess who controls the life-giving rains, she has both nurturing and destructive qualities.

◄ Coyolxauhqui
The Aztecs believed that the daily movements of the Sun and Moon symbolically reenacted a battle between Moon goddess, Coyolxauhqui, and the Sun, resulting in her decapitation.

SHAPESHIFTERS

Shapeshifting is a common theme in folklore and many cultures tell stories of people turning into ferocious animals at night, particularly during a full Moon. Symbolically these stories can be associated with the Moon's dark aspect and its links with the occult. They also represent a fear that humans are easily overtaken by base animal instinct. Involuntary shapeshifting signifies confinement, while voluntary forms symbolize liberation. Were-wolf myths were common in Europe, but elsewhere animal shapeshifters included were-jaguars, were-tigers, were-foxes, and were-badgers. Shamans and witches were credited with shapeshifting powers, traveling in this form between the human and spirit worlds.

WERE-JAGUAR

WERE-WOLF

WERE-FOX

THE PLANETS

The early astronomers noted that besides the Sun and the Moon, there were five small moving lights in the sky, which were only just visible to the naked eye. They called these lights *planetes*, meaning "wanderers," and named them after the gods of Ancient Rome—Mercury, Venus, Mars, Jupiter, and Saturn. The invention of the telescope in the 15th century led to the discovery of more distant planets—Uranus, Neptune, and Pluto. All the planets were given characteristics based on their color, movement, and size. Planets were thought to have some sort of connection with people, and to influence a particular day of the week. In medieval times alchemists matched them with metals. Andreas Cellarius's depiction of the cosmos, first published in the *Harmonia Macrocosmica* in 1660, is based on the system developed by the second-century astronomer Ptolemy that incorrectly placed the Earth at the centre of the cosmos.

1. Mercury
Named after the messenger god, Mercury is linked to reason, commerce, Wednesday, and the metal quicksilver.

2. Venus
Named after the goddess of love, Venus is associated with sexuality, desire, rebirth, and happiness. It is linked with Friday and copper.

3. Mars
Personified by a forceful male, Mars symbolizes violence, passion, fire, and bravery. Its day is Tuesday, and its metal iron.

4. Jupiter
Symbolic of balance and justice, Jupiter is associated with Thursday and the metal tin.

5. Saturn
Represented by a bearded elderly man, Saturn is about morality, melancholy, and rigidity. It is symbolic of Saturday and lead.

6. Planets as signs
As well as illustrating the planets as gods in his depiction of the cosmos, Cellarius also included the sign associated with each planet. Such signs are utilized in both astrology and alchemy.

THE NIGHT SKY

The awe-inspiring mystery and infinity of space has held sway over humans for thousands of years. Stars and planets—shining like beacons in the dark—were associated with supernatural forces symbolizing guidance, divine influence, and aspiration. Astronomy and astrology evolved from ancient times when observers noticed the wanderings of the planets across the night sky, and saw patterns (constellations) in the stars. Star symbols are used on flags, in religion, and to denote celebrity.

STARS

Representing divine guidance, guardianship, and hope, stars are hugely important symbols. American Indians believed that they represented the campfires of their ancestors, and other cultures thought they were gateways to Heaven or angelic messengers of the gods. In Christianity the Star of Bethlehem heralded the birth of Christ, and some saints are depicted with a star in Christian art. In heraldry the star is the ensign of knightly rank. The zodiac is made up of 12 star signs.

Scorpio

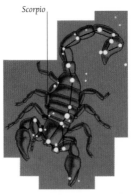

▲ Constellations
A constellation is a grouping of stars that forms a recognizable pattern. There are 88 known groups named after characters from classical mythology.

▲ Five-pointed star
Known as a pentagram, a five-pointed star drawn upward symbolizes aspiration, the spiritual world, and education; Christians see it as a symbol of Christ as "Alpha and Omega" (first and last). When inverted, the pentagram signifies the devil.

— *Male principle*

◄ Six-pointed star
Known as a hexagram or the Star of David in Judaism, this star is formed from two triangles, symbols of the male and female principles. It is a symbol for the link between Heaven and Earth and represents the union of opposites and creation. The symbol is also known as the Seal of Solomon, after a design on a ring owned by the prophet King Solomon.

Female principle

▲ Shooting stars
Representing sparks of heavenly fire, shooting stars were a sign of divinity. They acted as heavenly messengers, reminding people of the existence of a higher life. Seen as a good omen, they also signified birth.

MODERN STARS

Today stars are often used to symbolize our hopes and wishes. They are also associated with celebrity, and famous people are labeled as "stars." Stars are frequently used on flags, and rows of stars are a mark of quality. The first flag to use the five-pointed star was that of the newly formed USA in 1777.

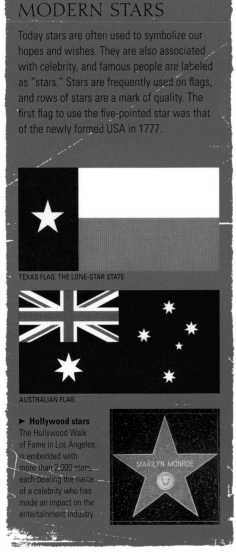

TEXAS FLAG, THE LONE-STAR STATE

AUSTRALIAN FLAG

► Hollywood stars
The Hollywood Walk of Fame in Los Angeles is embedded with more than 2,000 stars, each bearing the name of a celebrity who has made an impact on the entertainment industry.

MARILYN MONROE

STAR GODS

Heavenly symbols are linked to royalty and governance and indicate the divine presence. Early cultures believed that the stars influenced human life, often as divinities. Many stories are told about the symbolism of stars and there are numerous gods and goddesses associated with them. Stars also formed the crowns of several of the world's major fertility goddesses, including Ishtar from Babylon, and the Virgin Mary.

▲ Ishtar
The five-pointed star was the emblem of the Sumerian fertility goddess, Ishtar, in her warrior aspect as the morning star.

▲ Virgin Mary
As Queen of Heaven, the Virgin Mary is shown wearing a crown of stars. She is also associated with the six-pointed Marian Star.

▲ Star and crescent
The crescent emblem of Islam signifies divine authority and resurrection and, in conjunction with a five-pointed star, Paradise.

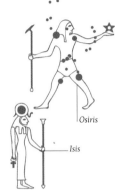

◄ Isis and Osiris
The Egyptian goddess of fertility and motherhood, Isis, was the wife of Osiris, Lord of the Dead, whose soul inhabited the star Orion. She was symbolized by the star Sirius, which heralded the annual flooding of the Nile, bringing renewed prosperity and fertility to the country; Sirius's appearance also marked the beginning of the new year.

Osiris

Isis

◄ Pole Star
In Ancient Egypt the soul of a dead pharaoh was thought to inhabit the Pole Star. It was also linked with the god Seth and the Phoenician god Baal Sapon.

► Maori doorway decoration
According to Maori beliefs, the star warded off evil. It was also linked with going into battle.

SKY-WATCHING

In primitive cultures sky-watching was an important part of life, and celestial phenomena were considered highly significant. When these coincided with events on Earth, they evolved into omens. Many myths and superstitions are associated with the aurora from which the dragon legends of the West and China are believed to have originated. St. Elmo's Fire, a continuous electric spark that occurs during thunderstorms, was regarded by sailors as an omen of divine intervention. The Maya thought that the Milky Way was a great white serpent writhing across the night sky.

▲ Northern Lights
The colorful, magical display of the Northern Lights is regarded as a sign of royal birth in some cultures. Elsewhere, it heralds war or the presence of ghosts. In Nordic mythology the aurora was seen as feminine.

► Milky Way
The Aztecs called the Milky Way Mixcoatyl (Cloud Serpent) and gave its name to the god of the Pole Star. Many cultures believed that the Milky Way was a road or river linking Earth and Heaven: to American Indians it was a pathway to the land of the dead, while the Inca imagined it was a heavenly river.

THE EARTH

Our view of the Earth has changed from early beliefs that it was flat or supported by animals, to the iconic symbol of a blue planet spinning in space. This modern view of the Earth has come to represent global unity. But the ancient ideas of a fecund Earth Mother remain embedded in our psyche. Its landscapes, violent eruptions, and raw materials, including soil itself are all strongly linked to symbolism, religion, and rituals.

THE EARTH

MOTHER EARTH

In early times the Earth was worshiped as the great Mother Goddess, a figure of sustenance and nurturing, and the source of all life. According to many creation myths, the first humans were made from clay, and coupling in furrows was a feature of some rural spring fertility festivals. The element Earth represents the feminine and passive, or the Yin of Chinese symbolism. It is traditionally portrayed by a circle.

◄ **Gaia**
The Universal Mother of Greek mythology, Gaia means "Earth." The Earth can also be seen as the goddesses Persephone, Demeter, or Hecate. Here Gaia is emerging from the Earth and handing her son to Athena as King Kekrops looks on.

► **Cihuacoatl**
The Aztec goddess of the Earth and childbirth, Cihuacoatl, devoured the dead to sustain the living. Her name means "Snake Woman" and she is sometimes depicted holding a child in her arms. Her roar signaled war.

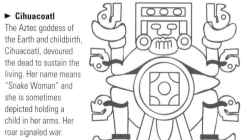

▲ **Venus of Laussel**
This 21,000-year-old rock carving from the Dordogne, France, shows the Earth Mother holding a bison horn, signifying the crescent Moon and the Universal Vulva, or life source.

▲ **Demeter**
The Greek Earth goddess is associated with harvest, grain, and with teaching humans how to sow and plow. As a fertility goddess, Demeter is sometimes identified with Gaia.

ROCK

Signifying strength, integrity, and refuge, rock is also associated with divinity. In ancient cultures, rocks were given sacred significance in the form of standing stones. Among American Indians, rocks represented the bones of Mother Earth and served as a focus for burial. In Christianity rock represents both Christ and the Church.

▲ **Mithra**
In Persia Mithra, god of light and the upper air, was born from a rock. He was usually portrayed slaying a bull, overcoming animal passions.

▲ **Bryce Canyon**
In Bryce Canyon, Utah, erosion has created distinctive pillars and spires within a spectacular amphitheater of red rock. The American Indian Paiute culture believed that these pinnacles were the Legend People, turned to stone by the trickster Coyote.

▲ **Cybele**
A goddess of nature and fertility, Cybele was worshiped in Rome in the form of a stone, having been born from a black rock hurled from the heavens.

LANDSCAPES

Whatever our relationship with the land, it is bound up with identity, nationhood, and life itself. The Earth's varied landscapes are rich in symbolism and meaning that reflect the origins, religious beliefs, and rituals of the people who live in them.

▲ Caves
A primal symbol of shelter, caves symbolize the womb and are linked to birth, rebirth, and the center of the universe. Darker interpretations of caves are associated with the Underworld, the gates of Hell, and the unconscious.

▲ Desert
Desert landscapes symbolize barrenness, desolation, abandonment, and the battle for survival—often against temptation. In both the Christian and Islamic religions they signify a place of retreat, meditation, and enlightenment.

▲ Valley
Representing fertility, the valley is where animals graze and people settle. Valleys signify a sheltering, feminine aspect. In Chinese symbolism the valley is the Yin, shadowy, gentle, feminine state, in contrast to the sunny Yang of the mountain. Valleys can also be seen as places of dread, such as the Valley of the Shadow of Death.

ACTIVE EARTH

Ancient stories often liken the violence of earthquakes and volcanoes to the awakening of a sleeping monster or the anger of the gods, and there is a rich vein of symbolism linked to the destructive power of the gods and the creative force. The Japanese thought the storm god, Susano-O, conjured up earthquakes, while the Greeks believed that Poseidon, the "Earth-shaker," was the culprit. Sacrifices were made to appease the gods. Often seismic activity was regarded as an omen of great change in religion or politics; the Bible tells of earthquakes heralding Christ's death.

◀ Japanese earthquakes
Some ancient cultures attributed violent earthquakes to the movements of the animals they thought supported the Earth. The Ainu of Japan believed their islands were supported by a giant catfish called Namazu who was restrained by Kashima with a stone.

Stone

◀ Mount Fuji
An iconic symbol of Japan, Mount Fuji is regarded as sacred in both Shinto and Buddhism. Thousands of people make an annual pilgrimage to its summit. One meaning of the name "Fuji" is "deity of fire."

▶ Volcano goddess
The Ancient Hawaiian volcano goddess, Pele, was volatile and capricious and lived in the craters of the Big Island's Kilauea Volcano. She caused earthquakes by stamping her feet and volcanic eruptions by digging with her magic stick.

▲ Hindu earthquakes
In one Hindu interpretation of the cosmos, the Earth was carried by four male elephants standing on a female tortoise, representing the two creative powers. It was their movement that set off earthquakes.

SEE ALSO
Reptiles & amphibians
  pp.64–65
Aquatic creatures pp.68–71
Fertility & childbirth pp.120–23
Greek & Roman deities
  pp.140–41
Hinduism pp.158–63
Tribal totems, heroes &
  tricksters pp.150–51

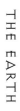

YIN-YANG LANDSCAPE

Chinese landscape painting has been a major art form since the T'ang dynasty (618–907CE). At a time of political unrest such paintings symbolized the peace and tranquility of our union with nature, and a human figure is often set against the backdrop of mountains and water. Each element of the painting is symbolic and the whole signifies order and harmony.

1. & 2. Yin and Yang

Yin (passive, cool, feminine) is found wherever there is fluidity and softness. It is symbolized here in the quiet valley, the water, and the graceful bending of bamboo. All forms of cloud and mist are symbols of Yin. Yang (active, warm, masculine) is represented as force and light. Here the thrusting mountains, hard rocks, sky, and the brightness of water are all Yang.

3. United elements

Taoists believe in a mystic sense of cosmic brotherhood that unites all the elements. As the philosopher Chuang Tzu put it, "Heaven and Earth and I live together, and all things and I are one." Here the dominant mountain is flanked by lesser mountains, and larger or smaller rocks and trees symbolize the belief that all elements within nature are related.

4. Human figure

People are often included in Chinese landscapes. Their size emphasizes the fact that humans are a small part of a vast cosmic creation. The figure shown here could be meditating or thinking; if men and women do not follow their proper wisdom, the whole cosmic order is damaged.

Shen Zhou, *Figure Sitting on a Riverbank*

▲ **Mount Sumeru**
Hindus and Buddhists regard the mythological Mount Sumeru, or
Meru, as representing the center of the universe. It is often found,
as above, in Tibetan mandalas, used to aid meditation.

MOUNTAINS

As near to Heaven as you can get on Earth, mountains are revered, sometimes feared, and regarded as sacred by the world's religions. They are often associated with gods, spirits, and prophets.

▲ Mount of Olives
In the Bible Jesus was said to have ascended to Heaven from the Mount of Olives outside Jerusalem.

Mountains command attention. Towering over us, their peaks often wreathed in clouds, they stand apart from our daily existence: remote, challenging, and mysterious. Seen as the embodiment of cosmic forces and life, for early cultures mountains represented the Earth's spiritual center and axis at the point where it joins Heaven: a divine meeting place for God and humans in a space and time apart. Men built temples in the shape of mountains to represent the spiritual ascent of the soul.

SACRED PLACES

High places have always been associated with sacred quests and are a symbol of spiritual transcendence, purity, and even eternity. Climbing a mountain is arduous, the air becomes thinner, causing breathing difficulties and hallucinations. Conquering the summit is a supreme achievement, and the view from the top offers a fresh perspective. This can be likened to a spiritual journey, at the summit of which the pure-hearted attain enlightenment.

Many mountains are considered sacred. In China there are nine sacred mountains that Buddhists venerate. Some mountains, such as Croag Patrick in Ireland or Mount Fuji in Japan, inspire people to climb them. Such sacred pilgrimages represent aspiration, renunciation of worldly desires, and enlightenment; spritually, mountain peaks are linked to the state of full consciousness.

▲ Mexican temple
These four-sided, mountain-like structures had stairs going up one or more sides, and flat tops where sacrifices took place. Old temples were not destroyed but simply built over so that they became many-layered.

GODS AND PROPHETS

Mountains have long been associated with biblical revelations, prophets, gods (especially Sun and weather gods), and heroes. Mount Olympus was the home of the Classical Greek gods, from where they ruled the world and human affairs. Moses climbed to the top of Mount Sinai to receive the Ten Commandments from God. Legend has it that the Prophet Muhammad turned the immutability of mountains into an allegory for humility when he ordered Mount Safa to move.

The American Indian Navajo thought certain mountains embodied important nature spirits, while in Mexico Mount Tlaloc was thought to personify an Aztec fertility and rain god.

For the Ancient Egyptians mountains represented Earth's desire for sky. They showed the body of sky goddess, Nut, curved over that of her lover. The upward-thrusting mountain symbolizes this physical desire. This belief is similar to the Chinese idea that a mountain's phallic shape makes it a masculine or Yang symbol signifying life.

TEMPLES AND TWIN MOUNTS

Temples built in the shape of mountains, such as those in Asia, Central America, and Mesopotamia, represent the cosmic center. Their terraces are associated with both spiritual ascent and gateways to Heaven. The Egyptian pyramids have similar cosmological significance. Mountains with twin summits are regarded as either the seat of astral or solar divinities or, as in China, Sumeria, and the Hebrew mountains of Sinai and Horeb, the seat of the Sun and the Moon.

◄ Mountains of the Immortals
This Chinese vessel shows the Taoist symbol of the Mountains of the Immortals. In China mountains are venerated and are the home of deities and spirits.

FIRE

Terrible and all-consuming, fire is the great destroyer. Symbolic of war and chaos, its qualities are active and masculine. It is also linked with the Sun. People or objects may be referred to as "fiery," and extreme emotions are associated with the color red.

Fire has a dual personality as it also symbolizes purification and regeneration, home, hearth, and divine love. When people learned how to make fire, it was life-changing and all early cultures had fire gods and fire-making legends.

FIRE GODS

Fire is associated with the space above us: it comes from the sky in the form of the Sun or lightning, and smoke drifts up to the heavens. It is easy to see why this all-powerful element, both violent and beneficent, was attributed to the gods. The worship or deification of fire is known from many religions and dates back to early humans. Fire gods feature in cultures around the globe. The Greeks and Romans had gods of both the forge and the hearth.

▲ **Raging fire**
The height and glowing red color of the flames of a forest fire emphasize its power. Fire can be a destructive or a creative force.

◄ Vulcan
The Roman god, Vulcan, is associated with fire, volcanoes, and craftsmanship. He made weapons for gods and heroes in his forge beneath Mount Etna, and was celebrated at the August Vulcanalia festival.

▲ **Chantico**
The Aztec goddess of volcanoes and the hearth, Chantico had a tongue of fire. She was patroness of the goldsmiths.

▲ **Chu Jung**
A Chinese fire god, Chu Jung punished those who broke the laws of Heaven. He is often depicted wearing armor, and is most famous for fighting his son to stop him from usurping the throne of Heaven.

▲ **Agni**
A Vedic god, Agni's name means "fire" in Sanskrit. He is shown with either one or two heads, indicating both his destructive and merciful qualities, and is seen as the life force of trees and plants.

▲ **Sehkmet**
Often depicted as a woman with the head of a lioness, and carrying a fire-spitting cobra, this bloodthirsty Egyptian war goddess destroyed enemies with fire arrows; her body shimmered like the midday Sun.

◄ Huehueteotl
An Aztec god of light and fire, Huehueteotl is often depicted as an old man with a red or yellow face and a censer (incense burner) on his head.

THE COSMOS

30

ETERNAL FLAME

An eternal flame is a light that is always kept burning. In ancient times they were fueled by olive oil or wood; modern versions use propane or natural gas. Eternal flames symbolize a person, group, or event of international significance, or even a noble goal such as world peace. The Olympic torch is lit in Greece, carried to the host city and kept alight during the Games. Many churches have an eternal flame on or above the altar.

► **Enlightening the world**
On Ellis Island in New York City, the Statue of Liberty holds her torch aloft, a symbol of freedom from oppression.

FIRE-MAKING LEGENDS

When people learned to kindle a fire they had the means to cook, keep warm, deter wild beasts and, later, to smelt ore. Numerous legends about how humans learned to make fire also describe the earliest fire-making tools. For example, the legendary Iranian king, Hushang, realized that fire could be created by striking flints together after throwing a flint-ax at a snake; it struck a rock instead, igniting sparks.

▲ **Prometheus**
The Greek god, Prometheus, tricked Zeus into eating bones instead of meat. As a punishment for his treatment, Zeus retaliated by withholding fire from mortals, which Prometheus later stole.

▲ **Maui**
The god Maui features in many Polynesian legends, especially those of the Maoris and the Hawaiians. In Hawaii the hawk is personified as Maui, who stole fire from the Earth Mother and was singed by the flames, which is why hawk feathers are brown. There is a similar Maori version of this story.

FIRE CEREMONIES

Its associations with regeneration, purification, and the divine ensured that fire played a ceremonial part in many different cultures and religions. It had a central role in the sacrificial rites of the Aztecs, who ritually burned tobacco and incense, along with body parts. Among Zoroastrians, who traditionally worship in fire temples, it represents the energy of the Creator. Other cultures, such as the North American Indians, used fire in their purification ceremonies and vision quests.

DIVINE FLAME

Fire is an important feature in many religions. In Christianity Hell is associated with fire and some saints are depicted with flaming hearts. In Christian churches candles represent God's presence, hope, and life. Old Testament stories tell of the burning bush.

FLAMING HEART   BURNING BUSH

▲ **Firecrackers**
In China the noise of fire crackers at New Year is designed to scare away evil spirits and misfortune. It also awakens the golden dragon so that it flies across the sky, bringing rain for the crops.

▲ **Zoroastrian**
Zoroastrian temples house the sacred fire, a symbol of the gods. This is kept constantly alight by priests; worshipers wear white linen masks to prevent their breath from contaminating it.

▲ **Aztec**
Aztec priests heralded potential world destruction every 52 years by dousing all fires and lighting a new fire within the chest cavity of a human sacrificial victim, symbolizing that out of sacrifice came life.

FIRE

31

WATER

Water constantly changes shape and transforms. Symbolically it is feminine and associated with the Moon and, as the origin of all life, with fertility. It may appear as rain or snow, as a raging torrent or placid lake. It also has various states, such as running, stagnant, stormy, or deep, each with its own symbolism. Although water is passive, it is influenced by the weather and can destroy, dissolve, wash away, or regenerate. It is also a source of purification and healing in many religions.

THE SEA

Regarded as symbolically maternal, the sea's depths represent the Earth's womb. All life sprang from its primordial waters, as reflected in the creation myths of numerous cultures. Often seen as mysterious, the sea also represents the unconscious mind, while deep waters have a symbolism related to the dead and the supernatural. There are many gods, spirits, and monsters associated with the sea and with natural phenomena such as whirlpools and tsunamis.

WATER AND WORSHIP

Water is central to many of the world's religions. In Christian baptism, pictured here, it symbolizes purification and the washing away of original sin. In Hinduism water is also used to bathe and purify ritual images of the divine.

▲ Neptune
The Roman name for the Greek god Poseidon, Neptune was the god of the sea. He was depicted as a bearded man holding a trident and sitting in a seashell accompanied by dolphins. His fiery temper supposedly manifested itself in storms and earthquakes.

▲ Sedna
In Inuit mythology, Sedna was a sea goddess and guardian of ocean animals. She ruled the Inuit underworld, Adlivun. Different Inuit groups call Sedna by different names. She was worshiped by those who hunted the waters, who relied on her goodwill to supply food.

▶ Nun
The most ancient of the Ancient Egyptian gods, Nun's name means "water." He represented the primeval water of chaos from which emerged creation. His qualities were darkness, boundlessness, and turbulence.

▲ Waves
Constantly driving forward through peaks and troughs, waves represent both constancy and changeability; people speak of waves of joy or sadness. Tidal waves symbolize destruction and regeneration; in dreams they may mean a fear of change.

◀ Charybdis
The daughter of Poseidon, Charybdis became a sea monster when Zeus stole her body, leaving only a mouth that became a whirlpool. In mythology Charybdis occupied one side of a narrow strait, while Scylla, another sea monster, took the other. Sailors navigating the strait too close to one side or the other risked death.

RIVERS

River symbolism is based around running water and reflects the creative power of nature and time. It signifies fertility and soil irrigation, giving life along its banks, yet is also a metaphor for the passage of time—a river flows from its source to the sea, as life flows from birth to death. A river can also symbolize a barrier between two realms, Life and Death. Great rivers are given personalities and many are considered sacred. Numerous cultures have river gods and spirits.

▲ Four rivers of Paradise
The Bible's Rivers of Paradise flowed out in the cardinal directions from the roots of the Tree of Life. Their waters symbolized life and nourishment.

▲ Styx
In Greek mythology the River Styx formed the boundary between Earth and Hades. Legends feature the ferryman, Charon, who took the dead across the River Acheron, which flowed into the Styx.

▲ Ganga
Representing the sacred water of the River Ganges, the Hindu goddess, Ganga, is shown sitting on a makara, a combination of fish and crocodile, denoting fertility and the wisdom of land and sea.

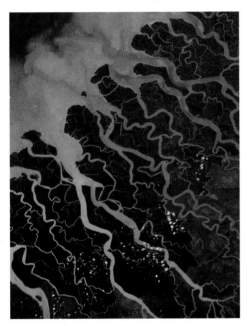

▲ Hapi
The Egyptian god of the Nile floods, Hapi, was portrayed as a man with a prominent belly, indicating the fertility of the land through flooding.

◄ Delta
A delta is symbolic of death and journey's end, marking a river's long meanderings from its source all the way down to where it spills into the sea.

◄ Spring
Springs like this one in Bali are often attributed with healing or magical powers. Often towns were built around springs and their name may reflect this. Bath, in England, is one example of a town that grew around a hot spring.

◄ Waterfall
Buddhists believe that waterfalls represent the "permanent impermanence" of the universe, which is partly why they play an important role in Chinese and Japanese landscape painting. In Shinto waterfalls are held sacred and standing under one is thought to purify the soul.

LAKES

Traditionally a lake represents peace and contemplation. Since its surface presents a reflection, there is also a strong link to mirror symbolism: in Greek legend Narcissus drowned while admiring his reflection in a lake. In China lakes signify wisdom, absorption, and passivity. In Hinduism and Buddhism lakes attached to temples represent creation and the transition to the next life.

WATER AND EVIL

In past centuries, women suspected of being witches were thrown into deep water. If they drowned, they were presumed innocent, but if the water rejected them and they floated, they could be condemned for witchcraft.

◄ Sacred lake
A sacred lake was central to most Ancient Egyptian temples. Pictured is the Temple of Amon at Karnak. The sacred lake was used for a daily ritual during which a goose, symbol of Amon himself, was freed at sunrise.

SEE ALSO
Egyptian deities *pp.138–39*
Greek & Roman deities *pp.140–41*
Hinduism *pp.158–63*
Buddhism *pp.164–69*
Taoism & Shinto *pp.170–71*
Witches & wicca *pp.192–93*

THE WEATHER

Changes in the weather have a fundamental impact on humans and can sometimes create life or death situations. People have long associated these vagaries with the whims of the gods, and blamed folklore personifications such as the North Wind for cold weather. As well as being linked with divine retribution and supernatural powers, the weather is also associated with benign forces and creativity.

◄ Ryujin
Ryujin is the most important of the Rajin, Japanese weather gods. He is usually portrayed as a demon, forming mists and black rain clouds, and beating drums to create thunder. He also devours children's bellybuttons.

This female figurine balances the symbol of lightning and is used in a dance to Shango, god of thunder and lightning

THUNDER, LIGHTNING, AND STORMS

Storms are often associated with warrior gods and supreme deities. Thunder was seen in many cultures as the creative power and harbinger of vital, fertilizing rain. In Bible stories it represented God's voice, while lightning delivered fecundity and illumination. A thunderbolt was the weapon of choice for the Greek god, Zeus, and the Hindu god of war, Indra. The Thunderbird of American Indian belief represents the Universal Spirit and is linked with war.

◄ Shango
Sacred to Nigeria's Yoruba people, Shango is a god of thunder and lightning. His symbol is the *oshe*, a double-headed ax representing the stone thunderbolts he hurls from the sky.

▲ Tala wipiki
This kachina, or spirit doll, represents lightning. It was made by the American Indian Hopis who lived in the desert lands of New Mexico. Due to its associations with rain, the tala wipiki kachina is considered benevolent today.

▲ Marduk
Marduk, the Babylonian creator god, placed the Mesopotamian god, Enlil, in the air and gave him the power to induce storms and spring breezes with his breath.

▲ Shiva
In Hinduism lightning or destructive fire is the third eye on the forehead of Shiva. It symbolizes divine force, cosmic intelligence, enlightenment, and the forces of destruction and regeneration. One of his weapons is a trident, representing lightning.

► Thor
Thor is the red-haired and bearded god of thunder and war in Nordic mythology. Often portrayed wielding a hammer or thunderbolt, his chariot was pulled across the sky by two goats with the unlikely names of Tooth-grinder and Tooth-gnasher.

▲ Rudra
The Vedic forerunner of the Hindu god, Shiva, Rudra was a god of storms and lightning who fired arrows of disease, but who also brought good health and performed good deeds. His name means "Howler" or "Red One" and he personifies untamed nature.

THE WINDS

In modern times wind has become a symbol of change and freedom, but traditionally it is linked with the four compass points, the gods, and even demons. Its role in pollination also makes wind a sexual symbol. The Apache American Indians believed that the whorls on the fingertips represented the wind's path as it entered the body at creation. In China wind is associated with rumor, a symbolism linked to hunting and "getting wind" of a scent.

BOREAS (NORTH WIND)

EURUS (EAST WIND)

ZEPHYRUS (WEST WIND)

NOTUS (SOUTH WIND)

◄ Greek wind gods
In Greek myth Aeolus, chief god of the directional winds, kept the winds in a cave and ruled over the four gods. Often shown as winged men with puffed cheeks, each wind brought different weather conditions, from light spring breezes to cold winter winds.

▲ Whirlwind
Symbolizing circular, solar, and creative movement, whirlwinds are often seen as a vehicle for divinity: in the Bible God spoke to Job from a whirlwind. In witchcraft evil spirits rode on whirlwinds.

▲ Cherub
These winged celestial beings (also known as "putti") are often portrayed as chubby-cheeked children, and in western art were used to represent wind, perhaps blowing a boat.

▲ Vayu
From the Sanskrit "blow," Vayu is the god of the winds in India; as one of the five elements, he is one of the most important deities in the Vedas (Hindu holy scriptures).

▲ Fujin
The Japanese Shinto god, Fujin, was portrayed as a fearsome-looking deity sitting on or traversing the clouds and carrying a sack containing the winds.

CLOUDS AND MIST

The symbolism of weather conditions from wispy mists to brooding storm banks can be varied. Rain clouds are linked with fecundity, hence the reference "pregnant with rain." In Judeo-Christian tradition they can indicate God's presence, while in China pink clouds symbolize good luck and happiness. In some cultures clouds are associated with gloom; people also link being out of touch with reality as having one's head "in the clouds." Mist is often associated with supernatural intervention, especially in Chinese landscape painting.

▲ Divine presence
Their heavenly associations have symbolically linked clouds to divine presence; in Christian iconography God is often shown as a hand emerging from a cloud.

▲ The indeterminate
Fog and mist are commonly used to symbolize the indeterminate, or the state that comes before revelation. Taoists link fog to the state humans must pass through before enlightenment, like the mental fog that precedes clarity of thought.

▲ The steeds of Valkyrie
In Greek mythology clouds represented the flocks of the god Apollo. In Nordic legend, however, they are the steeds of the Valkyrie, the god Odin's handmaidens who hovered over battlefields, escorting the slain to Valhalla (Paradise).

SEE ALSO
Fertility & childbirth
    pp.120–23
Celtic & Nordic deities
    pp.142–43
Nature spirits pp.148–49
Creation stories pp.156–57
Christianity pp.176–79
Angels pp.188–89

THE WEATHER

35

RAIN & SNOW

All precipitation, whether it comes as rain, hail, snow, or dew, is associated with water symbolism, and both life and death. It can result in destruction or generation. As rain, it represents fertility, while dew signifies a blessing. As ice and snow, its links with cold and impermanence are reflected in folklore and myth, while rainbows combine both solar and water symbolism. Due to its heavenly origin, precipitation is associated with gods of the sky. Human survival depended on cooperation between gods and humans, so that the weather's unpredictable and often violent power could be controlled.

RAINFALL

Rain has always been an important symbol of fecundity and in certain primitive cultures it is linked with divine semen. It is also associated with purification. For thousands of years people believed that the sky gods determined whether to withhold rain, unleash it with terrifying force, or release a gentle shower. Various rituals were carried out to invoke rainfall, and rain was associated with certain animals such as dragons, dogs, and even parrots.

▲ Dragon
In China dragons were associated with the weather and were thought to be rain-bringers; some of the country's worst floods were attributed to humans upsetting a dragon. Chinese dragons were believed to control water, vital for crops. In contrast, western dragons control fire.

▲ Torrential rain
When cold, penetrating rain pours down in torrents, it can bring misery and suffering as well as being a divine blessing. Heavy rain shares its symbolism with that of storms and the wrath of the gods.

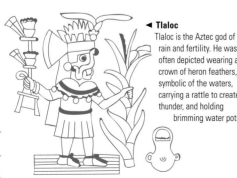

► Rain dances
Different interpretations of rain dances can be found in many cultures throughout the world. The American Indian Cherokee nation, for example, performed rain dances to invoke rain and to banish evil spirits. The stamping of feet imitates the patter of rain on hard ground.

◄ Tlaloc
Tlaloc is the Aztec god of rain and fertility. He was often depicted wearing a crown of heron feathers, symbolic of the waters, carrying a rattle to create thunder, and holding brimming water pots.

▲ Indra
The Hindu god of thunder, rain, fertility, and war, Indra, is often shown seated in his heavenly court, Svarga, in the clouds wreathing sacred Mount Meru. Indra is shown wielding a thunderbolt in one hand, symbolizing enlightenment, destruction, and regeneration.

▲ Zeus and Danaë
This painting illustrates a story from Greek mythology in which Danaë, the human mother of the hero, Perseus, is impregnated by the god, Zeus, in the form of a shower of coins. It is an erotic symbol of the divine fertility of rain.

SNOW AND ICE

Not surprisingly, snow and ice symbolism is almost entirely associated with themes of coldness and hardness. There are also references to purity and white, pristine beauty. Emotionally, snow and ice are linked with rigidity, frigidity, brittleness, impermanence, and a general absence of love; expressions such as "icily polite" are widely used. In contrast, melting ice represents a hard heart softening.

▶ Glacier
As a huge mass of perennial land ice that moves forward under its own weight, a glacier is symbolic of slow, relentless change. In common with ice, it is also associated with the polluted waters of Earth rather than the fresh waters of Paradise.

▲ Snowflakes
The fragile beauty of the snowflake is symbolic of impermanence, wisdom, truth, hardness, and purity. It also represents individuality because no two snowflakes are alike.

▲ Snow queen
This western fairytale symbolizes the triumph of good over evil. It tells the tale of two children who are parted when the Snow Queen kidnaps the boy, and how the girl risks everything to rescue him.

BRIDGE TO THE HEAVENS

Elusive, ethereal, and transient, the rainbow has a wide range of symbolic meanings. It has been seen as a sign of hope, peace, and divine covenant, an omen of war, an object of worship, and even fear. Rainbow legends and customs are widespread. The rainbow is a bridge to the heavens and wisdom is said to lie at its end.

▲ Iris
Goddess of the rainbow and messenger of the Olympian gods, Iris is often portrayed as a young woman with golden wings and a herald's rod. The rainbow represents her path between Earth and Heaven.

▲ Rainbow body
In Tibetan tantric Buddhism the rainbow body is the transitional state of enlightenment in which the practitioner's body literally disappears and is transformed into pure light. This usually happens after death.

▲ Crock of gold
In Irish folklore the leprechaun stores a pot of gold at the end of the rainbow; in the West the end of the rainbow is linked to finding one's fortune.

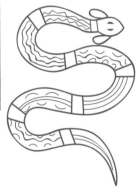

◀ Rainbow serpent
The rainbow serpent of Australian Aboriginal myth is linked to seasonal shifts and human reliance on water. The monstrous serpent inhabits the permanent water holes and therefore controls life's most precious resource.

▲ Navajo rainbow
The rainbow on the Navajo flag symbolizes sovereignty and the joining together of all the tribes into the Rainbow Nation. The copper outline represents their borders and the jagged shapes the sacred mountains.

▲ Kahukura
The Maori rainbow god, Kahukura, is invoked in war. It is also a symbol of man's mortality and a pathway from Heaven to Earth.

◀ Noah's rainbow covenant
After the biblical Flood, when God had safely delivered Noah and his ark, He sent a rainbow as a sign of His promise not to destroy humanity.

▶ **Noah's Ark**
The biblical story of Noah describes the Flood as God's punishment for human sin. Noah, a devout man, was instructed by God to build an ark, which ultimately survived, and he and his family went on to repopulate the world.

FLOODS

The story of a Great Flood sent by God, or the gods, to destroy
civilization in an act of divine retribution is a widespread theme
in mythology from cultures around the world.

Symbolically, floods represent death and
regeneration—the end of one cycle and the
beginning of another. They are associated
with the lunar powers of the waters, fertility,
and new life. They also have links with the
washing away of sin and the purification
of humanity.

UNIVERSAL THEME
Global flood stories are common to almost
every civilization around the world, from
China and Russia to Sumatra and Peru.
In general terms, they represent the chaos
that results when humans are out of harmony
with nature and the gods.

Many are similar to the famous biblical
flood story about Noah's ark: they include
themes such as divine retribution, advance
warning of a flood, the building of a boat to
house family and animals, and the release of
birds to determine whether the flood waters
had receded. The stories of Matsya in the *Purana* scriptures
of Hinduism, and Utnapishtim in the Babylonian *Epic of
Gilgamesh* are the most familiar
of these myths.

ORIGINS
Theories abound about the
origins of the biblical flood
story. However, it may have
originated in Mesopotamia

▲ **Matsya myth**
In this Hindu myth, Manu saved Vishnu in the
form of fish called Matsya, which later warned
him of a coming flood; Manu built a boat,
survived, and re-established life on Earth.

(now southern Iraq) where the Tigris and
Euphrates rivers join. This fertile region is
prone to severe flooding, and geological
evidence indicates floods may have caused
significant disruption of several human
settlements. To ancient cultures, a flood that
swamped them would have appeared global,
and spawned explanatory myths.

NOTABLE EXCEPTIONS
Areas where ancient cultures benefited from
annual flooding, such as the Amazon and the
Nile, do not have apocalyptical flood stories.
In Egypt the annual Nile floods made the
surrounding land extremely fertile, providing
food for the people. The floods were so
significant that they created a god, Hapi,
a positive figure who, together with the
pharaoh, was believed to control the rise and
fall of the water, bringing fertility to the
region. Without the use of the Nile's waters
for irrigation, Egypt's civilization would probably never have
developed in the sophisticated way that it did.

◄ **Nile inundation**
The Nile attracted valuable
game and this 2nd-century BCE
detail of a Nile mosaic shows a
rhinocerous stranded on a rock
during the annual flood.

◄ **Aztec creator god**
Meso-American beliefs include world cycles,
each destroyed by natural disasters such as
floods. Aztec weather and creator god,
Quetzalcoatl, repopulated the world after
one such event.

SEE ALSO
Water *pp.32–33*
Fertility & childbirth *pp.120–23*
Egyptian deities *pp.138–39*
Hinduism *pp.158–63*
Christianity *pp.176–79*

FLOODS

39

THE SEASONS

The seasons are universally seen as symbols of birth, growth, death, and rebirth, and therefore the passing of time. Humans have always reckoned time by the Sun and the lunar cycle, so the Sun and Moon feature in seasonal symbolism. Each season has its associated gods, animals, colors, and even emotions. In some cultures the seasons are symbolized by specific flowers, such as China's autumnal chrysanthemums.

SPRING

Fresh, verdant, and full of promise, spring represents rebirth and new life. Essentially it is nature unfolding. Baby animals, children, young women, and flowers are all recurring symbols of the season, signifying spring's youth, beauty, and heart-breaking brevity. In China and Japan the cherry blossom is an important seasonal symbol. In Celtic mythology the Green Man is connected with spring regeneration.

► Allegory of spring
In western art spring is traditionally represented by a beautiful young woman (symbolic of fertility) crowned in seasonal flowers and set in a soft, pastoral landscape. She may be seen accompanied by young children.

▲ Flora
In Roman mythology Flora was goddess of springtime and flowers. Her festival, the Floralia, was held in April or early May and signified the renewal of the cycle of life.

◄ Spring lamb
A symbol of springtime, the lamb represents Christ's crucifixion and resurrection; this links it with Easter, which falls on the first Sunday after the first full Moon after the spring equinox.

SUMMER

Summer is the season of ripening maturity, when the Sun is at its height. The Classical world associated summer with the Greek god, Apollo, and goddess Demeter (known to the Romans as Ceres). Its animals were the golden lion and the dragon. In China summer is symbolized by the lotus and peony.

► Ceres
The Roman goddess of agriculture and fertility, Ceres, was credited with teaching humans how to grow and use grain. She is often shown garlanded with wheat ears and holding a basket of fruit.

▲ Symbol of summer
This Classical figure represents summer, and shows a woman crowned in ears of wheat, and carrying a sheaf of corn and a scythe. Grain symbolizes rebirth, growth, and fertility.

AUTUMN

Autumn is traditionally depicted as either a child or a woman bearing a baskets of grapes, which symbolize hospitality and the abundance of the season. The seasonal animal is the hare. In western art the cornucopia (horn of plenty), overflowing with fruit, flowers, and grain, is an ancient symbol of autumnal bounty; it has long-standing links with fertility.

► Hare
The hare is a fertility symbol in many cultures—hence its link to the bounty of autumn. In Greco-Roman myth the hare symbolizes the abundance of the season; it also represents fertility in the autumn Chinese Moon festivals.

▲ Bacchus
The Greek god of wine and excess, Bacchus (also known as Dionysus), is associated with the celebrations of the autumn grape harvest.

▲ Persephone
The goddess Persephone symbolizes the grain, which comes up each year before returning to the Earth, in a constant cycle of renewal.

▲ Corn dolly
A figure made by plaiting wheat, the corn dolly is associated with Ancient European harvest customs and was used in Celtic fertility rites.

HARVEST FESTIVAL

Harvest thanksgiving festivals are common to all agrarian societies. They unite the community in ritual at a time when nature's bounty is celebrated and ancestors are remembered. Special food and drink, usually harvest related are consumed and people join in the festivities.

► Dewi Sri
The annual rice festival in Bali and Java is dedicated to the goddess Dewi Sri. She wears a crown and sometimes holds a lotus, symbolizing resurrection.

▲ Yaeyama dancer
On the Yaeyama islands of Japan traditional dances are performed to bring about a successful harvest. The dances reflect everyday activities. Here the dancer rides a hobby-horse into a mock battle.

▲ Chinese mooncakes
Mooncakes are eaten during a Chinese festival to celebrate the harvest. They may contain egg yolks, a symbol of the Moon.

WINTER

Winter is the dead time when cold winds howl, many trees are leafless, and the Earth appears hard and barren. Many cultures have their own stories to explain the changing of the seasons. In Ancient Greek mythology Persephone was abducted and taken to the Underworld, during which time the Earth grew dark and nothing would grow. Even after she was freed, Hades forced her to return to the Underworld for several months every year when the Earth became barren again. This period became winter.

◄ Winter personified
This Ancient Roman statuette shows a traditional interpretation of winter portrayed as an elderly man or woman, wrapped in a cloak to keep out the cold. Often the figure is shown hunched over, struggling against inclement weather.

▲ Duck
The duck is associated with Isis, Egyptian goddess of the dead, and is also traditionally linked with winter. The wild duck is also a popular winter game bird.

▲ Boreas
The bringer of the cold North Wind and winter, in Classical mythology Boreas was feared due to his destructive potential. The Athenian fleet prayed to him and held a festival, Boreasmi, in his honor.

▲ Salamander
The Ancient Roman writer, Pliny, said of salamanders, "This animal is so intensely cold as to extinguish fire … as ice does." A symbol of enduring faith and indestructibility, the salamander is also associated with fire.

SEE ALSO
The Moon *pp.18–19*
Mammals *pp.52–55*
Birds *pp.58–61*
Fertility & childbirth *pp.120–23*
Egyptian deities *pp.138–39*

Greek & Roman deities *pp.140–41*
Christianity *pp.176–79*

PRECIOUS STONES

Precious and semi-precious stones flash with color and light. The fact that they come from the Earth links them with divine energy as symbols of spiritual power and purity; some were credited with powers of healing and protection. They have been used for centuries to signify status. Transparent stones are linked with divination, while red ones indicate ardor and vitality. Some stones are linked to birth months and some have their own associations.

▲ Topaz
Reputed to be an empathetic stone, topaz symbolizes faithfulness, divine goodness, friendship, forgiveness, and love. Medicinally topaz was traditionally thought to banish nervous exhaustion and stimulate the appetite.

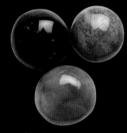

▲ Bloodstone
Regarded as a healing stone, bloodstone revitalizes relationships and purifies. It is sometimes seen as a warrior stone for overcoming obstacles and giving courage. Bloodstone was used to combat blood disorders and stop bleeding.

▲ Emerald
Its color associates the emerald with fertility, immortality, spring, and youth. The Egyptians buried an emerald with their dead to represent eternal youth. A Christian symbol of faith, emeralds also feature in folklore as a healing stone.

▲ Dragon protection
This 14th-century carving from China shows a dragon protecting hidden treasure. Traditionally, in Chinese culture, the Earth dragons guarded precious objects and jewels buried deep in the Earth. Such hidden treasure symbolized knowledge or truth.

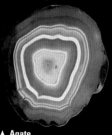

▲ Agate
Ancient cultures believed that agate rendered the wearer invisible. It represents courage, longevity, and prosperity; in the past, agate stones were tied to oxen horns to promote a good harvest.

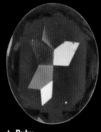

▲ Ruby
This gem symbolizes love, courage, and vitality. It has been linked with Saturn and Mars, the planet of passions. Royalty wore rubies as they were thought to temporarily darken when danger approached.

▲ Sapphire
Sapphires are a symbol of celestial harmony, peace, and truth. In Hindu tradition they were associated with Saturn and self-control. In some quarters they were thought to ward off evil.

▲ Jade
To the Chinese, jade is the Stone of Heaven and represents purity. A solar and Yang emblem, it also symbolizes justice, courage, harmony, and moral purity. Considered lucky, smooth jade also has sexual connotations.

▲ Diamond
Symbolic of purity, truth, and fidelity, the diamond is popular for engagement rings. Its radiance links it to the Sun. Diamonds are also believed to absorb the wearer's emotions and cleanse the soul.

THE COSMOS

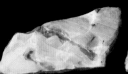

▲ Opal
The opal symbolizes divine insight, religious devotion, and fidelity. The Romans thought that opals fell from Heaven in a flash of lightning. Some cultures called the opal the "Eye Stone," believing it watched over royalty.

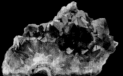

▲ Amethyst
The amethyst is a protective and spiritual stone and amethyst rings are worn by bishops in the Christian Church. It is also thought to give peace of mind and protect the wearer against drunkeness.

▲ Turquoise
Long seen as a talisman against evil, turquoise is symbolic of courage, success, and fulfillment. In Mexico it is a solar and fire symbol, and Tibetans regard it as a holy gemstone.

▲ Cornelian
Revered for its healing, spiritual, and creative qualities, cornelian is closely bound to religious symbolism. The Prophet Muhammad's seal comprised engraved cornelian set in a silver ring.

▲ Cat's Eye
Also known as Tiger's Eye, this stone symbolizes insight and mental clarity, and is therefore associated with meditation. It is thought to invoke good luck and protect the wearer against evil.

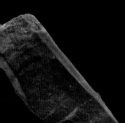

▲ Lapis lazuli
A blue stone with celestial symbolism, lapis lazuli represents power, wisdom, and inner strength. It was believed to enhance psychic abilities and insight. It is also a friendship stone.

▲ Onyx
Black stones are reputed to have protective energies. Onyx was traditionally worn to deflect negativity and symbolizes heightened senses, self-confidence, and spiritual strength. It is also linked with conjugal happiness and sincerity.

▲ Moonstone
With its pale iridescence, the moonstone has long been associated with the Moon and lovers. Its links with fertility induced Arabian women to sew them into their robes. Moonstones are also reputed to balance menstrual cycles.

◄ Crystal
Symbolic of purity, traditionally, crystals are important in magic—hence crystal balls and folk tales of magical crystal slippers. Their reputed ability to store and transmit energy makes them a healing and meditation tool.

▲ Garnet
A popular gemstone since the Bronze Age, the garnet is protective, repelling negativity, guarding against depression, and inspiring courage. It is also traditionally thought to symbolize energy, devotion, and fidelity.

▲ Aquamarine
The ancients believed that the energy of the sea was contained within the aquamarine so sailors wore the stones to protect them in heavy seas. Aquamarine is associated with creativity, communication, self-awareness, and confidence.

▲ Peridot
An emblem of fame, strength, and energy, the peridot is the birthstone for those born in August. In Hawaiian mythology peridot represents the tears of Pele, their volcano goddess.

BIRTHSTONES

Certain stones are associated with different months of the year and are thought to bring luck or influence to those born in those months. The selection varies, but a popular version is: Garnet (January); Amethyst (February); Aquamarine (March); Diamond (April); Emerald (May); Moonstone (June); Ruby (July); Peridot (August); Sapphire (September); Opal (October); Topaz (November); and Turquoise (December).

► Turquoise necklace
Turquoise (December) is traditionally associated with good luck and the promotion of friendship. Its bright color is also thought to enhance self-confidence.

► Inner radiance
Cut and faceted gemstones, such as this topaz, reveal their inner beauty and radiance. Symbolically, the process of working the stone reflects the gradual perfection of the spirits and progress towards divine wisdom, and represents the soul released from the base confines of the human body.

SEE ALSO
Dragons pp.78–79
Love & marriage pp.126–27
Amulets pp.194–95
Royalty pp.216–17
Jewellery pp.254–55

▲ The gilded idol
The Adoration of the Golden Calf serves as a symbol of idolatry and revolt against God. It relates to the Bible story in which the Israelites worshiped a golden calf.

GOLD

As lustrous and bright as the shining Sun, gold has excited passions since earliest times. As a result it is a powerful symbol of nobility, illumination, and sacredness.

▲ Sign of excellence
Universally recognized as a symbol of great human achievement, gold is often awarded in the form of medals, such as this Olympic medal, decorations, cups, and even entertainment awards.

Gold is the perfect metal: it has a brilliant sheen and is durable, malleable, and rust-proof. Its glorious color links it symbolically with the masculine Sun, perfection, and the heart. By association, it signifies the highest aspirations of the spirit, incorruptibility, and purity.

ASPIRATIONAL VALUE

Across the world gold has traditionally featured in the regalia of high office and monarchy. In the Inca empire new rulers were ceremonially covered in resin sprayed with gold dust, the historical origin of the mythical El Dorado (gilded man). Today gold is a symbol of the highest achievement or honor. Because of its qualities it has long had commercial value and has been used as currency and tribute since earliest times.

▲ Mark of enlightenment
Images of the Buddha are often gilded as a sign of enlightenment. Gold is valued for its purity and Buddhists earn merit by placing it on to sacred objects.

DIVINE GOLD

Gold is symbolically associated with various deities and religions. Jason's quest for the Golden Fleece in Greek mythology represents a search for spiritual illumination. In Christianity gold is an ambivalent symbol that can represent corruption, as in the story of the golden calf (*left*), or divinity. During coronations Christian medieval kings were

► Object of worship
Like the Mayans and Incas, the Aztecs worshiped gold and reserved it for high-ranking people and ritualistic use. To the Aztecs, gold represented the faeces of the Sun god, Huitzilopochtli.

given a golden crown, signifying Heaven's eternal light and divinely inspired authority. Divinity is represented by the gilding on the icons of Byzantine and Eastern Orthodox Christianity and the gold-leaf work in medieval art.

In both Buddhism and Christianity gold is a symbol of enlightenment. In Hindu belief it is regarded as a mineral form of light, a residue of the Sun itself. To the Egyptians gold formed the flesh of the most powerful of the gods, Re, known as the Mountain of Gold.

The ancient art of attempting to turn base metal into gold evolved into an allegory of spiritual purification becoming the alchemical Great Work. Chinese alchemists saw gold as the essence of the heavens, the harmonious Yang.

SYMBOL OF CORRUPTION

American Indian Sioux called gold "the yellow metal that makes the white man crazy," and it has attracted a certain level of negative symbolism. It was scorned in Communist Russia, where the "class enemy" was symbolized by a gold pocketwatch, traditionally worn by those of higher rank.

Some cultures feared gold, believing it to have malignant supernatural powers. Many traditional tales about gold serve as a warning against greed and temptation. The famous Greek myth about Midas, who came to regret asking the gods to grant him the gift of turning everything he touched into gold, is one such example.

SEE ALSO
The Sun *pp.16–17*
Precious matter *pp.46–47*
Egyptian deities *pp.138–39*
Buddhism *pp.164–69*
Christianity *pp.176–79*

Alchemy *pp.210–11*
Trappings of royalty *pp.218–19*
Jewelry *pp.254–55*
Colors *pp.280–83*

GOLD

PRECIOUS MATTER

In ancient times precious metal was thought to be solidified cosmic energy: it represented an earthly object with celestial potential. This belief led to the development of a cosmic hierarchy in which metals were paired with the seven known planets. Precious metals were also used both as sacred objects to symbolize divinity and as tools and weapons. Along with other precious commodities, including amber and pearl, precious metals were valued for their beauty and rarity and were often seen as status symbols.

▼ Pearls

Pearls are among the gemstones embellishing this 12th-century Byzantine crown, below. Symbolizing royalty, justice, wisdom, and purity, they were once exclusive to royalty. Representing perfection in Islamic and Hindu philosophies, pearls have long been a status symbol and have adorned rulers throughout the world.

Johannes Vermeer's portrait, *Girl with a Pearl Earring*, *(right)*, perfectly illustrates this luminous symbol of purity. Much prized as a sign of wealth, the pearl also represents the Moon, femininity, and spiritual wisdom. To the Chinese, pearls symbolically combine fire and water.

BYZANTINE CROWN

Johannes Vermeer, *Girl with a Pearl Earring*, c1665–66

▲ Lodestone
The magnetic properties of lodestone linked it with magic. Those who carried a lodestone were said to be able to pass safely among reptiles and see into the future.

▲ Lead sulphide
In alchemy lead represents the heavy, "sick" state of human existence or the soul. It is an attribute of Saturn, setter of boundaries. As the base metal it symbolizes the lowest level from which spiritual development is possible.

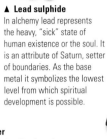

◄ Amber
Actually a fossilized sap from prehistoric trees, amber was traditionally regarded as a talisman for travelers. To early Christians it represented divine presence, while in China amber symbolizes courage or the soul of the tiger. It was also used to combat ailments such as arthritis.

▲ Iron
Iron represents strength and durability. Many cultures regarded iron smelting as spiritual, the forming of an object through smelting likened to a symbolic birth.

▲ Jet
An ancient fossilized wood, jet was regarded as a talisman against illness. It has been used as a treatment for migraines, stomach pains, and colds. Due to its color, it was often used in mourning jewelry in the West.

► Silver
This Byzantine cup is made of silver, which is linked to the Moon, Moon goddesses such as Diana, and queens. It signifies chastity, purity, wisdom, and the light of hope. In Ancient Egypt people thought that the gods' bones were made of silver. Used as currency, it also symbolizes wealth.

▲ Copper
This incense burner is made of copper, which is associated with Venus and is a symbol of the female. In West Africa copper served as a status symbol, as well as an object of cult and magic. Copper is also linked with healing; even today people wear copper bracelets to combat arthritis.

▲ Mother-of-pearl
Early societies valued mother-of-pearl more highly than actual pearls. Its iridescence symbolizes faith, charity, and innocence; it is also said to enhance focus.

▲ Coral
Coral is linked to Moon symbolism due to its watery origins. The Ancient Greeks linked it to rebirth; the Chinese with status and luck; and Christians, with Christ's blood.

▲ Ivory
Its color links ivory with purity, while its hardness signifies incorruptibility. The ivory tower represents the inaccessible; in Christianity, it symbolizes the Virgin Mary.

SEE ALSO
The Moon pp.18–19
Death & mourning pp.128–31
Christianity pp.176–79
Amulets pp.194–95
Colors pp.280–83

PRECIOUS MATTER

47

NATURAL WORLD

From soaring eagles to murky swamps, the natural world has fed our imagination ever since the first humans lived in caves. Literally and symbolically, plants and animals have fundamentally influenced the way we view the world. We have depended on both for sustenance and have always coexisted with animals, using them not just for food but also for clothing, labor, protection, and even tools. Consequently, all aspects of their lives have been imbued with symbolic significance, from the snake shedding its skin (rebirth) to a fish's watery habitat (life and fertility).

Animals—and even some plants—feature in creation stories, as ancestor figures, or are associated with gods, while earthly rulers used majestic species, such as the lion, to reflect their own glory. A common belief was that animals' highly tuned physical and sensory abilities associated them with supernatural powers that could be harnessed through shamanistic ritual. Some beliefs, such as birds being celestial messengers or souls, were so strongly held that they were incorporated into the major religions.

Animal species are infinitely varied and sometimes mirror our own behavior. Like humans, some are feared or revered; others simply amuse us as clowns or tricksters. Mythological hybrids and monsters were created, often representing complex psychological challenges; hence, "slaying the dragon" is a metaphor for good conquering evil, or mastering one's inner demons.

In common with animals, plants and trees are also a food source, which associates them with abundance, fertility, and the eternal cycle of life, death, and regeneration. Staple crops are especially important symbolically, and often feature in creation myths. Other foods, such as

LITERALLY AND SYMBOLICALLY, PLANTS AND ANIMALS HAVE FUNDAMENTALLY INFLUENCED THE WAY WE VIEW THE WORLD

tea and coffee, are connected to hospitality and ritual. Fruit—the culmination of a plant's productive powers—is associated with immortality because, although it has reached the end of one cycle, it contains the seeds for eternal renewal.

A vast number of plants are used in healing, while others are hallucinogens, poisons, or stimulants, which early societies regarded as magical, and which have a marked effect on our mental and physical well-being. Many plants are also fragrant or colorful, giving them an emotional resonance. The fleeting beauty of flowers symbolizes the glory and brevity of youth and there has also evolved a "language of flowers," which survives today; red roses, for example, remain a widely recognized symbol of love and passion.

In common with other plant life, trees are associated with fertility and the cycle of life, but their large size and longevity inspire additional themes of shelter, permanence, and immortality. Many were worshiped and the vast cosmic tree was thought to link Earth, Heaven, and the underworld; other sacred trees are usually regionally significant, such as the life-sustaining date palm in the Middle East.

Most plant symbolism is positive but where nature appears "untamed," as in woods and forests, psychological elements come into play that spawn a darker symbolism. As a dark and dangerous place in which one can easily get lost, the forest serves as a powerful metaphor for the transition to adulthood. Even today, we still try to find meaning in our world through signs and symbols.

MAMMALS

Since earliest times the lives of humans and animals have been intertwined, providing a rich source of symbolism. Animals have been worshiped as gods, linked with good or bad luck, and seen as sources of power and wisdom. Many are symbolically associated with a human quality. Hunter-gatherers respected and sometimes revered animals as being part of the natural world, which they viewed as sacred. To access their instinctual wisdom, specific animals were adopted as totems or ancestors.

▲ Wolf
In Ancient Rome the wolf was a symbol of maternal care, courage, or victory. In the West today it is associated with cunning, cruelty, lechery, and greed. American Indians invoked it in dance to guide spirits in the afterlife.

▲ Fox
Smooth-talking, sly, and treacherous, the fox embodies the qualities of a trickster. A shapeshifter in American Indian and Eastern cultures, it often appears in disguise in folklore and literature, too.

▲ Hyena
As a carrion-eater, the hyena is regarded as unclean, cowardly, and greedy. Due to an early belief that it could change gender, it came to symbolize sexual deviance.

▲ Jackal
The scavenging jackal represents destructiveness or evil in India, but in Ancient Egypt it was worshiped as Anubis, who received the dead on their way to the next world. In the Old Testament the jackal is a symbol of desolation.

◄ Coyote
In American Indian culture the wily coyote, shown here as a warrior's mask, is seen as a trickster, transformer, teacher, and cultural hero. It signifies both folly and wisdom, and the balance between the two.

► Racoon
A favourite in American Indian folklore, the racoon is a trickster and symbolizes mischief, dexterity, and adaptability. Its mask-like face represents an ability to assume disguise.

◄ Bear
In many shamanistic traditions the bear is associated with medicine, healing, and wisdom. Generally, it symbolizes strength and courage, and is linked with warlike divinities.

THE DOG

Since ancient times the dog has been seen as a companion animal symbolizing loyalty, protection, and hunting. Early societies associated it with the spirit world. African and American Indian cultures saw the dog as a master of fire and a rain-maker. However, Muslims regard the dog as unclean and use it as a derogatory term for an unbeliever.

► Hunting
The dog has been linked with hunting and its associated deities since earliest times. In Greek myth, the star, Sirius, symbolized Orion's hunting dog.

► Cerberus
As guardian of the gateway to the spirit world, Cerberus, the three-headed watchdog of Greek myth, symbolizes guardianship of the secret knowledge of death and resurrection.

▲ Coat of arms
Depicted on a coat of arms, the dog symbolizes courage, vigilance, and loyalty. Commonly featured breeds are the greyhound and mastiff.

▲ Tombstone
Many cultures regard dogs as faithful companions, even in death. They are often carved in postures of steadfast watchfulness on tombs.

▲ Squirrel
In medieval times, the red squirrel symbolized the devil because of its alertness and color. It was the emblem of Irish goddess, Medb.

▲ Flying fox
In Samoan folklore the flying fox, a fruit bat, is seen as a guardian of the forest, while in New Guinea it is a head-hunting symbol, often carved on war shields.

▲ Bat
In the West the bat is linked with vampires, the devil, and witchcraft. Seen as part bird, part rat, it symbolizes duplicity. American Indians regard it as a rain-bringer.

▲ Mouse
Although generally associated with timidity, Christians saw the mouse as the Devil, gnawing at the roots of the Tree of Life. Elsewhere, it is associated with frugality.

▲ Rat
In Asia the rat is revered as a symbol of good luck and wealth. However, it is more commonly associated with death, decay, and destruction.

▲ Beaver
An important animal in American Indian myth, this master builder signifies industry and perseverance, as well as home and family. In Christian symbolism the beaver represents chastity.

► Kangaroo
An emblem of Australia, the kangaroo can only move forward, which explains why it symbolizes progress on its country's coat of arms. Its speed and ability to go for months without water also associates it with energy and endurance. In shamanism the kangaroo represents family ties, while to the Australian Aboriginals the kangaroo is an ancestor and a tribal totem animal.

▲ Rabbit
A lunar symbol, the rabbit has ancient links with fertility and rebirth. Its alertness, speed, and timidity made it a Christian symbol of vigilance, fleeing temptation.

▲ Hare
The hare is a trickster, hero, or fertility symbol associated with the Moon. In Europe it was a witch's companion; in the East, it was a previous incarnation of the Buddha.

► Hedgehog
The hedgehog was an American Indian symbol of self-preservation. However, Christians associated it with evil and the Irish believed that witches took on hedgehog form to suckle milk from cows.

SEE ALSO
Sacred trees pp.96–97
The head pp.106–09
Fertility & childbirth pp.120–23
Tribal totems, heroes & tricksters pp.150–51
The dreaming pp.152–53
Shamanism pp.154–55
Chinese horoscope pp.204–05

MAMMALS

▲ Camel
Once believed to store water in its hump, the camel personifies the desert, temperance, humility, moderation, and stamina. Associated with royalty and wealth, its habit of kneeling has also made it a symbol of prayer.

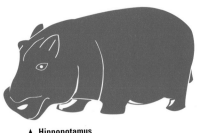

▲ Hippopotamus
In Ancient Egypt, where it wallowed in the fertile mud of the Nile, the hippopotamus symbolized rebirth and rejuvenation. Tawaret, goddess of childbirth and protection, was shown as a pregnant hippo, while the red hippo was associated with disharmony and the god, Seth.

▲ Goat
A masculine symbol associated with lust and fertility, the goat also represents agility; the climbing goat signifies determination. The goat is linked to the Ancient Greek gods Pan, Dionysus, and Zeus.

◀ Ox
The ox, shown here being ridden by Lao Tzu, the founder of Taoism, represents toil, strength, and wealth. To Christians it is the yoke of Christ, while Buddhists see the white ox as a symbol of contemplative wisdom.

▲ Cow
A symbol of maternal nourishment, the cow is seen as a personification of Mother Earth. Both lunar and astral, its crescent horns represent the Moon, and its milk the stars of the Milky Way. The cow is Hinduism's most sacred animal.

▲ Pig
The pig is associated with the Mother Goddess, representing fertility and prosperity, but is also associated with selfishness and ignorance. Jews and Muslims regard the pig as an unclean scavenger. Christians link its gluttony to Satan.

THE HORSE

A symbol of nobility, speed, freedom, and beauty, the horse is widely associated with conquering power, as represented by Classical equestrian statues. In the Ancient world the horse was an emblem of the life-force and was linked to Sun and sky gods. Different symbolism was attributed to white, black, or golden horses.

◀ White horse
A solar symbol of spiritual illumination, resurrection, and life, the white horse is a symbol of various gods. Muslims associate it with happiness.

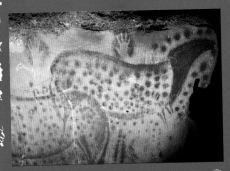

▲ Cave art
The spotted horse appears in the 20,000-year-old cave paintings at Pech Merle, France. An ancient symbol, the horse represents wind, rain, storm, fire, running water, and waves.

▲ Pegasus
In common with the white horse, the winged horse is a solar or spiritual symbol. Pegasus was the legendary winged horse of Greek mythology and often represents speed of thought.

▲ Galloping horse
Traditionally representing speed and vitality, the horse symbolically gallops "as fast as the wind," associating it with elemental power and freedom; it is also seen as a messenger.

▲ Stag
A solar emblem of fertility, the stag is associated with hunting and divine symbolism. Its antlers represent the Tree of Life and regeneration. The stag often features in heraldic motifs.

▲ Gazelle
A symbol of peace, speed, and grace, the gazelle was a mount for gods in African and Indian cultures. Fleeing from predators, it represents the soul taking flight from earthly passions.

▲ Lamb
The lamb is a universal symbol of innocence, gentleness, and meekness. It is strongly associated with Christianity which uses it to represent both Christ and sacrifice.

▲ Black sheep
Sheep symbolize meekness and, as part of a flock, require direction; the black sheep stands out as a nonconformist, hence the expression describing a maverick family member.

▲ Ram
A fire symbol and emblem of solar energy, the ram is associated with Sun and sky gods and also masculine virility. The spiral of the ram's horns represents thunder.

▲ Boar
The wild boar is an ancient symbol of strength, courage, and ferocity, especially in northern Europe. The Celts saw it as a sacred animal with supernatural powers and its meat was eaten ritually and buried with the slain. The boar features as a shapeshifter in several cultures including the Druidic, and in Melanesia. In Hinduism it was an incarnation of the god Vishnu.

◄ Elephant
Long associated with sovereign power in Africa and Asia, the elephant symbolizes strength, stability, and wisdom. The elephant-headed god, Ganesha, is worshipped by Hindus.

▲ Rhinoceros
A symbol of power and sovereignty, in heraldry the rhinoceros represents tenacity, vigor, and concord, while Africans regard the rhinoceros as a symbol of courage and fertility. It is hunted for its horn, which is used in medicine and as an aphrodisiac. The black rhinoceros has become a modern symbol for wildlife conservation.

▲ Monkey
In Christianity the monkey is associated with deception and vanity, but in Hinduism the monkey deity, Hanuman, was a great warrior, champion of Rama. In Japan the monkey is revered: the three Mystic Monkeys symbolize the correct way, "See no evil, hear no evil, speak no evil."

◄ Donkey
A donkey represents fertility, lewdness, obstinacy, humility, and patience. In *A Midsummer Night's Dream* Shakespeare gave a comic character called Bottom a donkey's head.

▲ Wild ass
In the West the ass is a symbol of stupidity and stubbornness, but in the East it symbolizes intelligence and strength. In Egypt the desert ass represents loneliness and isolation.

SEE ALSO

The night sky *pp.20–23*
Fertility & childbirth
  pp.120–23
Hinduism *pp.158–63*
Buddhism *pp.164–69*

Taoism & Shinto *pp.170–71*
Christianity *pp.176–79*
Chinese horoscope *pp.204–05*
Heraldic emblems *pp.318–23*

▲ **The power of good and evil**
As an eastern symbol of courage and strength, the tiger is sometimes depicted being
ridden by Chinese gods to signify their mastery over animal passions. The tiger is
a Yang animal with the power to drive out demons. Here it is the mount of a god
performing an exorcism during which he throws five poisonous animals from a bowl.

► Egyptian cat
In Ancient Egypt the cat was a form of the goddess Bastet.

CATS

From Ancient Egyptian times cats have captured our imagination. They have been worshiped as gods, persecuted as demons, and associated with an extraordinary range of both positive and negative symbolism.

The solar and lunar symbolism of cats is just one example of their contrasting associations. The lion, with its yellow coat and fiery mane, is a solar beast, although the lioness may also be linked to mother goddesses and so to the Moon. As solar symbols, lions are often carved into temple gateposts as guardians of the sacred space, and protective lion's heads may adorn buildings as gargoyles. By carrying water away from the walls, these solar conduits combine with the water to create a symbol of fertility. The domestic cat's aloofness and nocturnal habits give it the symbolism of both the Moon and darkness. Black cats are now considered lucky, but they were once associated with witchcraft as witches were often depicted with a black cat.

▲ Night eyes
As creatures of the night cats have been linked with magic.

KING OF BEASTS

In the West the lion is most widely known as the King of Beasts, while in the East that role is taken by the tiger, and in the Americas by the jaguar. All the big cats are fierce hunters, and for this reason they are feared and respected. In China, where they are regarded as symbols of courage, tigers represent speed, power, and beauty. The Hindu goddess, Durga, rides a tiger, symbolizing her mastery over animal passions, and Shiva wears a tiger's skin for similar reasons. Because of their courage and strength, lions and leopards feature in heraldic art, accentuating these qualities in noble lineages.

SACRED NATURE

Cats have had many sacred associations throughout the world. The jaguar is the incarnation of the supreme Aztec deity, Texcatlipoca, and Mayan reliefs depict priests wearing

◄ Jaguar
Thought by Meso-American cultures to be the lord of the night, the guardian, and the protector, the jaguar was often depicted in Aztec pottery.

jaguar skin costumes during sacrificial ceremonies. The jaguar is also associated with South American shamans, who may assume animal shapes or wear jaguar skins as a symbol of their power. After death shamans were thought to become jaguars. In the Classical world the leopard was an attribute of the Roman god Bacchus (Greek Dionysus), and was linked to his fertility cult, while in Egypt it was the emblem of Osiris, god of the underworld and vegetation, so its symbolism was again linked to fertility. The Ancient Egyptians revered cats and worshiped the cat goddess, Bastet.

CATS IN ART

Cats, and lions in particular, have appeared in many paintings. In Greek mythology one of the twelve labors of Hercules was to bring a lion's skin to King Eurystheus. He fought the lion with his bare hands and the scene appears in several paintings, as do other scenes in which a fierce lion is tamed by a good man. St. Jerome, for instance, is usually painted with a lion as his companion. He is said to have removed a thorn from the lion's paw, after which it renounced its fierce nature

▲ St. Jerome and the lion
By helping the lion, St. Jerome mastered his animal nature and demonstrated the strength of his Christian faith.

and lived peacefully as St. Jerome's follower. Such tales are much-loved for the story, but they also have added meaning as they symbolize our ability to overcome our animal nature.

CATS

BIRDS

Their ability to fly symbolically established birds as messengers between Heaven and Earth. They also represent souls because flying signifies release from the physical restrictions of the earthbound world. Bird-headed deities in Egyptian art symbolize the spiritual side of human nature. Traditionally, too, birds were linked with wisdom, intelligence, and rapid thought; the expression "a little bird told me" comes from the ancient belief that birds confided secrets.

▲ Albatross
The wandering albatross is symbolic of long ocean journeys. To Maoris, it represents power and beauty, while in the West it is thought to embody the soul of a dead sailor; to kill one is unlucky.

▲ Pelican
The legend that the pelican fed its young with blood drawn from its own breast resulted in it becoming a symbol of charity and love as well as of Christ's sacrifice.

▲ Heron
This solar bird shares much of the symbolism of the stork and crane and represents vigilance, quiet, and tact. In Ancient Egypt it was a symbol of the morning Sun and regeneration.

▲ Kingfisher
The kingfisher is associated with conjugal bliss, grace, and speed. It is also associated with the halcyon bird of Greek mythology, which symbolizes calm.

▲ Ibis
In Ancient Egypt the ibis was a symbol of wisdom and an incarnation of the god, Thoth, who was associated with scribes. It was mummified to give instruction in the afterlife.

Zeus disguised as a swan

► Goose
Signifying vigilance, the wild goose's migrations made it a symbol of freedom and renewal. In Hinduism it is the mount of Brahma, the creator. In folklore the goose represents family life, loyalty, and gossip.

▲ Stork
Its migratory habit associates the stork with spring and new life. It is also a herald of good news. Its symbolic link with childbirth goes back to Greek mythology where it was sacred to Hera, patron of childbirth.

▲ Flamingo
Ancient Egyptians revered the flamingo as a personification of the Sun god, Re. Because their color changes according to diet, flamingos were also associated with illusion and shapeshifting.

▲ Swan
The swan is a symbol of beauty and purity. A solar bird, it is associated with light and was linked to Apollo. Its habit of mating for life also makes it a symbol of fidelity. In Greek myth Zeus, disguised as a swan, seduced Leda.

▲ Duck
Regarded as a creator bird in the myths of various cultures, the duck is widely associated with immortality. In China the mandarin duck signifies wedded bliss and fidelity, while Celts believed the duck represented resourcefulness and honesty.

▲ Hoopoe
Symbolizing joy and affection in Ancient Egypt, the hoopoe also represents filial devotion since it is said to care for its aged parents. In China it is considered lucky.

▲ Ostrich
A heraldic symbol of faith and contemplation, in Ancient Egypt the ostrich's feather symbolized truth. To Zoroastrians it was a divine storm bird, whereas in Semitic and Babylonian cultures it was demonic.

▲ Crane
In Asia the crane's careful movements represent tact. In China it signifies immortality. It has also become a symbol of vigilance. The double-headed crane of Egyptian mythology signifies prosperity.

▲ Quail
The quail is associated with spring or summer, eroticism, and new life. Given as a lover's gift, a caged quail was a symbol of the imprisoned soul. To the Romans it symbolized courage and was used as a fighting bird.

▲ Kiwi
The national emblem of New Zealand and slang for a New Zealander, the kiwi has also been used as a military symbol. According to Polynesian myth, it was created from the calabash, a vine plant.

The owl was the symbol of Greek goddess, Athene, and of Athens, her city.

▲ Owl
As a nocturnal bird of prey, the owl is linked with darkness, death, wisdom, and witchcraft. Australian Aboriginals believe owls represent women's souls. Many cultures link the owl to spiritual symbolism.

▲ Hawk
An attribute of Sun gods, the hawk symbolizes the heavens, power, royalty, and wisdom. The Aztecs saw it as a messenger of the gods. In China it meant war and in Ancient Egypt it represented the soul.

▲ Falcon
The falcon is a solar bird symbolizing masculine power; its soaring flight signifies freedom of spirit. To American Indians it is a messenger of the ancestors. Used for hunting by the aristocracy, the falcon also represents nobility. In Ancient Egypt it was a symbol of divine kingship.

◄ Vulture
Because it scavenges on dead flesh, the vulture has mixed symbolism: on the one hand it symbolizes death and opportunism, while on the other purification. Tibetans and Parsees allow vultures to dispose of their dead and believe the birds can release or transport a corpse's spirit. The vulture also symbolizes maternal solicitude since when food is scarce it is rumored to feed its own flesh to its young.

▲ Condor
The condor is an important American Indian symbol. Seen as both creator and destroyer, its massive wingspan was thought to cause eclipses. The California condor is associated with healing and supernatural powers and was used in ritual sacrifice.

SEE ALSO
The Sun *pp.16–17*
Fertility & childbirth *pp.120–23*
Egyptian deities *pp.138–39*
Greek & Roman deities *pp.140–41*

BIRDS

▲ **Rooster**
A solar bird, the rooster is a symbol of the dawn, male pride, fertility, and courage. Crowing represents domination. It was sacred to several Ancient Greek and Roman gods, and its image was used in Shinto on drums calling people to prayer.

◄ **Peacock**
The peacock's splendor represents divinity, royalty, beauty, and love. In Hinduism, the bird is the mount of Kartikeya, god of war, while Buddhists equate the peacock with compassion and vigilance. Its tail markings have eye, star, and solar symbols. The strutting male peacock is associated with vanity.

◄ **Parrot**
Known for its mocking mimicry, the parrot symbolizes imitation. It was an attribute of Kama, Hindu god of love, as people in love mimic one another's behavior. American Indians see it as a carrier of prayers, a rain-bringer, and a seer.

▲ **Hummingbird**
The hummingbird is seen as a joyful messenger of the gods and, to American Indians, as a symbol of beauty, harmony, truth, and strength. Its feathers adorned Aztec and Mayan gods and were reputed to have magical properties. The hummingbird also symbolizes rebirth and healing.

▲ **Hen**
The traditional image of a plump hen fussing over her brood is generally associated with clucking maternal care. It also signifies procreation and divine intervention. In Hebrew law a hen and cock together symbolize a bridal couple.

▲ **Raven**
Regarded as a talking bird, the raven is associated with prophecy, but it attracts mixed symbolism. In some cultures it represents the Sun and wisdom and in others darkness and destruction. In Nordic mythology Odin, god of war, was accompanied by two ravens, while American Indians saw it as a creator and trickster.

▲ **Crow**
Like the raven, the carrion-eating crow has negative symbolism in Europe and is linked to bad luck, death, and evil. However, American Indians see it as a creative, civilizing, and solar bird. In Japan the crow symbolizes family love, while Christians associate its plucking out eyes from carrion with the Devil blinding sinners.

▲ **Jay**
Its reputation for nest-robbing and mimicry associates the jay with mischief and bad luck. American Indians see it as a trickster, creator, and guardian; its chattering warned of approaching enemies.

▲ **Nightingale**
The nightingale is renowned for its glorious song that continues through the night as well as throughout the day; it is associated with yearning, love, and death. In Christian tradition the nightingale's song represents a longing for Paradise, while its joyous dawn chorus symbolizes the coming of Christ's Light.

▲ **Magpie**
The garrulous magpie is an oracular bird. In the West its black and white plumage is associated with bishops, while in China it signifies good fortune and love, while Australian Aboriginals link it to happiness. However, in European folklore, a single magpie is seen as a bad omen.

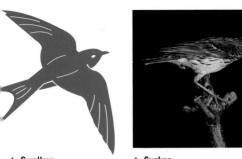

▲ Swallow
Harbinger of hope and springtime, the swooping swallow signifies good fortune. Its annual migration and habit of returning to the same nesting site associate it with both departure and return, representing death and resurrection.

▲ Cuckoo
A traditional herald of spring in northern Europe, the cuckoo symbolizes fertility. Its parasitical habit of laying its eggs in another bird's nest is associated with selfishness and infidelity, giving rise to the word "cuckold" for a man whose wife is unfaithful. However, Tibetans consider the cuckoo a sacred bird and attribute it with magical powers.

▲ Bird of Paradise
Famed for its extravagant plumage and elaborate mating rituals, the Bird of Paradise is a symbol of New Guinea; it flies across the red section of the national flag, representing the country's triumphant emergence into nationhood. Local tribes use Bird of Paradise plumes in rituals and as decoration.

▶ Dove
A universal symbol of peace and the soul, the dove returned to Noah bearing an olive branch, signifying God's forgiveness of humankind after the Flood. It is associated with the divine spirit and is symbolic of baptism. In Ancient Rome the dove was sacred to Venus, while in China it represented fertility. The turtle dove symbolizes both love and fidelity.

▲ Dodo
Extinct since the 17th century, the dodo symbolizes something that is dead or obsolete. It appears on the coat of arms of Mauritius, its native island, and is also an emblem of certain conservation organizations.

▶ Blackbird
Its alluring song and glossy black plumage make the blackbird a Christian symbol of sexual temptation.

▲ Goldfinch
In Christian art this bird's red face symbolizes the Passion of Christ as the goldfinch is associated with thistles and thorns. Elsewhere, it represents fertility and was a symbol of protection against the plague.

▲ Robin
In Europe the robin is a popular Christmas symbol associated with the winter solstice. Like the goldfinch, the robin is said to have plucked a thorn from Christ's crown, splashing blood over its breast.

▲ Wren
The tiny wren is a symbol of the spirit and was known in European folklore as "the King of the Birds." To American Indians it is a symbol of joy. The wren is traditionally seen as a symbol of the old year.

▲ Sparrow
The humble sparrow is a Christian symbol of lowliness; St. Francis of Assisi showed his love of all animals by addressing his sermon to these birds. The sparrow also represents fertility and is an attribute of Aphrodite, Greek goddess of love; in Japan it symbolizes loyalty.

SEE ALSO
The Sun pp.16–17
The head pp.106–09
Tribal totems, heroes & tricksters pp.150–51
Hinduism pp.158–63
Christianity pp.176–79

COAT OF ARMS

▲ **The double-headed eagle**
This detail of the coat of arms of Charles V, Holy Roman
emperor from 1519 to 1558 shows a double-headed eagle.
It represents Rome's western and eastern empires, with
one head gazing westward to Rome and the other, east
toward Byzantium.

EAGLES

An unambiguous and universally recognized symbol of power, the eagle is widely associated with solar and celestial symbolism and is linked to royalty and the gods.

Its size, strength, and authority has made the eagle an emblem of power, while its keen eyesight, speed, hunting prowess, and ability to wheel effortlessly through the heavens all contribute to its symbolic associations. The eagle is often paired with the serpent, bull, or lion, which are symbolically linked to spiritual victory.

SIGN OF POWER

The king of birds, the eagle is a "high-flier" symbolizing status, victory, and omniscience. Associated with power and leadership, it has been adopted as a symbol of sovereignty and national identity by nations including the US and Germany, as well as mighty civilizations such as the Roman Empire. The eagle was also the imperial emblem of the Russian and Austrian empires and was borne on the standard of Napoleon. The eagle's physical attributes, and its reputation as a formidable hunter, link it to warrior symbolism and war gods such as Scandinavia's Odin. The Chinese equate the eagle with courage, tenacity, strength, and fearlessness, while in Christianity it represents the power of God.

BIRD OF THE SUN

As a solar bird, the eagle is symbolic of the gods of the sky. It was the emblem of the Roman Sun god, *sol invictus*, meaning

▲ **United States presidential seal**
The mighty eagle appears here in the original design of 1888. The olive branch symbolizes peace, and 13 arrows (the 13 original colonies) represents willingness to defend the country.

"victorious over darkness," and was used to represent the Emperor. In American Indian culture the Sioux believed that eagle feathers represented the Sun's rays. The Aztecs saw the bird as the rising Sun, devourer of the serpent of darkness. In the Hebrew tradition it symbolizes the East and renewal. The double-headed eagle is an ancient solar symbol and is used in heraldry and coats of arms.

DIVINE MESSENGER

Soaring high in the sky, the eagle represents nearness to God and is associated with ascension.

In churches, the Bible is often placed on an eagle-shaped lectern, representing the power and inspiration of God's word. Symbolic of mystical power, the eagle is widely regarded as a divine messenger; it also represents spiritual protection and an ability to rise above the material world to see hidden spiritual truths. In American Indian culture the eagle signifies revelation. It is associated with numerous gods and is also a Celtic symbol of rebirth and renewal. To the Ancient Egyptians the eagle was a symbol of eternal life.

▲ **Eagle warrior**
This Aztec sculpture from New Mexico represents an eagle warrior, symbolic of courage in battle.

◀ **Chapungu bird**
A Shona word meaning "Bateleur Eagle," the Chapungu bird was revered as a protector, guiding spirit, and divine messenger. This carving of the bird is from the ruined city of Great Zimbabwe.

SEE ALSO
The Sun *pp. 16–17*
Egyptian deities *pp. 138–39*
Greek & Roman deities *pp. 140–41*
Judaism *pp. 172–73*
Christianity *pp. 176–79*
Heraldic emblems *pp. 318–23*

REPTILES & AMPHIBIANS

Ancient, mysterious, and often threatening, reptiles and amphibians have long captured the human imagination. They are associated with the Sun and Moon, and also cosmos and creation symbolism, and signify change and renewal because many cyclically shed their skin or change color. Amphibians and certain reptiles can survive in water as well as on land, representing the ability to move between the physical and spirit world. Their habits, appearance, and often bizarre defense mechanisms also contribute to their symbolism.

▲ Monitor lizard
A totem animal associated with magic, the monitor lizard represents shapeshifting, change, agility, and objective detachment. More generally, lizards were once thought to have no tongue and so symbolized silence; they also represent divine wisdom.

▲ Salamander
Usually portrayed as a small dragon or wingless lizard leaping out of the flames, the salamander is a symbol of fire; in heraldry it is associated with courage. Originally believed to be sexless, it also represents chastity.

▲ Alligator
An American Indian totem, the alligator represents maternal love (unlike most reptiles, it guards its nest), stealth, aggression, survival, and adaptability. In Columbia a mythological were-alligator links it to shapeshifting.

▲ Crocodile
Widely feared and revered, the crocodile was worshiped as the god Sebek in Ancient Egypt, where it was a symbol of sunrise and the fertile waters, and also guarded the threshold between life and death. Traditionally it is said to weep after eating men, which gave rise to the term "crocodile tears."

▲ Chameleon
Famous for its ability to change skin color, the chameleon symbolizes inconstancy. It can also move each eye independently—one eye is thought to see into the future, the other back into the past.

▲ Frilled lizard
In Australian myth the frilled lizard represents Gundamen and the need to adhere to tribal discipline. Originally a smooth-skinned man, Gundamen was punished for wrongdoing and transformed into a scaly lizard.

▲ Gila monster
According to American Indian Navajo legend, the gila monster was the first medicine man; his peculiar gait was associated with hand-trembling, a shamanistic ability to divine and heal serious illness.

FROGS AND TOADS

From Ancient Egypt to Japan, frogs and toads have long been associated with a wide range of symbolism, much of it concerning fertility and magic. Their metamorphic life cycle links them to lunar and water symbolism; they are also associated with birth and transformation, hence popular fables about frogs turning into princes. In 15th-century Europe both toads and frogs were linked to magic and witchcraft.

▲ Tadpole
The metamorphosis of the tadpole into a frog symbolizes resurrection. In Ancient Egypt the frog was a fetal symbol, while Heket, frog goddess of birth, is linked with evolution.

▲ Frog
In Celtic myth the frog was lord of the Earth and the healing waters, while Mayans saw it as a water god whose croaking invoked rain. In China it is a lunar, Ying symbol.

▲ Bullfrog
A large, aggressive amphibian famed for its vocal powers, the bullfrog personifies thunder in India, while in China it is thought to cause eclipses by swallowing the Moon. It is the state emblem of Missouri and Oklahoma.

▲ Swarm of frogs
In the Bible a terrible swarm of frogs represented one of the plagues of Egypt sent by God as a warning to His people to change their ways.

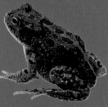

▲ Toad
In Europe the toad's toxic secretions link it to demonic symbolism. It is also an attribute of death and a witch's familiar. In China the toad is a rain-bringer, signifying good luck.

▲ Cane toad
To Australian Aboriginals the highly-toxic cane toad is a symbol of white man's stupidity because they introduced the species to the continent. It shares its symbolism with other toads, and as a prolific breeder, is associated with fertility.

◄ Gecko
A symbol of wisdom, agility, and adaptability, the harmless gecko (a small house lizard) is considered lucky; to Polynesians it is sacred. Its ability to discard and re-grow its tail represents renewal.

► Horned lizard
The horned lizard is an American Indian symbol of health and happiness; the Anasazi and Mimbre tribes of the Southwest United States often featured it on pottery and in petroglyphs. It is also the state reptile of Texas.

▲ Tortoise
Closely linked to lunar, water, and Earth Mother symbolism, the lumbering tortoise is often portrayed as supporting the world at the beginning of creation. It is associated with longevity and plodding slowness. In China it is believed to have oracular powers.

▲ Turtle
A turtle tattoo signifies a sailor who has crossed the equator. In Ancient Egypt the turtle represented drought, while in American Indian culture it was a cowardly braggart.

◄ Terrapin
In the sacred springs of North Africa terrapins are believed to embody powerful water spirits; it is therefore considered unlucky to kill one. The terrapin is portrayed as a trickster in American Indian myth.

SEE ALSO
The Sun pp.16–17
The Moon pp.18–19
Fertility & childbirth pp.120–23
Tribal totems, heroes, & tricksters pp.150–51

REPTILES & AMPHIBIANS

▲ The serpent in Paradise
The snake tempted Eve to taste the forbidden fruit on the Tree of Knowledge,
knowing it would cause her downfall. It represents deceit and temptation;
coiled around Eve, the snake symbolizes the male/female relationship.

SNAKES

With its unusual appearance and unique way of moving, the snake has always evoked both fascination and revulsion. The simple beauty of its form is at odds with its complex and powerful symbolism.

Self-contained, mysterious, inhabiting underground burrows, and shedding its skin, the snake is a chthonic creature, that is, one linked to the underworld. Its undulating movement reminded early cultures in many parts of the world of winding rivers, rolling hills, tangled roots, and even the spiraling cosmos. As a result, its myriad symbolism embraces themes of duality, fertility, the primeval life force, and creation.

▲ Medical symbol
The caduceus, a rod entwined with two snakes, is an ancient emblem of healing associated with Hermes, messenger of the Greek gods.

A DUAL POWER

In mythology and religion the snake is a dual power signifying both positive and negative symbolism. It is guardian and destroyer, light and dark, good and evil. Its venom can kill and it swallows creatures much larger than itself, yet its habit of shedding its skin links it to resurrection and healing. In Christianity the snake corrupts Eve by persuading her to taste the forbidden fruit. God cursed the snake who was then seen as the Devil. However, in Buddhism, the king of the snakes gave shelter to the Buddha and is seen in a more positive light. Being at home in dark places below the ground, the snake is associated with the underworld where it accesses the powers of the dead. In contrast it is also linked to deities and divine power.

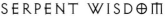

▲ Naga
The Hindu *naga*, or serpent, is a benevolent threshold guardian associated with rain, fertility, and renewal. It is often depicted with a human upper body and a snake tail.

SERPENT WISDOM

Ancestral and cosmic associations, combined with the snake's ability to glide through darkness, and its enigmatic, lidless gaze link it with wisdom. In Ancient Egypt the cobra represented both divine and royal wisdom. Maoris equate snakes with earthly wisdom while in many cultures snakes are the wise and cunning mediators between Heaven, Earth, and the underworld. In India serpents are associated with Shiva, Vishnu, and Ganesha. In Tantra the column of spiritual energy within the spinal column is symbolized by the "kundalini," or serpent.

FERTILITY AND BIRTH

Due to its shape, closeness to the Earth, and ability to shed its skin, the snake is a fertility and phallic symbol. It is associated with Mother Earth and in parts of Oceania it is linked to pregnancy. Elsewhere, it is a rain-bringer and represents a life force in tune with the Earth's mysteries. In Hindu mythology Vishnu rests on the serpent as it floats on the cosmic ocean. In Oceania, the snake is a creator figure; elsewhere, a mythical ancestor. As a rainbringer, like the Rainbow Serpent of Australian Aboriginal Dreamtime, it represents fertility and agricultural abundance.

▲ Guardian of the dead
Meretseger, guardian of the entombed dead shown as a coiled cobra at a burial site at Waset, Egypt; her name means "She who loves silence."

◄ Snakes and ladders
Originally an Indian board game in which virtues (ladders) allowed players to reach Heaven, while vices (snakes) set them back, Snakes and Ladders was later adopted by the British Raj and brought to the West.

SEE ALSO
Sacred trees *pp.96–97*
Fruits of the Earth *pp.98–99*
Fertility & childbirth *pp.120–23*
Greek & Roman deities
  pp.140–41
The Dreaming *pp.152–53*
Creation stories *pp.156–57*
Hinduism *pp.158–63*
Christianity *pp.176–79*
Professional symbols *pp.314–15*

AQUATIC CREATURES

Through the ages, aquatic creatures have been worshiped as gods, feared as monsters of the deep, and hunted for their flesh, skin, oils, bones, shells, and eggs. Their symbolism is closely bound to their behavior and appearance, the impact they have had on human culture, and their habitat. As a result, a great deal of the symbolism associated with these creatures is related to water, particularly to themes of birth, creation, and the Moon. Fish are widely linked to spiritual wisdom, fertility, and regeneration; swimming freely in water, they often signify harmony and marital bliss.

► Carp
In China and Japan carp-shaped kites symbolize courage and endurance, qualities associated with the carp because it swims against a river's flow. It also represents academic achievement and business acumen, and is a symbol of good luck and longevity.

► Crab
Associated with the astrological sign, Cancer, the crab's watery habitat makes it a lunar animal; reminiscent of the Moon's changing forms, it also casts its shell, symbolizing renewal. In China the crab's awkward, sideways gait represents dishonesty and unreliability.

▲ Lobster
The Japanese associate the lobster with longevity and happy events, such as New Year; to the Chinese it is a symbol of wealth and marital harmony, and is often eaten at wedding feasts. As a food, its high cost has made it a contemporary symbol of extravagance.

►
Seahorse
A popular emblem among seafarers and in heraldry, the seahorse symbolizes grace, confidence, the power of the ocean, and safe travel. In Greek myth seahorses pulled Poseidon's chariot across the ocean.

▼ Whale
A symbol of the womb and regeneration, as reflected in the Old Testament story of Jonah and the Whale, this ocean giant represents the might of the sea. It is also equated with plenty in Maori tradition.

▲ Shark
A symbol of masculine power, hunting prowess, and ferocity, the shark is revered in Pacific and African cultures. It is represented in male initiation ceremonies and also used as a totem. A popular ancestor figure in Oceania, Australian Aboriginals saw it as a creator figure.

▲ Dolphin
The dolphin is often seen as a psychopomp, a being who escorts souls to the underworld, and is associated with salvation, transformation, and love. It also has lunar and solar associations.

NATURAL WORLD

► Seal
Representing transformation, the seal was often changed into a mermaid or nymph in Greek and northern European myths. In Inuit tradition the seal is an ancestor figure and divine messenger.

◄ Sea urchin
A symbol of dormant force, the sea urchin is associated with the cosmic egg representing embryonic life, and with related symbolism concerning stones. In medieval compendiums, its habit of anchoring itself to a rock was interpreted as a storm warning.

▲ Starfish
The starfish is a celestial symbol and also represents divine love. In Christianity it is associated with the Holy Spirit and the Virgin Mary. Its remarkable ability to regenerate limbs links it to rebirth.

▲ Eel
Widely regarded as a phallic symbol, the Chinese associate the eel with carnal love. Elsewhere, the eel denotes a slippery individual. In Oceanic cultures the eel appears as a trickster and fertility symbol; it also replaces snake symbolism in countries that do not have snakes, such as New Zealand.

▲ Salmon
In Celtic culture the salmon represented wisdom and knowledge; it is also associated with fertility and bounty. A popular American Indian totem, it is a lunar symbol of renewal because it mysteriously returns from the ocean to its birth river to spawn and die.

▼ Octopus
Due to its transformational abilities, the octopus symbolizes the supernatural. Its ability to change color can represent inconstancy. Some American Indian tribes regard it as a spirit helper; in Hawaiian myth, it represents the creator god, Kanaloa.

THE SHELL

Linked to water and lunar symbolism, shells are regarded as feminine; their concave shape signifies the womb and birth. They are also associated with creation. Several deities have been portrayed emerging from a shell. In Christianity, shells are linked to baptism because they are used to sprinkle water.

▲ Cowrie
The cowrie is a fertility symbol associated with the vulva and sexual congress. It was one of the earliest symbols of wealth and was used as a divination tool.

▲ Shell as a chariot
The shell chariot is the symbol of an ocean god, such as the Greek god, Poseidon, shown here; it also represents a journey across the sea.

► Conch
Its shape associates the conch with the lunar spiral, the waters, or the rising and setting of the Sun. In Islam it represents the ear that hears the divine word. It is one of the eight auspicious Buddhist symbols.

► Scallop
In Christianity this shell came to symbolize pilgrimage after it was carried by those on the route to Santiago de Compostela. In Ancient Rome the scallop was linked to fertility and sexual passion.

Scallop shell

SEE ALSO
Water *pp.32–33*
Greek & Roman deities
pp.140–41
Creation stories *pp.156–57*
Buddhism *pp.164–69*
Western astrology *pp.200–01*
Heraldic emblems *pp.318–23*

THE BIRTH ⊕F VENUS

This icon of Renaissance art represents the moment when the goddess Venus emerges from the sea. She is blown to shore on a shell by the west winds, where a goddess of the seasons hands her a flowered cloak. Far from a simple representation of the myth, the artist has added many symbolic details to the painting.

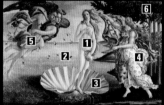

1. Venus
Traditionally, Venus was a symbol of birth and fertility, love, and sexual desire. Here the naked goddess is a symbol not just of earthly, but of spiritual love. Some have likened the image to that of the Virgin Mary.

2. Pink rose
Venus was the goddess of flowers and was associated with the pink rose in particular. This represents human sexuality and desire.

3. Scallop shell
The scallop shell upon which Venus stands was originally a symbol of the female sexual organs. Christianity transformed this fertility myth and made the scallop shell a symbol of the hope of resurrection and rebirth.

4. The nymph
Horae was a goddess of Spring, a season symbolizing fertility and birth. She wears Spring flowers and myrtle, a plant symbolic of happiness that was often used in marriage rituals.

5. The zephyrs (winds)
The zephyrs, Zephyr and Chloris, symbolize spiritual passion. They help bring together Spirit and Matter.

6. Gold
Used throughout the painting, gold accentuates the picture's role as a precious object and echoes the divine status of Venus. Gold is also symbolic of perfection, warmth, and love.

Sandro Botticelli, *The Birth of Venus*, c1482

CREEPY CRAWLIES

Bugs symbolize all that is small and insignificant in our world, yet the inescapable fact remains that without them, human life would soon die out. They perform an extraordinary array of vital functions in our ecosystem, including soil aeration, pollination, pest control, and the decomposition of dead materials; these habits and their diverse forms have inspired a rich vein of symbolism. Many insects are also associated with gods, spirits, and the underworld.

► Praying mantis
Seen as magical and holy, or demonic and devouring, the praying mantis attracts ambivalent symbolism. "Mantis" comes from the Greek word for "prophet," associating it with mystical powers. In Japan it is a popular Samurai emblem of courage and cunning.

▲ Fly
As disease-carriers, flies symbolize corruption and evil; Beezlebub, the Devil, originates from a Hebrew word meaning "Lord of the Flies." Among the American Indian Navajo, Dontso, "Big Fly," is a spirit messenger linked to healing.

▲ Dragonfly
In China the dragonfly's erratic, darting flight represents unreliability, while in Japan it is a symbol of joy as well as an imperial emblem. The dragonfly's iridescent colors associate it with magic and illusion.

▲ Butterfly
The butterfly's miraculous cycle of metamorphosis links it with transformation, resurrection, and the soul. It also signifies happiness and beauty; in Japan it is a symbol of the geisha but two butterflies together signify a joyful marriage.

▲ Moth
Usually nocturnal, moths are associated with darkness; in Bosnia it is believed witches may take the form of a moth. Their habit of hovering around a flame attracts ambivalent symbolism: as the soul seeking God, and also as insanity, rushing headlong towards doom.

▲ Wasp
From Ancient Egypt to Poland, the wasp has been widely regarded as evil and an inverted symbol of the bee, which traditionally represents goodness. In Hindu tradition the wasp is the lowest of all living creatures.

◄ Beetle
The scarab beetle was sacred to the Ancient Egyptians and was associated with the god of the rising Sun, Khepri. It represents regeneration, immortality, and divine wisdom.

▲ Ladybird
The ladybird's huge appetite for insect pests probably explains why it became a good luck symbol. It was traditionally associated with the Virgin Mary ("Our Lady's bird"), fertility, and motherhood.

▲ Grasshopper
The grasshopper's fertility made it a symbol of abundance in Ancient Greece, where the nobility wore golden grasshoppers in their hair. In Asia the insect's singing represents the chanting of the Buddhist monks, and in China the grasshopper is a symbol of good luck.

NATURAL WORLD

72

THE BEE

The bee is a popular symbol of order, diligence, immortality, and collaboration. These qualities contribute to its prolific use in Christian symbolism, as does honey, representing sweetness, and beeswax (used for candles), which signifies light. The bee is also associated with royalty and deities.

BUMBLE BEE

◄ Kama's bees
The Hindu god of love, Kama, is accompanied by honeybees, symbolizing the pain and sweetness of love. He appears as a winged youth bearing a bow and arrow, similar to Cupid, and riding a parrot; his bowstring is actually a line of bees.

◄ Beehive

An important symbol in both freemasonry and heraldry, the beehive denotes industry and cooperation. It also represents the Church, and in Greece, where hives were traditionally tomb-shaped, it can signify immortality. Beehives are also associated with an ordered community.

▲ Queen bee
Life in a hive revolves around the queen bee, making it an emblem of royalty; more recently, it has come to signify the female in charge. The queen bee also symbolizes the Virgin Mary and supreme mother.

◄ Coat of arms
The bee is widely used in Christian symbolism and represents, among other things, God's servant. The coat of arms of Pope Urban VIII (1623–44) features three golden bees chosen for their association with loyalty and diligence.

► Locust
Their ability to decimate crops associates locusts with calamity and destruction. In the Old Testament God sent a plague of locusts as a terrible punishment; in medieval bestiaries they symbolized spiritual torment, indecision, and ruin.

▲ Ant
Ant symbolism reflects its industrious, orderly behavior. In Mali, West Africa, ants signify fertility, and wells are often sunk near anthills as it is believed that ants know the location of streams.

▲ Termite
Termite and ant symbolism are intertwined in terms of fertility and industry. In India termite mounds represent the entrance to the otherworld, guarded by Nagas (divine serpents) and decorated with offerings.

▲ Spider
Seen as the Great Mother, a weaver of destiny, a solar symbol, and predator, the spider and its web are both symbolic. In Camaroon it represents diligence and wisdom. In China a spider on a thread is a symbol of good luck.

◄ Worm
Symbolic of the Earth, death, and dissolution, the worm is sometimes used in art to represent mortality. Cultures, including those of Ireland and China, link the worm to ancestor and creator myths.

◄ Scorpion
As an astrological sign, Scorpio, the scorpion is associated with Pluto, Lord of the Underworld. Generally, its lethal sting symbolizes death and destruction. Christians associate it with treachery, while in Africa many people use a euphemism when referring to it, believing that uttering its name would invoke evil. Among the Ashanti of West Africa, people wear scorpion talismans as protection against their sting.

▲ Snail
In heraldry the snail signifies deliberation and steadfastness but it is more widely associated with slowness. A lunar and feminine symbol, the spiral shell represents infinity and the

SEE ALSO
The Sun *pp.16–17*
Fertility & childbirth *pp.120–23*
Western astrology *pp.200–01*
Freemasonry *pp.260–61*
Shapes *pp.284–89*
Heraldic emblems *pp.318–23*

FABULOUS BEASTS

Regarded as symbols of supernatural power or different aspects of the human psyche, imaginary beasts have long played an important role in folklore, mythology, and religious imagery. They sometimes act as messengers or teachers, or represent dark, untamed forces in nature that must be overcome. As such, they may be fought by a hero figure, such as a knight slaying a dragon, allowing good to triumph over evil, or order over chaos. Fabulous beasts are often associated with deities, sometimes acting as their vehicle or mount. A hybrid beast— a composite animal or one that is part human—draws on its amalgamated symbolism to create new meaning.

▲ **Phoenix**
A legendary fire bird that resurrects itself from the flames, the phoenix originated as a myth to explain the cyclical rising and setting of the Sun; it later evolved into an emblem of resurrection.

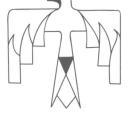

▲ **Thunderbird**
To American Indians the thunderbird is a mighty bird god that creates thunder by beating its wings, and hurls lightning as its weapon. It represents the powerful forces of nature, the sky, war, and transformation.

▲ **Griffin**
Part-eagle, part-lion, the griffin is a popular symbol in the Classical world as well as in medieval Christianity and heraldry. It evolved from an emblem signifying the Sun, strength, and vengeance into one of vigilant protection. In hieroglyphics it symbolizes divine retribution.

▲ **Basilisk**
With the wings, crest, and claws of a rooster and a reptilian body, the fearsome basilisk (or cockatrice) became a Christian symbol of the Devil; in the medieval period it was associated with lust and disease.

▲ **Simurgh**
Part-bird, part-mammal, the gigantic Simurgh is of Persian origin. A guardian with healing powers, it symbolizes the union of Heaven, Earth, and fertility.

◀ **Kinnara and kinnari**
A familiar Asian emblem, the fabulous kinnara originated in India. This human-bird hybrid is a mythological celestial musician associated with eternal lovers; the female version, kinnari (pictured), symbolizes beauty, grace, and accomplishment. In some Buddhist traditions kinnara represent four of the Buddha's animal incarnations.

◀ **Tengu**
A fearsome-looking man with clawed feet, wings, and a bird's head, the Japanese tengu is a mythological figure of Shinto origin with an antipathy for Buddhist worship, which he feels he should receive. This supernatural goblin is a trickster associated with the martial arts; he inflicts punishment on hypocrisy and arrogance.

GARUDA AND NAGA

The sun bird, Garuda, is the mount (*vahana*) of the Hindu god, Vishnu, while the naga are mythological serpents associated with the life-giving waters and fertility. These creatures also appear in Buddhist mythology as minor deities. In the West Garuda signifies the unfettered spirit, and the nagas, rooted Mother Earth.

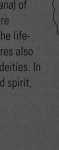

▲ Garuda
An eagle-man hybrid of Buddhist and Hindu mythology, the Garuda is also the national emblem of Thailand and symbol of their royal family. This version is called Krut Pha, meaning "garuda acting as the vehicle (of Vishnu)."

▲ Entwined in eternal battle
In the Hindu epic, the *Mahabharata*, Garuda is the nemesis of the nagas, who were originally cousins. Due to a bet, Garuda is forced to carry out the nagas' whims. In eternal battle, these creatures symbolize the opposition between the Sun and water; Garuda triumphs as the Sun evaporates moisture.

◄ Naga
Nagas are mythical serpents that guard treasures. In India they are revered as nature spirits, protectors of wells, springs, and rivers, and are associated with rain and fertility. In Buddhism, the naga is often interchangeable with the dragon and the serpent.

► Double-headed serpent
In Meso-American culture a huge, mythological double-headed serpent supports the Sun as it travels across the sky; the double-headed serpent bar acts as a sky symbol and an emblem of power. It represents control over both Earth and the cosmos.

▲ Hydra
The nine-headed monster of Greek myth, Hydra, is depicted as a serpent. If one of its heads was lost, another would grow in its place. Its ability to regenerate led to it being associated with fertility.

◄ Gorgon
In Ancient Greece the emblem of the Gorgon was often used to ward off evil. This monster-woman with writhing, venomous snakes for hair is associated with the ocean, the underworld, and Athena in her destructive, solar aspect.

► Makara
A composite aquatic dragon of Hindu myth, the Makara is part-animal, part-reptile, and part-fish. It symbolizes the astrological sign of Capricorn, called Makara in the Hindu calendar. It is also associated with Kamadeva, god of lust, and water, the source of life and fertility.

SEE ALSO
Sacred trees *pp.96–97*
Greek & Roman deities *pp.140–41*
Buddhism *pp.164–69*
Western astrology *pp.200–01*
Heraldic emblems *pp.318–23*

FABULOUS BEASTS

▲ Qitou

The mythical qitou is a Chinese tomb guardian and protector of the dead. It is an earth spirit with an ogre-like face, large elephant ears, wings, and a lion's body with a plume cresting its spine.

▲ Kirttimukha

According to myth, the Kirttimukha, or Face of Glory, is a demon who devoured himself at the order of Shiva, and whose image was placed above temple doorways as a symbol of devotion and protection.

▲ Chinthe (Chin-thei)

Often depicted in pairs guarding temple entrances to ward off evil, the Chinthe is a Burmese symbol of omniscient power and protection. Part-lion, part-dragon, the auspicious Chinthe is also associated with the astrological sign, Leo.

▲ Chimera

A composite goat-lion-serpent monster belching forth fire, the chimera of Greek mythology is portrayed here with all three animal heads emerging. Generally, it represents elemental fury and danger; however, since it is an imaginary creature it is also a symbol of non-existent or of wild fancifulness.

▲ Sphinx

The Egyptian sphinx is a human-headed lion symbolizing the power of the Sun and the ruling pharaoh. It was used to guard tombs, palaces, and sacred highways.

▲ Ky-lin

A guardian figure known as the Chinese unicorn, ky-lin is a composite creature with hooves, a horn on its head, and a scaly body. A Yin-Yang symbol, it represents fertility, kindness, and purity.

◄ Pegasus

The white, winged horse of Greek legend, Pegasus symbolizes the duality in human nature between animal instinct and spiritual aspiration. In myth, the hero Bellerophon riding Pegasus kills the monstrous chimera in a symbolic representation of light triumphing over dark.

▲ Unicorn

The magical and much-loved white unicorn is a mythical horse with a single horn and symbolized purity, courage, and courtly love; only a virgin was thought capable of catching one. It is associated with the Virgin Mary and is an attribute of St. Justina. Its horn was believed to be an antidote to poison.

MERMAID

Symbolically ambivalent, mermaids, sirens, and mermen are half-human sea creatures closely bound to water, lunar, and fertility symbolism. Water is a source of life but also death through drowning, and represents unconscious desires— hence stories of luring humans into the watery unknown.

▶ Mermaid
A beautiful marine hybrid, the mermaid is a symbol of doomed passion. She represents love, hope, transformation, safe passage, and allurement, but also loss of soul and treachery. To the medieval Church, mermaids personified base, unnatural desires, luring men away from salvation.

▲ Triton
Son of Poseidon the god Triton was a merman. He had the upper body of a man and the tail of a fish. Triton is usually depicted holding or blowing a horn or conch shell, and controls the power of the waters.

◀ Siren
Sirens were dangerous creatures who lured sailors to their deaths with their enchanting voices, lyres, and flutes. They represent illusion and the seductive powers of the senses. Originally, sirens were birds with women's heads associated with capturing souls, and later were sometimes identified with mermaids.

▶ Capricornus
Ancient cultures likened the sky to the ocean and devised stories of wondrous creatures comprising both elements—air and water—hence the hybrid goat-fish, Capricornus, a winter constellation associated with the winter solstice. It is also linked to Babylonian god, Ea-Oannes ("Antelope of the Seas").

Sea goat

▲ Sleipnir
An eight-legged horse, Sleipnir ("Gliding One") is the mount of Nordic god, Odin, and transports him between the physical and divine world. Its eight legs symbolize the compass directions and Sleipnir's ability to move through air and on land; they also symbolize the eight-spoked solar wheel.

Part-human, part-horse

▲ Centaur
In Greek myth centaurs have conflicting symbolism: some, like Chiron, were noble and gentle, others were wild, adulterous, and warlike. They symbolize the animal instinct combined with man's intellect.

▲ Harpy
These fearsome bird women with hideous faces, vulture's bodies, and claws are associated with death, fate, and divine punishment. Harpies are sometimes seen as demons that spirit away the souls of the dead.

▶ Minotaur
Part-bull, part-man, the minotaur of Greek legend was the mythological offspring of a Cretan queen and a white bull. Imprisoned in the labyrinth by Minos, it symbolized the savagery within.

SEE ALSO
Mammals *pp.52–55*
Celtic & Nordic deities *pp.142–43*
Hinduism *pp.158–63*
Western astrology *pp.200–01*

► **Chinese dragon with pearl**
This Chinese dragon is often shown with a pearl surrounded by branching flames (see center of image). The pearl and dragon can represent rolling thunder, the Moon as rain-bringer, or the "pearl of perfection," which is linked with Taoist philosophy. The Five-clawed Dragon represents the power of the Sun and the emperor.

DRAGONS

A symbolic fusion of serpent and bird, the mighty dragon is a complex and universal representation of awe-inspiring power, and appears in myths and legends around the world.

Originating from the Greek word for serpent ("drakon"), the dragon began as a benign symbol representing the fertilizing waters of the serpent and the divine "breath of life" of the bird; the latter also associated it with sky deities and rulers. Later the dragon became symbolically ambivalent, and was seen as both creative and destructive.

CREATOR DESTROYER

Mythology reveals the dragon as both creator and destroyer and involves epic themes such as cosmic chaos, creation, and rebirth. In nature the dragon symbolizes the life-bringing rain that follows thunder, as well as the destructive forces of lightning and flood.

The earliest known dragon myth tells of a Sumerian dragon, Zu, who stole the Tablets of Law that ensured cosmic harmony, only to be slain by sun god, Ninurta, to prevent darkness and chaos.

DRAGONS OF THE WEST

Medieval dragons combine air, water, fire, and earth symbolism and are portrayed as horned, fire-breathing monsters with scaly bodies, wings, clawed feet, and a barbed, serpentine tail. In western myth battles with dragons symbolize the struggle between good and evil or the mastering of man's base nature and reflect early Christian beliefs. Rescuing

▲ **St. George**
St. George's epic battle against a marauding dragon, in which he saves the princess and her people from an oppressor-figure, reflects Christian values and good triumphing over evil.

a maiden from a dragon represents the release of pure forces after vanquishing evil. Treasure-guarding dragons often signify the struggle to attain coveted inner knowledge. The dragon was also associated with kings and warriors.

EASTERN DRAGONS

Eastern dragons are seen as auspicious, benevolent, and wise. They are symbols of great power, spiritual and temporal, and are associated with wisdom, strength, and the creative forces of nature. They are revered and temples are dedicated to them.

The dragon appears in many forms, each with its own symbolism. Portrayed with the phoenix, for example, it represents the union of Heaven and Earth. Most important is the sky-dwelling turquoise Five-clawed Dragon, Lung, which symbolizes celestial and imperial power, the Sun, fertility, joy, spiritual knowledge, and immortality. The Four-clawed Dragon signifies earthly power, while the Three-clawed Dragon is a rain symbol.

The Chinese believe they are descended from dragons, and those born in the Chinese Year of the Dragon are especially blessed as they are thought to have health, wealth, and long life.

◄ **Welsh dragon**
The red dragon is the emblem of Wales. It originates from a legend about a struggle between the Welsh red dragon and a white dragon representing the invading Saxons.

▲ **Viking dragon**
The dragon figurehead on Viking longboats is a guardian symbol of protection and good fortune when away from the safety of the home harbor.

SEE ALSO
Precious stones pp.42–43
Fabulous beasts pp.74–77
Taoism & Shinto pp.170–71
Chinese horoscope pp.204–05
Heraldic emblems pp.318–23
Flags pp.324–29

PLANTS

Plants are associated with Mother Earth and the cycle of life. Many are attributes of fertility deities, and plant sap represents the fertilizing waters and motherhood. Some plants are seen as mythical ancestors, while others supposedly sprang from the blood of a god or hero figure—a reference to death and resurrection. According to ancient philosophy recorded in the *Doctrine of Signatures*, plant features that look like particular parts of the body can be used to cure ailments in that body part.

▲ Fern
Signifying solitude, the fern is also an ancient heraldic symbol associated with fecundity and loyalty. A national emblem in New Zealand, the silver fern means perseverance. The Maori fern frond symbol, koru, represents unfurling new life, ideas, and potential.

▲ Mistletoe
The evergreen mistletoe symbolizes immortality and new birth at the winter solstice. Druids believed mistletoe was sacred and associated it with protection, fertility, love, and health.

◀ Bamboo
A vital building material and food source in the East, the strong yet pliant bamboo has long been a fundamental part of Zen and Buddhist philosophy. It represents fertility, courage, and modesty. In China its upright yet flexible habit symbolizes the path toward enlightenment.

▲ Reed
The reed's habitat associates it with purification in Celtic tradition where it was thought to repel witches. The Egyptians associated reeds with royalty and the Nile; they were also linked to Greek music god, Pan.

▲ Mandrake
The mandrake is associated with magic; its roots resemble a human figure and it is said to shriek in agony when picked. Mandrake in Hebrew means "love plant." Some cultures believe it ensures conception.

▲ Shamrock
Also known as the white or three-leaf clover, the shamrock is the unofficial symbol of Ireland. Christians believe it represents the Trinity. Clovers were traditionally used in love, divination, incense, and the treatment of skin problems.

▲ Four-leaf clover
The rarity of the four-leaf clover associates it with good luck, and it was once believed that those who found one were able to see fairies. Its four leaves represent hope, faith, love, and luck.

▲ Deadly nightshade
Also known as the devil's berry, deadly nightshade symbolizes deception, danger, and death because the fruit looks tempting, yet is poisonous. Mixed with wolfsbane, this powerful hallucinogenic was used as an ointment by witches in the medieval period.

▲ Foxglove
The foxglove derives its name from its finger-like blooms which were thought to be fairy gloves. Widely used in healing, the foxglove's throat-like trumpets were associated with the treatment of mouth and throat ailments.

▲ Thistle
A heraldic emblem, the thistle is a Christian symbol of sin and Christ's suffering. It also represents austerity and vindictiveness. As Scotland's emblem, it is associated with protection from enemies.

▲ Acanthus
This thistle-like plant is widely used as a Classical motif in design and architecture. Its leaves symbolize wisdom and the arts. Its prickles and vigorous growth signify triumph over life's obstacles. The acanthus is also associated with immortality and is an ancient cemetery motif.

▲ Ivy
Chiefly associated with immortality, an ivy staff was carried by the Egyptian god, Osiris, as an emblem of virtue. In Sparta ivy signified fame and crowned athletes. Victorians equated it with fidelity. Elsewhere, its clinging habit represents dependence.

► Tobacco
American Indians regarded tobacco as sacred and smoked it ceremonially as a way of communicating with the spirits; it is associated with peace. The Pueblo Indians linked it to purification.

► Cannabis
Cannabis, or hemp, has been used as an aphrodisiac for millennia. It has also featured in religious ritual in Japanese Shinto and Rastafarianism and is variously associated with purity, fertility, and holiness. In the West, its distinctive leaf symbolizes youthful rebellion.

▲ Wolfsbane
According to Greek myth, poisonous wolfsbane, or aconite, fell from the saliva of the three-headed dog, Cerberus. Its name reflects its original use as poisoned wolf bait; it was also used to poison people and has associations with witchcraft.

▲ Myrtle
Evergreen myrtle represents immortality, and sprigs were often buried with the dead to help the soul on its journey. Associated with Venus, goddess of love, it signifies fertility and marital harmony. In China it symbolizes success.

FUNGI

Their bizarre appearance and occasionally poisonous or hallucinogenic properties have long associated fungi with magic and, in European folklore, with fairy enchantment. The Australian Arunta believe mushrooms are fallen stars, while the Chinese associate mushrooms with immortality. In modern times they have been associated with the nuclear bomb cloud.

ENOKI MUSHROOM   FLY AGARIC   COMMON STINKHORN

▲ Hawthorn
The hawthorn is associated with healing, fertility, weddings, protection, chastity, and fairies. It was also associated with gods, including the Roman goddess of flowers, Flora, and Greek god of marriage, Hymen, so was a popular bridal flower.

SEE ALSO
Love & marriage *pp.126–27*
Greek & Roman deities
  pp.140–41
Taoism & Shinto *pp.170–71*
Christianity *pp.176–79*

Witches & wicca *pp.192–93*
Heraldic emblems *pp.318–23*

FLOWERS

Flowers in full bloom are a symbol of nature at its glorious zenith. They reflect all that is passive and feminine and are associated with beauty, youth, and springtime, as well as spiritual perfection and peace. Much flower symbolism is linked to color, scent, and appearance; in the Victorian period a "language of flowers" developed and flowers were used to send hidden messages. Flowers have also been used in healing and ritual since ancient times.

◄ Chrysanthemum
Its late flowering associates the chrysanthemum with autumn, while in the East, because it flowers into the winter, it is an auspicious symbol of longevity, wealth, and happiness. Its radiating petals link the chrysanthemum to Sun symbolism, and to the Japanese imperial family. In Western art the chrysanthemum signifies decadence and death.

▲ Daffodil
A cheerful symbol of spring, the daffodil is also associated with resurrection and the Christian period of Lent. Its Greek genus, *Narcissus*, links it to a myth about a youth, Narcissus, who fell in love with his own reflection; the daffodil therefore came to represent self-love.

▲ Lily
Associated with purity and peace, the lily is linked to both virgin goddesses and fertility. In China the day lily was believed to alleviate grief, while the giant Gymea lily represents endurance to Australian Aboriginals.

▲ Tulip
A Persian symbol of perfect love, the tulip was later associated with Allah and became an emblem of Turkish Ottoman rulers. Widely linked to the Netherlands, it is a symbol of Amsterdam, wealth, beauty, and the spring.

▲ Hyacinth
When his beloved, Hyacinthus, was accidentally killed by a discus, the god Apollo named the flower that grew from his blood a hyacinth. The Hyacinth is a Christian symbol of prudence, perhaps because of this story.

▲ Primrose
Called the "prima rosa" as it flowers early, the primrose represents first love, youth, and purity. It is linked to the Nordic love goddess, Freya, while the Celts regarded it as a flower of the fairies. The primrose was traditionally used in healing.

▲ Crocus
The crocus is traditionally associated with spring, youthful gladness, cheerfulness, and fertility. People believed that wearing garlands of crocuses warded off drunkenness. The saffron variety is used to dye cloth yellow.

▲ Orchid
In the East the orchid is linked with beauty, passion, and fecundity. It also symbolizes feminine grace. In the West it represents luxury, beauty, and refinement, and is also a symbol of perfection. The spots on the orchid are thought to represent the blood of Christ.

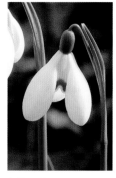

▲ Snowdrop
The pristine beauty of the snowdrop makes it a symbol of purity and hope, emerging to herald spring. The Victorians associated it with the buried dead, because it is low-growing. The snowdrop is also an emblem of the Virgin Mary and Christian Candlemass.

▲ Cyclamen
Due to the deep red at its center the cyclamen is associated with passion, and its root used in love potions. The red spot is thought to symbolize the bleeding heart of the Virgin Mary. It is also linked to resignation and saying goodbye.

▲ Passion flower
Spanish missionaries to the New World adopted the Passion flower as a symbol of the crucifixion: its corona, for example, represents the Crown of Thorns and the top three stigma represent the nails used to nail Christ to the cross. In Israel its appearance prompted the nickname "clock-flower."

◄ Violet
The expression "shrinking violet" is traditionally used to describe a timid person and alludes to the way the violet hugs the ground, half-hidden beneath leaves. In paintings of the Adoration of Christ violets represent Mary's chastity and the Christ Child's meekness. In the medieval period violets symbolized constancy.

▲ Peony
The imperial flower of China, where it is the flower of spring, the peony is also associated with beauty and femininity. The Japanese regard it as a symbol of fertility and link it to marital bliss. The peony was also widely used in traditional medicine.

▲ Pansy
The open-faced pansy is also known as "heartsease" and is associated with thought, love, and problems of the heart. Folklore maintained that anyone wanting to ensure their sweetheart's affections should carry a pansy.

▲ Honeysuckle
The honeysuckle's clinging tendrils symbolize a lover's embrace, while its scent is thought to invoke passionate dreams. According to folklore, if honeysuckle is brought into the house, a wedding will take place within a year.

▲ Iris
The iris represents hope and the power of light and is linked to Iris, the Greek goddess of the rainbow. In China it signals beauty in solitude; in the French *fleur de lys* its three petals represent faith, wisdom, and valor.

SEE ALSO
Love & marriage *pp.126–27*
Death & mourning *pp.128–31*
Greek & Roman deities *pp.140–41*
Celtic & Nordic deities *pp.142–43*

FLOWERS

83

ROSES

The complex and fragrant rose is a symbol of perfection and passion. It is universally associated with love, earthly and divine; attributed to goddesses, it signifies fertility, virginity, or beauty. Unfurling from a bud, it represents secrecy and the mystery of life. In Christianity the rose's symbolism is similar to that of the lotus in the East. Both red and white roses are associated with Christianity, and their thorns symbolize the crown of thorns and Christ's martyrdom. Elsewhere, different colored roses have specific meanings.

▲ **Forget-me-not**
According to European legend, "Forget-me-not" were the last words of a youth who drowned while picking this flower for his lover. This blue bloom is a symbol of remembrance, friendship, and fidelity, as well as desperate love. It is associated with various charities.

◄ **Buttercup**
The golden buttercup signifies wealth and is an emblem of Mars, originally a Roman fertility god. Its simplicity and low-growing habit symbolizes humility and neatness. Once thought to cure insanity, buttercups are also associated with mockery and childhood and playfully used to divine a liking for butter.

▲ **White rose**
The white rose is linked to purity, water, the Moon, reverence, and the Virgin Mary. Architectural ceiling roses traditionally denote confidentiality concerning anything said or done beneath them, deriving from the Latin for secrecy, *sub rosa*.

▲ **Yellow rose**
The yellow rose is linked to the Sun, making it a symbol of warm friendship and joy. Traditionally, it was also associated with jealousy and dying love. Today this flower is the symbol of the state of Texas. In Catholicism the golden rose is a papal emblem.

▲ **Red rose**
An attribute of Venus, goddess of love, the red rose denotes beauty, love, passion, and consummation, and is associated with the element of fire. In the Christian tradition it signifies the blood of martyrs and the resurrection. In Islam it represents the blood of the Prophet and his two sons.

▲ **Rose window**
Stained glass windows based on the rose design, rose windows are particularly associated with Gothic architecture and are full of symbolism, often concerning the Virgin and Child. This example comes from Chartres Cathedral in France.

▲ **Tudor rose**
The Wars of the Roses (1455–85) were a series of civil wars fought over the English throne between the royal houses of Lancaster and York. Each house had its own rose emblem; the Red Rose of Lancaster and the White Rose of York. These were merged to form the Tudor rose as a symbol of unity after the wars.

▲ **Daisy**
A solar emblem whose name evolved from its original description as the "day's eye," the daisy is a perfect symbol of modesty, and simplicity. It is also associated with innocence and loyal love. Traditionally, girls determined whether their suitor was true by plucking a daisy's petals and chanting "He loves me, he loves me not" until there was only one petal remaining.

▲ Sunflower
Its huge, nodding head constantly tracking the sun, the sunflower represents slavish worship; however, its ever-changing position signifies unreliability to some. It belongs to the genus *Helianthus*, which associates it with Helios, the Sun god. The Chinese believe the sunflower is linked to immortality.

▲ Poppy
In the West the blood-red poppy commemorates the war dead because poppies grew on the battlefields of World War I. The Chinese associate it with the evils of opium made from its seeds, while in Ancient Greece the poppy was linked to the gods of sleep and dreams, Hypnos and Morpheus. The poppy also symbolizes the Great Mother, as well as the death of winter and the fertility that follows.

▲ Lavender
Used since ancient times for perfume, cleansing, and healing, fragrant lavender has many symbolic associations. It has been seen as a lucky charm, a token of affection, and an aid to sleep. Used in potpourris to ward off evil, it is also associated with love.

◄ Carnation
The pink carnation symbolizes motherhood and the white carnation, pure love. Credited with aphrodisiac properties, the red carnation is a widespread symbol of love and fertility, associated with marriage. In paintings of Mary and child it often represents maternal love.

▲ Anemone
Derived from the Greek word *anemos* meaning "wind," the scarlet anemone, or windflower, represents the ephemeral quality of life, as its flowers are so short-lived, and is associated with mourning.

▲ Dandelion
The dandelion is associated with healing and divination; its fluffy seed-head is traditionally used as a love oracle, while dandelion tea is said to increase psychic abilities. Its golden, radiating petals represent the Sun. Elsewhere, it symbolizes bitterness due to the taste of its leaves.

▲ Marigold
A solar emblem known as the "Herb of the Sun," the marigold is a symbol of passion and creativity. In China it is associated with longevity and in India with the god Krishna. Early Christians also made offerings of "Mary's Gold."

SEE ALSO
The lotus *pp.86–87*
Death & mourning *pp.128–31*
Hinduism *pp.158–63*
Christianity *pp.176–79*

▲ Thousand-petaled lotus
In Buddhist cosmology the Buddha, the Chosen One, is often represented as the jewel in the lotus, seated on a lotus-flower throne, the pinnacle of perfection.

A thousand-petaled lotus is a potent symbol of spiritual enlightenment, especially in conjunction with the Buddha, who is sitting in the lotus position.

THE LOTUS

An ancient symbol of creation and fertility, the lotus is widely revered in India, Egypt, China, and Japan. It also symbolizes purity because it emerges unsullied from the murky waters.

▲ Jewel-like flower
The lotus opens its radiant petals as the Sun comes up, giving rise to many creation myths.

The long, winding stem of the lotus symbolizes the umbilical cord that binds man to his roots, and the flower bud represents human potential. The radiant petals of the lotus open at dawn then close again as the Sun sets, and this is seen as symbolic of the Sun emerging from the cosmic ocean.

THE SUN AND CREATION

One of the most widespread symbols in Indian culture, the lotus represents the Sun and creation, purity and perfection. It often features in Indian architecture and sculpture. In the central Hindu creation myth Brahma, the creator, emerges on a thousand-petaled lotus from the navel of the great god Vishnu as he sleeps upon the milky ocean and creates the universe afresh. The Sun god, Surya, is depicted holding two open lotus flowers, symbolizing enlightenment.

Often adorning the lintels of temple gates, the lotus flower bestows good fortune on all who enter. The petals at the base of temple columns indicate that the temple stands on an open lotus flower, representing the Earth and the cosmic ocean.

ENLIGHTENMENT

The lotus is pivotal in Buddhist philosophy. The muddy waters from which the plant grows represent ignorance and the wearisome round of birth and rebirth (*samsara*), while the stem of the plant, lifting above the water, symbolizes the core

▲ The golden lotus
A Buddha holds the symbol of purity and enlightenment in his left hand.

Buddhist doctrine that man is able to raise himself above his lower nature. The bud, opening up at the surface of the water, is considered an image of purity, and the open flower represents enlightenment.

The lotus also plays an important part in Buddhist iconography. Images of the Buddha are frequently seated on a stylized lotus throne in *padmasana,* or the lotus posture (*padma* means "lotus" in Sanskrit). Padmapani, a Buddhist deity, holds a lotus. The popular mantra, *om mani padme hum,* means "the jewel in the lotus." In esoteric Buddhism this is taken to mean the union of the male organ (the jewel) with the female organ (lotus), symbolizing the power of the creative force.

BIRTH AND REBIRTH

To the Ancient Egyptians the lotus, opening and closing with the movement of the Sun, was a symbol of birth and rebirth. It was associated with the god Nefertem and the Sun god, Re, who was sometimes depicted as a child or a golden youth lying on a lotus. The association of water and the Sun makes the flower a powerful image. According to one Egyptian creation myth, a giant lotus emerged from the primeval waters at the beginning of time. The Sun itself rose out of its center on the first morning.

The lotus was also an emblem of the early Christian Church, although it was later replaced by the water lily. In Buddhist legend lotuses bloomed at the feet of the newborn Prince Siddhartha, the future Buddha.

◄ Egyptian capitals
Egyptian columns often have capitals carved in the shape of lotus buds or flowers.

SEE ALSO
The Sun *pp.16–17*
Plants *pp.80–81*
Flowers *pp.82–85*
Egyptian deities *pp.138–39*
Creation stories *pp.156–57*
Buddhism *pp.164–69*

HERBS & SPICES

The distinctive taste and smell of herbs and spices has long associated them with cooking, but they have also been used for thousands of years for healing and religious ritual. Many herbs and spices are fragrant, so have emotional connections; others are considered sacred. Associations concerned with herbs and spices can be linked with magic or evil, as many have the power to harm or heal. According to traditional European lore, the symbolism of herbs, as with plants, relates to their appearance.

◄ Basil

From the African Congo to Tudor England, basil has been widely associated as a talisman against evil; in Greek myth, it was an antidote to the monstrous basilisk's venom. Elsewhere, it was linked to love and wealth, and was also used in funeral rites.

▲ Fennel

One of the oldest cultivated plants, fennel has symbolized courage since ancient times; Roman gladiators ate its seeds to promote courage, while Anglo-Saxons used it as a talisman. Fennel is also associated with perception, purification, and the Virgin Mary, and is used in herbal medicine.

▲ Parsley

According to folklore, parsley's long roots were thought to reach Hell, signifying evil. Seen by the Ancient Greeks as a symbol of oblivion and death, parsley became a funeral herb. However, in the Jewish tradition it is used as an emblem of renewal at Passover.

▲ Rosemary

Often planted on graves as a symbol of immortality, rosemary is associated with remembrance. In Europe it was a traditional emblem of fidelity, and was once included in bridal bouquets. Students in Ancient Rome used rosemary to boost concentration.

▲ Sage

Highly prized for its healing powers, sage derives its name from the Latin, *salvare*, which means "to save." Associated with immortality, protection, and wisdom, sage was a Christian symbol of the Virgin Mary. American Indians burned white sage in healing rituals.

▲ Thyme

Associated with courage, 15th-century English women embroidered wild thyme on tributes presented to knights. Roman soldiers were known to bathe in thyme to promote courage. It is also associated with healing, sleep, purification, love, and psychic power.

▲ Mint

Arabs regard peppermint as an aphrodisiac, but served as tea it is a traditional symbol of hospitality. Greek myth describes how Hades transformed the nymph, Menthe, into a mint bush to save her from his jealous wife. Mint was used ritually for protection, divination, and exorcism.

▲ Ginger
In Hawaii the flowering ginger is associated with the *kahili*, an emblem of royalty carried by chieftains. Its edible underground root is fiery hot, linking it to passion and success. Long traded as a spice, its high value associated it with wealth and power.

▲ Ginseng
Shamans searching for the elixir of eternal life experimented with ginseng, hence its link to immortality and longevity. A masculine, Yang herb, ginseng is linked to virility. Its name means "man-root," and legend says that the "Ginseng Child" living within serves those who eat it.

▲ Cinnamon
The phoenix was said to set itself alight on a pyre incorporating cinnamon— a belief that led to the spice becoming a yule symbol of renewal. Highly prized and valuable, it has been used as an aphrodisiac. In China it is a purification incense.

▲ Nutmeg
Originating in Indonesia, nutmeg is now largely grown in Grenada where it appears on the national flag. Widely used as an aphrodisiac, it became a symbol of wealth in Europe in the 18th and 19th centuries when those who could afford it carried a supply to grate on food.

▲ Cloves
Symbolic of love and protection, a clove tree was traditionally planted to mark the birth of a child; it also personified that child and, if the tree was felled, it heralded the child's death. A sought-after and costly spice, cloves also became a symbol of wealth.

▲ Betel nut
A mildly euphoric stimulant, chewing betel nut is an important part of Asian and Pacific cultures. Associated with hospitality, reciprocity, and fertility, the nut is seen as feminine, the leaves masculine. Vietnamese regard betel nuts as a symbol of love and marriage.

◄ Myrrh
As incense in religious ritual, myrrh symbolizes prayers rising to heaven. It is also associated with purity and sweetness. In Ancient Egypt it was used in mummification, linking it to death. Named after the Arabic word for "bitter," it came to symbolize suffering, repentance, and Christ's Passion.

▲ Garlic
The ancient superstition concerning garlic's protective powers against vampires persists, even today. Ancient Greeks left garlic offerings at crossroads for Hecate, goddess of the underworld, and associated garlic with strength. In China garlic is seen as lucky, and is linked to fertility.

► Saffron
Produced from the dried stigma of saffron crocus, saffron's color associates it with the Sun. Used to dye the robes of Buddhist monks, it has come to symbolize humility. It is also linked with love and magic.

SEE ALSO
Plants *pp.80–81*
Flowers *pp.82–85*
Love & marriage *pp.126–27*
Greek & Roman deities *pp.140–41*

Judaism *pp.172–73*
Amulets *pp.194–95*

HERBS & SPICES

▲ Psychological symbol
In this fairytale by the Grimm Brothers entitled *The Two Brothers*, the forest represents
the dark shadows of inner fears, which must be confronted and resolved. In this way,
fear fades away, ultimately leading to the symbolic illumination of self-discovery.

THE FOREST

Seen as both a place of fear and a spiritual retreat, the shadow-filled forest has long attracted mixed symbolism, and has deep-rooted psychological and spiritual significance in many cultures.

Forests have always gripped the human psyche. They stand, vast and mysterious, yet pulsating with hidden life. They are barriers between the known and the unknown—symbolically dark, mysterious, and feminine—and are associated with germination and the womb, initiation, and the supernatural.

A SPIRITUAL PLACE

Forests were among the first places in the natural world to be associated with spirits and deities, and offerings were strung from trees. Many cultures believed that trees housed spirits or souls; in Australia the Warlpiri people thought that souls gathered in trees, and the presence of many, possibly malevolent, trees with little light filtering through symbolized the unknown and death.

Tree trunks have been likened to the columns in temples and churches, and forest canopies to the sweeping, interior architecture of cathedrals; indeed, many places of worship have been built on the site of sacred groves, including Chartres cathedral in France.

In Christianity the forest is "untamed nature" associated with paganism and is symbolic of humankind lost in the

▲ Modern symbol
The rain forest has become a "final frontier" symbol of luxuriant, untamed nature facing annihilation by humans.

darkness without spiritual illumination. In Asia, however, it is a place of spiritual development and meditation; in the Hindu tradition a forest dweller is one who has retreated into a life of contemplation.

A PLACE ⊕F DANGER

In the forest distinctions are blurred between sight and sound, real and unreal, light and dark. The canopy filters out sunlight, making the forest symbolically opposed to the Sun's power—hence fear and coolness. Alive with potentially dangerous animals, it also represents untamed nature.

European fairy tales, such as *Hansel and Gretel*, are full of forest symbolism and tap into the ancient fear that the forest is a dangerous realm where one can easily lose the way.

A THRESH⊕LD

The forest is where fears are symbolically confronted and a true understanding of self emerges. This idea is echoed in Jungian psychological theory, where the forest is a threshold symbol for the unconscious fear that obscures reason. It also serves as a metaphor for overcoming inexperience and entering adulthood—a testing ground or place of initiation.

Today, global deforestation brings a new testing ground and a new symbolic threshold. The rain forest has become a modern symbol of nature under threat.

◄ Spiritual forests
Pine forests are often portrayed in Chinese and Japanese art and are believed to be home to forest spirits; the sacred pine represents immortality.

SEE ALSO
Trees *pp.94–95*
Nature spirits *pp.148–49*
Hinduism *pp.158–63*
Christianity *pp.176–79*
Fairy tales *pp.272–73*

RADHA AND KRISHNA

The Hindu god Krishna with his favorite *gopi* (cowherd girl), Radha, in a forest grove is a scene that is frequently illustrated in Indian court paintings from the 16th to the 19th century.

The Indian artist employed poetic symbols to charge his subjects with romantic ardor. Flowers were never merely flowers, nor clouds clouds: everything contained a deeper symbolism.

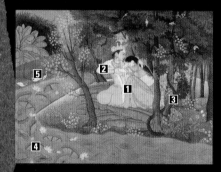

1. Radha
Radha's passion for Krishna symbolizes the soul's intense longing and willingness for the ultimate unification with God. Their embrace represents the Shiva and the Shakti; the male and female aspects of ourselves, longing to reunite with one another.

2. Krishna
The symbol of an able statesman, Krishna is a warrior, a great philosopher, and a teacher. Here he is represented as a beautiful young man; the symbol of love, devotion, and joy.

3. Tree creeper
The flowering creeper embracing a trunk suggests passion and romance and symbolically recreates the embrace of Radha and Krishna.

4. Lotus
The lotus flower represents beauty and non-attachment. It grows from the muddy waters without becoming dirty. This symbolizes the Hindu belief that one should live in the world without attachment to one's surroundings.

5. Herons
There are several white herons in the river, which are symbolic of vigilance, longevity, and happiness.

TREES

A source of sustenance, shelter, building material, and firewood, trees are associated with fertility, longevity, and strength. They represent dynamic life, death, and new growth, and symbolically link Heaven, Earth, and the underworld. Many are sacred and associated with specific deities or spirits, while fruit-bearing trees, such as the date palm, often represent the Tree of Life. Evergreens denote immortality, while deciduous trees signify rebirth; others serve as community focal points.

▲ Oak
The oak represents masculine strength and courage. For the druids it was a sacred tree associated with divination; revered by Celts, the oak is also linked to various thunder, sky, and fertility gods. To Jews it symbolizes the Divine Presence.

▲ Beech
Much prized in Siberia, the beech symbolizes stability, prosperity, and divination. In Celtic mythology Fagus (its genus name) was the god of beech trees. An emblem of Denmark, the beech also represents endurance.

▲ Willow
In the West the weeping willow symbolizes mourning and is associated with the Devil. In the East, however, it represents springtime and feminine grace; the Japanese Ainu believed the first men had spines of willow.

▲ Linden
A European symbol of happiness and beauty, the linden also represents friendship. Attributed to the goddess, Freya, and traditionally considered lightning-proof, lindens became symbolic village "guardians."

▲ Laurel
In North Africa the laurel is believed to repel evil, while in Greco-Roman tradition it represented victory, peace, purification, and divination. The laurel is also an attribute of the god, Apollo, and a symbol of eternity.

▲ Holly
A symbol of hope and joy, holly is associated with the German goddess, Holle; its red berries represent her blood, shed to grant it evergreen immortality. Holly was sacred to the god Saturn; it is sometimes seen as a Christian tree of the cross.

▲ Yew
An emblem of immortality, yews were grown in Celtic groves, some of which later became sites for Christian churches. The Celts thought the yew had magical properties and used it to make their wands and bows.

▲ Pine
The pine tree symbolizes strength of character and virility. An evergreen, the pine is also linked with immortality, as well as the Roman god, Bacchus. To the American Indian Iroquois the white pine is the tree of peace.

▲ Christmas tree
As an evergreen, the Christmas tree (traditionally a fir tree) represents the winter solstice. The tradition of dressing the tree dates back to 16th-century Germany. The lights in the tree symbolize the stars, Sun, and Moon lighting the Tree of Life.

▲ Cypress
A western symbol of death and mourning, the cypress is associated with gods of the underworld and was thought to preserve the body, hence its use in graveyards. In the East the phallic cypress represents endurance and immortality.

NATURAL WORLD

94

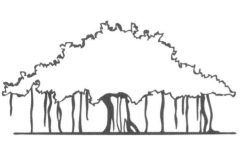

▲ Banyan
Sacred to Hindus, the banyan symbolizes eternity because of its vast canopy, while its aerial roots signify the spiritual world. In Philippine mythology the banyan houses mischievous spirits and demons; it also appears on Indonesia's coat of arms, where it stands for national unity.

▲ Baobab
Its majestic size, longevity, and endurance make the baobab a revered Tree of Life in African culture. It is a symbol of endurance, conservation, and creativity. The baobab tree is often a traditional village meeting place.

▲ Ginkgo
Described by Darwin as a "living fossil," the ginkgo is used in Chinese medicine to enhance longevity. It also symbolizes hope and love. The ginkgo leaf is a popular emblem in Japan; traditionally, it is a samurai symbol of loyalty.

▲ Tamarisk
Revered in the deserts of the Middle East as a Tree of Life, the tamarisk oozes a sweet resin that may have been the biblical "manna"—a Jewish symbol of divine grace. It was sacred to the Egyptian god, Osiris.

◄ Fig
A source of food since earliest times, the fig was regarded as a Tree of Life in parts of Asia, Oceania, and Egypt. It symbolizes fecundity, prosperity, and peace; in Buddhism it represents moral instruction. The fig leaf is associated with male genitalia.

▲ Acacia
In Judeo-Christian symbolism, the acacia represents immortality, and its sacred shittah wood was used to build the Ark of the Covenant; elsewhere, its white and red flowers denote life and death. Various parts of the tree are used to make incense.

▲ Palm
A Tree of Life in Arab and Egyptian cultures, the palm is a solar emblem associated with fertility and victory. In Greco-Roman tradition palm leaves were used to hail victors in battle or competitive events; in Christianity this symbolism evolved into victory over death.

▲ Olive
An ancient symbol of peace, glory, and immortality, the olive is sacred in Classical and Judeo-Christian symbolism. Its leaves crowned triumphant athletes, while an olive branch brought to Noah by the dove after the Flood signified peace.

▲ Almond
The Persian Tree of Heaven, the almond tree also represents divine grace, hidden truth, and virginity. In Chinese culture it symbolizes feminine beauty and resilience. As the first flower of the year to "awaken", the almond is also associated with vigilance.

▲ Peach
One of the Three Blessed Fruits of Buddhism, the peach is a highly auspicious symbol in Japanese and Chinese cultures. It signifies joy, immortality, and feminine charms. Peach wood was thought to repel demons, while fallen blossom represents femininity and prostitutes.

▲ Mulberry
This Tree of Life was thought by the Chinese to have powers that kept evil at bay; they also associate the mulberry with filial piety and industry. Its connection with silk (the leaves are eaten by silkworms) signifies wealth and sensuality.

▲ Plum
In Japanese culture plum blossom symbolizes happiness and good luck. It also represents spring, courage, and virtue overcoming difficulties, and is an emblem of the Samurai. In China it signifies virginity, beauty, and longevity.

▲ Cherry
A national emblem of China and Japan, cherry blossom symbolizes the ephemeral sweetness of youth, which, like blossom, is quickly shed. Its habit of flowering before leafing signifies man born naked into the world.

SEE ALSO
Sacred trees pp.96–97
Buddhism pp.164–69
Christianity pp.176–79

TREES

BAXTERS Patent Oil Printing, 11 Northampton Square.

▲ **Yggdrasil**
The Tree of Life in Nordic mythology was a giant ash, Yggdrasil,
which linked the realms of the gods, humans, and the underworld;
from its roots sprang a fountain from which rivers flowed.

SACRED TREES

▲ Bodhi tree
A sacred fig tree under which the Buddha gained Enlightenment, the Bodhi, or Bo, is associated with wisdom and mindfulness.

Trees have always been seen as powerful symbols of life, death, and renewal and some are deemed sacred. They are associated with fertility, knowledge, protection, and creation.

Trees have been revered since ancient times. Nourishing and sheltering, they represent the Great Mother. They stand as natural monuments to the eternal cycle of life, death and time itself, marking its passing in annular rings. Rooted in the soil of the world yet reaching skyward, they link Heaven, Earth, and the fertilizing waters, a symbol of the universe and creation.

COSMIC TREES

The cosmic or world tree appears in the mythology of many cultures and represents the dynamic life-force. The cosmic tree is usually a tree that is particularly significant in the region it serves as an axis, connecting the underworld, Earth, and Heaven. In many cultures the tree grows in Paradise, or at the peak of a sacred mountain. Its upper branches may contain birds, representing heavenly messengers, while a coiled snake at its base often signifies creative energy, drawn from the Earth. The cosmic tree may symbolize the means through which humans can overcome their base nature and ascend toward spiritual illumination. It is often linked to myths concerning the birth of humans.

▲ Egyptian Tree of Life
One of Egypt's sacred trees, the sycamore was a Tree of Life. On the threshold between life and death, it grew from a sacred mound that symbolized the beginning of creation.

LIFE AND KNOWLEDGE

The Tree of Life that grew in Paradise represents immortality and the beginning and the end of a cycle, and is another aspect of cosmic trees. With its roots in the moisture-laden underworld, its trunk in the world of mortals, and its leaves reaching to the heavens, it symbolizes growth, death, and regeneration, and therefore immortality. While the tree's shape suggests masculine, phallic associations, it is also associated with Mother Earth and fertility rituals since it is often fruit-bearing. The Tree of Life is known in many cultures, including that of Ancient Sumeria, India, China, and Japan. The Tree of Knowledge of the Judeo-Christian tradition is dualistic, combining good and evil, and represents the paradisal state from which humans can fall. Paired trees or those with split trunks also represent duality.

MYSTICISM AND MEDITATION

The inverted tree is a cosmic tree with its roots drawing spiritual sustenance from Heaven and spreading it, via its branches, down toward the Earth. It is a Jewish Kabbalah symbol and is often linked to mysticism. In the Kabbalah the inverted Sefirotic Tree may be shown as ten spheres, symbolic of the stages of revelation. For Buddhists it is a specific tree that has religious significance. The Bodhi tree is believed to be a descendant of the sacred fig tree under which the Buddha found Enlightenment while meditating over 2,500 years ago. The site of this original tree and of other trees grown from its shoots are regarded as holy sites.

◄ Tree of Knowledge
The biblical Tree of the Knowledge of Good and Evil represents duality and the separation of nature and the divine. The snake is temptation, while the fruit represents forbidden knowledge.

SEE ALSO
Trees *pp.94–95*
Creation stories *pp.156–57*
Buddhism *pp.164–69*
Kabbalah *pp.174–75*

FRUITS OF THE EARTH

Symbolic of fertility and immortality, fruit is a glorious product that encompasses the seed of the next generation. Fruit is associated with the Tree of Life, which provided food for the gods. It is also linked to the Tree of Knowledge of Good and Evil as an emblem of humans fall from grace. The smell and taste of fruit, packed with seeds and dripping juices, is linked to sensuality. This symbolism has often been used in art. Many fruits are also attributed to deities and have religious significance.

▲ Apple
In Europe the apple symbolizes love, fertility, youth, and immortality; its circular shape indicates eternity. It is widely associated with the Tree of Knowledge. To the Celts it was a symbol of the afterlife and fertility. In China it indicates peace. In the Bible the apple is the forbidden fruit eaten by Eve and symbolizes temptation and sin.

▲ Peach
In China and Japan the peach is associated with immortality and its blossom with the spring. Taoists and Europeans also linked it to virginity, and it was sacred to the Roman god of marriage, Hymen. When shown with the Virgin and Child in Western art, the peach symbolizes salvation.

▲ Lemon
Its bitter taste links the lemon with sourness and disappointment. However, in Hebrew tradition it symbolizes the heart.

▲ Orange
The simultaneous appearance of both its flowers and fruit associate the orange with virginity and fertility, making its fragrant blossom a traditional feature of weddings. The Chinese eat oranges on the second day of New Year to bring good fortune; they also link them to immortality.

▲ Pear
Its swollen sensuality links the pear to love and mother symbolism; the goddess Athena was considered mother of pear trees in Ancient Greece. The Chinese associate this long-lived tree with longevity, while Christians see it as an emblem of Christ's love for humanity.

▲ Fig
The fig is an almost universal symbol of fertility. Traditionally, the fig tree represents the Tree of Life and symbolizes both male and female; the fig leaf standing for male and the fruit for female. In Hebrew tradition the fig stands for peace and prosperity. The Kotoko of Chad associate it with childbearing.

► Pineapple
In the West Indies the pineapple was a dual symbol of deterrence and hospitality; it is known as a hospitality emblem in the United States.

▲ Melon
Melons represent fertility, sweetness, moisture, and vitality. Their sensual abundance also links them to luxury and gluttony, while their rapid growth signifies creative power. In China melons are traditionally associated with fertility and their seeds are sometimes seen at weddings. In northern Europe their rarity once suggested wealth.

▲ Gourd
The gourd has been used as a water bottle, ritual mask, musical instrument, and even a penis sheath. It is widely associated with creation and fertility myths in many cultures; Maoris use it in birthing rituals. Elsewhere, it is linked to healing and the supernatural.

▲ Mango
Sometimes described as the food of the gods, the mango is a Hindu symbol of love and fertility. Its leaf represents life and is used ritually to invoke good fortune. The paisley pattern is a mango motif copied from 15th-century Kashmiri shawls.

▲ Pomegranate
Shown here in a Roman mosaic, the pomegranate is a fruit bursting with glistening seeds. It is a solar emblem representing fertility (the womb) and life-blood. In China this theme evolved to signify the blessing of many virtuous children. In Greek myth the pomegranate is associated with rejuvenation.

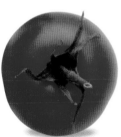

▲ Tomato
Known as the "love apple" when it was introduced to Europe, the tomato was considered an aphrodisiac. This was probably due to the large number of seeds inside the fruit. The Church promptly linked it to the Devil.

▲ Persimmon
Belonging to the plant genus *Diospyros* meaning "fruit of the gods,' the persimmon is a Chinese symbol of joy; used in traditional medicine, it is believed to regulate *ch'i*, or energy. In Japan it is believed to represent victory.

▲ Durian
Said to have the taste of Heaven and the stench of Hell, the Southeast Asian durian symbolizes the unpleasantness that obstructs the path to inner truth and beauty. The Malays regard it as an aphrodisiac, while in Hong Kong its costliness reflects status.

▲ Date
The date palm is an Arab Tree of Life and also represents endurance, providing food in the harsh desert habitat. Its fruit symbolized fertility in Ancient Egypt and the Middle East, while its distinctive palm frond was an ancient emblem of the tribes of Judea.

◄ Almond
The almond's association with purity originates from a Greek myth concerning the virgin birth of Attis; in China, it represents feminine beauty. An odd number of almonds are given for luck at weddings. The almond is also a biblical symbol of hastening old age.

▲ Grape
Its association with wine links the grape to the Roman god, Bacchus, along with its attendant themes of revelry, pleasure, and fertility. In the Christian tradition wine symbolizes the blood of Christ. Grapes are also traditionally associated with the autumn harvest and the gods of agriculture.

SEE ALSO
Trees *pp.94–95*
Sacred trees *pp.96–97*
Love & marriage *pp.126–27*
Greek & Roman deities *pp.140–41*

FRUITS ⊕ THE EARTH

FOODS OF THE EARTH

Since agriculture began, staple crops have been symbols of fertility and renewal to those who grew them. Grain became a powerful symbol of resurrection, ripening and dying back before magically reappearing in the spring. Some "foods of the earth" are associated with abundance or fertility; others, such as honey, represent the food of the gods. Many have a particular religious significance, or signify hospitality.

▲ Wheat
In Ancient Egypt wheat was associated with immortality. Elsewhere, wheat is linked to the summer, fertility, and an abundant harvest.

▲ Rice
A staple grain throughout Asia rice is a symbol of abundance and also symbolizes immortality, spiritual nourishment, purity, and knowledge. The custom of throwing rice at weddings originated in India and represents fecundity and happiness. It was also thought to ward off evil in Japan.

◄ Corn
Historically, a vital crop throughout the Americas, where it was seen as a symbol of life, corn (also known as maize) shares much of the symbolism of other grains and is associated with fertility and plenty. It plays a central role in many creation myths and was used in rituals.

▲ Sago
In New Guinea, where sago is a staple crop, it symbolizes life, while to the Asmat people of Irian Jaya, the sago tree represents the human body; its fruit is the head.

▲ Yam
This vegetable has a three-part tuber which some cultures equate to the human body. It is important in African and Pacific cultures, and New Guinea, and much ritual concerns yam growing and harvesting; it is also associated with male virility, sensuality, and status.

◄ Bread
Bread represents food for the body and soul, and unity. At Jewish Passover, unleavened bread signifies humility and sacrifice. The breaking of bread is associated with sharing and the Christian sacrament of Holy Communion, where it symbolizes the body of Christ.

▲ Leek
This famous Welsh emblem is associated with victory; the Welsh wore leeks to distinguish themselves from Saxons during a battle. In Hebrew "leek" resembles another word meaning "to be cut off," so leeks are symbolically eaten at Rosh Hashanah to "cut off" enemies.

▲ Onion
Its inner concentric rings associate the onion with eternity. Peeling away its layers represents revelation. In Ancient Egypt the onion was a funerary offering symbolizing immortality, while in medieval Europe it was used in lieu of rent.

▲ Egg
A universal symbol of fertility and the potential of life, the cosmic egg is central to many creation myths. In Buddhism breaking through the "eggshell of ignorance" signifies attaining enlightenment. In Christianity the egg symbolizes resurrection.

▲ Milk
A symbol of motherhood, milk is a life-food associated with fertility, abundance, and spiritual nourishment. It also signifies compassion, as "the milk of human kindness," and has been used in initiation ceremonies to signal rebirth.

► Honey
Golden honey represents immortality and was the food of the gods. Associated with fertility, it was thought to be an aphrodisiac. In Christianity honey represents the sweetness of the divine word; combined with oil, the Chinese equate it with false friendship.

▲ Chocolate
Regarded as an aphrodisiac, chocolate symbolizes sensuality and decadence. It was sacred to the Maya and Aztecs, and chocolate drinks played an important role in Mayan betrothal and marriage rituals. The Aztecs used cacao seeds as currency and chocolate-drinking was restriced to the elite; its luxury image remains.

▲ Coffee
Legend maintains that coffee was discovered by Ethiopian shepherds who noticed goats became skittish after chewing coffee berries. As its popularity spread and coffee houses proliferated, coffee came to symbolize sociability and hospitality.

◄ Salt
Once a precious commodity, salt was given in lieu of wages to soldiers in Ancient Rome. Its long association with meat preservation led to symbolism concerning purity and spiritual incorruptibility. In Christianity, it represents divine wisdom; in folklore, throwing salt over one's shoulder dispels bad luck.

► Tea
Symbolic of family, hospitality, and harmony, tea is ritually significant in the East. In China visiting diplomats are often presented with tea-making paraphernalia to symbolize peaceful resolution; in Japan the tea ceremony is a Zen-influenced art form that signifies discipline, respect, and tranquillity.

FOODS OF THE EARTH

101

HUMAN LIFE

We are set apart from animals by our ability to reason, to invent, and to create, as exemplified in our myths, symbols, and signs. For milennia, philosophers have debated the human place in the cosmos, and how we should deal with the fundamental issues of birth, life, and death. To create order and meaning in our lives, we have constructed various rituals and symbolisms to accompany the key milestones in people's lives, such as birth, puberty, marriage, and death.

In the ancient world the human body was often seen as the universe in microcosm; the Chinese believed that a healthy body represented Yin-Yang in perfect balance, while many religions associate it with Divine Power— hence, gods appeared in human form. Every part of the body has its own symbolism, inspired by its function or appearance. The head, for example, variously represents the life-force, the seat of reason, and spirituality; its importance is reflected by the fact that people in authority are called "heads", and royalty is crowned. The eye is all-seeing and the "window of the soul," whereas the nose is usually seen as phallic, and the hair is thought to be a sign of strength. Symbolically, the male is equated to fire and is phallic, while the female is related to water and is receptive. Together, they form a whole and, like the Sun and waters, symbolize creativity.

Early societies noticed that the human life cycle, particularly that of the female, had its parallel in the changing rhythm of the seasons. Gods and symbols were closely connected with the fertility of the soil and the seasonal patterns of growth, death, and regeneration. A golden wheat sheaf, for example, symbolizes

EARLY SOCIETIES NOTICED THAT THE HUMAN LIFE CYCLE, PARTICULARLY THAT OF THE FEMALE, HAD ITS PARALLEL IN THE CHANGING RHYTHM OF THE SEASONS fertility and abundance. Many cultures emphasize the male principle in fertility, and the phallus became venerated as a potent symbol of male fertility, represented in columns, obelisks, and maypoles.

However, in early agrarian communities a mother goddess embodying the female principle was seen as the source of all life.

Deities and symbols of childbirth and fertility helped promote conception, ease a painful labor, or ensure a healthy child; the vulva-like cowrie shell is one such symbolic talisman. Various complex social and religious rituals were also developed, such as naming a child, and initiation and marriage ceremonies. These rituals not only marked important transition points but also served as a means of regulating and unifying society.

Every culture deals with death differently and this is reflected in the way people bury their dead, and how they mourn and remember them. Great care is often taken to ensure the deceased would have a safe passage to the afterlife, and there are numerous myths about life beyond death. Some afterworlds are joyous places, others places of limbo or dread; often this is seen as either a reward or a punishment for an individual's behavior during his or her lifetime.

Death and mourning rituals are also laden with symbolism, from the placement of graves to the color of mourning clothes; other symbols also evolved that spoke of death, such as the Grim Reaper or rotting fruit, and serve as a reminder that life on this Earth is short.

THE HEAD

In many cultures the head is considered the most important part of the human body because it contains the brain. It is symbolic of the life force within. The head is the seat of reason, wisdom, intellect, and spirituality. Such is its significance as a symbol of life that heads are bowed as a sign of respect, crowns are placed on the heads of royalty, winners are given crowns of glory, and people in authority are known as "heads."

MULTIPLE HEADS

Mythology is full of creatures—whether men, spirits, or gods—with many heads, each of which represents an aspect of its owner. Hecate was first depicted as a three-headed deity in the 5th century. Her heads show three sides of her character and are sometimes replaced with a dog, a horse, and a serpent. Multiple-headed beings, such as Brahma, are more common in the East, especially in Hinduism and Buddhism.

▼ Shiva
Usually shown with only one head, Shiva has three here. The one in the center is Shiva himself; the right head represents his consort, Parvati; the left head is Bhairava, Shiva's fierce aspect.

▲ Hecate
Statues of the Roman goddess Hecate were often found at forks in the road. Her three heads symbolize her ability to see in all directions, offering protection to travelers at these dangerous junctions.

◄ Janus
As the Roman god of beginnings and endings, Janus is depicted with two faces so that he can look in two directions at the same time, as well as into the past and the future. These two heads guarded exits and entrances.

▲ Brahma
In Hindu art Brahma usually has four heads. These are said to represent many aspects of Hinduism, such as the four Vedas (the most religious texts for Hindus), the four varnas (the caste system), and the four yugas (the divisions of time).

THE EARS

Symbolically, the ear's shape associates it with the spiral and the shell. The shell is a birth symbol linked to the vulva and this accounts for the idea of birth from an ear, which occurs in Hindu mythology: Karma was born from his mother's ear. The ear is also linked to the breath of life; in Egyptian symbolism the right ear receives the "air of life" and the left ear the "air of death." In Africa ears are symbols of sexual nature, while in Buddhism and Jainism long ears relate to wisdom.

► Satyr
The goat-like satyrs, the followers of Dionysus, are depicted with prominent, pointed ears. The goat symbolizes male sexuality, and these ears highlight the satyrs' wild, uncontrollable spirit, as well as their attraction to sensual pleasure.

▲ Ear-stelae
Ears in Egyptian funerary art were thought to aid the gods in hearing prayers. They were relatively common, especially in a class of reliefs called ear-stelae. These stelae were dedicated to certain gods in appreciation for their goodwill.

▲ Ears of the Buddha
Elongated earlobes are a feature of the Buddha. A symbol of his wisdom, they also remind us that he was once a prince who wore heavy earrings. Even after he stopped wearing them, his lobes carried the scars of his old worldly possessions.

THE EYES

Symbolic of gods, especially Sun gods, as all-seeing beings, eyes represent perception and spiritual enlightenment. Two eyes often correspond to the Sun and the Moon. A third eye can mean fire. Eyes are also capable of destruction but in Egypt, the eye is used as a protective talisman. In Buddhism it symbolizes wisdom, while others believe in the evil eye—the curse of a single glance. Through the ages, eyes in works of art have been mutilated through fear of their power.

▲ Eye of Providence
In Christianity the Eye of Providence represents God's omniscience and omnipresence. From the late Renaissance the eye was often pictured within a triangle that signifies the Holy Trinity.

▲ Right Eye of Horus
Resembling the eye of a falcon, this symbol, the *wadjet* (or *udjat*), is usually said to represent the right eye of the Egyptian falcon god, Horus, and as such it is associated with the Sun.

▲ Left Eye of Horus
The mirror image of, or left, Eye of Horus represents the Moon, and together, the two eyes represent the whole universe. The Eye of Horus is a sacred symbol that is found in almost all works of Egyptian art.

▲ Osiris
The Egyptian hieroglyph for the god Osiris is an eye above a throne, meaning "the place of the eye." According to myth, Horus gave the eye to Osiris as a gift, to help him rule the underworld.

▲ Enlightenment
In Hinduism and Buddhism the third eye, or Eye of Wisdom, located on the sixth chakra (or brow chakra) of a deity, signifies enlightenment.

▲ Cyclops
In Greek mythology the Cyclops were a race of brutish giants, each with a single eye in the middle of its forehead. This is considered by some to indicate the subhuman condition and diminished consciousness.

▲ The prow of a boat
The evil eye is one of the most widespread superstitions, and talismans in the form of eyes are used to protect against it. In the Mediterranean, eyes are sometimes painted on boats to ward off the evil spell.

▲ Peacock feathers
The Greek giant Argos had 100 eyes, and only a few slept at any one time. On Argos's death, Hera, queen of the gods, set his eyes into the peacock's tail, which came to signify a preoccupation with the external world.

THE NOSE

Widely seen as a symbol of sharpness, the nose means discernment and perceptiveness. It is also characterized as a symbol of prying or meddling. Because it is used for the sense of smell, it is respected by hunter-gatherer tribes, who collect the snouts of the beasts they have killed. It is widely seen as a phallic symbol, so men prefer a large nose, whereas women prefer a small nose, indicating femininity and sexual awareness.

▲ Tengu
In Japan priests who seek fame and misuse the Buddhist scriptures become *tengu*—long-nosed mountain demons—after their deaths. Proud people in Japan are shown with long noses and are also called *tengu*.

▲ Pinocchio
In the Italian novel *Pinocchio* by Carlo Collodi the eponymous puppet's nose grew longer whenever he lied. A hand gesture pulling out from the nose now signifies that a person is lying.

◄ Raised or wrinkled nose
In Europe a raised or wrinkled nose conveys arrogance and disgust, as in phrases such as "to turn one's nose up." In Japanese *hanataka* ("high nose") means proud.

◄ Ethiopian portraits
Ethiopian art is distinguishable from the art of many other indigenous peoples by the large eyes seen on all its human subjects. The significance of this is an emphasis on the eyes as windows of the soul.

SEE ALSO
Egyptian deities *pp.138–39*
Greek & Roman deities *pp.140–41*
Hinduism *pp.158–63*
Buddhism *pp.164–69*
Amulets *pp.194–95*
Picture writing *pp.300–05*

THE HEAD

107

THE HAIR

Since ancient times hair has been seen as symbolic of inner strength and power, lasting even after the person dies. Cutting hair can mean surrender and sacrifice. Hair radiating from the head is a symbol of the Sun's rays. It is also associated with the Earth, grass being the "hair" of the Earth. Simple agricultural societies equated hair growth with crop growth, so they cared for their hair to ensure abundant harvests.

▲ Zeus
Several Ancient Greek heroes had long hair, and Greek soldiers wore their hair long in battle as a sign of aristocracy. Here the luxuriant locks of Zeus, king of the gods, symbolize his divine power and virility.

▲ Shiva
Often shown with a pile of densely matted hair resembling a crown, Shiva never cut his hair because it was believed to hold a magical source of power and energy. It is usually decorated with a crescent.

▲ Samson and Delilah
In the Old Testament Samson's full head of hair symbolized power and virility, and he was famous for his feats of extraordinary strength. Samson's name meant "like the Sun," and long hair was a symbol of the Sun's radiant power. When Delilah betrayed him by cutting his hair, she made him weak and vulnerable.

▲ Mary Magdalene
In much medieval Christian art Mary Magdalene is shown as having long red hair, which she wears down over her shoulders. This was generally considered to be a sign of sexual impropriety in women at the time, as well as being indicative of penitence.

▲ Buddhist topknot
The Buddha is usually shown with an *ushnisha*, a protuberance on his head which signifies spiritual knowledge. This may have derived from the topknot he wore before abandoning his princely life.

▲ Egyptian gods
The Egyptian hieroglyph for a god is a bearded figure, since the beard was considered a divine attribute. Egyptian kings wore beards in their official images whether or not they had beards in real life.

THE TONGUE

As the organ of speech, the tongue can destroy or create. It is often likened to a flame because of its darting movement and red color. To the Ancient Egyptians, the tongue was the visible manifestation of the spoken word, through which the god Ptah created the universe. In many cultures images of a face with a "stuck-out" tongue are used to ward off harmful spirits.

◄ Gorgon
The most widely used image to avert evil in Ancient Greece was the Gorgoneion, the head of the Gorgon. This fearsome image, with goggling eyes, snake hair, and a protruding tongue, was placed on doors, walls, and tombstones in the hope of protection against evil.

▲ Egyptian god Bes
A minor god of Ancient Egypt, Bes is represented as a dwarf with a large head and protruding tongue. Bes was a household protector who battled evil. He came to be associated with childbirth because he was thought to fend off harmful spirits during labor.

▲ Maori war cries
Before battle, the Maori tribespeople of New Zealand would perform a haka dance to invoke Tumatauenga, the god of war, and warn the enemy of their fate. The dance involved fierce facial expressions and the poking out of tongues as far as possible as a symbol of aggression and challenge.

▲ Goddess Kali
Statues of Kali, the Hindu goddess of destruction, are often terrifying due to her crazed eyes and a protruding tongue that looks like a flame. Her facial expressions show the extent of her power to destroy, and her flickering tongue symbolizes mockery of human ignorance.

THE TEETH

Because teeth are used for chewing and tearing food, they symbolize animal strength and aggression. Protruding teeth are a feature typical of Buddhist deities in their wrathful aspect. But there is global variation regarding the symbolism of the teeth. In some cultures tooth filing as a sign of beauty features in coming-of-age rituals, while in others long teeth are a sign of ambition.

◄ **Cadmus**
In Ancient Greece teeth were a symbol of fertility. Hardened warriors called Spartoi ("sown men") grew from where Cadmus planted dragon's teeth in the ground, and the city of Thebes was founded on this spot.

▲ **Wrathful deity**
Protruding teeth often feature on Shivaite and Buddhist deities, such as Kali and Yama, in their wrathful aspects. Sharp, prominent teeth represent power and force and are seen in statues of the deities as protectors against evil. Large, fang-like teeth are a feature of Asian demons.

▲ **Toothlessness**
The absence of teeth is a sign of lost youth, as well as the loss of the ability to fight and defend oneself. It is a symbol of frustration and weakness, since a healthy jaw denotes vigour and confidence. The word "toothless" has become synonymous with anything that is lacking in force.

▲ **Dracula**
Fanged teeth have come to symbolize bloodsucking vampires. Prolific in folklore, the most famous vampire is Bram Stoker's Count Dracula, who uses his fangs to pierce his victims' flesh before sucking out their blood. The sexual symbolism of sharp teeth incising human flesh is implicit.

THE MOUTH

The mouth is the channel through which we talk, eat, and breathe. It is seen as a symbol of creative force. But the ability to reason and speak our thoughts can be undermined by what we say. Our words can lead us into either an elevated world or a lower, debased world. The mouth is sometimes depicted as the lips of an angel or the jaws of a monster.

THE LIPS

The full, reddened lips of a woman are considered attractive because they mimic the sexual swelling of the female genitalia. Full lips are appealing because the more estrogen a woman has, the fuller her lips will be, thereby signalling fertility. Lipstick mimics this, giving the impression of sexual arousal.

◄ **Mouth of Hell**
In medieval Christian art the entrance to Hell is often shown as the gaping fiery mouth of the huge reptilian monster Leviathan. In this Doom painting, those unworthy of Heaven are taken by demons to the mouth of Hell, beyond which lies eternal pain and torment.

SEE ALSO
Egyptian deities *pp.138–39*
Greek & Roman deities *pp. 140–141*
Hinduism *pp.158–63*
Buddhism *pp.164–69*
Christianity *pp.176–79*
Picture writing *pp.300–05*

▲ Scalping

To the American Indians, a man's scalp symbolized his life force. It was removed not only as a trophy of war but also to verify the courage of the warrior who won it. Occasionally, the victim of a scalping survived, though with severe injuries. Many rituals surrounded the bringing home of scalps from war, and their drying and decoration.

HEAD TROPHIES

▲ Skull cup
Used in Tibetan Buddhism, the skull cap is a decorated cup or bowl made from a human skull. It represents impermanence.

The skull is one of the most striking of all symbols. A widely-held belief that the power of the human soul resided in the head made skulls, and heads, prized trophies in many cultures.

The image of a grinning skull is a visual metaphor for mortality, particularly in the West. It appears as a warning on toxic products, for example, or as a grim icon on a memorial stone. But in some cultures attitudes are very different and people honor the skull as powerful source of life and fertility, rather than fearing it as a terrifying symbol of death.

SACRED SKULLS
Because of its association with the soul and the afterlife, the skull has strong religious connotations. The cult of the skull as a sacred object was widespread among ancient peoples. In Nordic mythology, the skull of the giant Ymir became the vault of Heaven after his death; in pre-Columbian America, the skull was honored by the Aztecs and other tribes. Skulls also appear in the iconography of many Hindu and Buddhist deities, often in garlands or on a sceptre. As a Christian emblem, the skull is associated with penitence and is a pious reminder of the transience of life.

▲ The place of the skull
The crucifixion of Christ occurred at Golgotha, said by some to be the spot where Adam's skull lay buried. Christ's blood dripping on it was said to cleanse man of Original Sin.

HEADHUNTING RITUALS

◄ New Guinea clubhouse
A huge ceremonial clubhouse erected on the island of New Guinea, north of Australia, in which the skulls from headhunting expeditions were displayed.

Until recently, taking human heads as symbols of power was common among certain peoples in parts of Southeast Asia, Oceania, and South America. The custom arose from the belief that the soul resided in the head; through decapitation, the headhunter sought to transfer the victim's soul, or life force, to himself, his land, and his community. Headhunting was an important means of renewing fertility and spiritual power after a death in the community, or a failed harvest. In some cultures heads were tokens of manhood, and young men could marry only after taking their first head. In Southeast Asia and Melanesia among tribes such as the Iban, Ilongot, and Dayak, headhunting was a ritual, as well as an act of war. The Maoris preserved their enemies' heads by smoking them after removing the skull. In China, too, Qin soldiers collected their enemies' heads. As most of the soldiers were slaves, they gained their freedom by returning from war with such trophies.

SHRUNKEN HEADS
Of the many headhunting cultures worldwide, only the Jivaro clan, of the Amazon forests of Ecuador and Peru, is known for the practice of shrinking human heads, or *tsantsa*. By acquiring a head in battle, a Jivaro warrior increased his own personal power, or *arutam*, but the dead man's soul was still considered dangerous. Shrinking the head destroyed its power and prevented the victim's avenging spirit from returning. The head was also thought to improve the growth of crops.

▲ Shrinking a head
To shrink a head, first the skull was removed, and the skin was filled with hot sand or pebbles. The head was then massaged until it shrank.

SEE ALSO
Death & mourning *pp.128–31*
Hinduism *pp.158–63*

111

MAN AND THE UNIVERSE

The relationship between people and the Universe was an important issue in Renaissance thought. Da Vinci's famous drawing of the Vitruvian Man was based on an idea by the Roman architect Vitruvius. It can be interpreted as an analogy between the structure of the human body and the structure of the Universe. To alchemist and writer, Agrippa of Nettesheim, the body was the microcosm that contained the macrocosm—that is, the Universe.

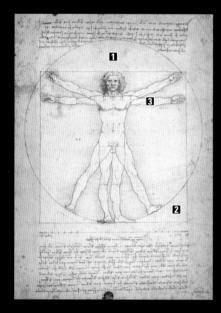

1. The circle
During the Renaissance humanists likened the perfection of the circle to God. They believed that a person, represented here by Leonardo's figure, formed the circle, or spiritual world, by the circular motion of his/her body, which symbolized the creative spirit that lifted people above the limitations of the physical world, or square.

2. The square
The figure stands within the square that is superimposed on the circle. Some people believe that Leonardo was not only providing an exercise in proportion but also showing symbolically how someone can be simultaneously in the natural and spiritual worlds.

3. Divine proportion
Following Vitruvius's lead, Leonardo's main intention in this drawing was to illustrate the concept of what is known as the Divine Proportion. According to this principle, each separate part of the body is a simple fraction of the whole. For example, the head measured from the forehead to the chin is exactly one tenth of the total height, and the outstretched arms are always as wide as the body is tall. The Divine Proportion of the human body reflects the symmetry that occurs throughout the Universe.

Man the microcosm
Agrippa of Nettesheim (1486–1535) was the foremost Renaissance author on the subjects of magic, astrology, and esoterica. His best-known work, the three-part *De Occulta Philosophia,* examines the concept—widely held at the time—that the Universe is built on the model of a man and has a soul. Agrippa visualized a man, the microcosm, in the same shape as a pentagram representing the Universe, or macrocosm. In this drawing, the five points of the pentagram jointly represent the parts of the body and the planets, shown as symbols, that were known to astrologers at the time, At the top are the head and the planet Mars; the arms correlate to Venus (left) and Jupiter (right); the legs correlate to Mercury (left) and Saturn (right). The Moon appears at the center of the pentagram, near the genitals.

Leonardo da Vinci, *The Vitruvian Man,* 1492

HUMAN BODY

The human body was considered in many traditions to be the microcosm of the universe: everything that existed outside of a person was represented within. Most cultures allocated symbolism to every part of the body and gave these parts meaning beyond their biological functions. In many religions the human figure symbolized the Divine Power and was the principal symbol of the sacred. Gods appeared in human form, and the Old Testament states that "God made man in his own image."

THE SKELETON

The grim image of a human skeleton is the personification of Death. In Classical antiquity skeletons are present at banquets as a reminder of life's fleeting pleasure. The skeleton is often depicted sitting next to both priests and peasants as a reminder that Death treats all people equally.

◄ **Tarot card of Death**
In tarot the Death card shows arms and heads growing in the field of life, while a skeleton is scything one of the heads. The card can mean change and transformation as well as death.

HUMAN SKELETON

◄ **Day of the Dead**
In Mexico death is viewed as one more misfortune to contend with, but also as the ultimate liberation. Mexicans venerate the skull and skeleton during Day of the Dead ceremonies. Even toys and sweets are seen in the form of a skeleton. This macabre couple was made for a wedding cake.

THE BONES

As the framework of the human body, bones represent strength, stability, and determination. The Amazonian Yanomana tribe believed the soul resided in bone marrow, so they ate the marrow of deceased relatives to ensure their spirit lived on. For this reason, bone marrow symbolizes immortality and resurrection.

◄ **Ribs**
The Bible's book of Genesis tells how God took a rib from Adam to make Eve. The rib has therefore come to symbolize woman, born of man.

DJED

PRIMARY CHAKRAS

▲ **Spine**
The pillar-like *djed* represents the backbone of Egyptian god Osiris. In Tantric Buddhism the primary chakras (centers of energy in the body) run down the spine and open to release energy during meditation.

THE ⊕RGANS

In Egypt, during mummification, four organs—the liver, lungs, stomach, and intestines—were placed in separate canopic jars. Each was protected by one of the four sons of Horus and associated with one of the four cardinal directions. In China the organs are associated with the seven bodily orifices.

ENDLESS KNOT

HUMBABA

▲ Intestines
The endless knot, a symbol of longevity and eternity, is thought to be a stylized image of the intestines, while the giant Humbaba in Assyrian mythology is said in some accounts to have had a face resembling the coiled entrails of men and beasts.

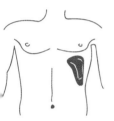

▲ Spleen
The spleen is regarded as the seat of the humors—laughter and melancholy. In the East it means only cheerfulness, and in China is one of the Eight Treasures linked to Yin energy.

▲ Liver
For Ancient Romans the liver was considered the seat of passion. In China the liver is one of the Eight Precious Organs of the Buddha and is represented by the lotus flower.

THE LIMBS

Our legs and arms are seen as the most active parts of the body. Legs are a sign of balance and onward movement. They symbolize good luck and are depicted in the four-limbed swastika and in three-legged signs, portraying fertility and regeneration. The arm shows strength, power, and protection and is the instrument of justice.

◄ Legs
Perhaps the most famous leg symbol is the triskelion, seen on the flags of the Isle of Man (*left*) and Sicily. It means good luck, fertility, and regeneration, with its image of constant movement and footsteps.

THE HEART

Long used to symbolize the spiritual and emotional core of a human being, the heart is widely associated with love, while the word "heart" is used poetically to refer to the soul. Stylized depictions of hearts are used to represent love, and the Sacred Heart, often wrapped in a crown of thorns and situated on the chest of Christ, is a popular motif in Christian art.

▲ Weighing the heart
The heart played a fundamental part in Ancient Egyptian beliefs. In the Hall of Judgment the heart of the deceased was weighed against an ostrich feather of Ma'at, goddess of truth and justice.

▲ The winged heart
The winged heart, meaning ascension, is a symbol of the Sufi movement, a mystic branch of Islam. It indicates that the heart is between soul and body, a medium between spirit and matter.

▲ Human sacrifice
For the Aztecs the heart was the center of their life force and religion. Thousands of human hearts, often still beating, were offered up to the Sun god to ensure the renewal of crops and regeneration of the soil.

▼ Arms
Arms are lifted in battle as a sign of surrender and are raised up to God in prayer or supplication. In Hinduism the multiple arms of deities such as Vishnu (*below*) symbolize their many roles.

THE COSMIC FORM OF THE GOD VISHNU, c1800

RAISED ARMS IN SAYDEH MURAL

EGYPTIAN HIEROGLYPHIC ARM SIGN

SEE ALSO
The lotus *pp.86–87*
Death & mourning *pp.128–31*
Hinduism *pp.158–63*
Buddhism *pp.164–69*
Taoism & Shinto *pp.170–71*
Christianity *pp.176–79*
Islam *pp.180–83*

HANDS & FEET

Hand and footprints are, to many, a personal reminder of being in a specific place. In Buddhism footprints purporting to have been left by the Buddha are revered. The action of the hand is full of symbolism, and different hand positions are used in many cultures to enhance meditation and religious rituals. Feet represent balance, the Earth, and travel, marking the path a person has taken and, therefore, symbolizing free will.

THE HANDS

The hands are infinitely expressive and capable of displaying a wide range of gestures, each with different meanings. Hands can be an instrument of command but may also signify protection, creation, blessing, power, a pledge, strength, and teaching. Healers work by the "laying on" of hands; people holding hands convey love and affection; we shake hands when meeting others; and we offer a "helping hand" to those in need.

► Hand of God
A hand reaching out from Heaven is often a depiction of the hand of God. Traditionally, God's left hand is concerned with justice, and His right with mercy. The hand of God creates and protects, but if His laws are not obeyed, it also punishes.

◄ Hamsa hand
This ancient hand symbol, most commonly known as the Hamsa or Hamesh, is used as a protective amulet by both Jews and Muslims to guard against the evil eye. In some instances, a stylized eye appears in the center of the palm of the hand.

▲ Creator gods
The hands of the Egyptian creator gods, Ptah and Khnum, are symbols of creative power. Ptah created the heavens and Earth, while Khnum (*shown here*) made people.

▲ Faith and justice
In heraldry a hand on a crest or shield is a pledge of faith, sincerity, and justice; two joined right hands represent union and alliance. The open hand may also signify the Sun.

▲ Hand washing
The washing of hands indicates innocence, and stems from Pontius Pilate washing his hands after the trial of Christ. Clean hands imply a pure and sin-free soul.

► Hands on gravestones
Many meanings are seen in hands on gravestones. Shaking hands are a farewell to Earth; an upward index finger is the hope of Heaven; clutching an arrow means "mortality"; and hands held over a broken chain mean the loss of a family member.

HANDSHAKE

INDEX FINGER POINTING UP

CLUTCHING AN ARROW

HANDS ABOVE A BROKEN CHAIN

▲ Clasped and hidden hands
n China clasping one's hands together, often hidden by long sleeves,
denotes respect and amiability, since the hands cannot then be used
n aggression. Hands raised, palms together, as a form of greeting are
also symbolic of respect being shown.

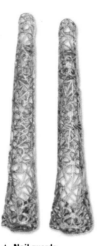

▲ Nail guards
In Asia, long fingernails were
considered a sign of wealth,
since only the rich could
preserve their nails by being
idle. These intricately carved
gold nail guards are from China
and would have been used to
preserve long fingernails.

▲ Unit of measurement
The hand as a unit of
measurement dates back to
Egyptian times. Today this
unit of measurement is used
primarily in defining the height
of horses, though in Bali
a man's house is still built
according to his own size, based
on hand width and arm length.

THE FEET

The power of mobility and a "solid foundation" is symbolized by our feet.
In Hinduism, feet are seen as a point of divine contact between human
beings and Earth. In the Middle East one showed respect for a visitor or
friend by washing their feet, while in Asia feet are considered unclean, so
t is taboo to point the soles of your feet toward another person.

▲ Bare feet
n the West bare feet are a
sign of humility and poverty.
Christ and the Apostles,
Franciscan friars, and saints
are all depicted in art without
footwear. Eastern nations
customarily perform all acts
of religious worship with bare
feet. In antiquity bare feet were
also a sign of mourning.

▲ Feet washing
Washing a pilgrim's feet is the first symbolic act of hospitality
performed in monasteries along the pilgrimage roads. The washing
itself recalls Christ's own actions at the Last Supper. He washed
the feet of His disciples at the meal as a means of expressing His
humble service and love. The humility is implied due to the perception
of the feet as unclean parts of the body.

▲ Vishnu's giant steps
The feet and footprints of Vishnu
are worshiped after a myth that
tells how, in his dwarf
incarnation, he requested King
Bali grant him as much land as
he could cover in three steps.
On reverting to full size, he set
one foot on Earth, one in the air,
and one on the king's head.

▲ Demonic feet
The foot is said to support the
soul, since it serves to keep
the entire body upright. For this
reason, demonic beings are
often depicted with feet that
differ from those of a person—
either hairy, emphasizing the
demon's animal nature, or
turned the wrong way.

SEE ALSO
Death & mourning pp.128–31
Hinduism pp.158–63
Satan & demons pp.190–91
Amulets pp.194–95
Heraldic emblems pp.318–23
Symbolic gestures pp.334–37

BUDDHA'S F⊕⊕TPRINT

Buddha's footprints, *Buddhapada*, are found at many Buddhist temples and are seen as signs of the Buddha's presence. It is believed that he left them to guide us to enlightenment. Many are decorated with symbolic images, including the 32, 108, or 132 distinctive signs of the Buddha. These footprints from the Indian stupa of Amaravati are surrounded by symbolic motifs.

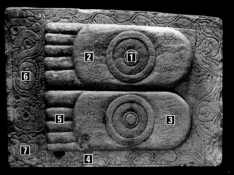

1. Center of the sole
In the center of the sole is a 1,000-spoked wheel (*dharma-chakra*), edged with a band of four-petaled flowers. The wheel is a symbol of the Buddha's teachings and is one of the Eight Auspicious Symbols.

2. Swastika
The swastika means "the auspicious" and is an Ancient Indian symbol.

3. Triratna
The triratna mark is a felicitous symbol in which a three-pronged element surmounts a flower motif; it symbolizes the three jewels of Buddhism—the Buddha, Buddhist Law (*dharma*), and the community of monks (*sangha*).

4. Lotus flowers
The feet are surrounded by intertwined lotus flowers. The lotus is another of the Eight Auspicious Symbols. The roots of a lotus are entrenched in the mud, the stem grows up through the water, and the flower lies in the sunlight, symbolizing purity and enlightenment.

5. Toes
Long, straight toes that are all the same length are one of the 32 signs of Buddhahood.

6. Knot
The knotted shape symbolizes the infinite wisdom of the Buddha.

7. Small figure
A benevolent spirit, or *yaksha*, sits in the area around the toes. His umbilical cord is a vine on which grows jewels in the form of fruit.

FERTILITY & CHILDBIRTH

Throughout human history people have revered fertility and birth symbols, from phalluses to patron saints. Every ancient civilization had important rituals focusing on the creation of new life and plentiful harvests. The Mesopotamians are believed to have made figurines for use in fertility rites, while the Egyptians had countless gods to call upon to aid fertility. Major pagan rituals occurred in spring, celebrating rebirth and fertility. The arrival of Christianity did not end the belief in fertility symbols. Indeed, they are so deeply rooted in our culture that many are still used today.

FERTILITY GODS

From the earliest times and in every culture, the regular birth of children ensured survival. Cultures developed many deities to watch over and promote fertility. By paying homage to deities, worshipers were calling forth specialized energy to aid them in their endeavour. These gods represented the fertility of people and the land upon which they lived.

◄ Min
Egyptian deity Min was the god of fertility in animals and crops, and as such he was in charge of the rain. At harvest time he was praised in the hope that he would bless the crops with his favor. Min is always depicted with an erect penis.

▲ The linga
In India Shiva, the supreme god of creative energy, was often represented by and worshiped as a phallic symbol called the linga. It is a potent depiction of the god's invisible presence at the core of creation.

► Astarte
This exaggerated gold figure depicts Astarte, or Ashtart, a Semitic goddess of sexual love, maternity, and fertility. It dates from c16th century BCE.

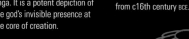

▲ Priapus
Priapus was a Greek fertility god symbolized by an exaggerated phallus. The son of Aphrodite and either Dionysus or Hermes, he was the protector of livestock, fruit plants, gardens, and male genitalia.

► Lotus-headed goddess
The mysterious goddess Lajja Gauri is depicted with a lotus for a head and legs open and raised, suggesting either birthing or sexual availability. She is the elemental force of all life.

FERTILITY SYMBOLS

Certain animals and plants have long been associated with fertility because of their reproductive habits or their appearance. As a result, their image was sometimes used as a fertility talisman. Examples include the bull, the rooster, and the rabbit, as well as the many-seeded pomegranate.

◄ Peacock
The peacock has long been associated with fertility as it was thought to dance before rainfall. Its fan-shaped tail has been said to be a symbol of the Sun; alternatively, it represents the vault of Heaven, and the "eyes" upon it are the stars.

▲ The Venus of Willendorf
The Venus is an idealization of the female figure. This statuette was discovered in 1908 at a Palaeolithic site near Willendorf, Austria. Her pronounced vulva, breasts, and belly suggest a strong connection to fertility.

► Easter egg
Much of the symbolism of present-day Easter celebrations is not Christian in origin. The Easter bunny and chocolate eggs are echoes of ancient spring fertility rites, and the name "Easter" comes from Eostre, the Anglo-Saxon goddess of fertility.

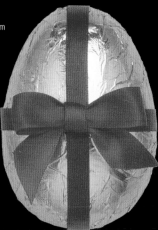

▲ Pine cone
Pine trees were powerful fertility symbols in many cultures. The Celts gathered pine cones for use as fertility charms by a woman hoping to conceive. Often they were put under her pillow as she slept.

▲ Acorn
Like the oak, the tree that bears it, the acorn has been considered a powerful fertility symbol dating back to pagan times. The strongest bringers of fertility were acorns that had been gathered at night.

▲ Hazelnuts
With its nourishing nuts and tendency to grow near water, hazel was a traditional symbol of fertility and female wisdom. Strings of hazelnuts would be hung in rooms to bring fertility to the occupants.

▲ Pomegranate
Its abundance of seeds led to the pomegranate's use as a symbol of fertility, birth, and eternal life. Ritual items, such as jars, pendants, and scepters, are often seen in the shape of the pomegranate.

▲ Cowrie shell
These shells were viewed as common symbols of fertility, birth, and womanhood because of their resemblance to the vulva. They were given to brides to guarantee offspring and provide a safe delivery.

▲ Fish
Used for millennia worldwide as a religious symbol associated with the pagan Mother Goddess. The fish symbol was often drawn by overlapping two very thin crescent moons.

▲ Cornucopia
The word "cornucopia" literally means "horn of plenty," from *cornu* (horn) and *copiae* (abundance, plenty). The cornucopia was used to evoke abundance in Ancient Greek and Roman art, and it was often shown overflowing with fruit, wheat, and flowers.

◄ Wheat sheaf
The sheaf of wheat signifies a good harvest, fertility, and a closeness to the Earth and her resources. To early agricultural people, a good wheat harvest assured plenty of the bread that would keep the community alive throughout the winter.

◄ Sheela na Gig
Carvings of women with an exaggerated vulva are commonly found on churches of the medieval period. They were seen as protective fertility symbols.

SEE ALSO
Aquatic creatures pp.68–71
Fruits of the Earth pp.98–99
Hinduism pp.158–63
Christianity pp.176–79

121

PHALLIC SYMBOLS

The phallus, the erect male sex organ, is a symbol of fertility and strength. Phallic symbols are among the most ancient objects excavated in both Asia and Europe, indicating a longtime concern with fertility. The phallus can be seen in deities, such as the Greco-Roman god Priapus, or objects, like the Shiva linga of India. It was also glorified through fertility rites centred around the maypole and the pillar.

► Cerne Abbas
The Cerne Abbas giant, or "Rude Man," is the largest hill figure in Britain. Carved into the earth to expose the chalk beneath, the giant is 180ft (55m) long. His monstrous phallus and huge club symbolize fertility and renewal.

◄ Bull's horn on chain
The bull is a potent symbol of the masculine principle in nature, full of procreative power, and was worshiped in Egypt, India, and parts of the Mediterranean. Today a bull's horn on a chain is a popular jewelry item among young men.

► Herm
The street corners in Ancient Athens each had a herm, dedicated to Hermes. A herm was a square column topped with the god's head, on which were sculpted erect penises, which passers-by would touch for luck.

◄ Maenad and thyrsos
Sacred to the Greek god Dionysus, the thyrsos, an ivy-twined, pine-cone-tipped staff, is an obvious phallic symbol. Dionysus's companions were made up of bands of maenads and satyrs. In their fertility celebrations each dressed in animal skins and carried a thyrsos.

MODERN PHALLIC SYMBOLS

The phallic symbol is just as prevalent in modern culture as it ever was in ancient times, though its association with regeneration has diminished in the western world. Objects that are phallic in shape tend to be linked to power. In the 20th century the theories of psychologist Sigmund Freud had a huge impact on western culture. Freud believed that in our subconscious, all elongated objects represented the male organ.

▲ Gun
The gun is one of the most recognized of modern phallic symbols. Slow-motion visuals in instances of "gunplay" in movies are thought by some to symbolize ejaculation, while to lose one's gun is emasculating.

◄ Guitar
The electric guitar, regarded since the 1950s' advent of rock 'n' roll as a symbol of rebellion and youth, can also be seen to represent male virility. Some performers play the guitar in an aggressively sexual manner.

▲ Rocket
The rocket is a classic phallic shape, and even the language associated with it, such as "thrust," is pseudo-sexual. It may be interpreted as a male desire to conquer—in this instance, space.

▲ Sports car
Psychologists claim that any vehicle—such as a car, motorcycle, or scooter—has the potential of a phallic symbol, and for many the sports car is the ultimate. It represents sexual potency and generative power with its expense, length, and high-octane engine.

BIRTH SYMBOLS

Bringing a child into the world is the ultimate act of procreation and regeneration, and as such it has been revered and mythologized throughout history. Childbirth has many accompanying symbols and rituals designed to protect the mother, to assure the health of the child, or simply to celebrate the miracle of birth. One of the most potent universal symbols of birth is water, which is associated with the feminine principle and the universal womb.

▲ Scorpio
The zodiac sign for Scorpio rules the male and female sex organs and therefore has close links to reproduction. All arrowed zodiac symbols are linked to the masculine.

◄ Hippopotamus
In Ancient Egypt the part-hippo deity, Tawaret, was goddess of all things feared by man. But once it was understood that the female hippo's aggression was to protect her young, Tawaret became overseer of childbirth.

◄ Ka
The Egyptian hieroglyph *ka* is usually translated as "soul," or "spirit." The *ka* came into existence when an individual was born and acted as an invisible double, representing that person's life force.

▲ Stork
Long associated with childbirth, the stork is a fertility symbol that is also linked to birth and springtime. The concept of a stork delivering newborn babies to their mothers is taught to children throughout North America and Europe.

GUARDIANS OF CHILDBIRTH

Because childbirth has always been a risky and important event, it is unsurprising that so many guardians and goddesses are called upon for help. Most cultures had some kind of protector at this time, whether a goddess of childbirth, such as the Romans' Lucina, a guardian of both mother and child, the Greek goddess Juno, and the Egyptians' Isis and Hathor; or the many Roman Catholic saints.

◄ Frigg
A Nordic goddess of women, motherhood, and household management, Frigg was the wife of Odin and the patron of childbirth, granting aid to women suffering the pains of labor. Scandinavians used the plant lady's bedstraw (*Galium verum*) as a gentle sedative during a difficult birth, dubbing it "Frigg's grass."

◄ St. Anne
According to apocryphal Christian literature, St. Anne was the mother of the Virgin Mary. She is the saint to whom pregnant women pray for a safe pregnancy and delivery and enough milk to feed the newborn child. Over the centuries, St. Anne has become one of the most popular saints.

▲ Ixchel
In Mayan culture Ixchel was the goddess of pregnancy and childbirth. She was also called the goddess of becoming. As a fertility deity, she made women fruitful and sent fertilizing rains to the Earth.

▲ St. Gerard Majella
Many hospitals dedicate their maternity wards to the patron saint of pregnancy and expectant mothers. In life, he devoted himself to pregnant women after being falsely accused of fathering a child.

▲ Hecate
In addition to her role as protector of travelers at road junctions, Hecate was also a goddess of childbirth. In this guise, she was often called upon to ease the pains of labor, as well as to guarantee the health of a child. As a midwife, she carried a sacred knife to cut the umbilical cord.

SEE ALSO
Birds *pp.58–61*
Greek and Roman deities *pp.140–41*
Celtic and Nordic deities *pp.142–43*
Meso- and South American deities *pp.144–45*
Western astrology *pp.200–03*
Picture writing *pp.300–05*

▲ Circumcision
The ritual of circumcision has a long history and is practiced in many traditional communities. The Ancient Egyptians, seen here in this carved stone panel, regarded the circumcized penis as a symbol of fertility.

INITIATION RITES

Between the two fixed points of birth and death humans go through significant changes. Milestones in life, such as entry to the adult world, are often marked by symbolic rites.

▲ **Baptism**
The rite of purification with water is usually associated with acceptance into the Christian faith.

Among the most important events in the human life cycle is the passage of an individual from one status to another. Occasions such as a child acquiring a name or passing into adulthood are often defined by ceremonies to introduce the person to their new status and wish them well.

NAMING CEREMONIES

A ceremony observed in almost every culture is the naming of a child. Many Christians baptize their children in a symbolic purification rite that confers membership of the Christian Church. In Greece babies are named in a ceremony that takes place either on the fifth or seventh day after birth. Traditionally, when a boy is born, the family hangs a crown of olive leaves above their door to symbolize success. At Islamic naming ceremonies an animal is sometimes sacrificed as a symbol of thanksgiving to God for the gift of the child.

RITUAL HAIRCUTTING

Around the world, initiation rites vary according to belief and culture. However, some, such as ritual haircutting, are common to a wide diversity of societies and religions. Jewish boys, for example, have their first haircut at the age of three, as a sign that they are ready to start learning. Hindu babies have their heads shaved to remove the hair they were born

▲ **Life transition**
After spending time in the bush, gaining knowledge, these ocher-painted Australian Aboriginal boys are awaiting circumcision.

with, which is thought to carry negative influences from a previous life. The shaving symbolizes cutting off the past and preparing the child for the future.

ADOLESCENCE

Life's milestones are often recognized in a religious ceremony, such as Bar Mitzvah in Judaism. In some societies a young person on the brink of maturity undergoes character-testing rituals during which he or she experiences a symbolic "death," only to reappear as an adult. Usually, the rites include a period of trial and learning, when the initiate is separated from the community. For adolescent boys, circumcision (removal of the foreskin of the penis) is often the final stage of such ceremonies. The painful rite is symbolic of the child's entry into manhood; in some cultures circumcision represents the removal of "female" aspects of the male.

Female circumcision is less common and girls are more likely to celebrate the onset of menstruation. In Ghana the girl is ritually bathed and given new cloth; in Nepal a Buddhist ritual keeps the girl away from sunlight and men for 12 days. Zulu girls smear clay on their bodies to represent a return to the innocence of infancy, after which they emerge as adults.

◀ **Bar Mitzvah**
Meaning "Son of the Commandment," Bar Mitzvah marks the initiation of the 13-year-old Jewish boy into adherence to the Torah. For girls, the similarly named Bat Mitzvah occurs at the age of 12. This boy is being initiated at the Western Wall in Jerusalem.

▲ **Puberty ritual**
In the *dipo* puberty ritual performed by the Krobo people of Ghana, young girls spend time in seclusion before appearing at a public ceremony dressed in traditional clothes and jewelry.

SEE ALSO
Hinduism *pp.158–63*
Buddhism *pp.164–69*
Judaism *pp.172–73*
Christianity *pp.176–79*

LOVE & MARRIAGE

The earliest, and perhaps strongest, social ties experienced by people everywhere are those of the family. Marriage therefore plays a vital role in society and symbolizes order and stability. In the West it is declared that love is what makes the world go round, and it is certainly central to the life and well-being of many people. Symbols of love have evolved almost everywhere—from the English red rose to the maple leaf of Japan and China.

LOVE TOKENS

Love tokens have long been used in bids to woo women, because they were considered a genuine and respectable way to show one's affection. Many love symbols and tokens have their origin in ancient times—the Moon and stars are emblematic of passion, seduction, and fidelity, for example—but lovers through the centuries have also turned to flowers, perfumes, gemstones, animals, tarot imagery, and color to help them express their feelings.

▲ **Heart pierced by arrow**
Many cultures believe that the heart is the seat of human emotion, particularly love. When Cupid (Eros) shoots an arrow into a heart, it causes the victim to fall passionately in love. This is why love is said to be both pleasurable and painful.

▲ **Turtle doves**
Turtle doves mate for life and are therefore seen as a symbol of love, fidelity, and peace. The dove is associated with Venus as sign of spring and sensuality. In association with the olive branch it is a sign of peace and renewed life.

▲ **Mistletoe**
The mistletoe is sacred in some places and is widely associated with mystery, magic, and wisdom. People kiss under the mistletoe because it is neither tree nor shrub and so is equated with freedom from restrictions.

▲ **Maple leaf**
In China and Japan the maple leaf is an emblem of lovers. North American settlers used to place maple leaves at the foot of their beds to ward off demons, as well as to encourage sexual pleasure and peaceful sleep.

▲ **Red rose**
The red rose represents all things sensual, pure, and romantic. In Ancient Greece and Rome the rose was sacred to Aphrodite (Venus) and was her emblem of beauty. In the West it symbolizes passion, desire, and love.

▲ **The Moon and the star**
This West African Adinkra (symbol) of the Moon (male) and star (female), known as *Osram ne nsoromma*, signifies harmony and love. It is based on the story that the Pole Star has a deep love for her husband the Moon and awaits his return.

▲ **Love spoons**
Ornately carved love spoons are traditionally given by young Welsh suitors as tokens of affection. Made from a single piece of wood, a love spoon may incorporate several romantic symbols, such as hearts ("my heart is yours").

VALENTINES

The earliest surviving written valentine is a verse by Charles, Duke of Orleans. It was sent to his wife in France while he was held at the Tower of London, following capture at the Battle of Agincourt in 1415. Today, cards are sent on St. Valentine's Day, February 14. The first literary link between this day and romance was probably in Geoffrey Chaucer's *Parliament of Fowls* (1382).

◀ **Valentine's Day card**
The Victorians took Valentine's cards to elaborate lengths, depicting any or all of the symbols associated with love and lovers: turtle doves, lovers' knots in gold or silver, bows and arrows, rings, red roses, Cupids, hands, forget-me-nots, and bleeding hearts.

MARRIAGE

Marriage is one of the earliest social institutions created by man, and marriage rites are observed in almost every historically known society. Formed for the purpose of procreation, it is the union of opposites—male-female, Yin-Yang, god-goddess—to form a whole. People marry within their own group or outside it. Alliances are made between families and strong social ties are formed. Marriage rites vary from extremely elaborate to low-key and simple, and they may be secular events or religious ceremonies.

▲ Gold ring
The wedding band symbolizes eternity by having no beginning or end. Traditionally, both spouses wear one on the third finger of the left hand, the vein of which was believed to lead to the heart, thereby linking the couple's destiny.

▲ Russian wedding ring
These rings intertwine bands of three different colors of gold: rose, yellow, and white. They are believed to represent the Holy Trinity and are still very popular today. Elizabethans wore a version of this ring called the gimmal ring.

▲ Puzzle ring
In the Middle East puzzle rings were worn by wives to show faithfulness to their husband. It is made up of many rings that, when worn correctly, form a band ring. The complexity of this design meant that they were rarely taken off.

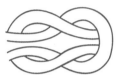

◀ Love knot
According to Roman lore, this knot symbolized the legendary fertility of Hercules. Also known as the marriage knot, it is a symbol of eternal love and was incorporated into a bride's protective girdle, to be untied by her groom.

▲ Kiddush
At a Jewish wedding ceremony, the bride and groom drink from a Kiddush cup to symbolize their love. Traditionally, a drinking glass is broken at a Jewish wedding to represent the end of their single life and beginning of their union.

▲ Loving cup
The use of the loving cup is an ancient tradition that has its roots in Celtic and Jewish cultures. The bride and groom share their first drink together as husband and wife, demonstrating the coming together of two families.

▲ Hennaed hands
For the Hindu bride, Mehndi Day is when the bride's hands and feet are decorated with intricate henna designs, signifying the strength of love in marriage. A deeply colored design is a sign of good luck. The names of the bride and groom are often hidden in the pattern.

▲ Shiro-maku kimono
The white Japanese wedding kimono, *shiro-maku*, takes its name from the words for "white" and "pure," signifying innocence. The bride also wears a white *obi* (sash), which represents female virtue.

▲ Veil
Worn in many cultures, the veil was thought to disguise the bride from malevolent spirits and ward off evil, but it also symbolizes innocence. The ceremonial removal of the veil represents revelation and light.

▲ Tying wrists
The ancient tradition of binding newlyweds' wrists together with ribbon or cord is intended to create the infinity symbol between the bride and groom. It is said that the phrase "to tie the knot," meaning to marry, originated with this ritual.

▲ Rice and confetti
Throwing things at a newly married couple is a very old tradition that dates back to Ancient Rome or Egypt. As a symbol of abundance, rice was thrown in the hopes that the couple would be prosperous and have a fertile marriage.

▲ Bridal bouquet
In times gone by, it was thought a bride could pass on good luck, so wedding guests would try to touch her. In her bid to escape, she would toss her bouquet. Today the single woman who catches it is said to marry next.

▲ Wedding cake
The wedding cake is a key symbol of western marriage. Newlyweds make the first cut together to symbolize their shared future. In Britain wedding cakes contain fruit and nuts, symbolizing fertility.

SEE ALSO
Flowers *pp.82–85*
Human body *pp.112–15*
Greek & Roman deities *pp.140–41*
Christianity *pp.176–79*

DEATH & MOURNING

People live in the shadow of death and the unknown. How each culture deals with the fear of death depends upon its beliefs, myths, and practices. Some have developed a belief in the afterlife, others in immortality or rebirth. As a result, the ritual procedures of death—the tending of the corpse, the way it is disposed of, commemorative ceremonies, and mourning—are of great importance. Death is laden with symbols that reflect foreboding, sorrow, the journey to another life, and the joy this might bring.

SYMBOLS OF DEATH

Images of death range from the blunt depictions of the Grim Reaper to more subtle depictions of the fragility of life. The human skull is a symbol of death found in many cultures and religious traditions. The passing of time is represented by clocks, candles, hourglasses, and sundials. Certain animals, such as crows, cats, owls, vultures, and bats, are also associated with death—some because they feed on carrion, others because they are black or are creatures of the night.

▲ Ravens
Despite being viewed in many cultures as a symbol of wisdom, hope, and fertility, to Christians the raven is the antithesis of the innocent white dove. Eaters of carrion, ravens were messengers of death, pestilence, and battle, and were associated with Satan.

▲ Vultures
A reputation for scavenging and eating dead matter made the vulture a symbol of death. In Tibet, they are used for "sky burials," in which they feast on corpses.

▲ Grim Reaper
In western cultures, death is often dubbed the Grim Reaper. He is depicted as a skeletal figure carrying a large scythe— a harvesting tool for cutting life short—and wearing a hooded midnight-black cloak.

◄ Owls
As a creature of the night, the owl can represent misfortune and spiritual darkness. Some cultures believe that owls swoop down to Earth to eat the souls of the dying. Their loud screeching cry and glassy-eyed stare are thought to be omens of death and disaster.

▲ Angels
In Christian tradition angels are the messengers between God and humans, symbolizing the transition between Heaven and Earth. This image is of St. Michael, who is believed to rescue the souls of the faithful from the power of Satan, especially at the hour of death.

▲ Flags at half mast
Originally a naval custom, a flag at half mast is a sign of mourning. The flag is moved halfway down the pole, usually slowly and with ceremony. Some countries lower it by just one flag width, making room for the invisible "flag of death."

▲ Poppies
Long before World War I, the red poppy was already a symbol of sleep, death, and the Blood of Christ. Each poppy on Remembrance Day in the UK is said to represent the soul of a fallen soldier.

▲ Cypress trees
In Mediterranean countries the cypress is seen as a funerary tree, due to a close association with the Roman god Pluto, ruler of the underworld. But when linked with Zeus, Venus, or Apollo, it can also mean life.

▲ Bells
The sound of the "passing bell" is the herald of death, calling attention to the fact that a soul is passing into the next world, and asking for your prayers. It was believed that the bell also frightened away evil spirits.

▲ Danse macabre
This allegorical scene first appeared at the time of the Black Death. Also known as the dance of death, it depicts Death leading revelers, showing that the end is both inevitable and the equalizer.

▲ Candle
The candle is representative of the passage of time and the brevity of human existence, which will eventually burn itself out. It was often incorporated into vanitas paintings, a type of still life full of symbolism.

BURIALS

Throughout history and in every human society, the disposal of the dead has been accompanied by symbolic ritual. Funerary rites deal not only with the preparation and disposal of the body, but also with the well-being of the survivors. The various methods are linked to religious beliefs, climate, and social status. Burial is associated with beliefs about the afterlife; cremation is sometimes viewed as liberating the spirit of the deceased.

▲ Ga tribe of Ghana
In coastal Ghana the Ga tribe believe that after death they move on to another life. Their coffins symbolize their lives, so this fish coffin is for someone with close ties with the sea.

▲ Jazz funeral
This unique funeral tradition, arising from African spiritual practices in the United States, has become symbolic of New Orleans. The funeral includes somber dirges, but ends with upbeat music and dancing in a communal celebration of life.

▲ Mayan tomb
The Mayan dead were placed in graves that faced North or West, the direction of the Mayan heavens, to allow for easier access to the other world. The tombs had nine stepped platforms that represented the nine levels of the underworld.

◄ Coins
In Greek and Roman mythology the River Styx was the boundary between Earth and the underworld. Charon the ferryman would guide the dead in return for a monetary fee, so to pay for safe transit to the afterlife, coins were placed on the tongue or eyes of the deceased in many burial rituals.

▲ Jewish coffin
In the Jewish faith the deceased is buried in a simple unpolished box with no handles or padding. This symbolizes that in death all are equal, despite personal wealth. The funeral is always a simple affair.

▲ Mummification
Ancient Egyptians developed mummification to preserve the body and so ensure immortality in the next life. The mummy was then placed in a series of gilded wooden coffins.

▲ Ship burials
The Anglo-Saxons used ships or boats in royal funerals, since the womb-like, water-borne craft symbolized the king's rebirth. The vessel would also be loaded up with goods for the deceased to use in the afterlife.

CREMATION

Funeral rites by cremation were widely practiced in ancient civilizations, and the funeral pyre was part of the burial ritual of the Ancient Greeks and Romans. Almost alone among ancient peoples, the Jews forbade cremation on the grounds that it is a desecration of the body. Hindus are always cremated; the fire helps free the soul from the body, ready for reincarnation.

◄ River Ganges
For Hindus the Ganges is the sacred river. To wash in its waters is to cleanse the soul, and to release a person's ashes on to its tide is to ensure a favorable reincarnation.

▲ Balinese cremation
Cremation is an important ritual in Balinese religion and is both expensive and elaborate. The form of the animal-shaped sarcophagus is symbolic of the family's caste.

SEE ALSO
Birds *pp.58–61*
Flowers *pp.82–85*
Trees *pp.94–95*
Greek & Roman deities *pp.140–41*
Hinduism *pp.158–63*
The home *pp.238–41*

DEATH & MOURNING

MOURNING

While death unites everyone in grief, its expression depends on cultural beliefs. In some societies the mourning period can last for years, while in others there are no mourning rituals at all. Generally the focus is on honoring the dead and comforting the living. Symbolically, in western culture, this includes memorial plaques on benches and gravestones, and in memorial gardens. It also carries over into clothing, commonly black, which symbolizes night and grief. Some cultures, including Buddhist and Hindu, mourn in white, signifying the light reached by the deceased.

▲ **Widow's cap**
In 19th-century England, a widow wore a distinctive black cap and "weeping veil" without ornament. She was expected to mourn for over two years. An elderly widow might remain in mourning for the rest of her life.

▲ **Queen Victoria**
After the death of her husband, Prince Albert, Queen Victoria went into deep mourning. She wore her trademark widow's dress for the remainder of her long life, greatly influencing 19th-century mourning customs.

► **Black armband**
In Victorian times men in mourning wore black armbands, which remained commonplace up to the 1940s. Despite falling out of fashion, they are still worn by sports teams following the death of a teammate or community member.

◄ **Mourning clothes**
White was once the color of mourning among European royalty and, although black has replaced it in the West, many cultures still wear white to signify grief. Here, a group of women in Macau—where most of the population is Buddhist—are wearing white mourning dress.

MOURNING JEWELRY

Mourning, or memorial, jewelry was worn from medieval times and served a very real purpose. It was worn in memory of those who were departed and was highly sentimental. Many pieces had inscriptions or contained a lock of the loved one's hair. Favorite symbols used in Victorian mourning jewelry included flowers such as forget-me-nots, hearts, crosses, and ivy leaves. These became more popular than the more macabre symbols of skulls, coffins, and gravestones, which were intended to ward off death and sinister occurrences.

▲ **Rings**
Mourning rings were status symbols in the 17th and 18th centuries. Skull rings, often made of gold and black enamel, acted as a reminder of death.

▲ **Lockets**
Locks of the deceased's hair were often either set into rings or lockets or woven into braid for necklaces. Hair is a symbol of life, and cutting it is linked to funerals in many cultures.

▲ **Brooches**
Mourning jewelry was most often black and ideally matt in finish. Jet, a deep black coal, was popular in the manufacture of much mourning ornamentation.

MEMORIALS AND FESTIVALS

Every culture honors and remembers its dead. This is usually done by choosing where to bury the deceased—in simple graves or elaborate tombs and pyramids—and by holding annual festivities. These can either be joyous events, such as Mexico's Day of the Dead, or more somber affairs, such as Memorial Day. Many of these festivals have deep religious roots, appeasing the spirits of the dead ancestors, giving comfort to the surviving friends and family, or ensuring the loved one's well-being in the afterlife.

▲ **Pyramids**
According to one theory, Ancient Egypt's pyramids represented the first land, rising from the primeval waters. The pyramid's tip was linked to the Sun, and as a burial chamber it ensured the pharaoh's successful journey to a prosperous life in the next world.

▲ **Taj Mahal**
This mausoleum is one of the most famous monuments in the world and is a symbol of both India and mourning. Grief-stricken when his third wife, Mumtaz Mahal, died during the birth of their 14th child, in 1631 Shah Jahan began planning its construction, which was finished around 1648.

▲ The Cenotaph
Meaning "empty tomb" in Greek, the Cenotaph in central London was initially a wood-and-plaster construction for the first anniversary of the Armistice in 1919. Such was the extent of public enthusiasm, it was decided that it should become a permanent memorial and symbol of the fallen.

▲ Day of the Dead
The Day of the Dead is celebrated in Mexico on November 1, coinciding with the Catholic observation of All Saint's Day. It is a uniquely Mexican event, honoring the spirits of the departed, who are invited to return to Earth to join in the revelry.

▲ Obon
The Japanese Buddhist festival of the dead, Obon is the time when the souls of the departed return to the world of the living. Families light paper lanterns and hang them in front of their houses to help the spirits find their way home.

GRAVESTONES

Thousands of different religious and secular symbols and emblems have adorned tombstones through the ages, indicating different attitudes towards death and the hereafter, membership in a fraternal organization, or an individual's trade. In Christianity winged angels represented the soul rising towards Heaven, skulls and hourglasses were reminders that mortal life was short, and biblical scenes expressed a range of ideas, such as the Resurrection, strict adherence to the Word of God, or the sinfulness of humans.

▲ Lamp
Lamps, including the type of oil lamp on this gravestone, symbolize immortality, faith, the light of wisdom, and the knowledge of God.

▲ Lion
The lion's eternal watch guards the tomb against evil spirits and signifies courage, strength, and resurrection. A statue of a lion was often placed on the gravestone of a guardian or fallen hero.

▲ Hourglass
The traditional symbol of Father Time, the hourglass represents the passage of time, while a flying hourglass was a reminder that time flies. An hourglass on its side meant that time had stopped for the deceased.

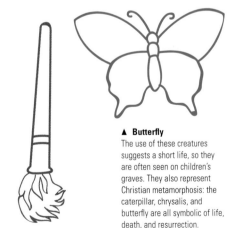

▲ Butterfly
The use of these creatures suggests a short life, so they are often seen on children's graves. They also represent Christian metamorphosis: the caterpillar, chrysalis, and butterfly are all symbolic of life, death, and resurrection.

▲ Torch
The torch of triumphant life signifies immortality and life versus death. It can be passed from hand to hand, as in a relay race, and when shown upside down it indicates that life has been snuffed out.

▲ Five-pointed star
A five-pointed star symbolizes the Star of Bethlehem, offering divine guidance and protection to the deceased. It may also represent the five wounds of Christ.

◄ Oak leaf
Oak leaves, which are often seen on military tombs, can mean power, authority, and victory. The oak signifies strength, glory, and durability, while its fruit, the acorn, symbolizes the promise of maturity and strength.

SEE ALSO
Trees pp.94–95
Hands & feet pp.116–19
Sacred places pp.232–33
Colors pp.280–83
Shapes pp.284–89

DEATH & MOURNING

131

▲ **A Vanitas Still Life with a Nautilus and a Lute**
This work by Matthys Naiveu contains references to perfection
(nautilus shell), the passing of time (hourglass), the vanity of our
existence (globe), the brevity of life (musical instruments, wilting
flowers), and the inevitability of death (snuffed candle and skull).

VANITAS

Vanitas still-life paintings serve as reminders that the power, the pleasures, and even the beauty of this earthly life are transient and that, ultimately, all things must pass.

As a style of painting, vanitas rose to prominence in the 16th and 17th centuries, primarily in the Netherlands, Flanders, and France. The term "vanitas" refers to the vanity of all worldly things, such as riches, beauty, pastimes, and learning, and it is derived from the Latin, meaning emptiness or futility. The ultimate root of the genre takes as its inspiration the Bible's Ecclesiastes 1:2: "Vanity of vanities; all is vanity."

MORAL MESSAGE

Designed to work on several levels and not simply to be viewed as exquisite works of art, vanitas paintings are full of symbolism, inviting the viewer to reflect upon the inevitability of death and the consequent foolishness of all human ambition. The paintings were moralizing in intent and served as reminders—admonishments, even—not to attach meaning or importance to the things of this world. Traditionally in vanitas paintings, attributes that symbolize material wealth, knowledge, nature, and the material or temporal things of this earth, tend to be juxtaposed with objects that embody the hope of Christ's resurrection and everlasting life.

▲ **Vanitas with a Sundial, French School**
Timepieces, including sundials, signified the passing of time and often sported mottos such as *ultima forsan* ("perhaps the last [hour]").

MORTALITY

Other elements that were commonly included were rotten fruit, which symbolizes aging; bubbles, which suggest the suddenness of death; and snuffed candles and watches, which remind us of the brevity of life. However, the most often used macabre symbol of death in vanitas painting was the skull. In the Shakespeare play *Hamlet*, the eponymous prince holds the skull of Yorick, a former servant, and bemoans the pointlessness and temporary nature of worldly matters. Death is unavoidable; the things of this life are inconsequential.

VANITAS SYMBOLS

In this artistic style, objects are seldom what they seem. A glass of red wine may simply be included as a vessel containing fermented grape juice, but it could also represent the blood of Christ (particularly if it is situated next to a loaf of bread), or it might refer to the human sense of taste, or even to debauchery. The elements of vanitas still lifes typically belong to one of three categories: the accoutrements of mortal life, such as books, tools, purses, or deeds; objects that reflect the impermanence of this life, such as skulls or hourglasses; and objects that suggest the promise of salvation and eternal life, such as ears of wheat or branches of laurel or ivory. Symbols of wealth included seashells and purple cloth, while a disordered pile of dishes might hint at the foolishness of a life that is focused on earthly concerns as opposed to one focused on the soul's redemption. The mirror was used to represent wisdom and knowledge, though when covered with dust, it assumes the meaning of a spirit clouded by ignorance.

▲ **Three Monkeys**
The monkey symbolized greed and lechery. Here, painted by Frans Snyders, the monkeys' attitudes toward food warn of being led by animal instinct.

▲ **Young Man Holding a Skull**
In this Frans Hals painting, sometimes thought to be of Hamlet, the skull voices a warning, calling on the spectator to think upon death, even in youth.

SEE ALSO
Head trophies *pp.110–111*
Death & mourning *pp.128–131*
Colors *pp.280–83*

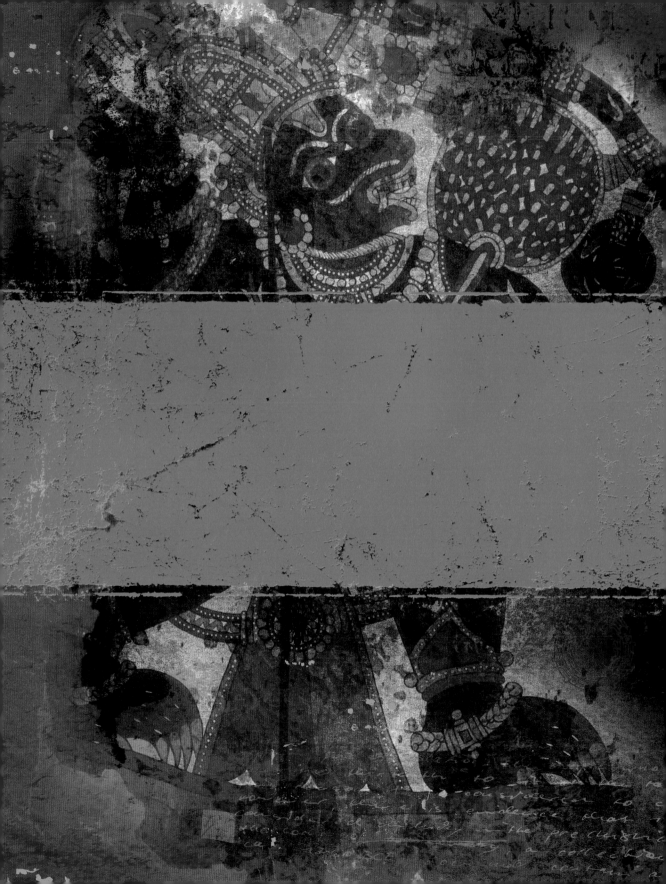

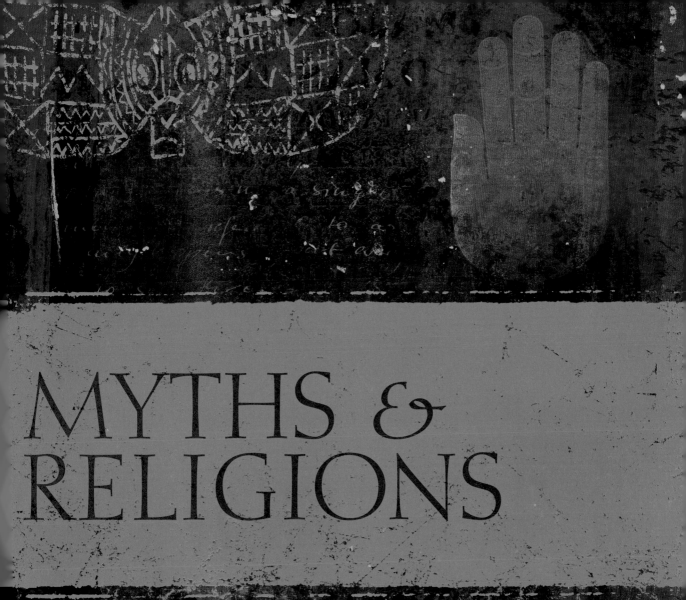

MYTHS & RELIGIONS

Fearful of the unknown, we have created religions and peopled the cosmos with deities who guide us on our life's journey and beyond. Each culture has its own symbols, creation stories, and tales of ancestors, providing deep, shared roots and reinforcing our sense of identity.

From earliest times, cultures have invented various deities who each represent different attributes—Eros, the Greek god of love, for example. Symbolic mythological figures also occur in all cultures and include heroes and tricksters who feature in ancient stories about creation. Divination—the ability to see into the past and future—has also been practiced for millennia, and ranges from the use of crystal balls to astrology.

Over thousands of years, a few belief systems have captured the imagination and spread beyond their place of origin to become, in some instances, world religions. Hinduism is a religion that has evolved through the amalgam of many beliefs, but more commonly the great religions have a founding father, a prophet, or teacher, such as the Buddha, Christ, Muhammad, and Sikhism's Guru Nanak, who revealed the doctrine and whose teachings were later enshrined in a holy book.

In some cultures a system of beliefs and symbols has developed in isolation that can appear obscure to outsiders. The Australian Aboriginal "Dreaming" is one such example. Symbolism within many American Indian groups is similarly insular, but despite differences in belief, ritual, and tradition, the same fundamental concerns with life, death, and the afterlife are present in all cultures.

In many societies, such as China, the cult of the ancestors plays a major part in dealing

EACH CULTURE HAS ITS SYMBOLS, CREATION STORIES, AND TALES OF ANCESTORS, PROVIDING DEEP, SHARED ROOTS

with after-death issues. When a person dies they join the ranks of the ancestors, who then watch over their descendants and are honored and often present in spirit at ceremonies, battles, and festivals. Their presence is evident on a daily basis, through their images and through symbols carved on weapons and houses, ensuring a sense of continuity within the society.

In some cultures around the world the influence of the spirits remains strong regardless of official religious beliefs. Spirits are believed to inhabit the mountains, trees, waters, rocks, and fields and must be appeased with small offerings to maintain harmony; even

homes have their own house spirit, set beside a shrine to the Buddha or the ancestors. The making of symbolic offerings originates from the same basic instinct as the ritual performing of sacrifice to please the gods.

Each culture has its mediators—priests or shamans who, through their higher spiritual awareness, commune with deities or spirits, often through the use of symbols. Some, such as Catholic priests, conduct rituals and teach the word of God, while others, such as shamans, commune with the spirits and use "magical" powers. Many work for the good of the community but others also practice black magic and invoke fear among their followers. All such practitioners are generally respected, however, as people throughout the world still feel the need for intermediaries with the deities; they deal with the spiritual aspects of the community, allowing ordinary people to get on with their daily lives.

EGYPTIAN DEITIES

Egyptian gods developed from the merging of two earlier cultures, one of which worshiped gods in human form while the other had animal-shaped gods. Gradually, a religion emerged that focused on the cult of the dead and was highly orientated toward symbolism. The Egyptian gods nearly always carry or wear symbols of power, such as a crown or a crook and flail. Some also carry the ankh, symbol of eternal life. These religious symbols are not the same as those found in Egyptian hieroglyphs (writing).

▲ Osiris
A symbol of rebirth and fertility, Osiris's role relates to the underworld. His body was cast into the Nile, then dismembered and stamped into the earth by his jealous brother, Seth, but it reformed. This rebirth was seen as a symbol of the burial, germination, and growth of wheat from the fertile soil of the Nile valley. As judge of the dead, Osiris holds a crook and flail as a sign of his power and sovereignty.

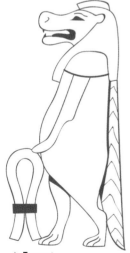

▲ Tawaret
One of several hippopotamus deities, Tawaret is usually depicted standing. Her swollen belly and breasts are symbolic of her role as protector of women in childbirth. The ankh signifies life and immortality.

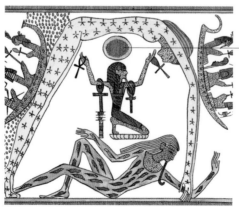

▲ Nut and Geb
A creator goddess, Nut personified the vault of Heaven and was a symbol of resurrection. Each day she swallowed the Sun at night and gave birth to it again in the morning. Here she is shown bent over the Earth god, Geb, who is leaning on one elbow with his knees raised to signify valleys and mountains. They are separated by Shu, god of the air, who holds several ankhs, symbolic of eternal life. Two solar barques, one for night and one for day, symbollically cross the heavens.

Disc representing the Sun

▲ Amun
Hidden from humans but believed to be the soul or essence of all matter, Amun was the creator god who later merged with the Sun god, Re, and became visible to mortals as Amun-Re. When depicted in human form he wears a headdress with feathers, symbolic of the sky and his associations with the wind. However, he may appear as a Nile goose or serpent, symbolic of the waters of renewal, or, as here, as a ram with protective curved horns, a symbol of fertility.

MYTHS & RELIGIONS

▲ Horus
Signifying kingship and represented by the falcon, Horus was "Lord of the Sky." The Eye of Horus (*ujdat*) was worn as an amulet to ward off evil.

Ankh   Was scepter

▲ Seth
The god of chaos and adversity, Seth, is depicted here as a mythical animal carrying an ankh and a "was" scepter, which is symbolic of power.

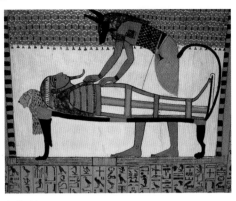

▲ Anubis
The jackal-headed mortuary god, Anubis, oversaw the embalming of the dead. His death symbolism may stem from the fact that jackals scavenged around graveyards particularly at night. Anubis is always depicted as black, although jackals are not, because it is symbolic of death and the color of mummified flesh.

▲ Sobek
The Nile god, Sobek, has a crocodile's head and wears a crown of ostrich feathers with a horned sun disk, symbolic of a pharaoh's power.

▲ Sekhmet
A goddess of war and terror but also protection and healing, Sekhmet's lion head is symbolic of her fierceness. Her caring nature is signified by the reed scalpels in her hands.

▲ Bastet
Bastet was a Moon goddess and is depicted here with a cat's head. She carries a small shield as a sign of her fierceness and symbolic of her close affinity with the goddess Sekhmet.

▲ Isis
The throne-shaped crown of Isis indicates that she originally personified the throne of the pharaohs. Isis rescued Osiris and restored him to life, an act symbolic of resurrection.

▲ Thoth
The Moon god Thoth, gave people the art of writing and is associated with wisdom and magic. Often symbolized, as here, with the head of an ibis, or depicted as a baboon.

▲ Re (Ra)
One of several creator gods, Re is depicted as the solar falcon with the Sun disc on his head. He carries an ankh as well as several symbols of power—a crook, flail, and "was" scepter.

► Ma'at
Symbolic of divine protection when depicted with wings, Ma'at may wear a feather in her headband, which is symbolic of truth. When people died, their hearts were weighed against the feather—only those that were lighter could enter the underworld.

SEE ALSO
Birds *pp.58–61*
Amulets *pp.194–95*
The head *pp.106–09*
Picture writing *pp.300–303*

EGYPTIAN DEITIES

139

GREEK & ROMAN DEITIES

The Ancient Greek civilization is associated with many powerful gods who squabbled, felt hatred, and loved, very like the humans living below. Later the Romans adopted these gods, giving them Roman names, such as Jupiter instead of Zeus, and sometimes also combining their attributes with those of other deities. Cronus, for example, in becoming Saturn swapped his scythe for a sickle. Today we still know the major deities because their various strengths and qualities are symbolized in Classical painting and architecture throughout the western world.

► Zeus/Jupiter
King of the gods and god of the skies, Zeus's many amorous conquests reflect the Greek conquest of neighboring regions and the absorption of their mother goddess cults. Among his symbols is the eagle, which signifies his power and royal status.

▲ Hades/Pluto
As god of death and ruler of the underworld, Hades is often depicted wearing a crown and carrying a scepter with two prongs that symbolize life and death. He is accompanied by the three-headed dog Cerebus who guards the gates of Hades.

▲ Nike/Victoria
To the Greeks Nike was a symbol of superiority and victory in battle. She has wings, when depicted on her own, which signify the fleeting nature of victory. A stylized version of one of her wings is now a well-known sportswear logo.

▲ Aphrodite/Venus
Aphrodite, personification of the Spring, was the goddess of beauty, sexual love, and fertility. She is often depicted naked, causing havoc among her fellow gods. Her symbols or attributes include a swan, a scallop shell, dolphins, and a flaming heart.

▲ Eros/Cupid
The god of love, Eros, carries a quiver, bow, and arrows with which he pierces his victims. His golden arrows signify true love and the leaden ones signify passion. He is sometimes blindfolded as a symbol of the blindness of love.

▲ Dionysus/Bacchus
The god of vine-growing and wine-making, and to the Greeks also a god of fertility, Dionysus is often shown wearing a crown of grapes or ivy, symbolic of everlasting life.

▲ Hera/Juno
A powerful goddess, Hera's symbols include the peacock (*shown here*), which she supposedly created, and the lotus, which is linked to her role as the goddess of marriage.

▲ Poseidon/Neptune
The god Poseidon symbolizes the power and uncontrollability of the sea. He is portrayed as an old, bearded man, and among his attributes are a trident, the symbol of lightning, and a dolphin, the sign of a calm sea and savior of the shipwrecked.

► Ares/Mars
Ares is the god of war and fittingly his attributes are his helmet and spear. In the Trojan war he was defeated by the goddess Athena, symbolizing the victory of wisdom over violence. Sometimes he is accompanied by a wolf, probably because his twin sons were raised by wolves.

She-wolf with Mars's sons, Romulus and Remus

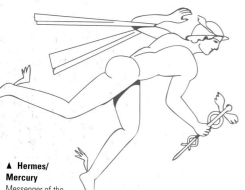

▲ Hermes/ Mercury
Messenger of the gods, Hermes wears a winged cap and has winged heels, which signify his swiftness. He also carries a winged staff, called a caduceus, which is symbolic of balance and harmony.

▲ Cronus/Saturn
Cronus is a grain god and the sickle that he carries to harvest crops has become his symbol. However, this was altered to a scythe for Saturn, symbolic of the death and destruction preceding rebirth.

► Pan
The god of shepherds and hunters, Pan's horns, hooves, and tail are a sign of his animal sexual nature. Sometimes depicted playing bewitching music on his pipes, he could also instill an uncontrollable fear in people, from which the term "panic" is derived.

► Apollo
The god of light and of the arts, Apollo, is the embodiment of male beauty. His attributes are a lyre, bow and arrows, and sometimes a snake or a wolf. They signify his pastoral origins and power over the predators of sheep. He was the lord of the Delphic oracle.

▲ Athena/Minerva
Originally a goddess of wisdom and learning, Athena adopted warlike attributes in Mycenaean times. Often depicted in a warrior's helmet and holding a shield and/or spear, she was the patron of Athens and her symbol is an owl.

SEE ALSO
Snakes *pp.66–67*
Aquatic creatures *pp.68–71*
Creation stories *pp.156–57*
Professional signs *pp.314–15*

GREEK & ROMAN DEITIES

141

CELTIC & NORDIC DEITIES

The pre-Roman gods of Celtic and Nordic people were creator and mother goddesses, or gods of nature who signified fertility, war, and/or love. Symbolic of a power greater than that of humans, the gods were assigned responsibility for anything that people did not understand, such as thunderbolts that were thought to originate from Thor's magic hammer, Mjollnir. Celtic deities were immortal, but Nordic gods were not; they maintained their youth by eating special apples grown by Idun, the goddess of youth.

▲ **Thor**
Riding his goat-drawn chariot across the heavens, Thor is the god of war and ruler of the skies. Associated with the swastika, which may have derived from his hammer, his emblem is the hazel tree a symbol of fertility, divination, and wisdom.

Silver wheel

◄ **Arianrhod**
A Welsh chthonic goddess and a star and Moon deity, Arianrhod is called "Silver Wheel" because she carried souls to the afterlife on her silver wheel, which is symbolic of birth and rebirth.

▲ **Cernunnos**
The "Horned One," Cernunnos is a chthonic god, having powers over the underworld. He is often depicted in a yogic posture holding a torque, or twisted necklace, and a serpent, female and male symbols respectively. The serpent is also a symbol of resurrection. Cernunnos signifies the sacrificial stag, itself a symbol of sexuality, whose blood must be spilled if harmony is to be maintained.

▲ **Brigid**
As a Celtic solar goddess and patroness of smiths, Brigid's attributes include fire, with which she is depicted here. She is also linked with the healing properties of sacred springs.

▲ **Morrigan**
A Celtic goddess of war, fertility, and vegetation, Morrigan is linked with horse symbolism. She is also associated with the crow as she assumed its form to foretell the outcome of battles.

▲ **Rhiannon**
A Celtic goddess of horses and the underworld, Rhiannon rides a white mare, symbolizing the powers of nature. Linked with the earth, she is associated with fertility and regeneration.

▲ **Cocidius**
A British warrior and hunting god, Cocidius is depicted here with a shield in one hand and a spear in the other. The small horns on his head are symbolic of virility and fertility.

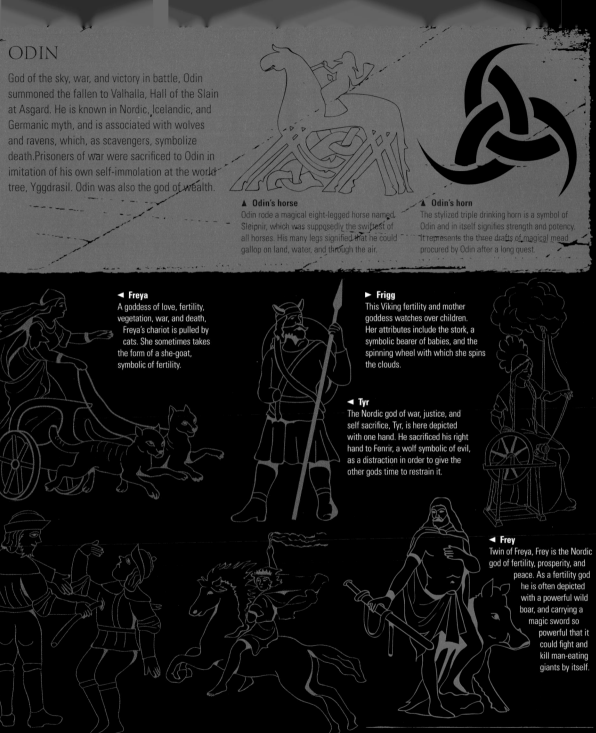

ODIN

God of the sky, war, and victory in battle, Odin summoned the fallen to Valhalla, Hall of the Slain at Asgard. He is known in Nordic, Icelandic, and Germanic myth, and is associated with wolves and ravens, which, as scavengers, symbolize death. Prisoners of war were sacrificed to Odin in imitation of his own self-immolation at the world tree, Yggdrasil. Odin was also the god of wealth.

▲ Odin's horse
Odin rode a magical eight-legged horse named Sleipnir, which was supposedly the swiftest of all horses. His many legs signified that he could gallop on land, water, and through the air.

▲ Odin's horn
The stylized triple drinking horn is a symbol of Odin and in itself signifies strength and potency. It represents the three drafts of magical mead procured by Odin after a long quest.

◄ Freya
A goddess of love, fertility, vegetation, war, and death, Freya's chariot is pulled by cats. She sometimes takes the form of a she-goat, symbolic of fertility.

► Frigg
This Viking fertility and mother goddess watches over children. Her attributes include the stork, a symbolic bearer of babies, and the spinning wheel with which she spins the clouds.

◄ Tyr
The Nordic god of war, justice, and self sacrifice, Tyr, is here depicted with one hand. He sacrificed his right hand to Fenrir, a wolf symbolic of evil, as a distraction in order to give the other gods time to restrain it.

◄ Frey
Twin of Freya, Frey is the Nordic god of fertility, prosperity, and peace. As a fertility god he is often depicted with a powerful wild boar, and carrying a magic sword so powerful that it could fight and kill man-eating giants by itself.

Baldr
Protected from death by all except mistletoe, Baldr was killed by his brother after the trickster, Loki, persuaded him to make a spear from the plant. Baldr's death symbolizes the mortality of Nordic gods but his emblem, the evergreen, is suggestive

▲ Dagr
The Nordic god of daytime and lord of the light, Dagr rides his glittering white stallion, Skinfaxi, across the skies every day, so the horse's brilliant mane can light up the Earth below. The cycle of day and night is symbolized by his birth from the

SEE ALSO

The weather *pp.34–35*
Sacred trees *pp.96–97*
Tribal totems, heroes & tricksters *pp.150–51*
Satan & demons *pp.190–91*

MESO- & SOUTH AMERICAN DEITIES

The vast continents of the Americas with their extremes of climate and terrain spawned many cultures and gods. The great Mayan, Aztec, and Incan empires of Meso- and South America were highly structured, wealthy kingdoms whose great pyramids and temples provided a rich display of symbolism. These cultures were dominated by cults in which people placated their many gods through human and animal sacrifice, as the spilling of blood was thought necessary to regenerate and maintain the natural order.

MAYAN DEITIES

The great Mayan civilization flourished in Central America between 2000 and 900BCE. Mayans developed a writing system using symbols, as well as complex astrological charts and calendars. Cities, such as Teotihuacan, were built as microcosms of the universe with pyramids that signified the Sun and the Moon. Mayan deities included gods of the elements, crops, birth, and death, who can be recognized by their various attributes.

Corn symbol

Black spot

▲ Suicide goddess
Known as Ixtab, the suicide goddess is always depicted hanging with a rope around her neck. She was worshiped because taking one's own life was perceived by the Mayans as a route to Paradise.

▲ God of death
The skeletal form of Yum Cimil symbolizes his role as god of death. The black spots signify decomposition. His adornments are made of bones and he holds the symbol for corn to represent regeneration and rebirth.

▲ Spider Woman
A Mayan goddess of the underworld, Spider Woman has an elaborate headdress, and sometimes wears a nose plate covering her nose and mouth, symbolizing her transformation into an arachnid. The water dripping from her hands signifies an association with water.

► Kukulcan
Known as "the plumed serpent" because he was half-rattlesnake and half-quetzal bird, Kukulcan is a creator god who restored the world after its destruction. The snake symbolizes the Earth and the bird the sky and divinity. Kukulcan was called Quezalcoatl by the Aztecs.

MYTHS & RELIGIONS

AZTEC DEITIES

The Aztecs gradually took over power in Meso-America after the demise of the Maya. Their empire was hierarchical and dominated by the warrior class. The gods of war, death, and fire were prominent among their deities. These gods, like the Mayan gods before them, had physical attributes or adornments that were highly symbolic of their role.

▲ Huehueteotl
Also called "the Old One," the fire god, Heuhueteotl, is usually depicted as an old, bearded man supporting an incense brazier on his head to symbolize the sacrificial fire ceremonies he presided over.

▲ Huitzilopochtli
The god of the Sun and war, Huitzilopochtli is depicted as a warrior. He has a headdress of hummingbird feathers, symbolic of fallen warriors, and holds a shield of eagle feathers in one hand, symbolizing the Universal Spirit and light, and a serpent-like staff in the other, which signifies the fertility of the Earth. His temple was painted red, symbolizing war.

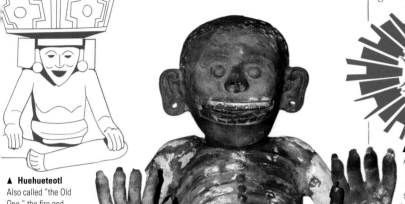

▲ Mictlantecuhtli
The Aztec god of death, Mictlantecuhtli, is usually depicted as a skeleton with staring eyes and protruding teeth. As ruler of the underworld, he is also painted white to signify the color of the dying Sun and the night.

INCA DEITIES

The Incas of Peru were prominent between 1100 and the Spanish conquest of the 1530s. They were a warlike people and as such had cruel gods, including Inti, who demanded many symbolic animal and human sacrifices. The Inca ruler was supposedly a reincarnation of the Sun god. Their deities were used as a means to terrify and control the people they conquered, but they also adopted gods of the vanquished, such as Pachacamac.

▲ Inti
As god of the Sun, Inti is represented symbolically as a shining disc with a human face surrounded by bright rays. He was feared for his great power. Solar eclipses were thought to symbolize his anger and gold signified his sweat.

▲ Viracocha
A Pre-Inca Sun, creator, and storm god, Viracocha is thought to be the Inca representation of Kukulcan. He is usually depicted as a small man with an aureole around his head, symbolic of the Sun, and carrying thunderbolts in his hands, which are symbolic of his role as a storm god.

▲ Pachacamac
A pre-Inca god of earthquakes and fire, here carved in wood, his link with agriculture is signified by the corn cobs on his robes.

SEE ALSO
Fire pp.30–31
Fabulous beasts pp.74–77
Picture writing pp.300–05

ANCESTORS

In many parts of the world ancestors are revered and even deified. They are thought to watch over and guide their descendents, for whom they signify a sense of identity and unity. For this reason people make offerings to their ancestors and add their image to ritual items, such as masks, to imbue them with protective strength. In some countries ancestors are mummified, while in others their names are passed from one generation to the next. They are usually symbolic of power; for example, the Egyptian pharoahs claimed descent from the gods.

◄ **Chimu mummy**
Human remains are a powerful symbol of kinship. The Chimu people of Peru kept mummified remains of their ancestors in sacred rooms, and brought them out during feasts and ceremonies.

Tjemen

HONORING THE ANCESTORS

For many peoples, respect for one's ancestors is part of accepting their society's traditions and structure. They are symbolic of the antiquity and past events of a particular group of people, and by honoring them their descendents affirm their place in society and their belief in its values, which are upheld by the ancestors.

◄ **Zairean mask**
For the Kuba of Zaire, grass-skirted masks such as this one are symbolic representations of their spirit ancestors. Boys were formerly introduced to their ancestors during initiation rites. By crawling between the legs of the dancers, the initiates were linked as men with their tribal origins.

◄ **Bjis poles**
The Asmat of New Guinea erect bjis poles that are carved with ancestral figures. The side projection, called a *tjemen*, which means "penis," signified fertility. These poles have powerful protective symbolism and are used in rituals associated with headhunting and the fertility of crops.

CONFUCIUS

Confucius, who lived in the 6th century BCE, remains for many Chinese a symbol of classical Chinese values. A great teacher, he propounded a doctrine based on loyalty and duty to parents, clan, and state. By stressing loyalty to one's clan, Confucius emphasized the importance of the ancestors already popular in China. His image is placed in many household shrines, and in some popular religious temples, alongside that of the clan and family ancestors.

DESCENT FROM ANIMALS

Some groups of people believe they come from animal, or part-animal, ancestry. For this reason such peoples feel a bond with the animal world. The qualities of the ancestor creature are important symbolically, so a bird may signify closeness to the gods or keenness of vision, and animals may represent courage, strength, or stealth.

▶ Bear
The Micmac of North America claim descent from a bear, an animal that symbolizes stength, courage, and renewal. One myth tells of a girl marrying a young man and finding that his village is a bear village. She gives birth to bear twins that can change shape.

▲ Dhakhan
The Kabi Australian Aboriginal people claim descent from Dhakhan, a giant serpent symbolic of creation. Dhakhan is often depicted as a rainbow, a form he assumes when traveling between his lairs.

▲ Turtle
The Elema people believe they are descended from a giant turtle, having arrived in southern Papua by sea many years ago. This ceremonial mask, called a semese, depicts a sea monster spirit that signifies this journey.

▲ Menolo
Some Solomon Islanders revere the shark-god, Menolo, from whom they claim descent. He symbolizes the sea, which they depend on, and represents speed, ferocity, and beauty. Because Menolo is an ancestor, the islanders do not hunt sharks.

DESCENT FROM GODS

Dynasties often linked their names to that of a deity and some claimed direct descent from the gods to reinforce their legitimacy as rulers. Because divine descent signifies a godlike status, it acts as a deterrent to most pretenders. Descent from a deity is also symbolic of the status of the ruler as an intermediary between Heaven and Earth, or between gods and humans. It was the ruler and his priests that interpreted the will of the gods.

Isis

Osiris

▲ Osiris and Isis
The Egyptian pharaohs claimed descent from Osiris and Isis. Since both symbolized rebirth and renewal, this claim reinforced the pharaohs' belief that they would rule forever. Isis is also the symbolic mother of the pharaoh. Here she is wearing a solar disc, symbolic of the Sun.

▲ Amaterasu
The Japanese emperors trace their descent to Amaterasu, goddess of the Sun. From her they received the light-giving symbolism of the Sun. To this day the emperor is treated with the reverence usually accorded to a deity.

▲ Moai
Facing inland to keep watch over their people, the moai are the giant stone figures of Easter Island. They are symbolic representations of ancestral chiefs who were thought to be direct descendants of the gods. There are about 900 moai on the island; a few of them have a red stone on their heads, which may represent a headdress.

SEE ALSO
The Sun *pp.16–17*
Mammals *pp.52–55*
Reptiles & amphibians
  pp.64–65
Head trophies *pp.110–11*

Egyptian deities *pp.138–39*
The Dreaming *pp.152–53*

NATURE SPIRITS

In almost all countries nature spirits have been venerated at some time. They symbolize the essence of rivers, the sea, mountains, trees, and animals, and are called upon for protection and good fortune. Their anger is appeased by the paying of respect. In Africa nature spirits may be invoked by wearing masks during ceremonial dances, while in the Americas symbolic dolls or pottery figures are made. Whilst for many revering nature spirits is in the distant past, for others it is still very much alive: wayside shrines are seen in many places, and nature spirits are a central part of Japanese Shinto, for example.

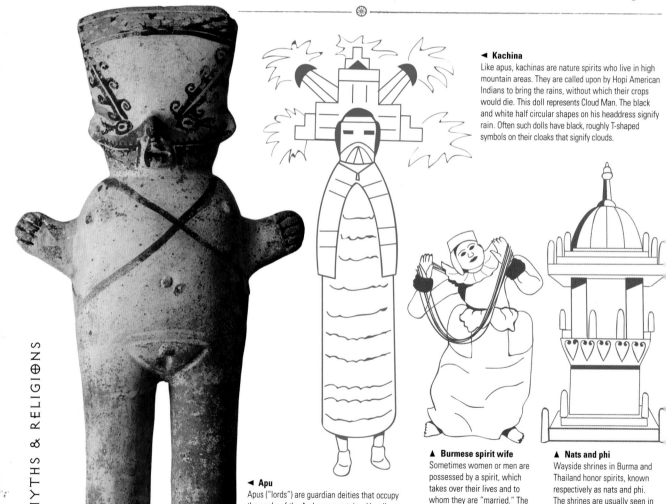

◄ Kachina
Like apus, kachinas are nature spirits who live in high mountain areas. They are called upon by Hopi American Indians to bring the rains, without which their crops would die. This doll represents Cloud Man. The black and white half circular shapes on his headdress signify rain. Often such dolls have black, roughly T-shaped symbols on their cloaks that signify clouds.

◄ Apu
Apus ("lords") are guardian deities that occupy the peaks of the Andean mountains. Usually male, they are regarded as sacred and powerful. Offerings of natural objects wrapped in white paper, called *despachos*, are made to apus as a symbol of love and as a sign of our links to all other things.

▲ Burmese spirit wife
Sometimes women or men are possessed by a spirit, which takes over their lives and to whom they are "married." The spirit forces them to act out of character, act in lewd and unacceptable ways, and dance wildly, which perhaps symbolizes the wild side of their nature in a conventional society.

▲ Nats and phi
Wayside shrines in Burma and Thailand honor spirits, known respectively as nats and phi. The shrines are usually seen in dangerous places, including accident blindspots. By making symbolic offerings at these shrines, travelers passing by ensure safe passage to their various destinations.

▲ Bwa flying spirit
This mask from Burkino Faso is worn to call upon the protection of the hawk, a solar and heavenly bird. The zigzag lines symbolize the path of the ancestors and the checkerboard patterns signify both knowledge and ignorance, and light and dark.

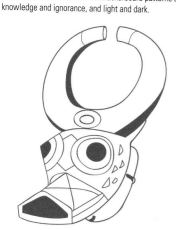

▲ Buffalo spirit
Among the Nuna people of Burkino Faso, the buffalo symbolizes power and strength. The protective spirit and blessings of the animal are called down and enter the person wearing the mask during sacred ritual dances.

▲ Elephant spirit
When used in sacred dance, masks personify and activate a spirit. Although there have been no elephants in Nigeria for some time, highly stylized masks, like this one, that capture the sacred powers of the elephant spirit are still made for ritual purposes. The mask shown above is being used as a symbol of ugliness.

◄ Water spirit
This hippopotamus mask is from the Degema region of Nigeria. It symbolizes the spirit of the water and is believed to signify righteousness. The mask is used in ritual dances at annual festivals, to bring fertility to the people.

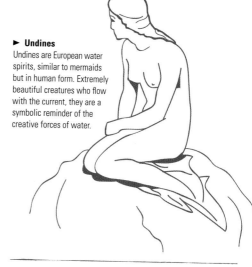

► Undines
Undines are European water spirits, similar to mermaids but in human form. Extremely beautiful creatures who flow with the current, they are a symbolic reminder of the creative forces of water.

▲ Gnomes
The word "gnome" probably derives from the Greek *genomos*, meaning "earth dweller." Gnomes were said to guard treasure deep in the Earth, so are symbolic of fertility, protection, and good luck.

▲ Elves
The elves were nature spirits popular in Germanic and Nordic legend. Living in wells, springs, and forests, they were variously described. In Nordic mythology, for example, elves are light and angelic or dark skinned like dwarves. The elf cross symbol is worn to protect one against mischievious elves.

SEE ALSO

The weather pp.34–35
Tribal totems, heroes & tricksters pp.150–51
Taoism & Shinto pp.170–71
Amulets pp.194–95
Masks pp.270–71

NATURE SPIRITS

149

TRIBAL TOTEMS, HEROES & TRICKSTERS

Every culture has figures in its mythology who are regarded as having affected that culture in some way, either by being an ancestral figure, rescuing the community from danger, or giving them gifts. Sometimes the figure might combine two or more of these roles and has often come to signify that culture's origin. The symbolic stories told about these figures allow people to learn of the creation of the world and their culture's first inhabitants.

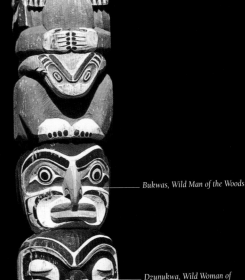

Thunderbird

Sea Bear holding killer whale

Woman holding frog

Bukwas, Wild Man of the Woods

Dzunukwa, Wild Woman of the Woods

TRIBAL TOTEMS

Animal ancestors are the most common form of totem, but some plants are also considered sacred. Found in hunting societies, tribal totems are symbolic of a particular community, and regarded with awe or ritual respect by its members. In many cultures animal ancestors are carved into totem poles, which signify the community's origins and essence. Killing a totem animal is taboo because the animal is related to the people and therefore regarded as a brother.

► Totem Pole
All figures on a totem pole are symbolic. This Kwakwaka'wakw totem pole from Canada has a thunderbird at the top, which is symbolic of power, a killer whale, the symbol of strength and bravery, and a frog, the sign of prosperity. Bukwas is linked to the dead, particularly those who drowned, and Dzunukwa symbolizes the spirits of those drowned or lost in the forest.

► Bear
The bear, symbolic of strength, protection, and the sweetness of truth, is a sacred animal in many countries. In North America it is the Guardian of the West, and several American Indian peoples, such as the Ouataouaks, have a bear totem.

CULTURE HEROES AND TRICKSTERS

Culture heroes are mythical figures, sometimes animal, who helped to create humans or gave them skills, such as making fire or growing crops. They stand in the public consciousness as a symbol of that society and its worth, and signify the ultimate example of doing good for the community. A trickster is a mischievous, cunning, often amusing figure, who subverts the natural order, either to help humans or out of spite. Tricksters are super-human but they also reflect human nature in that they are amoral and break the rules of gods or nature. They can be funny or foolish but ultimately their actions help humans and so usually signify some commitment to the community.

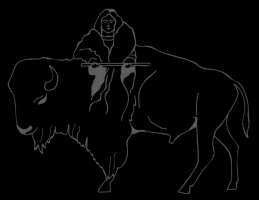

▲ **White Buffalo Woman**
The buffalo was an important animal in American Indian culture, a symbol of power and strength, providing food and skins. A white buffalo was considered sacred, signifying answered prayers. White Buffalo Woman, a culture hero of the Lakota people, brought them the sacred ritual pipe, an important symbol of their culture.

▲ **Chi Wara**
The antelope Chi Wara gave agriculture to the Bambara people of Mali. The thunder of his hooves denotes the coming rain and so symbolizes fertility.

▲ **Raven**
A well-known American Indian trickster that is symbolic of beginnings. The raven found humans inside a clam and used trickery to help them find food.

▲ **Anansi**
This West African sign is symbolic of a spider's web and represents the spider hero and trickster, Anansi, who helped to create humans.

▲ **Coyote**
An important trickster in the Americas, Coyote is a sign that something is about to happen. For the Hopi he created the Milky Way by leaving the lid off a sealed pot and allowing the stars to escape. He also gave humans fire, flood, and night.

▲ **The Mimi**
Living in caves and crevices in Arnhem Land in Australia, the Mimi are trickster spirits. They are cultural symbols personified as thin, matchstick figures. The Mimi taught people how to hunt and gather, as well as correct ritual and social behavior.

▲ **Loki**
Loki, or Sly One, is an Icelandic trickster symbolic of cunning. Known as "the contriver of all fraud," he was close to the god Odin, but through his trickery brought about the death of his son, Baldr, embodiment of innocence, peace, and beauty.

◀ **Brer Rabbit**
In West Africa the rabbit is an artful trickster who, like the coyote, stole fire to give to humans; he outmaneuvers the deceitful hyena but he also breaks friendships and symbolizes fear. As Brer Rabbit he migrated to Jamaica and the United States with the slave ships.

▲ **Squirrel**
In Scandinavia the squirrel is a trickster that symbolizes mischief; it caused trouble between the eagle and the serpent in the boughs of the World Tree, Yggdrasil.

▲ **Renard the fox**
A trickster from France and Belgium, Renard the fox symbolized craftiness. He made the aristocracy and the clergy the butt of many of his jokes, and thus became a folk hero.

◀ **Nanabush**
A culture hero and trickster of the Ojibway people of the Great Lakes region in North America, and symbolic of their culture, Nanabush recreated the world after a flood. His attributes include long rabbit-like ears.

SEE ALSO
Fire *pp.30–31*
Mammals *pp.52–55*
Birds *pp.58–61*
Sacred trees *pp.96–97*
Celtic & Nordic Deities *pp.142–43*

▲ **Man's Dreaming**
Although abstract to the uninitiated, Australian Aboriginal paintings are full of
symbolism. Here wavy lines signify running water; footprints indicate the artist's
journey through The Dreaming; and concentric circles represent still water or campsites.

THE DREAMING

Australian Aboriginals share a unique relationship with
the land and are linked to it naturally, morally, and spiritually
by the symbolism of what they refer to as The Dreaming.

▲ Bark painting
Wandjini spirits symbolize rainfall and storms. Their haloes are symbolic of clouds and lightening.

Describing the cosmos and the myths relating to it, The Dreaming, which has its own rich symbolism, provides an ideological framework for living in harmony with nature. There is not just one Dreaming but an intricate network of Dreamings that belongs to places, groups, and individuals.

ANCESTRAL ⊕RIGINS
According to Australian Aboriginal legend, The Dreaming is symbolic of a time when the first ancestral beings created the Earth. Emerging from a featureless land, they traveled far and wide, shaping the landscape and creating its form and features. They were able to change shape and so some became humans; others became animals, trees, and so on. Once their work was done, the beings returned to the land—as the clouds or the oceans—or simply rested, dormant, below the Earth's surface. Today the land's natural features are symbolic of this ancestral activity—a cave entrance signifies the hole through which an ancestral being emerged; the mountains and rivers signify features that formed as the ancestors traveled. The land, or "country," remains central to an Australian Aboriginal's being; it can feel, hear, smell, and fear, and is a constant reminder of his or her origins. The symbolic heart of this mythological landscape is Uluru (Ayers Rock).

▲ X-ray painting
A long tradition of "X-ray" paintings, in which internal structures of animals and people are visible, exists on rocks and cave walls. These paintings probably had a ritual significance.

A RICH LEGACY
As the ancestral beings journeyed, they played music, sang, danced, and told stories; they also painted and engraved rocks and cave walls, and these traditions have become integral to Australian Aboriginal religion. Among the ancient examples are rock paintings and engravings held to be the work of the ancestral beings themselves, or at least depictions of them. Such is the energy of these paintings, that they are ritually re-painted, symbolically releasing their spiritual power as a form of worship.

These images are not only symbolic of the creation of the Earth, they also signify a moral and social code that is founded in a deep respect for the land. The ancient art lives on today in bark painting, body painting, rock painting, and engraving, through which different clans have cultivated their own interpretations of The Dreaming.

SY𝕄B⊕LIC C⊕NNECTI⊕N
Almost all art of The Dreaming features the land and contains symbols that represent natural forms, including broken lines for rain, curved lines for a rainbow, footprints for a journey, animal tracks for various animals, an elipse for a shield, and concentric circles for a campsite or waterhole.

For thousands of years such art has been an outward manifestation of the artist's connection to his or her individual Dreaming and the land, symbolizing the Australian Aboriginal's strong link to his or her ancestral past.

◄ Body painting
Integral to Australian Aboriginal ceremony, body painting often contains symbolism that relates to a specific ancestral being. It might also be used to signify a person's status – his position in a particular community or his origins, for example.

SEE ALSO
Tribal totems, heroes, & tricksters *pp.150–51*
Shapes *pp.284–89*

153

SHAMANISM

A shaman is a traditional priest or spiritual leader who can control spirits, make "out-of-body" journeys, and effect cures using magic. Shamans can divine the future through sacrifice or other methods that involve the use of symbolism. Within the community, shamans are extremely powerful bridges between the natural world and the spiritual world. The role is often inherited and shamans usually wear distinctive clothing. Although shamanism is of Arctic or Siberian origin, similar intermediaries exist in every continent.

ESSENTIAL ATTRIBUTES

Once a child, usually a boy, was acknowledged as a possible shaman, he was consecrated and began his training. The process lasted for several years, during which time he received ritual and symbolic items, such as a drum, rattle, bones, and teeth. All of these attributes gave him the added powers associated with the metal used for the instrument or the birds and animals whose bones and teeth he wore.

Metal medallion

Rattle

Drum

Antler

◀ Mongolian shaman
As the spiritual focus of communities, the shaman is the link between his people and their gods. The drum is symbolic of the rhythm of the universe and has powers of enchantment, as spirits dwell in between the drum beats.

▲ Bells
Antlers are a symbol of defense and here one has been combined with bells and feathers for added symbolism and power. Metal objects, thought to be cosmic energy in solidified form, signify the power of the Earth. Feathers symbolize spiritual flight and links with the heavens.

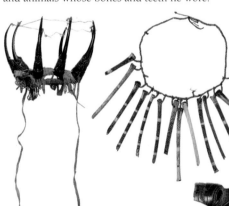

◀ Animal bones
Wearing animal figures or bones in his costume symbolically empowers the shaman with the strength of those animals. They also signify life, death, and renewal.

Runes

▲ Headdress
Worn only during shamanistic rites and symbolic of these rites when worn, the shaman's headdress may contain feathers or wings, which signify the shaman's spiritual journey, or animal claws to give the shaman that animal's power.

▲ Rattle
A sacred tool, the rattle was used to deflect evil. Its rattling sound was believed to frighten off all evil spirits, and it could also be used to imitate the sound of rain in rain-calling rituals. Rattles were often carved with symbolic images of animals or birds, such as this raven with a sparrow hawk on its underside, to increase their strength.

▲ Apron
The symbolic animal and ancestor talismans on a shaman's apron added to his authority and protected him during rituals and dangerous spiritual journeys. For some peoples these objects symbolize spirit helpers.

▲ Rune drum
Used in rituals to foretell the future, the rune drum was made of animal skin and marked with symbolic runes. The shaman would shake a ring on to a rune drum and make his pronouncements according to the rune it landed on.

SPIRIT HELPERS

Most shamans have spirit helpers, which, among other things, guide and protect them during their various journeys to the spirit world. Spirit helpers may be animals, plants, or tribal ancestors. The bear is one of the most common spirit helpers, probably because it is symbolic of great power and strength. The type of bear varies with geographical location; for example, Inuit shamans have a polar bear as their spirit helper, its white coat having additional symbolism, being a sign of purity.

▲ **Nenet Spirit helper**
When they made journeys to the spirit world, the Nenet shamans of Siberia were often accompanied by a boar, a symbol of strength and wildness.

▲ **Inuit spirit helper**
For the Inuit the shaman's spirit helper was the polar bear, symbolic of power and resurrection due to its habit of sleeping over the winter and of females emerging with new cubs in the Spring. The polar bear is an ancestor figure and embodiment of the supreme being. In prehistoric times its bones were ritually buried with human remains.

NATURAL WORLD

Shamans are symbolic of the spiritual life of their community. They have a deep understanding of the natural world and utilize its plants and animals in a variety of ways. Some shamans induce out-of-body experiences through the use of hallucinogenic drugs, such as cohoba powder, which both signify and enable journeys to the spirit world. Others dress in animal skins to make these symbolic journeys or carry ornate magical staffs as tangible signs of their power.

▲ **Carrying a staff**
The carved staff or wand carried by a shaman not only symbolizes his power, it also signifies the boundary between the natural and spirit worlds. Batak shamans of Sumatra, known as datus, have staffs that contain a powerful magical substance called pukpuk.

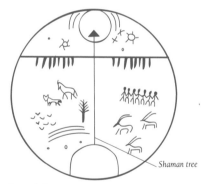

▲ **The shaman's tree**
Yakut and Evenk shamans have a tree as a symbol of meditation. Depicted here on a drum, it is their form of the world tree. The roots, trunk, and branches all signify and unite the paths of the lower, middle, and upper worlds respectively.

Shaman tree

◄ **Wearing animal skins**
Shamans, such as the Blackfoot shaman shown here, often dressed in animal skins, usually bear, wolf, or buffalo. The skin allowed the shaman to assume the power and protection of the animal he wore. It also served as a visible sign of these animal attributes to anyone the shaman encountered.

▲ **Cohoba powder**
Caribbean shamans sniffed cohoba powder to enter a trance-like state before symbolically flying with mythical bird helpers to the spirit world. Here they induced the illness-causing spirits to cure their victims. The shamans' return to normality, unaided, was thought to signify their power.

SWEAT LODGE

Among American Indian Plains tribes, the sweat lodge ceremony is an important and symbolic ritual of purification and rebirth. A sweat lodge is a small, enclosed space, made from wood of deciduous trees, which signify death and rebirth. It contains the elements fire, air, water, and earth, for inside the dark lodge hot rocks are sprinkled with water to create a steamy atmosphere similar, it is thought, to conditions within the womb and from which people are symbolically reborn.

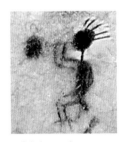

▲ **Ritualistic rebirth**
People symbolically die and leave the mortal world when they enter a sweat lodge. After spending hours inside, in the dark and heat, they emerge again, reborn.

SEE ALSO
Mammals *pp.52–55*
Plants *pp.80–81*
Sacred trees *pp.96–97*
Initiation rites *pp.124–25*

SHAMANISM

► **The Beginning**
This 12th-century illumination shows God creating the world over six days. First he made Earth, then water, land and plants, stars and the Sun, fish and birds, and finally animals and people.

PRINCIPIO CREAVIT DEUS CELVE TERRAM

CREATION STORIES

Every culture has stories that attempt to explain the act of creation.
For many they are not a literal account of events, but may be perceived
as symbolic of a deeper truth.

Although the origins of most creation stories have been lost in time, there are a number of common themes. Often if a creation story exists, there is also a tale about a great flood that swept away all that existed before, signifying a new beginning. Other stories involve the action of gods, semi-gods, or animals, each with its own symbolic overtones.

UNIONS AND THE EGG

The concept of "birth" features in various creation stories—often involving symbolic mother and father figures. In Greek mythology, for example, the union of the Earth goddess, Gaia, with the sky god, Uranus, signified one universe. They produced many children who created, among other things, plants and animals.

Another theme involves the hatching of a cosmic egg, symbolic of the universe. The Chinese creator, P'an Ku, was incubated in such an egg and organized matter into Yin and Yang, Sun and Moon, and water and land. When the egg hatched, he died of his labors. A Fijian myth recounts how Turukawa, the hawk, laid two eggs from which a boy and girl hatched. The serpent Degei taught them to talk, make fire, and cook, and created food for them.

ORDER FROM CHAOS

Various creation stories describe harmony being wrought by a mighty force from a state of chaos. In Babylonian mythology such chaos was signified

◄ P'an Ku
Symbolically incubated in a cosmic egg for 18,000 years, P'an Ku created the universe. He died when the egg hatched, his limbs forming all the Earth's natural features.

▲ Gaia
The Greek goddess, Gaia, symbolized "Mother Earth" and many portrayals of her show her in semi-nudity, surrounded by nature, or even emerging from the earth.

by Tiamat, the bloated mother of gods and monsters, who was symbolic of the waters beneath the earth. She was slain by the god Marduk, who made the sky from her upper body and the Earth from her lower half. Tiamat's tears represented the waters of the Tigris and Euphrates rivers.

Among the many Hindu creation myths is one in which Vishnu reclines on the snake Ananta, symbolic of eternity, while floating on a vast ocean. Vishnu gives rise to Brahma, who creates the universe from the primordial waters. At intervals the ocean is restored, when Rudra, a destructive aspect of Vishnu, appears and devours everything. Afterwards Vishnu the creator, called Vishnu Anantasayana, awakens and the cycle is repeated.

CREATION BY A GOD

Often the mainstay of a religious belief is the idea that an all-powerful being created the world from nothing. In the Old Testament, God's creation of the world in just six days is symbolic of His command over all. Jews observe the Sabbath as a symbol of God's seventh day, when He rested from his labors. Sikh, Muslim, and Mayan creation stories are also based on one or more supreme beings creating the universe, before which nothing else existed.

▲ Tiamat
This scene from the Assyrian Tablets of Creation shows Marduk fighting Tiamat. It symbolizes the victory of order over chaos that led to the creation of Earth and sky.

SEE ALSO
The Earth pp.24–25
Floods pp.38–39
Dragons pp.78–79
Hinduism pp.158–61

HINDUISM

Gods and goddesses abound in Hinduism as a result of the merging of many different cultures. Each of the deities represents a different aspect of Brahman, the universal or totality of being. Vishnu, for example, is the embodiment of preservation, and Brahma the personification of creation. Some gods are associated with meaningful postures, such as Shiva's dance (Shiva Nataraja), and all of them hold symbolic objects. Each god rides a different animal *vahana* (vehicle), which signifies unity with nature and mastery over animal passions.

SHIVA

The destroyer, Shiva, is also associated with creativity and fertility and is often worshipped in the form of a phallic pillar, or linga. He appears in many guises, such as a wandering ascetic, teacher, or dancer. Shiva's attributes include a trident, which is symbolic of his three roles of destroyer, creator, and preserver.

▲ Wedding of Shiva and Parvati
Shiva's consort is Parvati. Both have fierce aspects, but they are depicted here as a loving couple, waited on by attendants and riding Shiva's white bull, Nandi, "the happy one," a symbol of fertility. Shiva's lower left hand is in gift-bestowing mudra, the lower right hand is dispelling fear.

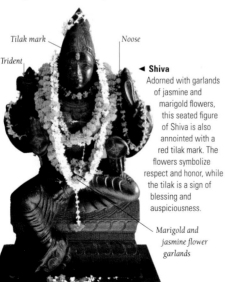

Tilak mark

Noose

Trident

◄ Shiva
Adorned with garlands of jasmine and marigold flowers, this seated figure of Shiva is also annointed with a red tilak mark. The flowers symbolize respect and honor, while the tilak is a sign of blessing and auspiciousness.

Marigold and jasmine flower garlands

▲ Shiva Nataraja
Here, in a wheel of fire, Shiva adopts the dancing posture of Natajara. Part of his divine duty is dancing out the round of birth, death, and rebirth. His streaming hair represents the River Ganges, while his feet stamp on a dwarf, who symbolizes ignorance.

Begging bowl

Trident

Hourglass-shaped drum

◄ Shiva Bhairava
As a destroyer of enemies, Shiva Bhairava is a fierce manifestation of Shiva that is associated with annihilation. In this form he is often shown accompanied by a dog, an animal that is generally considered to be unclean, and carrying a begging bowl made from a skull, symbolizing death.

VISHNU

Starting out as a minor god, Vishnu was gradually elevated to major status, and later manifested himself through a series of incarnations. He is the preserver of the universe and the maintainer of the existing order. Recognizable by his attributes of conch, mace, discus, and lotus, four-armed Vishnu is often depicted riding the man-bird Garuda.

Discus Ananta Conch

◄ Vishnu
Often depicted as dark skinned and dressed in yellow robes, Vishnu carries a different object in each of his hands. The conch symbolizes creation, the lotus is creation and purity, the mace is a sign of authority, and the discus is the wheel of existence or speed of thought. Closely associated with Vishnu is the many headed cosmic serpent, Ananta, representing infinity.

Mace Lotus

VISHNU'S AVATARS

In his efforts to avert evil, Vishnu has descended to Earth in various incarnations (*avatars*) in order to destroy demons and restore order. He has appeared nine times, as Matsya the fish, Kurma the tortoise, Varaha the boar, Narasimha the man-lion, Vamana the dwarf, Parashurama the warrior priest, Rama the prince, Krishna the cow-herd, and Buddha the sage. Vishnu has not yet appeared in his final reincarnation as Kalki the horse.

▲ Vamana
In a dwarf incarnation Vishnu confounded the all-powerful King Bali by claiming, and winning, all the land he could cover in three steps. Vishnu's steps covered the entire globe, affirming his dominance over the world.

▲ Rama
Usually depicted with blue skin and with a bow, Rama overcomes evil in the form of the demon king, Ravanna, and his army. Rama is widely revered, and in its Hindi form the name "Ram" has become synonymous with the word for God.

▲ Narasimha
As a man-lion Vishnu defeated a prophecy by defending a devotee from his arrogant father, King Haranyakasipu.

▲ Kurma the tortoise
As a tortoise, Vishnu supported Mount Mandara when the gods and demons churned the Milky Ocean to obtain *amritsa*, the elixir of life.

▲ Krishna
For many Hindus, Krishna is the most revered deity. Usually depicted with blue skin, he may appear as a child, a cow-herd, or as a pastoral deity. He is also a great sage, who in the *Bhagavad Gita* imparts wisdom on the nature of love and duty.

▲ Vishnu Anantasayana
When resting on the serpent Ananta, as shown here, Vishnu is called Vishnu Anantasayana. Drifting on the Milky Ocean at the dawn of time, the god Brahma, seated on a lotus, emerges from Vishnu's navel and creates the world anew, once every *kalpa* (4,320 million years).

BRAHMA

Although he is the creator god, Brahma is less widely worshiped than either Vishnu or Shiva. His four heads face the four directions and symbolize the four *vedas*, or holy books; his fifth head was struck off by Bhairava, a form of the god Shiva.

► Brahma
Unlike other gods, Brahma has no weapons. Instead he holds a sacred text, a water pot representing the waters of life, a rosary symbolic of the eternal cycle of time, and a spoon for ritual purification in sacrifice. Brahma's mount is a goose or swan.

HINDUISM

GODS AND GODDESSES

Besides the deities Vishnu, Shiva, and Brahma, there are many other Hindu gods and goddesses who can be called upon at different times for different reasons. Ganesha, for example, is the remover of obstacles. The gods each have a different appearance by which they can be recognized. Each is also associated with specific attributes, which symbolize their powers. The goddess Lakshmi, for example, is depicted with lotus flowers and coins, while the warrior god, Hanuman, holds weapons.

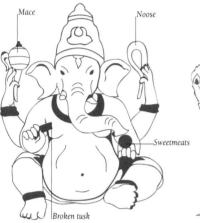

Mace

Noose

Sweetmeats

Broken tusk

▲ Ganesha
The elephant-headed god Ganesha often holds his own broken tusk, which he writes with, and a bowl of sweetmeats in his lower hands. In his upper hands he holds a noose, symbolizing worldly desire, and a mace or an elephant goad with which he propels humans along the path of life.

▲ Kartikeyya
The god of war, here shown in his six-headed form, is a boy god known variously as Kartikeyya, Skanda, Kumara, and Subrahmanya. He rides a peacock, which is symbolic of his royal rank and immortality, and carries weapons, including a hatchet, spear, and sword, to fight the powers of evil.

▲ Hanuman
A symbol of loyalty and heroism, Hanuman is revered throughout the Indian subcontinent. He wears red and saffron clothing, the colors of which are symbolic of strength and sacrifice. The monkey warrior is depicted using many weapons. Here he is carrying his favorite, the gada, or mace, a divine weapon used to destroy evil. He may also carry a bow, a club, a rock, or a staff.

▲ Apsaras
These sensuous nymphs emerged from the waters during the churning of the Milky Ocean. Their voluptuous bodies stress their link with fertility. They personify rain clouds and mists, and appear around temple doorways as symbols of abundance.

▲ Kali
In the form of Kali, the goddess symbolizes both despair and hope. In her two left hands she holds a sword to cut through ignorance and a severed head, symbolizing death, while her right hands make the signs for dispelling fear and gift-bestowal. The garland of skulls around her neck symbolizes impermanence.

▲ Lakshmi
A benign form of the mother goddess, Lakshmi symbolizes wealth and generosity. Seated on a lotus growing from a lake, she is being purified by white elephants, symbolic of good fortune and abundance. The cascade of gold coins signifies prosperity, as does the gold embroidery on her red clothing.

▲ Durga
Durga is a beautiful but fierce goddess. Here she is depicted riding her tiger, which is symbolic of her unlimited power. Killing the Titan buffalo and expelling the demon within symbolizes mastery of her animal senses, and also perhaps the strength of the goddess cult.

THE ACT OF WORSHIP

Worship (*puja*) is considered a sacred duty that involves prayer, chanting of symbolic mantras, making offerings in the home and in the temple, and the act of *darshan*—exchanging glances with the deity. Gods are often garlanded with flowers as a sign of respect. Sometimes pilgrimages are made to specific sites, such as Varanasi where a ford on the River Ganges is considered symbolic of crossing from one world to another.

◄ Diwali
The festival of light celebrates the return from exile of Rama (*center left*) and Sita (*center right*), incarnations of Vishnu and Lakshmi. For five nights people light lamps, a sign of wisdom and knowledge, to welcome Lakshmi, whose attributes include good fortune, into their homes.

▲ Shrine
The sacred center of every home is the household shrine. Fresh offerings of fruit, incense, and flowers, all symbolic of abundance, are placed before the god, their essence carried to Heaven by the smoke of burning incense.

▲ Temple
The architecture of a Hindu temple is symbolic. The central tower represents the sacred mountain, home of the gods, and the image of the god is housed in the inner sanctum, the *garbhagrah*, which has maternal symbolism. The temple itself may be dwarfed by the surrounding gateways, emphasizing the importance of the threshold as a link between the secular world and the sacred one.

▲ Sadhu
The ascetic life is part of the culture of Hinduism. This sadhu is a follower of Shiva, as signified by the three lines on his forehead and the buffalo horns on his staff. It is a Hindu ideal to live as a sadhu in later life.

▲ Aum (Om)
The a, u, and m symbolize the three *gunas*—essence, activity, and inertia—and the Trimurti, which comprises the three main Hindu gods, Brahma, Shiva, and Vishnu. Aum is the seed of all divine mantras, powerful words or sounds.

▲ The River Ganges
The holiest of India's rivers, the River Ganges rises in the Himalayas, home of the gods, and is personified by the goddess Ganga. Pilgrims come to Varanasi to wash away their sins and to place the ashes of deceased relatives in the holy waters, which are thought to merge eventually with the cosmic ocean.

SEE ALSO
Death & mourning *pp.128–31*
Religious architecture *pp.228–31*

KALI AND SHIVA

This 19th-century Indian painting features the goddess Kali sitting upon the inert body of Shiva. It is set in a cremation ground and depicts Kali and Shiva surrounded by jackals and carrion birds. Kali is offered sacrificial blood by her worshipers while Brahma and Vishnu look on.

1. The Black Goddess
Kali is known as the "Black Goddess." This absence of color symbolizes her transcendence of all form. Her nudity suggests she is free from all illusion.

2. Kali's three eyes and teeth
Kali's three eyes represent the Sun, the Moon, and fire; she can see into the past, present, and future. Her fang-like teeth, like those of an animal or demon, and her lolling tongue signify her all-devouring nature.

3. Human skulls
Kali's necklace is made of human skulls. It symbolizes the certainty of death and, consequently, rebirth.

4. Kali's four arms and hands
Like most deities, Kali has four arms to signify both her god-like nature and her many attributes. She clutches a sword symbolizing the destruction of ignorance and a severed head symbolizing death. Her skirt is made of dismembered arms.

5. Recumbent Shiva and Parvati
Shiva lying under the feet of Kali represents the potential of creation that can only be released by Kali, her "Shakti" or universal feminine creative principle. Kali is action incarnate to Shiva's transcendent being. Next to Shiva is Parvati, another aspect of the Mother Goddess, tempting Shiva into the domestic world.

6. & 7. Vishnu and Brahma
In Hindu cosmology Brahma created the world. He and the god Vishnu (the Preserver) worship Kali from the side.

8. Harmonious pattern
The picture appears gruesome, but it is arranged in a harmonious pattern. This symbolizes awareness of life and death as part of the same pattern.

In northern India in the mid 6th century BCE Prince Siddhartha renounced his worldly life in search of an existence free of suffering and of *samsara*, the endless round of birth and rebirth. When he achieved his goal, through meditation and asceticism, he became the Buddha or Enlightened One. Buddhist art has many scenes and postures which symbolize his teachings and which encapsulate visually different aspects of the complex doctrine of Buddhism.

✺

ASANAS

The Buddha appears in four different poses—seated, standing, walking, or reclining—which are known as *asanas*. Each pose signifies a different event of his life, the seated Buddha being the most common as he was sitting at the moment of his Enlightenment and sat to meditate. Everything about the Buddha is symbolic, from his physical appearance to his smile and hand gestures.

▲ Reclining Buddha
At the age of 80, the Buddha died after a lifetime of teaching, never to be reborn. This is symbolized by the parinirvana posture in which the Buddha is shown reclining on his right side.

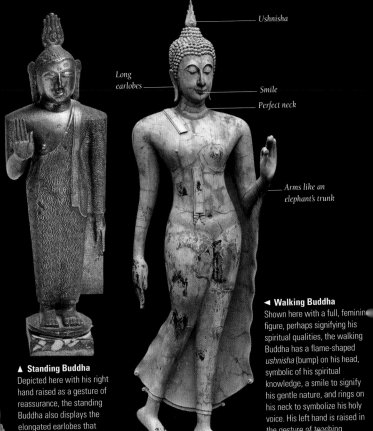

Ushnisha

Long earlobes

Smile

Perfect neck

Arms like an elephant's trunk

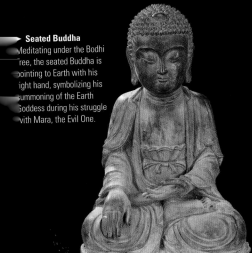

► Seated Buddha
Meditating under the Bodhi Tree, the seated Buddha is pointing to Earth with his right hand, symbolizing his summoning of the Earth Goddess during his struggle with Mara, the Evil One.

▲ Standing Buddha
Depicted here with his right hand raised as a gesture of reassurance, the standing Buddha also displays the elongated earlobes that signify his Enlightenment.

◄ Walking Buddha
Shown here with a full, feminine figure, perhaps signifying his spiritual qualities, the walking Buddha has a flame-shaped *ushnisha* (bump) on his head, symbolic of his spiritual knowledge, a smile to signify his gentle nature, and rings on his neck to symbolize his holy voice. His left hand is raised in the gesture of teaching.

HAND GESTURES

The Buddha is always depicted using hand gestures, called *mudras*. Some, such as the bhumisparsa mudra, are used only by the Buddha, while others are more widely used: the dhyana mudra, for example, during meditation. Mudras are reminders of the Buddha's teaching.

▶ Dhyana mudra
A meditating hand gesture in which the right hand is placed on the left, both with palms upward. The Buddha is often depicted in this mudra, which may also include a begging bowl.

▲ Bhumisparsa mudra
This hand position, called the "earth touching gesture," is regarded as symbolic of the Buddha's Enlightenment.

▲ Varada mudra
This gesture, which can be made with either hand, symbolizes the bestowing of knowledge or granting of a wish or blessing to a devotee.

▲ Dharmachakra mudra
After attaining Enlightenment, the Buddha gave his first sermon in the deer park in Beñares. This gesture signifies "the setting in motion of the Wheel of Law" during that sermon.

▲ Vitarka mudra
This is a teaching gesture, in which the thumb and index finger touch. It can be performed with one or both hands and is the symbol of the Buddha's teaching.

▲ Abhaya mudra
The hand raised, palm toward the spectator, is a symbol made to dispel fear. It signifies reassurance to those who follow the ways of the Buddha.

EIGHT AUSPICIOUS SYMBOLS

Deriving from Indian iconography, the eight auspicuous symbols of Buddhism are very old. Each symbol signifies some aspect of Buddhist teaching, but their meaning may differ from one country to the next. They are particularly popular in Tibet, Nepal, and China where they are often depicted in paintings, ceramics, and lacquerware. They also feature in ritual, either singly, in pairs, or in groups, where they are symbolic of protection and goodwill.

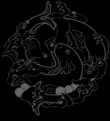

▲ Golden Fish
Symbolic of an enlightened person's ability to move freely and without fear, the golden fish also signify India's two sacred rivers, the Ganges and Yamuna.

▲ Parasol
A symbol of spiritual power, the parasol is carried over images of gods and important people during rituals and processions.

▲ Conch
A white conch (shell) signifies power and authority, the power of teaching, and sounds out the truth of the dharma.

▲ Wheel
A wheel symbolizes the Buddha's turning of the Wheel of Law in his first sermon.

▲ Lotus
The lotus flower is a symbol of purity, and its blossom signifies wholesome deeds.

▲ Drawing
The right-angled lines form an endless knot, symbolic of the infinite knowledge of the Buddha, and the union of compassion and wisdom.

▲ Banner
This symbol signifies the victory of the mind over the negative forces within; also the victory of the Buddhist doctrine over harmful influences.

▲ Vase
This well-known symbol represents abundance. In this instance, it signifies the infinite wisdom and spiritual richness of the Buddha.

SEE ALSO

Aquatic creatures *pp.68–71*
The lotus *pp.86–87*
Sacred trees *pp.96–97*

BODHISATTVAS

There are two types of bodhisattva, both are closely related to enlightenment. The first is Guatma Buddha up until the point of Enlightenment, and in all his previous lives. The second is one, who having attained enlightenment, puts off entering Nirvana until all living beings have been enlightened. Bodhisattvas are usually depicted in sumptuous clothes and jewelry, and carrying various symbolic attributes.

Lotus

▲ Maitreya
The Buddha of the future age, Maitreya, is often depicted as the fat, laughing Buddha. His fat is symbolic of happiness, and his belly holds the wisdom of the universe. He carries a purse as a sign of abundance.

Rosary

▲ Avalokiteshvara
A widely depicted bodhisattva, Avalokiteshvara signifies supreme compassion. His hand mudras and the objects he holds are symbolic of his many powers. The rosary, for example, signifies the cycle of life.

▲ Tara
Avalokiteshvara has a female aspect called Tara. Here her right hand mudra symbolizes the gift of wisdom, while her left hand signifies teaching. She guides people to enlightenment by dispelling ignorance.

▲ Kuan Yin
In China Avalokiteshvara is female and is known as Kuan Yin. As bodhisattva of mercy and compassion she has many forms. Here she is shown in flowing white robes, which are a symbol of purity and womanhood. Her right hand is in vitarka mudra, a teaching gesture symbolic of the Buddha's doctrine.

▲ Manjusri
The youthful Manjusri, wisdom incarnate, is often dressed with a decorative belt and a distinctive tiger's claw necklace. In his left hand he carries a lotus, the sign of purity, which has a book of sutras (scriptures) on top of it, signifying wisdom. His left hand mudra, with an open palm facing forward, signifies compassion and charity.

THE FIVE BUDDHAS

Also known as the Great Buddhas of Wisdom, the five buddhas are central to Tibetan Buddhism. These directional Buddhas—the four quarters and a central Buddha—are transcendent beings who symbolize divine forces and can be focused on during periods of meditation. Each is symbolically associated with a particular direction, element, color, and attitude, and each also symbolizes a particular virtue. For example, Amoghasiddha fights envy and jealousy, Vairocana ignorance, and Aksobya anger and hate.

▼ West: Amitabha
With a name meaning "infinite light" and discriminating wisdom, Amitabha's attributes include the element fire, the color red, which signifies the setting Sun, the peacock, symbolic of compassion, and the lotus, a sign of purity.

◄ North: Amoghasiddhi
His name means "almighty conqueror" and his wisdom is all accomplishing. Attributes of Amoghasiddhi include the element air, the color green, which is a sign of wisdom, and the mythical creature, the Garuda.

► Center: Vairocana
The wisdom of Vairocana embodies that of the four surrounding Buddhas. He is associated with the color white, signifying purity, the wheel, symbolizing the Wheel of Law, and space. His animal is the lion, a sign of strength and bravery.

► South: Ratnasambhava
A buddha with the wisdom of equality, Ratnasambhava controls the element earth. His color is yellow, which is symbolic of the Sun's illumination, and he holds a jewel that is symbolic of a liberated mind.

▲ East: Aksobya
The mirror-like wisdom of Aksobya is coupled with his symbol, the thunderbolt, and his element, water. His other attributes include the color blue and the elephant, which supports his throne and is a symbol of steadfastness and strength.

MYTHS & RELIGIONS

SYMBOLS OF THE BUDDHA

Early in the development of Buddhism, the Buddha's presence was indicated in art by objects associated with episodes in his life. For example, he was often symbolized by a Bodhi tree, a footprint, or an alms bowl. Other symbols, such as the Dharma Wheel, signify both the Buddha and his teachings.

▲ Alms bowl
After his Enlightenment the Buddha renounced all material things by wearing a simple robe and carrying an alms bowl. For monks their alms bowl is a reminder of humility, while for donors it signifies the good karma they will receive from their acts of charity.

▲ Bodhi leaves
The Buddha attained Enlightenment beneath a Bodhi tree, an event that led to the development of the tree and its leaves as signs of devotion. As a symbolic reminder, Bodhi trees are grown in Buddhist centers around the world.

▲ Lion
A symbol of the Buddha, the lion was the emblem of his clan, the Sakyas, and its roar symbolic of the strength of his words. These lions stand on the site where the Buddha first preached at Sarnath. They were erected by King Ashoka, who also had the lion as his symbol.

▲ Empty throne
As well as being a sign of the Buddha's royal ancestry, the empty throne is also a symbol of the Buddha as spiritual leader. Here there are deer carved around the base of the column and these too have symbolic meaning (*see below*).

▲ The Wheel of Law (Dharma)
An important icon, the Dharma wheel symbolizes Buddha's teaching and its parts signify different aspects of its practice—the rim signifies concentration, the spokes wisdom, and the hub discipline. The spokes of the Dharma Wheel are also symbolic of the Noble Eightfold Path to Nirvana—right understanding, right thought, right speech, right action, right livelihood, right effort, right mindfulness, and right concentration. The deer symbolize the Buddha's first teaching in a deer park.

THE MONKHOOD

A symbolic journey imitating that made by Prince Siddhartha may be undertaken by boys entering the monkhood. On entering the monastry initiates adopt the same appearance as the other monks, which is as a sign to others of their calling. The monkhood, or sangha, is one of the three gems central to Buddhism, the other two being the Buddha himself and dharma (his teachings).

▲ The Great Departure
This frieze depicts Prince Siddhartha leaving his palace, having renounced the worldly life. Known as the "Great Departure," Buddhist boys symbolically re-enact this scene before donning the robes of a monk and entering a monastery as a novice.

◄ Appearance
Recognized by their saffron or red colored robes and shaved heads, monks are not priests and are not obliged to conduct services. Their clothing symbolizes the simple life they lead, following the teachings of the Buddha, and their bald heads signify renunciation of worldly things. They spend most of their time in contemplation.

◄ Prayer wheel
Originating in Tibetan tradition, prayer wheels symbolize people's prayers. Sacred verses, called mantras, are inscribed on them and on leaves that are placed inside the cylinder. Each rotation of the prayer wheel represents one recitation of the mantra.

SEE ALSO
Sacred trees *pp.96–97*
The home *pp.238–39*

BUDDHISM

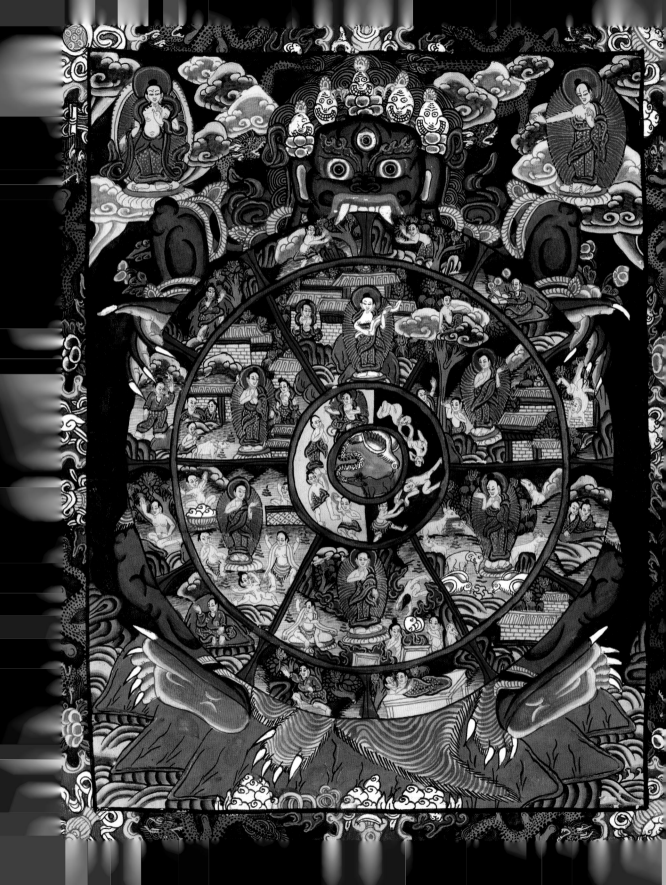

BUDDHIST WHEEL ⊕F LIFE

The Buddhist Wheel of Life symbolizes the constant circle of action and change to which we are subject. It represents the law of *karma*, according to which delusions and desires lead to actions that keep us on the ever-turning Wheel of Life, unable to detach ourselves and attain enlightenment.

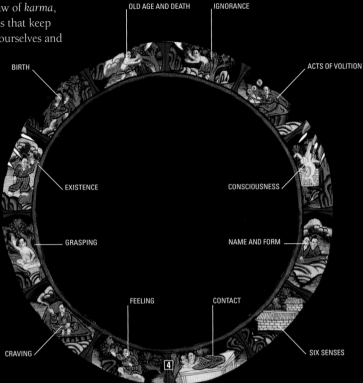

OLD AGE AND DEATH

IGNORANCE

BIRTH

ACTS OF VOLITION

EXISTENCE

CONSCIOUSNESS

GRASPING

NAME AND FORM

FEELING

CONTACT

CRAVING

SIX SENSES

1. Center of the Wheel
At the heart, in the very center of the Wheel of Life, is a rooster, which symbolizes ignorance, a snake (hatred), and a pig (greed). Each creature is chasing and biting the other's tail, giving rise to the endless cycle of rebirths. These are the three delusions that prevent us from attaining *Nirvana*.

2. Inner ring
Encompassing the innermost circle is another circle with white and black backgrounds. This represents beings rising and falling according to their deeds. Those who have lived good lives are seen to be ascending, while those who have lived bad lives are descending into ignorance and darkness.

3. Middle ring
The areas between the spokes form the middle ring of the Wheel and symbolize the different realms of existence. The top half portrays the higher realms of existence: humans, gods, and demi-gods. The lower half shows the lower realms of existence: animals, demons, and hungry ghosts. In each realm a Buddha promises release.

4. Outer ring
The depictions in the outermost circle represent the 12 links of the chain of dependence. In this realm are shown all the important themes of human life—birth, the religious life, old age, sickness, and death. From the top of the circle these are ignorance (a blind person), acts of volition (a potter at his wheel), consciousness (a monkey in a tree), name and form (men in a boat), the six senses (a house with empty windows), contact (a couple embracing), feeling (a man with an arrow in his eye), craving (a person drinking alcohol), grasping (a woman picking fruit), existence (a pregnant woman), birth (a woman crouching), and old age and death (an old man carrying a burden).

5. & 6. Yama and the Buddha
Turning the wheel is Yama, Lord of Death, who signifies the certainty of death for us all. At the top right the Buddha points the way to enlightenment that is reached by following his doctrine, which is set out in the Wheel of Law.

TAOISM & SHINTO

Taoism and Shinto are Chinese and Japanese religions that emphasize living in harmony with nature. The landscape around us, the oceans, mountains, lakes, and flowers are all part of a well-ordered balance of life. This harmony is symbolic of both religions, and followers strive to maintain it. Taoist gods can control the forces of nature and other aspects of life; Shinto spirits are everywhere and inhabit places such as caves and springs.

TAOISM

Philosophical Taoism is an ancient system of thought that began with the teachings of Lao Tzu, who is said to have written the *Tao Te Ching* between the 6th and 4th centuries BCE. He wrote that everything in nature was symbolic of the natural order of things, from mountains and rocks to trees and the veining in their leaves. Taoism speaks of non-action (*wu-wei*), meaning taking no action that is contrary to nature. Yin and Yang are the terms used to signify opposite but balanced "forces," such as male and female.

▲ Taoist painting
The elements of earth, wood, fire, metal, and water are used in art in a symbolic form to represent the essence of an object. Clay signifies the earth, fire is symbolically used by painting with soot, and water is mixed with painting materials.

▲ Yin and Yang
The natural world is seen in terms of the complementary but differing forces of Yin and Yang. Shown here in symbolic form, they represent the two halves of the Tao. Yin is female, dark, yielding, low, and night, while Yang is male, light, strong, high, and day. Yin would be signified by valleys, for example, whereas mountains signify Yang.

▲ The uncarved block
Lao Tzu speaks of the uncarved block, the continual ceaseless mass of change. In art this mass is often symbolized by a misshapen rock with forms that never repeat themselves. Such stones are often collected and placed in gardens as symbols of the universe in miniature.

▲ Veins of nature
Of great significance in Taoism is an understanding of the lines and veins that run through natural objects, such as trees and leaves, and the "dragon" veins of metal that run through the Earth. All are symbolic of the oneness of life and the natural balance of Yin and Yang.

◄ Jade
In Taoism jade is the essence of Heaven, and is said to be formed from a dragon's semen. Jade symbolizes nobility, perfection, and immortality.

Fan   Aura

◄ Lao Tzu
Lao Tzu's teachings are fundamental to Taoism but little is known about him. Supposedly born old, he had a gray beard and long earlobes that signified wisdom. He is shown here holding a fan, symbolic of how Taoism can be disseminated and salvation sought. It may also symbolize completion of the universe. He is deified by Taoists and the aura around his head signifies his holiness.

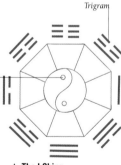

Trigram

Yin and Yang

▲ The I Ching
The Book of Changes, also called *I Ching*, is a classic work. Its trigrams and hexagrams signify Yin and Yang properties that are still used for divination purposes, signifying when to act and when not to in order to follow the path of nature. Eight trigrams make up one hexagram.

SHINTO ⊕

The origins of Shinto are ancient and intimately connected with Japanese mythology. The religion is centred on its many spirits (*kami*), which signify the different elements and forces of the natural world. Any imbalance, caused, for example, by felling a tree or killing an animal, is restored symbolically through ritual and purification.

◄ The Shinto shrine
The focus of worship in Shinto is the shrine. The torii, or sacred gateway through which everyone passes to enter a shrine, is an instantly recognizable symbol, marking the passage into the sacred realm. This gateway links water with sky and land, signifying the balance of nature.

Magatama bead of compassion

Sword of strength

Mirror of truth

▲ Symbols of Shinto
Three symbols are found in Shinto shrines: a necklace of magatama beads, signifying compassion, that was carried by Amaterasu, the Sun goddess; the metal mirror of truth with which she was lured from her cave; and a sword of strength that was found by the god Susa-No-O and later owned by the first Japanese emperor.

◄ Daikoku
Japanese gods of wealth are associated with symbols of financial wealth and abundance. Here the Shinto god Daikoku is depicted sitting on a sack of rice, holding a mallet that is used to grant wishes or to bring good fortune.

► Garden or flower arrangement
The Shinto ideals of harmony with nature underlie traditional customs, such as garden design and flower arranging, which symbolize on a small scale the harmony of the universe.

SHINTO SPIRITS

In Shinto sacred beings that signify anything extraordinary or awe-inspiring are referred to as *kami*. Amaterasu is the most important of them. However, the name is given to all spirits regardless of whether they are good, as is Inari, or bad, as is Kagu-Zuchi when he allows houses to burn.

▲ Inari
Responsible for good harvests and prosperity, Inari holds a wish-fulfilling jewel and has two white foxes, symbolic of power, as his messengers.

▲ Amaterasu
The brightness of the Sun goddess, Amaterasu, is often signified by sun-rays emanating from her head. She was believed to be an ancestor of the emperors.

▲ Mountain gods
Most mountains and volcanoes have their own gods or spirits that personify and symbolize their power. The goddess of Mount Fuji, for example, is Sengen-Samba.

◄ Fire gods
The fire spirit, Kagu-Zuchi, is feared and respected by the Japanese. He is always depicted as a tall young man, often bare chested, but always accompanied by flames over which he has sole control. As fire is a real threat to wooden houses, the god is regularly placated with ritual.

SEE ALSO
The Sun *pp.16–17*
Fire *pp.30–31*
Ancestors *pp.146–47*
Divination *pp.196–99*
Gardens *pp.244–47*

JUDAISM

Judaism is an ancient religion founded in the Caanan region of western Asia some 3,500 years ago. Jews believe they are the chosen people that were led by God (Yahweh) from slavery in Egypt to the Promised Land. Today Jews are scattered across the globe and so the symbols of their religion are an important unifying factor. All aspects of Jewish life—from foods eaten at festivals and garments worn for prayer to ritual objects used in the synagogue—are imbued with a significance reflecting a rich past and a deep love of God.

NATION AND LAW

Jewish identity is bound up with the concept of nationhood. To a people that were without a home for thousands of years, the longing for a country of their own assumed great significance. Hence the bitter struggle over the state of Israel, which for most Jews is the symbol of Judaism. The Law, now called *halakah*, is believed to have been given by God to Moses and embodies the moral structure of the Jewish nation.

▲ Star of David
Instantly recognizable throughout the world as a popular symbol of Judaism, the Star of David is a powerful sign of Jewish identity and unity. Used on Jewish tombstones in the late 17th century and adopted by Zionists in the 1890s, it now features on the nation flag of Israel.

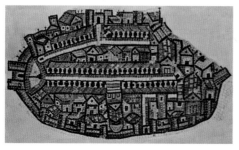

▲ Jerusalem
The ancient and holy city of Jerusalem stands at the heart of Judaism. Since King David became the city's ruler, some 3,000 years ago, it has been a focus of prayer and a symbol of Jewish nationhood.

▲ The Western Wall
The Temple of Jerusalem was destroyed by the Romans in 70CE. The Western Wall, also known as the "Wailing Wall," is all that remains. For Jews it is a place of pilgrimage and symbolizes the Jewish nation.

◄ Ark of the Covenant
Originally signifying God's presence, this wooden chest is thought to have housed the Ten Commandments. Today every synagogue has a symbolic ark—it is the sacred chest in which the Torah scrolls are kept.

Lion   Crown

▲ Torah
The Law of God and central to the Jewish faith, the Torah is a handwritten scroll comprising the first five books of the "Hebrew Bible." The staves, called Azei Hayyim, on which the scrolls are wound signify the Trees of Life.

▲ Torah mantle
The Torah is protected by a mantle of cloth, traditionally embroidered with symbols of Judaism. Here a crown, symbolic of the regal status of the Torah, is flanked by two lions, a common symbol with links to the Tribe of Judah.

MYTHS & RELIGIONS

FESTIVALS AND PRAYER

Prayer is fundamental to the Jewish faith, with devout Jews praying three times a day. Saturday—the Sabbath—is of particular significance, but there are also a number of festivals during which Jews celebrate both their history and traditions and affirm their faith in God. Because prayer is such a central part of Judaism, there are various symbolic objects and rituals associated with it.

Tefillin

► Sabbath
The Jewish Sabbath (*Shabbat* in Hebrew) begins on Friday evening and ends at nightfall the following day. Orthodox male Jews wear two tefillins, small leather boxes containing passages from the Torah, a kippah (skull cap), symbolic of God's presence, and a prayer shawl, or tallit, with 613 tassels, symbolic of the Ten Commandments.

Tefillin attached to the arm with a leather strap

Prayer shawl or tallit

Mezuzah scroll

◄ Silver prayer book
Several items are associated with praying, including the prayer book, which both symbolizes and contains God's word. The ornately decorated covers signify the sacredness of the text inside. Prayer books are commonly given to boys at their Bar Mitzvah, a ceremony that celebrates their coming of age at 13.

◄ Mezuzah
A small container, called a mezuzah, is often attached to the front doorpost of Jewish houses as a symbol of the occupier's faith. It is traditional to kiss one's fingers and touch the mezuzah on entering the home as a symbol of one's devotion to God. Each mezuzah contains a small scroll with biblical text written on it.

◄ Sukkoth
During the festival of Sukkoth, which remembers God's care of the people as they sought the Promised Land, festive huts, symbolic of the tents erected in the desert, are built, and leaves of palm, willow, and myrtle are woven together to make lulavs (*shown here*). They are waved in all directions in the synagogue to signify God's mastery of the universe and to call for rain in the coming year.

PASSOVER

Passover celebrates the Jews' liberation from Egypt. The rituals associated with this festival are heavy with symbolism, not least the Passover meal, or seder, which comprises a number of different elements (*shown below*), each with its own symbolism for the event.

▲ Matzoh bread
Unleavened matzoh bread symbolizes the speed with which the Jews left Egypt —not having time to wait for their bread to rise.

A bitter herb, such as horseradish or romaine lettuce, symbolizes the bitterness of slavery.

A hard-boiled egg symbolizes new life.

A lamb shank represents the lambs sacrificed at the Jewish temples during festival time.

Parsley represents the lowliness of the Jewish slaves.

Charoset, a fruit and nut paste, signifies the mortar made by the Jews for Egyptian palaces.

THE PASSOVER MEAL

▲ Salt water
Salt water for dipping bitter herbs signifies the tears of the Jews during their slavery in Egypt.

▲ Shofar
The ram's horn symbolizes God's pleasure in Abraham's loyalty and represents the ram that God allowed him to sacrifice in place of his son. The Shofar is also symbolic of Rosh Hashanah, the Jewish New Year.

▲ Menorah
A seven-branched candelabrum is one of the oldest symbols of Judaism. The menorah may have its origins in the ancient symbol of the Tree of Life. Its light symbolizes the eternal light of the Torah.

SEE ALSO
Sacred trees *pp.96–97*
Initiation rites *pp.124–25*
Kabbalah *pp.174–75*
Shapes *pp.284–89*
Flags *pp.328–29*

JUDAISM

KABBALAH

Followers of Kabbalah, a branch of Jewish mysticism, explore hidden meanings in the Torah—the first five books of the Old Testament—in order achieve a more spiritual relationship with God. Making use of diagrams, symbols, and numerology, Kabbalah is a highly complex, esoteric system. It was originally an oral tradition but from around the 13th century it appeared in literature, among which the Zohar, or Book of Splendor, is considered the most significant work.

THE KABBALAH G⊕D

Kabbalists have a dualistic concept of God: God the infinite, nothingness, who is not addressed in prayer; and God manifest, an active God with whom the faithful develop a relationship. A significant element of Kabbalah is the use of meditation, during which a Kabbalist might focus on or visualize one of the many symbols or diagrams used to represent God.

CROWN (KETER)
INTELLIGENCE (BINAH)
WISDOM (CHOCHMAH)
POWER (GEVURAH)
LOVE (CHESED)
COMPASSION (TIFERET)
MAJESTY (HOD)
ENDURANCE (NETZACH)
FOUNDATION (YESOD)
KINGDOM (MALCHUT)

▲ **The Sefirot**
The above diagram is a symbolic representation of the Tree of Life, which in Kabbalah is often inverted and so rooted in Heaven. This tree portrays the Sefirot, which are central to Kabbalistic thought and signify God in his progression from the infinite, unknowable God to the active God that created the universe. Each of the ten stages, or Sefirah, is symbolic of a different aspect of a person's relationship with God and is connected to others by channels so forming groups.

WORLD OF EMANATIONS (ATZILUTH)
WORLD OF CREATION (BERIAH)
WORLD OF FORMATION (YETSIRAH)
WORLD OF ACTION (ASSIAH)

▲ **Four worlds**
One way in which the Sefirot can be interpreted is through grouping the ten emanations of God into "four worlds," as shown above. Each world signifies a separate stage in the creation process.

▲ **72 names of God**
Among the various symbols used for Kabbalah meditation are the 72 names of God, said to have enabled prophets to perform miracles, such as Moses's parting of the Red Sea. The 72 names derive from three verses in Exodus, each of which contains 72 Hebrew letters. By taking a letter from each verse, working from left to right with the first verse, right to left with the second verse, and left to right again with the last verse, the 72 three-letter names of God are formed.

◄ **Ein Sof**
This symbol represents "Ein Sof," the infinite aspect of God considered by Kabbalists to have existed before creation—an unknowable nothingness—which then manifested as the God of creation and worship, via the ten sefirot (see far left). Ein Sof is often symbolic of God's Light.

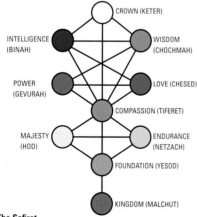

GEMATRIA

Gematria is a Hebrew form of numerology, used in Kabbalah to find hidden meanings in words, and the relationship between the ten Sefirot and the Hebrew alphabet. It is an extremely complex art, applied in a number of different ways. Each letter of the alphabet is deeply symbolic, both in the sound it makes and in its position in a word. The glyphs also have a numerical significance and one can reinterpret words by adding the numerical values of the letters. Words have a special link to other words that share the same total; the second word bringing new meaning to the first.

Glyph	Hebrew	Decimal
א	ALEPH	1
ב	BET	2
ג	GIMEL	3
ד	DALED	4
ה	HE	5
ו	WAW	6
ז	ZAYIN	7
ח	HETH	8
ט	TETH	9
י	YODTH	10
כ	KAPH	20
ל	LAMED	30
מ	MEM	40
נ	NUN	50
ס	SAMEKH	60
ע	AYIN	70
פ	PE	80
צ	TSADI	90
ק	QOPH	100
ר	RESH	200
ש	SHIN	300
ת	TAW	400
ך	KAPH	500
ם	MEM	600
ן	NUN	700
ף	PE	800
ץ	TSADI	900

► Tetraktys

The Kabbalistic tetraktys is a symbol of the cosmos, based on the original by the Ancient Greek philosopher Pythagoras, which arranges ten points in descending order and symbolizes the process of creation from the one to the many. This version uses the letters of the Hebrew alphabet that spell out the tetragrammaton (the four-lettered name of God) YHWH, and forms the basis for the Kabbalistic Tree of Life—the Sefirot.

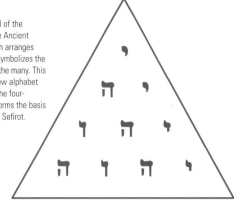

► The Hebrew Triad

Represented by the Hebrew letter "shin," the Hebrew Triad is a graphic rendition of the first three Sefirot. It symbolizes the crown in the center, the father on the left, and the mother on the right.

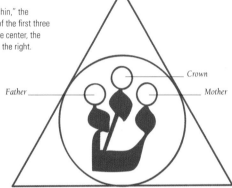

Father — *Crown* — *Mother*

THE RED BRACELET

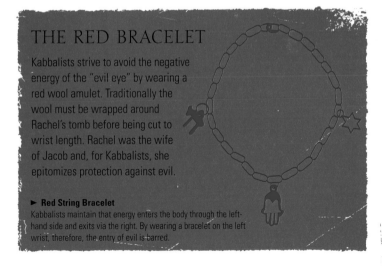

Kabbalists strive to avoid the negative energy of the "evil eye" by wearing a red wool amulet. Traditionally the wool must be wrapped around Rachel's tomb before being cut to wrist length. Rachel was the wife of Jacob and, for Kabbalists, she epitomizes protection against evil.

► Red String Bracelet

Kabbalists maintain that energy enters the body through the left-hand side and exits via the right. By wearing a bracelet on the left wrist, therefore, the entry of evil is barred.

◄ Hebrew alphabet

There are 22 letters in the Hebrew alphabet, five of which appear twice, depending on whether they are used at the beginning and middle of a word, or at the end.

SEE ALSO
Judaism *pp.172–73*
Amulets *pp.194–95*
Numerology *pp.206–07*

CHRISTIANITY

Christianity, which appeared about 2,000 years ago, has its roots in Judaism. Christians believe that Christ died on the cross to redeem the sins of the world. The cross is therefore the supreme symbol of the Christian faith, being worn by followers of the faith to signify their belief, and reflected in the shape of many of its churches. Biblical stories have given rise to a number of symbols, such as the dove of peace, while martyrs, who died for their beliefs, and apostles have given rise to others.

SYMBOLS OF FAITH

Representational art has always been a part of Christianity and many symbols of the religion are a part of Christian consiousness. As well as the cross, the halo, or nimbus, which encircles the head of Christ and the saints, frequently appears as a symbol of sanctity. Other symbols include the fish, which appeared during the Roman period when Christians were being persecuted for their beliefs and is still in use today, and the dove, which now has a more universal appeal and is a sign of peace.

▲ The standing lamb
The sacrificial lamb is a symbol of Christ. Standing with a banner, the lamb signifies Christ's triumph in rising from the dead after being crucified.

▲ The lying lamb
When lying on a cross and the Book of Seven Seals, the recumbent lamb symbolizes the triumph of the Christian faith at the Last Judgement.

▲ Virgin and child
As a baby, Christ is often depicted naked and sitting on a white cloth to symbolize his innocence, purity, and holiness. The presence of the Virgin Mary signifies her motherly nature and the human aspect of Christ.

▲ The Virgin Mary
Mary is depicted here in a traditional red tunic over which is worn a blue robe symbolic of Heaven and her position as its queen. Over her heart she has her hands clasped in prayer, a sign of sincerity and humility.

▲ Nativity scene
This scene depicts Christ's birth in a stable. The visit of the shepherds and the three wise men, or magi, symbolizes the acceptance of Christianity by people of all backgrounds and all nationalities.

◄ Fish
The first letters of the words Jesus Christ, Son of God, and Saviour, spell *Ichthus*, or "fish" in Greek. It was used by early Christians as a secret sign. One person drew one arc of the fish and a second completed it.

► Jesus Christ
Believed by Christians to be the son of God, Jesus Christ was born of the Virgin Mary. In this Russian icon, the haloed Christ is depicted with his right hand raised to bless the faithful. The three fingers that touch are a sign of the Holy Trinity (*see above right*), while the two free fingers symbolize Christ's humanity and his coming to Earth in human form. In his left hand he holds the sacred book.

▲ Fleur de lis
To Christians, the fleur de lis is symbolic of the Holy Trinity (the Father, Son, and Holy Spirit), the purity of the Virgin Mary, and the Angel Gabriel.

◄ Dove
Symbolic of the Holy Spirit, the third member of the Trinity, the dove is also a symbol of peace, having returned to Noah's ark carrying an olive branch.

▲ Crown of thorns
Placed on Christ's head to signify his humiliation, the crown of thorns is seen by Christians as a sign of Christ's suffering to save humanity.

▲ Three nails
Used in the crucifixion of Christ to secure his hands and feet to the cross, three nails, like the crown of thorns, are symbolic of Christ's supreme sacrifice.

CHRISTIAN SAINTS

Humans who lived particularly devout lives and have been canonized by the Church after death are called saints. Many saints are symbolic of a particular characteristic, such as devotion, as well as being recognized by their attributes. Some emblems signify the manner in which the saints were killed, others such as the crossed keys of St. Peter the apostle are so well known that they may be used to symbolize St. Peter himself.

▲ St. Sebastian
The arrow is a symbol of the plague and of St. Sebastian. It is the attribute of St. Sebastian because he survived being shot with arrows, and because arrows leave scars that are similar to the marks left by the plague. He was later stoned to death.

▲ St. Francis of Assisi
The patron saint of animals and birds, St. Francis of Assisi is often depicted in their company to signify his love of nature.

▲ St. Catherine
Martyred on four flaming wheels for her beliefs, St. Catherine has become a symbol of devotion. Her emblem is the spiked wheel, also known as the Catherine wheel.

► St. Paul
Converted to Christianity on the road to Damascus, St. Paul carries a cross-hilted sword in his right hand to signify his teaching of God's word as the "Sword of the Spirit." He also carries a letter, symbolic of the many letters he wrote to the churches he founded.

► St. Peter
Usually depicted carrying the keys of Heaven, St. Peter is symbolized by crossed keys, which represent the locked door of excommunication and the open door of absolution. The keys signify his power to forgive sinners.

THE ACT ✠ WORSHIP

Practicing Christians go to church to worship and attend various services, including baptisms and funerals. Catholics may pray using rosaries, and for confirmed followers of the faith, attending mass and receiving holy communion is central to their beliefs, symbolizing their union with God.

◄ Rosary
Taking its name from the white rose, symbol of the purity of the Virgin Mary, the rosary marks out repetitions of the prayer "Hail Mary."

▲ Church
Churches are symbolic at many levels. In cross-shaped churches the western arm is called the nave, from the Latin for "ship," after early descriptions of the church as an ark.

◄ Communion
The sacred rite of communion, taken by confirmed Christians, began at the Last Supper, when Christ ate his final meal with the disciples. He said that the bread and wine he shared with them were his body and his blood. Many Christians take this literally, while others believe it to be a symbolic truth.

SEE ALSO
Angels pp.188–89
The Holy Grail pp.208–09
Religious architecture pp.228–31
Symbolic gestures pp.334–37

THE CROSS

Although the cross has had many associations in the past, it is perhaps most widely recognized as a symbol of the Christian faith, where it signifies Christ's sacrifice in dying on the cross to save humanity. Even making the sign of the cross is symbolic—of the Holy Trinity—and is given as a blessing by priests during religious services. The sign is made in the air, the vertical part being drawn first followed by the horizontal. Over time many visual variations of the cross have evolved. Each has a particular symbolism, which has led to the adoption of specific crosses by different organizations and Christian orders. The Maltese Cross, for example, is symbolic of protection and is the emblem of US firefighters.

► **Crucifix**
The image of Christ on the cross, the crucifix is an object of Christian devotion.

▲ **Latin Cross**
With its long upright and shorter cross beam, The Latin cross is symbolic of the cross on which Christ was crucified. Although early Christians considered it gruesome and used the fish instead, it gradually became an accepted symbol of Christ.

▲ **St. Andrew's Cross**
This X-shaped cross, also known as a saltire, signifies the cross on which St. Andrew was crucified. Symbolic of resolution and endurance of hardship, this cross has been adopted as the emblem on both the Scottish and Jamaican flags.

▲ **St. Peter's Cross**
Named after St. Peter, who was crucified upside down, this cross is the symbol of humility for Christians. However, in modern times it has acquired satanic significance, being used in mockery of the symbolism of the Latin Cross.

▲ **St. Anthony's Cross**
Formed from the last letter of the Hebrew alphabet transcribed into Greek and so also known as the Tau Cross, this was the standard form of cross used by the Romans for crucifixion. It is symbolic of redemption and well-being.

▲ **The Chi-Ro Cross**
Made up of the letters X and P, the first two letters of the name "Christ" in Greek, this cross was adopted by the Roman Emperor Constantine. Of ancient origin, it was previously the symbol of Chronos, the Greek god of time.

▲ **Coptic Cross**
The Coptic Cross, derived from the Egyptian ankh, was used by early Egyptian Christians after the introduction of Christianity by St. Mark. A variation of the form was later used as a symbol by Ethiopian Christians.

▲ **The Celtic Cross**
In this ancient form of the cross, the cross element is surrounded by a circle, said by some to be a symbol of unity and God's eternal love, and by others to signify a halo. The Celtic Cross predates Christianity in Ireland.

▲ **Greek Cross**
The Greek Cross has four arms of equal length. It is instantly recognizable, and was in common use as a Christian symbol from the 4th century. It symbolizes the spread of the gospel to all parts of the world.

▲ **The Maltese Cross**
Similar to a Greek Cross but the four arms widen out into swallowtail shapes. The resulting eight corners symbolize rebirth. An emblem of honor and protection, it is symbolic of various Christian organizations.

CROSS OR CRUCIFIX

The cross is symbolic of Christianity as a whole, but different branches of the religion use different types of cross. Protestants, for example, have adopted a plain cross, symbolic of Christ having risen from the dead. Catholics have adopted the crucifix—a cross with the crucified Christ—as symbolic of Christ's sacrifice. His presence on the cross is also symbolic of God's work as ongoing rather than ending with his death and resurrection. Some Catholic crosses have a skull at the base, symbolic of Golgotha, the "place of the skull" (commonly called Calvary), where Christ was taken to be crucified.

▲ **Plain cross**
This modern Methodist church in Singapore displays a large plain steel cross like that seen in most other Protestant churches.

▲ **Crucifix**
This 14th–15th century crucifix from a Catholic church in Croatia shows Christ on the cross with God looking down on him from above.

▲ **Budded Cross**
This takes the form of the Latin Cross but terminates with buds in the shape of a clover leaf. The three buds signify the Holy Trinity. It may be derived from a Druid cross in which the trefoil signifies earth, sea, and sky.

▲ **Russian Orthodox Cross**
Symbolic of the balance between salvation and damnation, this cross has been adopted by the Russian Orthodox Church. The lower bar indicates that repentent sinners go to Heaven, while others descend into Hell.

▲ **Julian Cross**
The emblem of traveling bards, this cross is made up of four Latin Crosses at right angles to each other, each pointing to the four corners of the world. For this reason it is sometimes known as the Missionary Cross.

▲ **The Papal Cross**
This cross may be used only by the Pope. Its three bars signify Heaven, the Earth, and the Church, which are the three domains of his authority. The cross is carried ahead of the Pope in all papal processions.

▲ **The Cross of Lorraine**
A heraldic cross that has two cross bars, traditionally of equal length, is used by the Catholic Church to signify a Cardinal. This cross was carried into battle by Joan of Arc and later became a symbol of the Free French.

▲ **Camargue Cross**
From the Camargue in the South of France, this cross has three elements: the cross, the anchor, and the heart, symbolizing Faith, Hope, and Charity (or love). The anchor also serves as a symbol of the local fishermen.

▲ **Anchor Cross**
This is correctly termed the St. Clement's Cross, since St. Clement was supposedly tied to an anchor and thrown into the sea. It symbolizes the anchor that holds Christians steady through the storms of life.

▲ **Brighid's (Bride's) Cross**
This Irish cross probably predates Christianity in Ireland, as St. Brighid may have evolved from a Celtic goddess. This type of cross is usually woven of straw for Candlemas, and is symbolic of prosperity and protection.

◄ **Baptismal Cross**
This eight-armed cross is made from an X superimposed on to a Greek Cross. It is often used for baptisms because the number eight symbolizes rebirth. It also signifies the eight-day period between Christ's entry into Jerusalem and his resurrection.

SEE ALSO
Head trophies pp.110–11
Greek & Roman deities pp.140–41
Celtic & Nordic deities pp.142–43
Satan & demons pp.190–91
Amulets pp.194–95
Shapes pp.284–89
Picture writing pp.300–05
Heraldic emblems pp.318–323
Flags pp.324–29

ISLAM

Followers of the Islamic faith, Muslims, believe in one God and that Muhammad is his prophet. Islam is a religion that avoids human representation in art; however, a variety of objects, such as the star and crescent and the hand of Fatimah, have become symbolic of the faith. The color green, a symbol of Spring, is particularly important: the Koran states that the inhabitants of Paradise will wear garments of green silk.

MOSQUES AND MECCA

Muslim places of worship, called mosques, are where the faithful gather to pray at least once a week. Although mosques do not have to be of a particular design, many have a dome and/or tall minarets that, because of their prominance in city skylines, have themselves become symbols of the Islamic faith. Some mosques incorporate five pillars, representing the Five Pillars of the faith (*see Hand of Fatimah*), and contain a niche that indicates the direction of Mecca. As the symbolic heart of Islam, Mecca is a place that all Muslims try to visit at least once in their lifetime. The Hajj (pilgrimage) is one of the Five Pillars.

▲ **Star and crescent**
In the 14th century the crescent Moon was adopted as a symbol of Islam, followed by the star, which signifies sovereignity and dignity. They are also a reminder of the lunar calender by which Islamic religious life is ordered.

▲ **Hand of Fatimah**
Traditionally worn by women as an amulet to protect them from evil, the Hand of Fatimah, daughter of Muhammad, also has other meanings. Each finger symbolizes one of the Five Pillars of Islam—Shahada (affirmation of the faith), Salat (set prayers), Zakat (giving of alms), Sawm (fasting through Ramadan), and Hajj (pilgrimage to Mecca).

▲ **The Dome of the Rock mosque**
Mosques symbolize the heart of Islamic religion and community. The dome, an ancient feminine symbol, represents the arc of the heavens, and by passing through the arched doorway the faithful symbolically pass into another state of being. Caliphs built mosques as an overt sign of their piety; some mosques, such as the Dome of the Rock, enshrine specific holy places. This is the spot to which the Angel Gabriel brought Muhammad prior to his Night Journey to Heaven.

▲ **Mosque lamp**
Ceramic or metal lamps are often suspended from chains in mosques. The light they produce is symbolic of eternal truth, wisdom, and the power of God. It is also a sign of the divine presence within.

▲ **Minaret**
The minaret, from which the faithful are called to prayer, is an integral part of many mosques and a potent symbol of the Islamic faith. God's name may be placed at the top to signify his supremacy over all things.

▲ **Ka'ba**
It is toward the Ka'ba in Mecca, symbol of Muslim unity and the oneness of God, that all Muslims face in prayer. Pilgrims circle the Ka'ba seven times, an act that symbolizes Muhammad's seven ascents to Heaven.

PRAYER AND THE WRITTEN WORD

Prayer constitutes the second Pillar of Islam (Salat) and is undertaken five times a day. Cleanliness is an important aspect of this ritual and, before each period of prayer, practicing Muslims wash in a prescribed and ritual way. As in many religions this action is symbolic of the washing away of sin and self purification. Because representational art is avoided, ingenious ways of praising God visually have been devised, ranging from the beautiful calligraphy seen as decoration everywhere in Muslim countries, to the lighting of colored lanterns during Ramadan.

▲ Daily prayer
Fives times a day, Muslims face Mecca to pray. First they raise their hands palm outward to signify that they are putting everything behind them but God. Later they touch the ground with their foreheads and intone the words, "Allah is great," symbolically submitting to God.

▲ Prayer mat with compass
Cleanliness is important when praying. The prayer mat signifies a clean place and the compass indicates the direction of Mecca.

▲ Prayer beads
The Muslim *subha* consists of 99 beads, which symbolize the 99 divine names of God. Sometimes a special elongated bead, called a "leader," is added for the hundredth name, that of the Essence, which can only be found in Paradise. Muslims intone the names of God, chanting "Allah" with the hundredth bead.

▲ The Koran
The sacred text of Islam, the Koran, or Qur'an, sets out God's word as revealed to the prophet Muhammad. It is thought to symbolize the prophethood of Muhammad and the truth of the religion. Written in Arabic, the language in which its words were revealed to the prophet, the text is often enclosed by beautiful borders and scrollwork.

▲ Ceramic tile
Islamic decoration is epitomized by the use of ornamental tiles. In the above example of Islamic craftsmanship, the star shape symbolizes the divinity and supremacy of Islam.

◄ Ramadan
Ramadan occurs during the ninth month of the year and those who are able fast during the daylight hours. Signs that Ramadan has started include the use of attar, a pungent perfume, and the preparation of traditional sweet dishes using *simahi* (vermicelli), which are consumed after sunset. In Egypt the festival is associated with the lighting of colored lanterns, called *fanoos*, which symbolizes people's gratitude to God.

▲ Calligraphy
Symbolic of beauty, power, and unity, Islamic calligraphy is an exquisite art form. Words from the Koran and the name of God decorate all kinds of objects, including the tiled walls of mosques.

SEE ALSO
Shapes *pp.284–89*
Sacred places *pp.232–33*

ISLAM

181

ISLAMIC CARPET

There is a rich tradition of symbolic geometric patterns in Islamic art, many of which are incorporated in traditonal crafts. In Islamic carpets the range of compositions and colors is enormous. Owners of rugs are often able to trace the origins of their carpets back to a particular tribe, area, or town.

1. Patterns and symmetry
The symmetry of the patterns used in Islamic carpets symbolizes balanced proportions. The design of shapes and their position is usually the same on both sides of the central axis. The repetition of the patterns is used to symbolize unity in multiplicity.

2. Borders
There are often several borders in the design of an Islamic carpet and their number is symbolic. Three, five, seven, and nine are sacred numbers, which are used to determine how many borders a carpet will have. The three borders shown here symbolize earth, sky, water, holiness, productivity, and fertility.

3. & 4. Shapes
Stars are hugely symbolic, and the number of points of a star determines its meaning. An eight-pointed star symbolizes the line of life from birth to death. The dot in the center of the carpet symbolizes one God and the role of Mecca as the center of Islam toward which all Muslims face to pray.

5. Colors
Each of the colors in an Islamic carpet has a different meaning. For example, yellow symbolizes an abundant and wealthy life while blue shows an unattainable depth and mythical infinity of sky and sea. Green represents spring and paradise.

SIKHISM

Sikhism is a monotheistic faith founded in northern India in the 15th century by the Guru Nanak and built on by nine successive gurus or teachers. Sikhs respect the equality of all people, regardless of their faith, and emphasize service to others, humility, and daily prayer. They do not place statues of God or the gurus in their temples, but instead a number of objects and practices have important religious symbolism. Depictions of the gurus are always very symbolic, as is the appearance of practicing Sikhs who adopt the five Ks.

◄ Guru Nanak
The first of the ten gurus, Guru Nanak embodies the wisdom of Sikhism. He is always depicted with prayer beads, which, with the halo around his head, are a symbol of his holy status. His half-closed eyes are a sign of spiritual ecstasy and his long, white beard is symbolic of wisdom.

THE FIVE KS

These are the five items of dress and physical appearance beginning with the letter K that were set down by Guru Gobind Singh, the tenth and last guru in 1699, to act as overt markers of followers of his rules of discipline. They are the *kirpan, kangha, kara, kachhera,* and *kesh.* Today, by adopting the five Ks, Sikhs signal a belief and pride in their religion.

Sword

Shield

Kirpan

► Kirpan
The ceremonial weapon, or *kirpan,* is a symbol of courage and rectitude, and a sign of every Sikh's readiness to defend the weak and oppressed. It is worn close to the skin as a reminder of human mortality, and represents justice, order, and morality.

▲ Kangha
The wooden comb, known as a *kangha,* symbolizes moral and spiritual control and cleanliness. Sikhs wear the comb in their hair and use it twice daily. By combing their hair, they distinguish themselves from Hindu ascetics, with their unkept, matted locks.

▲ Kara
The steel bracelet, or *kara,* signifies strength and integrity and is always worn on the right wrist. Its circular shape symbolizes perfection and unity with God and is a continual reminder of the vow taken by all Sikhs to do nothing that might bring shame on their religion.

▲ Kachhera
Cotton shorts, not unlike boxer shorts, *kachhera* are worn as an undergarment at all times by Sikh men. Although they allow free movement, *kachhera* are nevertheless a symbol of self control and sexual restraint, and are a reminder of the prohibition of adultery.

◄ Kesh
Uncut hair, called *kesh,* is a symbol of saintliness. All Sikh men wear their hair long, as they believe that by keeping hair in its natural state they live in harmony with God. They cover their hair with a distinctive turban, which is a recognizable sign of Sikhism.

THE GURDWARA

In Sikhism God is not thought to have a physical form and he is worshiped without use of the symbols of other religions, such as incense or candles. There are no priests and anyone can lead a service. However, each *gurdwara* (temple) has one person, a *granthi*, appointed to read and take care of the book of scriptures, called the Guru Granth Sahib. The *gurdwara* is the focal point of religious life for Sikhs and a symbol of worship.

◀ Gurdwara entrance
Some Sikh *gurdwaras* have four doors. These are the Door of Livelihood, the Door of Learning, the Door of Grace, and the Door of Peace. They symbolize the fact that people are welcome from all directions. A light is always visible in the temple for the same reason.

▲ Gurdwara duties
Community service, such as cooking (*shown here*), is an important part of the Sikh faith, a symbolic reminder of the virtues of humility and service.

◀ The Golden Temple
Founded by Guru Ram Das, the fourth guru, and extended by Guru Arjan Dev, the fifth guru, the Golden Temple at Amritsar is constructed on a sacred lake, the waters of which symbolize creation and abundance. It was built to house the holy book.

▼ The holy book
Called the Guru Granth Sahib, the holy book contains hymns by the gurus and other writers on which the Sikh religion is based. The book has an appointed guardian in every temple. A sacred whisk, or *chauri*, symbol of honor and sovereignty, is waved over the text whenever it is read.

EMBLEMS AND NAMES

The power of the one God and equality are central tenets of the Sikh religion. The *khanda* emblem is made up of three elements that symbolize these principles. One way in which Sikhs signify their equality is by adopting the name "Singh" for men and "Kaur" for women.

Two-edged sword or khanda   *Circular chakra*   *Single-edged sword*

▲ The khanda
The emblem of the Sikh faith, the *khanda* is made up of a two-edged sword, symbolic of truth and justice, and two outer swords that represent the power of God. The circle represents a weapon, the chakra, and symbolizes eternity.

▲ Ek Onkar
Meaning "God is one," these first two words in the Guru Granth Sahib are the ones most repeated by Sikhs. They are one of the cornerstones of Sikhism, and in their written form make up one of the most famous symbols of the Sikh religion.

▲ Gobind Singh
All Sikh males take the name "Singh," meaning "lion," while women have the name "Kaur," meaning "princess". The disciples of the tenth guru, Gobind Singh, first adopted the name "Singh" and others followed. This uniformity symbolizes the Sikhs' emphasis on equality and rejection of the caste system, which could be identified from last names.

SEE ALSO
The head *pp.106–09*
Tools & weapons *pp.224–25*
Sacred places *pp.232–33*
Headwear *pp.250–51*

▲ **Altar of Mama Wati**
During a ritual ceremony altars are traditionally richly laden with
candles and symbolic items and gifts that relate to the loa being
invoked. Here the image of Mama Wati has snakes entwined around
her arms, symbolic of fertility and renewal.

VOODOO

A belief system that concerns the power of spirits over the
natural world, voodoo was practiced in secret by slaves
who used symbolism to disguise their religion.

The word "voodoo" stems from the West
African *vodun*, which means "spirit." The
religion originated in Haiti, during the
slave era of the 18th century, and
combines elements from a number
of different West African faiths.
The slaves kept their beliefs alive
by combining them with Christian
rites, often giving Christian names
to the old spirits while retaining
their symbolism. Largely
misunderstood, voodoo has
long been regarded with
suspicion by outsiders,
and associations with
evil spirits and the
living dead abound.

▲ Voodoo dolls
Made of natural fiber and
with an animal's head, this
voodoo doll signifies the
bounty of the natural world
and counters infertility. A
doll is made to effect a
change in a person; what is
done to the doll supposedly
also happens to the person.

THE LOA

The concept of the "spirit" is
essential to voodoo culture
and manifests itself in a
number of different ways. Beneath the supreme
divine being, the Gran Met (Great Master), are a
multitude of "loas" (literally "mysteries"), each one is
an ancestral spirit of some magnitude; for example,
a king, a high priest, or a hero in past life. Each of
these loas signifies a different aspect of the natural
world—health, death, love, forests, streams—and
has the power to influence whatever they
symbolize for better or worse. Loas are, therefore,
the focus of voodoo worship. Believers in voodoo
invoke loas at the beginning of a ceremony by
drawing a ritual symbol, known as a "vever," on
the ground. Each loa has a different symbol made up of a
unique combination of motifs signifying different aspects of
their personality and powers. There is a reciprocal element to
the relationship between believers and their loas, and this

forms the focus of the ceremony. In return for food, which
is symbolically represented through a gift of animal
sacrifice, the loa provides worshipers with good fortune,
health, and protection from evil spirits.

VOODOO RITUAL

Symbolic rituals are held in gratitude for recent
luck or to ask for help at a time of misfortune.
The worshipers signify their desire to connect to the
spirit world by dancing to a chant and drumbeat,
specific to a particular loa, until one or more of
them is possessed by the spirit. Entering a trance-
like state signifies the worshippers' devotion
and for other believers signals the apearance
of the spirit. The loa then communicates his/
her will through the possessed.

VOODOO MAGIC

There are two groups of loa: the "rada," or sweet
spirits, are thought to be of African origin, whereas
the "petro," or the bitter spirits, may be of Caribbean
origin and are more vengeful. Practitioners of rada
are thought to practice white magic in the form
of beneficial charms, or "wanga," including the
making of love potions or the use of healing herbs.
A more sinister form of voodoo centers on the
petro spirits and is more closely associated with
black magic or sorcery.

◄ Vevers
Made from cornmeal at the start of voodoo rituals, vevers are unique
to the loa they symbolize. The vevers shown here signify Papa Legba (*top*),
Damballah La Flambeau, Ayizan, Brigitte, and Ogoun (*bottom*). A number of
loas may be called upon in any one ritual.

SEE ALSO
Satan & demons *pp.190–91*
Witches & wicca *pp.192–193*

ANGELS

The embodiment of heavenly purity and benevolence, angels feature in the Old and New Testaments, and the Koran. They are regarded by Jews, Christians, and Muslims as messengers of God, and are most commonly perceived as spiritual, superhuman beings that mediate between God and humans, reflecting God's will on Earth. In the Bible angels are always described as being youthful and beautiful—a symbol of their high status—and dressed in white—a sign of their spirituality and purity.

▲ Archangel Gabriel
Known to Christians for announcing Jesus' impending birth to Mary, and in Islam for revealing the Koran to Muhammad, Gabriel (Jibra'il) is often depicted with a trumpet, symbolic of his role as herald.

ANGEL ATTRIBUTES

All angels—excluding those who have fallen from grace—are holy and without sin. There are various descriptions of them in the Bible and, over the centuries, common themes have developed in the way that angels have been portrayed in the arts, for example, with wings or haloes. There is great symbolism in an angel's appearance, in many cases their physical attributes representing spiritual ones.

▲ Wings
An angel's wings are symbolic of its spirituality and of its closeness to God. They also signify an angel's ability to fly from Heaven to Earth to carry out God's bidding.

▲ Harp
Numerous angels surround God in Heaven and are referred to as the "heavenly host." They are often depicted with musical instruments—specifically the harp—as a sign of the harmony they create in praising God.

▲ Censer
Used for burning incense, the fragrance from censers is said to carry people's prayers to Heaven. An angel might be depicted wafting the incense in the direction of a holy figure as a symbol of veneration.

◄ Halo
The halo is symbolic of light and divinity. Accounts of angels in the Bible often mention them as bright beings or surrounded by an aura of some kind, and in many images of angels (and other holy figures) this is represented as a halo around their heads.

CELESTIAL HIERARCHY

The "heavenly host" includes various ranks of angels, each with different duties and imbued with its own symbolism. A 5th-century Greek scholar, Dionysus the Areopagite, describes the angels as belonging to three "choirs": the First Choir (comprising the Seraphim, Cherubim, and Thrones); the Second Choir (Dominations, Virtues, and Powers); and the Third Choir (Principalities, Archangels, and Angels).

▲ **Archangel Michael**
Particularly associated with God's "armies" of angels, and with ridding Heaven of Satan, Michael signifies chivalry in both the Christian and Jewish faiths; he is also considered "protector of Israel."

► **The Seven Archangels**
A sign of the importance of the archangels is that they include the only named angels in the Bible. They most closely represent God's will on Earth, through their duty to relay messages to people.

Cherubim
God
Archangel

▲ **Archangel Raphael**
For Christians the Archangel Raphael is symbolic of healing (his name in Hebrew means "God heals"). For Muslims he signifies the coming of Judgement Day, as it is he who will bring the news.

▲ **Cherubim**
Being close to God, cherubim signify a deep knowledge of God's will and, therefore, wisdom. They were responsible for the expulsion of Adam and Eve from the Garden of Eden.

▲ **Seraphim**
The highest ranking angels that are closest to God, four Seraphim fly above God's throne, singing his praises. Extremely bright and with six wings, they symbolize love and light.

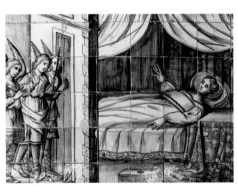

▲ **Guardian angels**
A symbol of God's care for his people, guardian angels protect an individual, offering his or her prayers to God, and providing guidance through the journey of life.

CHERUBS

Often confused with the Cherubim, cherubs or putti (from old Italian *putto*, meaning "child") were Classical images of rounded, naked baby figures, always male, and often with wings. Symbolic of innocence and purity, their wings, if present, added spiritual significance. Cherubs became popular during the Renaissance: some, such as Cupid, were a sign of love and romance, and therefore had mythological symbolism, while others were depicted, for example, welcoming people to Heaven and therefore had religious symbolism. Cherubs are sometimes depicted with items such as musical instruments or a skull for symbolic emphasis.

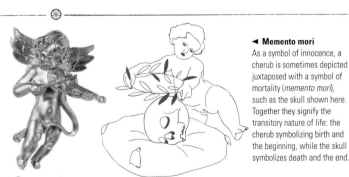

▲ **Baroque putto**
During the Baroque period it was not unusual to see sculpted and carved putti in both architecture and furniture designs. They may be gilded to signify their heavenly status.

◄ **Memento mori**
As a symbol of innocence, a cherub is sometimes depicted juxtaposed with a symbol of mortality (*memento mori*), such as the skull shown here. Together they signify the transitory nature of life: the cherub symbolizing birth and the beginning, while the skull symbolizes death and the end.

SEE ALSO
Death & mourning *pp.128–31*
Vanitas *pp.132–33*
Greek & Roman deities *pp.140–41*
Satan and demons *pp.190–91*
Gardens *pp.244–47*

SATAN & DEMONS

Most cultures, whether ancient or contemporary, feature the Devil or demons in their mythology and religion. At best demons signify ill-fortune and poor health; at worst they are manifestations of evil and death. Such figures are also associated with darkness and the unknown; they prey on our greatest fears, especially Satan who is symbolic of Hell as opposed to Heaven.

◄ Cult of Satan
Recent times have seen the development of several satanic cults. The Church of Satan, for example, rejects organized religion and instead honors Satan. He does not symbolize evil here, but simply stands in opposition to God.

SATAN AND SATANISM

In the biblical sense, Satan is God's rival. As the angel Lucifer, he was cast from Heaven for challenging God's authority. As such, Satan is symbolic of pure evil, a master of deception, and the embodiment of temptation. During medieval times the Devil came to signify those who revolted against Christianity. Many of the popular images of Satan that exist today originate from this time, and each has its own symbolism.

◄ Seth
For the Ancient Egyptians the god Seth symbolized evil: he was god of chaos, storms, and war. The term Satanism probably derives from "Seitanism", used to describe worship of Seth.

▲ Ahriman
Zoroastrianism, the religion of the ancient Persians, was one of the first to acknowledge Good and Evil as opposing forces. Ahriman, who was symbolic of Evil, also influenced the concept of Satan in Judaism and Christianity.

◄ Trident
In medieval times, the Christians "demonized" attributes associated with pagan gods to discredit them. The trident, which in Ancient Greek and Hindu religions was a weapon against evil, instead became a symbol of the Devil, and a tool of evil.

▲ The Sigil of Baphomet
The three downward points of a Baphomet signify the (rejected) Christian Trinity; the two upward points are the horns of the goat face, which symbolizes carnality.

▲ Cerunnos
Medieval Christians not only associated Satan with the trident (*see left*), they may have given him the horns of the Celtic god, Cerunnos. By making horns symbolic of the Devil, they discredited the pagan god.

▲ Black mass
Traditional Satanists perform the "black mass" in which much of the Christian symbolism is reversed: the cross hangs upside down and blood not wine is drunk from the cup. There may be sexual overtones, or a sacrifice, to signify the dominance of our carnal nature.

▲ Satan as a serpent
Adept at changing his form in order to deceive, Satan is assumed to be the serpent that tempted Adam and Eve to eat the forbidden fruit in the Garden of Eden. God's cursing of the snake made it a potent symbol of the fall from grace.

◄ The Grimoire of Honorius
Books of black magic were not uncommon during medieval times. This book of spells, symbols, and formulae was published in the 17th century and sets out instructions for saying mass to conjure demons. Because it parodies the Christian mass, it symbolizes profanity.

MYTHS & RELIGIONS

DEMONS AND DEVILS

Demons have featured in the beliefs of many civilizations over time, and are often regarded as a manifestation of bad luck and mischief. They are also perceived as signifying the darker side of an individual and have been used to explain mental illness. In many cases, demons are inextricably linked to religious superstition and to people's need to understand why bad things happen in a world in which God, who is inherently good, is supposedly omnipotent. Much of the symbolism associated with demons and devils is, therefore, related to the battle between Good and Evil.

▲ Galla
In Mesopotamian mythology, there were seven demons called Galla, who were symbolic of death and gloom. They roamed at night looking for victims to drag down to the underworld.

▲ Medieval demon
In medieval times, Christian legends—like that of St. Anthony the Great, who was relentlessly pursued by demons—symbolized the power of faith in God over temptation by the Devil.

◄ Mara's daughters
In Buddhism the demon Mara symbolized temptation. It was he who tried to distract the Buddha from his meditation. He even sent his beautiful daughters to try and distract him. The Buddha went on to attain Enlightenment and to formulate his doctrine.

▲ Tokoloshi
In South Africa demons are symbolized in the form of tokoloshis. Fear of these demons is widespread and people are known to raise their beds on bricks to avoid an attack from these evil spirits at night.

▲ Hawaiian god Ku
In many cultures gods, such as Ku, have a demonic appearance to create fear and awe among their worshipers. This makes it difficult for "outsiders" to distinguish between the godly and the demonic.

▲ Babylonian demon
In Babylon it was commonly held that a person with mental or physical illness, or who had suffered a deep loss of some kind, had upset the gods. Their misfortune was symbolic of this and proof of demons at work.

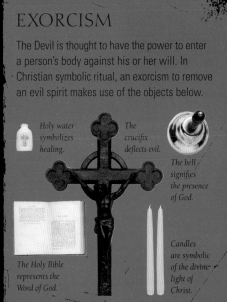

EXORCISM

The Devil is thought to have the power to enter a person's body against his or her will. In Christian symbolic ritual, an exorcism to remove an evil spirit makes use of the objects below.

Holy water symbolizes healing.

The crucifix deflects evil.

The bell signifies the presence of God.

Candles are symbolic of the divine light of Christ.

The Holy Bible represents the Word of God.

▲ Ten-headed Ravana
To Hindus, Ravana embodies evil and signifies the ego. He is depicted with ten heads and many arms that symbolize his strength and greed. Effigies of Ravana are burned at the festival of Dusshera.

▲ Asuras
In Hindu mythology *asuras* were power seekers that constantly battled with the gods. Although often referred to as demons, these figures were not symbols of pure evil, but rather of drought, flood, and famine.

▲ Rahu
Rahu was an *asura* who was beheaded for drinking from the cup of immortality. He was the symbol of eclipses because he chased and swallowed the Sun and Moon, but they reappeared through his open neck.

SEE ALSO
The Moon *pp. 18–19*
Egyptian deities *pp. 138–139*
Celtic & Nordic deities *pp. 142–43*
Angels *pp. 188–89*
Witches & wicca *pp. 192–93*
Musical instruments *pp. 274–75*

WITCHES & WICCA

Witchcraft is an ancient tradition, practiced in various forms as far back as Ancient Egypt and in all regions of the world. To the Celts "wicca," meaning "witch," had close ties to nature, but also to magic and the occult. Traditionally respected as symbols of wisdom and knowledge, witches were pursued by the Christian Church from the 15th to the 17th century. At this time their practices were deemed heretical and much of their symbolism became associated with the Devil.

◄ Use of poppets
Made to symbolize a specific person, a poppet has magic properties that allow the maker to influence that person's life or cause him/her harm.

WITCHES

Magic is the mainstay of witchcraft and, over the centuries, symbolic images of witches have developed based on the various tools, signs, and familiars (animals) associated with their rituals of casting spells and spiritual healing. Although the ugly old woman dressed head to foot in black is a stereotype, there is much symbolism in the many physical attributes that are commonly used in the portrayal of witches today.

▲ Broom
Made of birch, symbolizing birth and rebirth, hazel, signifying fertility and knowledge, or yew, which is symbolic of death and resurrection, brooms are used to sweep away negative energy and have phallic symbolism. Witches are said to ride their broomsticks during fertility rites.

▲ Wand
The wand is commonly associated with witchcraft and is symbolic of a witch's energy and power. Made of any material, the most common are crafted from wood, which is an effective conductor of energy. A magic wand might be used for channeling and directing energy as part of a spell or during certain rituals.

► Cauldron
Central to certain rituals, the cauldron is highly symbolic. It signifies the womb, fertility, and rebirth. When in use, it also signifies the four elements: earth, water, fire, and air.

▲ Cup or chalice
Frequently used when making predictions, the chalice signifies a witch's psychic powers, intuition, and emotions.

▲ Spells and potions
Spell-making can be beneficial or harmful. Even the ingredients are symbolic: use of a toad, for example, would signify ill-doing.

DETECTING WITCHES

The image of the witch as a devil worshiper was encouraged in the 15th to 17th centuries, and witch hunts were commonplace. Thousands of witches (and sometimes their pets) were executed. A manual, the *Malleus Maleficarum,* set out rules on how to detect witches, with signs of Satan (usually a birthmark) and fear of the persecutor among them. Sometimes victims were tied up and left in the water to see if they drowned. Survival of this ordeal was a sign that confirmed they were witches.

▲ Spell books
A symbol of power, the witch's spell book probably derives from the magic books, or grimoires, that existed in medieval times.

▲ Black Cats
Once thought to be a gift from the Devil, a black cat belonging to a witch is symbolic of the night and bad luck.

▲ Raven
Common in witchcraft, the raven symbolizes healing and omens. It is also associated with shapeshifting.

▲ Toad
Connected to the underworld and symbolic of death, darkness, and poison, the toad is a common witch's familiar.

WICCA

Wicca is one form of witchcraft practiced today. Taking inspiration from the Celtic tradition of witchcraft, it has many symbols. Some, such as the triple circle, are used during rituals, others signify gods and a few have uncertain origins.

◄ Pentacle
A pentagram within a circle, the pentacle has five points: four of them symbolize air, fire, earth, and water, and the fifth is ether, which signifies the spirit. The circle is symbolic of unity, and the symbol as a whole embodies the integration of body and spirit.

▲ Cerunnos
This sign represents Cerunnos, the ancient Celtic horned god of the forests and forest animals. The sign symbolizes the male power of wicca.

▲ Mother goddess
The female power of wicca is sometimes represented as a symbol based on the Egyptian Mother Goddess. Cerunnos, the horned god, is her consort.

▲ Triple Circle
This symbol, used in ritual to call upon the triple goddess (mother, maiden, and crone), signifies the mind, the body, and the spirit.

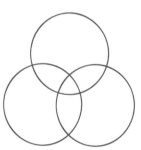

◄ Witch's sign
The exact meaning of this sign is unknown. One idea is that the square signifies Earth, and the triangles signify mind, body, spirit, man, woman, and child.

▲ Heptagram
Drawn with a single unbroken line, the seven points of the heptagram symbolize, among other things, the seven planets.

▲ Triple Moon
Symbolizing the triple goddess as the waxing, full, and waning Moon, the sign as a whole signifies the cycle of life.

▲ Spirit circle
All Wiccan rituals require the casting of a circle, as shown here. Each quarter is symbolic of one of the four elements.

SEE ALSO
Birds *pp.58–61*
Reptiles & amphibians *pp.64–65*
Fertility & childbirth *pp.120–23*
Egyptian deities *pp.138–39*
The Holy Grail *pp.208–09*

WITCHES & WICCA

AMULETS

Symbolic of beneficent power, amulets have been worn
for protection and strength for many thousands of
years. Often made from natural substances, such as
ivory, gemstones, and wood, these small objects, also
known as talismans, are worn as charms or carried by
individuals for good fortune, protection, and strength.
Amulets may also have religious or superstitious origins,
and are often symbolic of the desire to ward off evil.

◄ **Azabache**
In South America newborn
babies are sometimes given a
gold bracelet on which hangs a
clenched fist made from black
or red coral. A symbol of
resistance, the charm protects
the child from the *mal do ojo*
(evil eye) associated with
excessive admiration.

▲ **Silver charm bracelet**
Popular with young girls since
the beginning of the 20th
century, silver charm bracelets
were given at birthdays, with
additional charms following in
subsequent years. Each silver
charm has a different meaning:
for example, a horseshoe was
a symbol of luck; Cupid signified
love; and a stork symbolized
the birth of a child.

► **Pomander**
Common in medieval times,
pomanders contained scents
and spices and were usually
worn around the neck. Symbolic
of sweetness and protection,
they were worn as a safeguard
against contagious diseases.

▲ **The Eye**
Seen throughout the Middle
East, this amulet also protects
the wearer from the "evil eye,"
which is said to result from the
envy of others. The eye symbol
deflects the stares of onlookers.

Metal amulet

► **Metal
amulet**
Assyrian kings
wore necklaces
with metal amulets,
bearing the protective
symbols of the gods.
Metal was a sign of the
Earth's strength.

▲ **Knight's amulet**
Medieval knights often wore
amulets in battle. This example
comes from the belt of a Polish
knight and symbolizes abundant
health, wealth, and power.

▲ **Pazuzu**
During childbirth Assyrian
women wore amulets bearing
an image of Pazuzu. According
to legend, the ancient demon
prevented miscarriage and
infant death.

▲ **Red and white string**
According to tradition, Bulgarians
tie a piece of red and white
string around their wrists as a
charm to speed up the arrival of
Spring. Together, the colors red
and white are symbolic of joy.

EGYPTIAN AMULETS

Symbolism was a significant part of life in Ancient Egypt, and featured particularly in the use of amulets. Made from ceramics, gems, and metals, amulets signified attributes of specific gods or animals. They were worn as symbols of praise, protection, and fortune, and were entombed with mummies for the journey into the afterlife.

▲ Scarab beetle
The scarab beetle symbolized the Egyptian Sun god, Khepri, who rolled the Sun across the sky much as a scarab rolls its dung. Scarabs were also thought to protect the heart and as such were worn as amulets.

▲ Ankh
The ankh was associated with the Sun and symbolized eternal life. Often made from gold or copper, it was commonly placed in tombs of the deceased to symbolize the breath needed for the afterlife.

▲ Eye of Horus
The right eye of Horus symbolizes the Sun and the left eye the Moon. As a symbol the eye signified protection from evil and was also used to grant the wearer healing powers.

◀ Jeweled amulet
Symbolic of hidden truth and light, jeweled amulets were buried with the deceased as protection from evil and as identification, so they could reach the correct level in the afterlife.

▲ Locket
Once used as containers for herbs to ward off sickness and evil, lockets became symbolic of love when they contained a lock of hair or picture of a loved one.

▲ Tiger tooth
Amulets of animal origin, such as claws and teeth, signify the positive qualities of that creature. This tiger's tooth symbolizes courage and strength.

▲ Rabbit's foot
Long considered a symbol of good luck in the West, a rabbit's foot is also believed to bring a person fertility and, for the Chinese, prosperity.

▲ St. Christopher
Sometimes worn as protection from the "Black Death," St. Christopher amulets are more symbolic of safety, especially when traveling.

▲ Hei Tiki
The Hei Tiki is a Maori talisman, shaped as a human figure and symbolizing an embryo. The charm is worn by women to encourage fertility.

► Buddha talisman
Buddhists often wear an amulet of the Buddha as an outward sign of their devotion. He appears in a number of postures, each with its own symbolism. Here his right hand is touching the Earth, a sign symbolic of the moment of the Buddha's Enlightenment.

▲ Crucifix
An amulet signifying Christ's crucifixion has long been a symbol of the Christian faith. The epitome of "good," a crucifix protects the wearer against evil.

▲ Ichthys
Used in ancient times as an amulet signifying fertility, the ichthys (fish) subsequently became a Christian symbol. It was used as a secret sign and later worn as a talisman. In North America the fish is a totem animal, symbolic of hidden knowledge, and worn for protection.

SEE ALSO
The Sun pp.16–17
The head pp.106–09
Fertility & childbirth pp.120–123
Egyptian deities pp.138–39

Tribal totems, heroes, & tricksters pp.150–51
Buddhism pp.164–69
Christianity pp.176–79

DIVINATION

Since ancient times the practice of divination—attempting to foretell the future or explain portents—has been found in all cultures. The methods used include everything from the casting of sticks or stones, and the examination of tea leaves and animal entrails, to palmistry and tarot readings. Some forms of divination rely on a "sign" of some sort to answer a question, such as a pendulum swing to the left or right, while others are more complex and use systems of symbols and configurations that need interpreting in order to arrive at an appropriate conclusion.

⊕BSERVING MⓄVEMENT

A question that requires a "yes" or "no" type answer can rely on the simplest "sign from above," whether it be in interpreting the swing of a pendulum, the patterns flocks of birds make as they fly, or the crossing over of two dowsing rods. Such forms of divination have been used for many years and date back at least as far as Ancient Egyptian times.

◄ Chicken-watching
Roman seers consulted sacred chickens, often before battles. The way the birds ate their food and scratched the ground was symbolic. Eating was a good sign; if they refused to feed, the omens were bad.

◄ Pendulum
The use of a pendulum is a form of dowsing. The diviner asks a series of simple questions and the direction the pendulum moves in signifies the yes/no answer.

CRYSTAL BALL

Often used in divination, a crystal ball concentrates the rays of the Sun or some other light and in doing so is symbolic of divine light and celestial power. The diviner then empties his/her mind and gazes into the depths of the crystal from which he/she may receive flashes of insight signifying scenes from the past or future events yet to happen.

❂ READING SIGNS

There are numerous ways in which "readers" can divine the future or interpret a given situation by reading "signs." This might involve watching the shapes made by rising smoke, observing the forms of molten wax as it solidifies, or looking at the patterns made by tea leaves or coffee grounds. In all instances, the resulting shapes are symbolic of a deeper meaning: for example, a forked line signifies a decision to be made, while smoke rising in a straight line promises a positive outcome.

 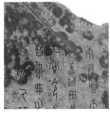

▲ Tea leaves
The art of tasseography involves reading the pattern made by the tea leaves left in a cup after the tea has been drunk. Patterns in the bottom of the cup represent the past, and at the top the future. Each shape—a raven or an acorn, for example—has a symbolic meaning—bad news, success, or danger.

▲ Oracle bones
An Ancient Chinese form of divination, a number of symbols were inscribed on an animal bone and several holes drilled partway through. When heated, the weakened bone cracked. The lines made, and their relation to the various symbols, were then interpreted to divine a meaning.

◄ Divination bowl
The Yoruba people of Nigeria fill a bowl with sand and then tap it with a stick. The significance of the resulting sand pattern is interpreted by the diviner.

I CHING

Also known as the Book of Changes, the *I Ching* is the foundation of Chinese philosophy. It is also used for divination, based on the interpretation of hexagrams, which are made up of eight trigrams (shown here). Consisting of three broken (Yin) and solid (Yang) lines, randomly generated by tossing coins or dice, each trigram signifies different aspects of the universe—a different element, direction, relationship, figure, and body part.

▲ Trigram of Earth (*Kun*)
A symbol of receptiveness, *Kun* comprises three Yin lines and so is feminine, representing the "mother." It is associated with the earth element, the West, and the reproductive organs.

▲ Trigram of the Mountain (*Ken*)
More Yin than Yang, this symbol of beginnings and endings signifies the "youngest son." It is linked with the earth element, the West, and the hands.

▲ Trigram of Water (*Kan*)
Kan symbolizes hard work, warning against stagnation. It signifies the "middle son," and is linked with the Moon, water, the East, and the ear.

▲ Trigram of Wind (*Sun*)
A symbol of gentleness, *Sun* signifies the "eldest daughter." It is associated with soft wood, the East, and the hips and buttocks.

▲ Trigram of Thunder (*Chen*)
This is a symbol of growth and vitality. It represents the "eldest son," and is associated with hard wood and softness, the East, and the feet.

▲ Trigram of Fire (*Li*)
This is a symbol of light and signifies glory. It represents the "middle daughter," and is associated with fire, the Sun, the East, and the eye.

▲ Trigram of Lake (*Tui*)
This is a symbol of joy and pleasure. It represents the "youngest daughter," and is associated with soft metal, the West, and the mouth.

▲ Trigram of Heaven (*Chien*)
A Yang symbol of creative energy, *Chien* is masculine and signifies the "father." It is linked with hard metal, the West, and the head.

CASTING METHODS

Many cultures use the casting of lots, stones, sticks, or similar objects for divination. The *I Ching* is probably the best-known method, but there are many more, including runes, dice, and even coconut shells. The method may involve using just one stick, as in Kau Cim, or casting up to 24 runes. The essence of casting is that the result is random and the symbolism interpreted afresh each time.

◄ Dice
Possibly the most recognized symbols of chance are dice. There are various ways of throwing them for divination purposes. One involves throwing three dice. Each is taken in turn and thrown; the number showing when it comes to rest is interpreted accordingly.

◄ African bone reading
Once commonly used, bone reading is less popular nowadays. This method of divination involves throwing sets of bones, usually between four and fourteen, and interpreting the pattern in which they fall and the direction they point in. Each bone is symbolic of something different—a bird's wing bone, for example, signifies travel, while the breast bone symbolizes love.

▲ Coconut
In some parts of Africa four pieces of coconut are cast and questions answered depending on whether the pieces fall flesh-side up or vice versa. There are only five outcomes, which range on a sliding scale from positive to negative. Coins can be used in the same way.

► Kau Cim
A number of "fortune sticks" are held in a tube and shaken until one (or sometimes more) falls out. Each has a specific symbol or meaning, which is then interpreted in the context of the question that is being asked.

▲ Rune stones
The casting of runes dates back to medieval times. The 24 stones are arranged in any of a number of formations, and the reading given according to the symbol each rune carries and its position in the arrangement.

SEE ALSO
Precious stones *pp.42–43*
Shamanism *pp.154–55*
Taoism & Shinto *pp.170–71*
Voodoo *pp.186–87*

PALMISTRY

Another ancient form of fortune-telling is palmistry. All aspects of the hand are considered: the general shape of the palm and fingers, the dominant lines and the mounds at the base of the fingers and thumb; even relative finger length and the length and depth of the lines are significant. Each element signifies some aspect of a person's life. For example, the fingers relate to confidence, discipline, creativity, and communication, while the mounds relate to pride, imagination, love, and sadness. This, together with the shape and color of the hand and how it is held, enables a palm reader to discover not just the present, but also the future.

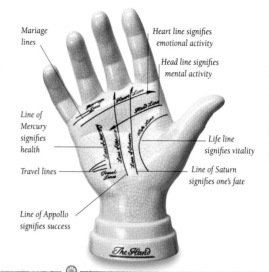

Mariage lines

Heart line signifies emotional activity

Head line signifies mental activity

Line of Mercury signifies health

Travel lines

Line of Appollo signifies success

Life line signifies vitality

Line of Saturn signifies one's fate

The Hand

▼ Oil in the hand
In Arab countries a traditional method of fortune-telling is by reading the formation of a pool of oil in the palm of the hand. The way in which the oil runs into the lines signifes a person's character as well as foretelling the future.

THE TAR⊕T

Card reading, or cartomancy, has been known since at least the 15th century. A Tarot deck comprises 22 picture cards, called the Major Arcana (*shown here*), and the Minor Arcana, which is organized in four suits (cups, coins, swords, and rods). The Major Arcana is most often used in fortune-telling. The cards are shuffled by the person whose fortune is being told, and can then be arranged by the teller in a number of different ways, depending on the nature of the question asked. The result of the reading is complex: each card is symbolic of a stage in the person's life, but the card's position in the spread, the cards around it, and whether it is the right way up or inverted, may modify that symbolism.

▲ The Fool or Jester
Depicted with his possessions on his back, the Fool signifies innocence and a carefree nature, and often represents the fortune seeker and/or a new journey. Inverted, the card represents naivety and foolishness.

▲ The Magician
Symbolizing willpower and the ability to achieve, the Magician is depicted with a table and the various cups, coins, rods, and swords of the Minor Arcana. Inverted, the card signifies an abuse of such skills.

▲ The High Priestess
Often depicted sitting on a throne in contemplation, the High Priestess symbolizes wisdom and sound judgement. Inverted, the card can mean lack of vision and an inability to make good judgement.

▲ The Empress
Signifying creation and growth, the Empress is depicted with an orb and the symbol for Venus on her shield. Inverted, the Empress card indicates inaction and indecision.

▲ The Emperor
Usually seated on a throne, the Emperor symbolizes material things and worldy authority; he is always in absolute control. Inverted, the card represents gullibility or immaturity.

▲ The Hierophant
Seated before two pillars that represent Heaven's gates, the Hierophant has a three-tiered staff and crown and is symbolic of peace and harmony. Inverted, the card can signify vulnerability.

▲ The Lovers
Symbolic of affairs of the heart, the Lovers also reflect an inner harmony. In this example, Cupid hovers above them. Inverted, the card signifies temptation or separation.

▲ The Chariot
Symbolic of a struggle and a need to focus, the Chariot also signifies bridling disparate wills in order to succeed. Inverted, it can indicate a failure to see something through.

▲ **Justice**
Depicted as a woman with the sword and scales of justice, this card symbolizes balance, and specifically equilibrium between the spiritual and the material. Inverted, the card signifies a lack of balance and injustice.

▲ **The Hermit**
Often pictured holding a lantern, the Hermit represents introspection and self-examination. It can signify a need for advice. Inverted, the card represents obstinacy and a refusal to take advice.

▲ **The Wheel of Fortune**
A wheel on which beasts revolve, this card represents motion, the beginning of a new cycle, and unexpected good fortune. Inverted, it is a sign of bad luck and an unforeseen change for the worse.

▲ **Strength**
This card is symbolized by a young woman holding a lion's mouth open; it represents inner strength and determination. Inverted, the Strength card represents a lack of confidence and weakness.

▲ **The Hanged Man**
This card, symbolic of meditation and self-sacrifice, always shows a man hanging in the same way, with one foot tied and the free leg bent, his hands behind his back. Inverted, it represents selfishness.

▲ **Death**
Often depicted as a skeletal figure, Death represents a transformation and getting rid of the old to make way for the new. Inverted, the card symbolizes lethargy and an inability to move on.

▲ **Temperance**
This card shows an angel pouring fluid from one cup to another. It symbolizes moderation and self-control. Inverted, the card signifies a lack of self-control or some kind of conflict of interest.

▲ **The Devil**
Depicted with two people in shackles, the Devil represents subordination or a lack of success. It can also signify destruction. Inverted, the Devil card is symbolic of release from something binding.

▲ **The Tower**
The falling tower represents a radical change—a move to somewhere new or a change in faith, for example. Inverted, the Tower suggests a resistance to change and being stuck in a rut.

▲ **The Stars**
Signifying hope and fulfillment of wishes, the stars shine above a naked woman pouring water from an urn. Inverted, the Stars card symbolizes self-doubt and unfulfilled dreams.

◄ **The World**
This card shows a woman standing in an oval wreath surrounded by an angel, an eagle, a bull, and a lion—symbols of the apocalypse. The World card symbolizes great accomplishment. Inverted, it signifies a failure to achieve.

▲ **The Moon**
Shown both full and as a crescent, the Moon represents a deception of some kind and the need to tread carefully. Inverted, the card signifies that all will be well in the end.

▲ **The Sun**
Symbolizing contentment and satisfaction, the Sun card can also signify the attainment of a personal goal. Inverted, the Sun card can indicate delays over future plans.

▲ **Judgement**
An angel blowing a trumpet as people rise from their graves signifies an acceptance of the past and letting it go. Inverted, the Judgement card represents an unwillingness to move on.

SEE ALSO
The night sky pp.20–23
Human body pp.112–15
Hands & feet pp.116–19
Greek & Roman deities pp.140–41

WESTERN ASTROLOGY

As a form of divination, western astrology has been traced to Mesopotamia as far back as 3000BCE. Based on the position of the Sun, the Moon, planets, and stars in the sky at the time of a person's birth, and using the symbolic qualities attributed to them, astrologists are able to define a person's personality traits to compile his or her horoscope. They can use the same system to determine that person's fortune in life.

SUN SIGNS

Central to western astrology is the zodiac, which comprises the 12 major star constellations in the ecliptic belt around the Earth—that is, the path of the Sun as it moves through the sky. Referred to by astrologists as "Sun" signs, the zodiac starts with Aries and ends with Pisces, each signifying an approximate four-week period, as it takes the Earth one year to complete its orbit of the Sun. Each sign is represented by a symbol, such as the scales for Libra, and is used to determine a person's fortune. By compiling a horoscope—a chart of the positions of the Sun, Moon, and other planets when a person is born—the major influences in his or her life can be determined, based on the relationships of the celestial bodies to each other.

▲ **Aries**
(March 21 – April 20)
A fire sign with Mars as its ruling planet, Aries is symbolized by the ram. Typical traits include courage, leadership, impetuosity, and enthusiasm.

▲ **Taurus**
(April 21 – May 21)
An earth sign, with ruling planet Venus, Taurus has the bull as its symbol. Typical character traits include loyalty, creativity, and stubbornness.

▲ **Gemini**
(May 22 – June 21)
An air sign, ruled by the planet Mercury, Gemini is represented by twins, which symbolize a dual personality. Typical traits include good communication and acting on impulse.

▲ **Cancer**
(June 22– July 22)
A water sign, with the Moon as its ruling planet, Cancer is symbolized by the crab, whose shell signifies a love of the home. Cancerians are typically secretive and private.

▲ **Leo**
(July 23 – August 23)
A fire sign, with the Sun as its ruling planet, Leo has a lion as its symbol. Typical character traits include a warm and sunny disposition, generosity, and a powerful personality.

▲ **Virgo**
(August 24 – September 23)
An earth sign, with ruling planet Mercury, Virgo is symbolized by the virgin, who represents purity. The typical Virgoan is naturally inquisitive, practical, and fastidious.

▲ **Libra**
(Sepember 24 – October 23)
An air sign, with ruling planet Venus, Libra is symbolized by the scales, which represent balance and harmony. Typical Librans are charming, just, diplomatic, and fair-minded.

▲ **Scorpio**
(October 24 – November 22)
A water sign, ruled by the planet Pluto, Scorpio has the scorpion as its symbol. Traits include curiosity, proneness to jealousy, and a desire to control.

▲ **Sagittarius**
(November 23 – December 21)
A fire sign, with ruling planet Jupiter, Sagittarius has the centaur as its symbol. Typical traits include honesty and an insatiable appetite for learning.

▲ **Capricorn**
(December 22 – January 20)
An earth sign, with ruling planet Saturn, Capricorn is symbolized by the goat. Typical traits include tenacity, intuition, and a tendency to be deliberate.

▲ **Aquarius**
(January 21– February 19)
An air sign, ruled by Saturn, Aquarius is the water bearer symbolic of independence and unpredictability. Aquarians are idealistic and unconventional.

▲ **Pisces**
(February 20 – March 20)
A water sign, with ruling planet Neptune, Pisces is symbolized by a pair of fish. Typical traits include a psychic ability, compassion, and intuition.

MYTHS & RELIGIONS

◀ **Zodiac tapestry**
The importance of astrology in European courts from medieval times to the Renaissance is indicated by this fine zodiac tapestry from Flanders. Astrology was not only part of cultural life but also a branch of learning and a matter of politics.

ASCENDANT AND DESCENDANT

To construct a horoscope, astrologists mark the "ascendant," or rising sign, on the eastern horizon at the time of a person's birth. It signifies his or her childhood and upbringing. Opposite, on the western horizon, astrologists find the "descendant" sign, which symbolizes personal relationships. Once the positions of these two signs have been determined, the remaining ten signs can be entered in the chart to give an even fuller reading.

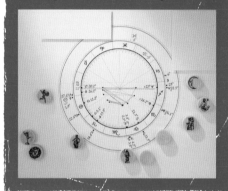

PLANETARY RULERS

Astrologists can determine more about a person and his or her fortune by looking at the positions of the planets at the moment of birth. Each Sun sign has only one planetary ruler, though the same planet may rule more than one Sun sign. Venus, for example, rules both Taurus and Libra. Each planet has its own symbolism, and intensifies a person's major characteristics.

▲ **Sun**
A symbol of masculinity, the Sun represents rulers and fatherhood, power, authority, and self expression.

▲ **Moon**
A symbol of femininity, the Moon signifies motherhood, inner feelings, and links with the past.

▲ **Mars**
A symbol of force and energy, Mars is associated with the head and signifies ambition, drive, and aggression.

▲ **Venus**
A symbol of love and beauty, Venus is linked to the kidneys and signifies relationships, harmony, and cooperation.

▲ **Mercury**
A symbol of communication, Mercury is linked with the nervous system and signifies thought, logic, and education.

▲ **Jupiter**
Signifying expansion, exploration, and a search for knowledge, Jupiter governs the liver.

▲ **Saturn**
Order, responsibility, limitation, and a search for knowledge are linked with Saturn, as is the skin and the skeleton.

▲ **Uranus**
A symbol of rebellion and change, Uranus represents innovation, idealism, and individual freedom.

▲ **Neptune**
A symbol of mysticism, Neptune is linked to dreams and fantasy. It represents spirituality and psychic ability.

▲ **Pluto**
A symbol of transformation, Pluto is associated with regeneration, and represents life, death, and renewal.

SEE ALSO
The Sun *pp.16–17*
The Moon *pp.18–19*
The night sky *pp.20–23*
Chinese horoscope *pp.204–05*

ASTROLOGICAL CHART

The word "astrology" is a Greek term meaning "science of the stars."
The Greek zodiac, the basis of our modern standard zodiac, was adapted
from an earlier Babylonian system. Ancient astronomers identified animals
and mythical characters among the star constellations, some of which later
became the 12 signs of the zodiac. Originally a device for measuring time,
the zodiac was later employed to make predictions. The first known
horoscope using the zodiac "Sun signs" dates from about 410BCE. This
16th-century chart is part of a portolan (a set of navigation charts) and
combines celestial, calendrical, and astrological information, reflecting
the links believed to exist between them.

1. & 2. Zodiac signs and symbols
The 12 signs of the zodiac are derived from the names of
their respective star constellations but they can also
be represented symbolically. Scorpio, for example, can be
depicted as both a scorpion and an arrow sign. The derivation
of the sign is unclear, though some people say it resembles
the sting of the scorpion.

3. The lunar cycle
Each zodiac sign covers a four-week period that relates to the
lunar cycle and because of this it does not equate to the 12
months of the Gregorian calender. Instead each sign includes
parts of two months. Libra, for example, starts on September
24 and finishes on October 23.

4. The planets
The planets are also important in determining a person's
horoscope but at the time this chart was compiled—in the 16th
century—the Universe was not well known. Only a few of the
planets are indicated here and their association with the zodiac
signs is not clear.

Novel interpretation
In 1661 a star atlas called the *Harmonia Microcosmia* was
published that included pictures in which the traditional zodiac
signs had been "christianized." The 12 zodiac signs were
replaced by the 12 apostles and the northern and southern
constellations were substituted with figures from the New
and Old Testaments respectively.

CHINESE HOROSCOPE

The ancient Chinese system of astrology is closely linked to Chinese thought regarding natural science and philosophy. Some 5,000 years old, it is a form of divination based on the path of the celestial bodies, such as the Sun, the Moon, the planets, and comets, through the sky. In its simplest terms any one event, or a person's personality and their destiny, is interpreted depending on an element aspect—wood, earth, fire, air, or water—an animal aspect, and whether these are symbolic of Yin or Yang.

ANIMAL SIGNS

Referred to as the 12 "earthly branches," the animal signs are the most widely recognized symbols of the Chinese horoscope. They relate, not to months, as in Western astrology, but to years, which recur five times in a cycle of 60 years, and are linked to the orbit of Jupiter, which takes 12 years to complete. Each cycle starts at the Chinese New Year in February, which also marks the beginning of the lunar calendar. Starting with the Rat and ending with the Boar, each of the 12 animal signs is symbolic of a different type of personality, specifically those character traits that make up the outward manifestation of a person. Each is also influenced by an element, and by Yin (feminine) or Yang (masculine) qualities.

▲ **Rat**
1960, 1972, 1984, 1996
Ambitious and hard-working, the Rat, which is a Yang sign, is also shy and reserved. Rats are likely to accumulate money.

▲ **Ox**
1961, 1973, 1985, 1997
Dependable, methodical, and patient, but also stubborn, the Ox is a Yin sign. Slow to arouse, feelings nevertheless run deep.

▲ **Tiger**
1962, 1974, 1986, 1998
Impulsive and unpredictable, generous and affectionate, the Tiger is a Yang sign. Tigers take risks, but are usually lucky.

▲ **Rabbit**
1963, 1975, 1987, 1999
Artistic, thoughtful, intelligent and lucky, the Rabbit is a Yin sign. A typical Rabbit often pursues a comfortable lifestyle.

▲ **Dragon**
1964, 1976, 1988, 2000
Strong-willed and fiery, Dragons can also be arrogant and over-bearing. A Yang sign, typical Dragons are usually successful.

▲ **Snake**
1965, 1977, 1989, 2001
Sensual, creative, cautious, and responsible, the Snake is a Yin sign. Snakes may be secretive, self-doubting, and distrustful.

▲ **Horse**
1966, 1978, 1990, 2002
Popular, good-humored, and physically and mentally agile, the Horse is a Yang sign. Typical Horses can be fickle and gullible.

▲ **Sheep**
1967, 1979, 1991, 2003
A Yin sign, Sheep are moody, indecisive, and easily hurt, but are also popular, understanding, and compassionate.

▲ **Monkey**
1968, 1980, 1992, 2004
Inquisitive, inventive, and quick-witted, the Monkey, a Yang sign, can be competitive, conceited, and suspicious.

▲ **Rooster**
1969, 1981, 1993, 2005
A Yin sign, the typical Rooster is disciplined and a good organizer. Roosters can be eccentric, but are usually witty.

▲ **Dog**
1970, 1982, 1994, 2006
Honest, loyal, and affectionate, the Dog is a Yang sign. The typical Dog can also be cynical and inflexible.

▲ **Boar**
1971, 1983, 1995, 2007
Sociable, loyal, and reliable, the Boar is a Yin sign. Typical Boars are passionate in nature, but can be naive and self-indulgent.

FIVE ELEMENTS

Referred to as the ten "heavenly stems," the elements metal, wood, earth, fire, and water play a significant role in Chinese astrology. Each of the five elements is repeated—once in a Yin mode and then again in Yang for every month over a 60-year cycle, starting with Wood (Yang) Rat and ending with Water (Yin) Boar. These elements are not fixed to a particular animal, as there are two more animal signs than Yin and Yang elements in each year. Four of the five elements (metal, wood, fire, and water) are also linked to the hour and year of birth. In this context, the elements are unchanging with regard to the animal sign they represent.

▲ Chinese zodiac wheel
The symbols for Yin and Yang, signifying perfect balance, are at the center of this zodiac wheel. Around the outside are the 12 animal signs, which are also identified by their Chinese characters. The four-colored ring in between signifies the fixed element for that animal sign. For example, Fire is associated with the color red and rules the Snake, the Horse, and the Sheep.

▲ Wood
Signifying the planet Jupiter, the east, and the color green, Wood is linked with the gall bladder and liver. Typical characteristics include a warm and generous disposition.

▲ Fire
Representing Mars, the south, and the color red, Fire is linked with the heart and circulatory system. Typical characteristics include a competitive and energetic nature.

▲ Earth
Representing the planet Saturn, the center, and the color yellow, Earth is linked to both the stomach and the spleen. Typical characteristics include ambition, tenacity, and reliability.

▲ Metal
Symbolic of the planet Venus, the west, and the color white, Metal is associated with the lungs. Typical characteristics include a determined and self-reliant nature.

◀ Water
Symbolic of the planet Mercury, the north, and the color black, Water is associated with the digestive system. Typical characteristics include compassion, intellect, and creativity.

INNER AND SECRET SIGNS

A person's characteristics comprise outer signs, inner signs, and secret signs. The outer signs are those determined by the year in which a person is born, described as the person's "outer animal" (*see left*). The same person's "inner animal" is determined by the month of birth, according to the Chinese agricultural calendar, which divides the year into 12 approximate four-week periods. Using the 12 animal signs, the inner animal symbolizes a person's inner feelings and relationships. The "secret animal" is determined by the hour of birth, again signified by the animal signs—this is held to be that person's true manifestation.

SEE ALSO
Fire *pp.30–31*
Water *pp.32–33*
Mammals *pp.52–55*
Snakes *pp.66–67*
Taoism & Shinto *pp.170–71*
Western astrology *pp.200–03*
Alphabets *pp.306–09*

NUMEROLOGY

Through the ages many different civilizations have used numerology to explain the past and foretell the future. It featured in Ancient Chinese divination, for example, with the "magic square," which has also been associated with Ancient Egyptian and Indian divination. Other nations, including the Ancient Greeks, Jews, and Babylonians, developed systems of digit summing, adding together particular number sequences, such as the four digits in a particular year. Various forms of numerology continue to be in use today. The basis of numerology, whatever the system, is the idea that each number from 1 to 9 has it own symbolic meaning, which can then be interpreted to define a person's major characteristics, to explain specific events in the past, or to predict events in the future. In some practices 11 and 22 are also significant, and intensify the symbolism.

ADDING DIGITS TOGETHER

One of the most widely used forms of numerology today is that of adding digits together to arrive at one single significant number. The simplest method is to add together the digits that make up a person's date of birth. For example, December 2, 1984 is calculated as follows: 0+2+1+2+1+9+8+4 = 27. These two numbers are then added together to give a single digit as follows, 2 + 7 = 9. Similarly, summing July 17, 1941 yields a significant figure of 3. The Ancient Greek philosopher, Pythagoras, applied the same principle to the letters of the alphabet, where A = 1, B = 2, and so on. Again, when the letters reach double figures, as for Z (26), they are added together giving, in this case, an 8 (see full alphabet/numbers below). Following this system it is possible to assess any important set of numbers or words in a person's life, to give greater meaning to the events and circumstances that influence it.

A	B	C	D	E	F	G	H	I
1	2	3	4	5	6	7	8	9

J	K	L	M	N	O	P	Q	R
1	2	3	4	5	6	7	8	9

S	T	U	V	W	X	Y	Z
1	2	3	4	5	6	7	8

THE MAGIC SQUARE

Magic squares have held a symbolic significance for a number of civilizations, the most recognizable of which originated in Ancient Chinese mythology and is called Lo Shu. Here a square to the order of three—that is with three rows and three columns—contains the digits 1 to 9 arranged in such a way that the sum of each row, column, and diagonal comes to 15 (referred to as the "magic constant"). Other nations have been known to apply the same principle using different numbers or larger squares, resulting in different magic constants.

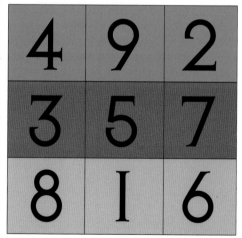

▲ Lo Shu
The numerical value of the Lo Shu was derived from *I Ching*, there being a symbolic link between the three lines of a trigram and the rows of figures in the square. The colors are also symbolic. From left to right green represents intellect, reasoning, and judgement; purple emotions, feelings, and intuitions; and orange life, finance, and business.

WHAT THE NUMBERS MEAN

Based on date of birth and/or the letters of a name, a person may discover that he or she has a series of significant numbers in his or her life, each with its own symbolism. The numbers reveal information about a person's character as well as his or her talents, aims, and motivations. Some numbers may recur, in which case their significance is intensified. There are no good or bad numbers, but each number has both positive and negative qualities in equal measure, which can be expressed as a person's strengths and weaknesses respectively.

Once numbers have been identified as potentially having a negative influence on a person, their effects can be tempered or blocked by his or her subsequent actions. For example, he or she can work to control certain character tendencies and has a choice in how his or her various abilities are used. In some cases, the symbolism of a given number may already be evident in a person's life, or be something that will manifest itself later on.

1

▲ **Creativity and Confidence**
The number 1 represents a creative spirit, a strong sense of individuality, and courage or determination. If blocked, the same number can symbolize addictive behaviour, aggression, or a dominating force.

2

▲ **Cooperation and Balance**
This number represents an ability to adapt and to work with others—the 2 is a symbol of partnership—as well as being a skilled mediator. If blocked, the same number can represent a shy and self-conscious nature.

3

▲ **Expression and Sensitivity**
The number 3 represents self-expression, either verbally or creatively, and an inspiration to others. If blocked, great optimism and a fun-loving nature give way to harsh criticism and moodiness.

4

▲ **Stability and Progress**
This number represents the building of a solid foundation on which to move forward, good organizational skills, and an ability to manage. If blocked, the same number can symbolize inflexibility and an inability in a person to progress.

5

▲ **Freedom and Discipline**
The number 5 represents a versatile and expansive nature with a tendency to act quickly in any given situation. If blocked, the number can symbolize an impatient and restless nature.

6

▲ **Vision and Acceptance**
This number represents beauty, purity, high ideals, and a well-balanced, unselfish disposition. If blocked, the number 6 can symbolize an obstinate, domineering nature and a tendency to be judgemental.

7

▲ **Trust and Openness**
The number 7 represents uniqueness, a desire to learn, a scientific mind, and a tendency toward perfection. If blocked, a person's natural charm may give way to aloofness, and a sarcastic and derisory nature.

8

◀ **Abundance and Power**
This number signifies a strong sense of authority, an ability to make decisions, and forcefulness. If blocked, a natural work ethic can give way to over-ambition, mismanagement, and an abuse of power.

9

◀ **Integrity and Wisdom**
The number 9 represents natural charisma, good leadership qualities, and a certain selflessness. If blocked, the number can symbolize a negative, possessive nature, and lack of direction.

SEE ALSO
Taoism & Shinto pp.170–71
Divination pp.196–99
Numbers pp.294–97

NUMEROLOGY

▲ **The Grail and the Round Table**
The French poet Robert de Boron made the
quest for the Grail a central theme in the
legends of King Arthur and his Knights of
the Round Table. His Grail is that of Joseph
of Arimathea, who is said to have brought
the cup from the Last Supper to England.

THE HOLY GRAIL

A potent symbol of Christian mythology, with origins in medieval storytelling, the Holy Grail signifies the ultimate goal, a quest for immortality, and a deep-rooted spirituality.

▲ Gundestrup cauldron
In Celtic mythology the cauldron represents the cosmic center of all things.

A recurring feature in medieval art and literature, the Holy Grail has been described variously as a bowl, a chalice, or a plate. For centuries it has fascinated people, some of whom have themselves tried to discover its exact location and meaning. For many, however, the word "grail" is more a symbolic concept than a physical object.

NATURE OF THE GRAIL

Symbolically, the origins of the Holy Grail are thought to have an association with the cauldron of Celtic mythology. Central to pagan ritual, the cauldron is a symbol of fertility and abundance. In some stories the Grail is described as a wish-fulfilling plate or dish; in others it has powers of divination, not unlike the oracles of Greek mythology; in others still it is an object made of stone. By medieval times it was widely accepted as being the bowl or cup from which Christ drank at the Last Supper and in which Joseph of Arimathea caught Christ's blood as he hung on the cross, making the quest to find it a spiritual one. Central to some of the Grail legends is the cup's association with a lance that drips blood, which is symbolic of the piercing of Christ's side. Whatever form the Grail takes in these stories, this is always of less importance than what the Grail signifies— in essence, the quest for a higher truth.

▲ Joseph of Arimathea
The Holy Grail has inextricable links to the blood of Christ and this has imbued the Grail with a deep, spiritual symbolism.

THE QUEST FOR THE GRAIL

Popular stories of the Holy Grail include the medieval accounts of Percival the lowly Welshman, and the legends of the Knights of King Arthur's Round Table. Such is the nature of the Grail in these stories that it can only be attained by the most pure, noble, and worthy of men. Each protagonist embarks on a long and challenging journey of self-discovery in which he is put to the test a number of times. It is only at the point of enlightenment that he is able to attain the Grail. As such, the Grail is a symbol of absolute truth and goodness, and the finder's reward is perpetual youth and abundance.

MODERN CONTROVERSY

A more recent theory is based on the French translation of Holy Grail—*San Greal*. Moving just one letter changes the meaning to "royal blood" (*sang real*), leading to the idea that the Holy Grail was symbolic of Mary Magdalene's womb and that she married Christ and bore him children—the "blood of Christ" therefore signifying his bloodline. Revived in Dan Brown's *The Da Vinci Code* in 2003, the theory has prompted much discussion and, although rejected by serious historians, is testimony to our lasting fascination with the Holy Grail.

► The Last Supper
The symbolism in Leonardo da Vinci's painting has been much debated, not least the gender of the person sitting to the right of Jesus. Most historians identify the figure as John, the apostle, but the idea put forward in *The Da Vinci Code* has led to some renewed speculation that it is Mary Magdalene.

SEE ALSO
Christianity *pp.176–79*
Witches & wicca *pp.192–93*
The home *pp.238–41*

ALCHEMY

Developed in Europe during medieval times, western alchemy was influenced by practices both in Ancient Egypt and Mesopotamia. Essentially an attempt to turn base metals into gold or silver, alchemy also has a deep symbolic significance for those who practice it: transforming a metal into gold would signify a change from something impure to pure. As such it is symbolic of a spiritual journey for the alchemist, from ignorance to enlightenment.

ALCHEMIC SYMBOLISM

Alchemists used planetary signs, such as Sun and Moon, to represent some alchemic symbols, but during medieval times, fearful of persecution, they invented their own complex vocabulary of signs to record and pass on their knowledge. Because of this secrecy, alchemy became associated with fraud and extortion, which detracted from some of the scientific discoveries made.

Heavenly symbols surrounded by faces of angels

Distinct division between Heaven and Earth

Phoenix holding fire and air

Eagle holding Earth and water

▲ **The Opus Medico Chymicum**
This illustration, taken from the 1618 *Opus Medico Chymicum*, shows the four elements (earth, water, air, and fire), as well as other alchemic symbols, such as the king, queen, Moon, eagle, lion, and phoenix.

THE QUEST FOR GOLD

The alchemist's quest for gold was symbolic of his desire for spirituality. In order to achieve this, an alchemist had to find what is referred to as the "philosopher's stone." Actual stone or dry red powder, this substance was said to have various mystic qualities and was integral to the process of turning base metal into gold. Sometimes called the "elixir of youth," the philosopher's stone signifies purity and immortality, and brings a conclusion to the alchemist's "Great Work."

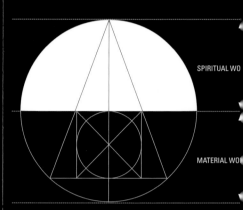

SPIRITUAL WO

MATERIAL WO

▲ **Philosopher's Stone**
This complex symbol represents the philosopher's stone and embodies a number of key principles relating to alchemy, among them a triangle signifying the three heavenly substances (salt, sulfur, and mercury) and a square representing the four elements. The circle symbolizes the philosophical concept that "all is one."

◄ **Seal of Solomon**
The seal of Solomon is a six-pointed star that features in various faiths, most notably Judaism. In combining the symbols for fire and water, it signifies the union of opposites and final transmutation of alchemical processes.

◄ **Sun and Moon symbols**
Used to represent gold, the Sun symbol was the sign of perfection for alchemists. The dot at the center signifies completion of the "Great Work." Used to represent silver, and called the "Lesser Work," the Moon symbol signifies intuition, fertility, and the body as opposed to the Sun's soul.

SUN

MOON

MYTHS & RELIGIONS

▲ Earth symbol
One of the four elements of alchemy, earth represents the dry and cold aspects of the process. It symbolizes birth and creation and is associated with the metal copper.

▲ Water symbol
Second of the four elements of alchemy, water represents the cold and moist stages of the process. It symbolizes the process of purification and is associated with the metal tin.

▲ Air symbol
Third of the four elements of alchemy, air represents the hot and moist stages of the process. It symbolizes the breath of life and is associated with the metal iron.

▶ Fire symbol
Last of the four elements of alchemy, fire signifies the hot and dry stages of the process. It is associated with the metal lead and symbolizes the final transformation.

▲ Sulfur symbol
Sulfur is one of the three heavenly substances that make up base matter. Its dry, fiery force reacts with the fluidity of mercury and is symbolic of the desire to achieve a higher spirituality. Sulfur was sometimes linked with masculine qualities, as opposed to the feminine qualities of mercury.

▲ Mercury symbol
Along with salt and sulfur, mercury is one of the three heavenly substances. Its fluidity represents the transition from base metal into gold and is symbolic of the union between the spiritual and the material.

▲ Alchemic illustrations
This watercolor taken from the alchemic text *Splendor Solis*, published in 1598, includes the colors black, white, red, and gold, which have symbolic implications. Black, for example, represents the first stage of the process, which then moves through various processes, represented by white, then red until it reaches the end product, gold.

THE ANIMALS

A number of animals feature in alchemy, each imbued with its own symbolism. The four elements, for example, are represented by animals—the eagle (air), lion (earth), fish (water), and dragon (fire). Animals are also used to represent each stage of the alchemical process, starting with the blackening (crow or raven) and ending with the final product (phoenix).

▲ Phoenix
By laying its egg in the ashes before dying in the flames, the phoenix symbolizes the last stage of the alchemical process—the change into gold and philosophical perfection.

▲ Uroborus
Forming a circle, the uroborus is a serpent eating its own tail. As such, it symbolizes continuity and immortality, as well as the alchemical principle that "one is all."

▲ Caduceus
Signifying a union of opposites as symbolized by mercury and sulfur, the rod of the caduceus represents the power of transformation, while the wings symbolize the balance that results from the process.

▲ Green lion
Representing green vitriol, a highly corrosive liquid used in many alchemical processes, the lion in green form is shown here swallowing the Sun. It is symbolic of the end product of the alchemical process—gold.

◀ Eagle
Symbolizing the transmutation of base metal into gold, and therefore the death of the impure and the birth of the pure, the eagle with its wings outstretched represents the air and mercury to the lion's earth and sulfur.

SEE ALSO
Gold *pp.44–45*
Precious matter *pp.46–47*
Eagles *pp.62–63*
Fabulous beasts *pp.74–77*
Shapes *pp.284–89*

ALCHEMY

211

SOCIETY & CULTURE

Symbols lie at the very heart of our social and cultural identity. They may be drawn from nature or man-made, be animate or inanimate, and may take many different forms, ranging from images to rituals and storytelling. Symbols serve a vital function because they help to bind us together, creating a common codified system that reflects status, nationality, cultural activities, and much more.

In some ancient civilizations rulers were identified with the gods—and in some countries this reverence remains, as in Japan and Thailand. Royalty and its ceremonial pomp and regalia are steeped in a symbolism that serves to elevate and enhance, setting the ruler apart from his or her subjects.

Nationality is an obvious means of grouping people together and this is enhanced by the use of common culture and national symbols. These icons might take the form of animals or birds, such as the New Zealand kiwi, flags, postage stamps, or even dates that celebrate historic events, such as Britain's Guy Fawkes Night.

From earliest times, the aspirations of every culture and society have been expressed through its architecture. From ancient Classical buildings celebrating the might of the empire to the heavenly symbolism represented by the spires and domes of churches and mosques, architects have created buildings that make a universal visual statement. Ordinary buildings may seem purely functional by comparison but they, too, are associated with deeply held beliefs about home and hearth. Womb-like and feminine, the home stands for sanctuary and security, its walls keeping the outside world firmly at bay. Stairs are linked with the ascent to spiritual enlightenment, while windows are the "eye of the soul," letting in the light of truth.

THE NEED TO
BELONG IS
FUNDAMENTAL
TO ALL HUMAN
SOCIETIES AND
ENHANCES
OUR SENSE
OF CULTURAL
IDENTITY

Such symbolism is commonly associated with religious buildings. Every culture also has symbolically sacred places, which may be man-made, such as Britain's Stonehenge, or natural, such as India's River Ganges.

In common with homes, gardens are regarded as havens but they also represent myriad other ideals, from signs of status to a Paradise on Earth where the gardener is the creator figure. Other seemingly random items, such as tools and weapons, assume significance symbolically when linked to politics, religion, or folklore. Cultural activities, such as music, dance, and theater, have their roots in ancient times, while fairy tales, handed down through the generations, are variously associated with religion, psychology, or the cosmos.

Clothing and costume reflect various aspects of our society and culture, including nationality, job, religion, personality, aspirations, and status. Western dress is heavily influenced by fashion, but people worldwide still wear traditional styles that are imbued with symbolism, such as the Indian sari.

Jewelry has always been a sign of status as well as the identifying mark of a tribe, while body adornment is traditionally associated with tribal, military, or religious communities. The need to belong is fundamental to all human societies and enhances our sense of cultural identity. Whether it is by birth, group affiliation, or religion, "membership" is symbolized by clothing, rituals, celebrations, and cultural icons—all ties that bind people together.

ROYALTY

Ruling elites of ancient civilizations were revered as gods living on Earth. In Egypt only gods, kings, and queens were allowed to carry the powerful ankh symbol, or "sign of life," which bestowed on them the right to give or take away life. Even today certain royalty are still revered—King Bhumibol Adulyadej of Thailand, the longest serving monarch ever, is revered as the country's "guiding light." Rituals and symbols of statehood continue there, as they do in the world's 30 other monarchies.

LOUIS XIV

▲ Queen
The queen is a compelling symbol of power and femininity. Queen Elizabeth I was adept at cultivating her public image. Her numerous portraits combined assured majesty with varying symbols of chastity, wealth, and peace.

▲ King and queen
The combined rule of a king and queen, as with King William III and Queen Mary II shown here, symbolizes balance and harmony. This commemorative plate of 1689 (with symbolic crowns and ermine) celebrates their ascension.

▲ Pharaoh
Tutankhamen was worshiped as a god and intermediary between Earth and Heaven. His mask is gold because the flesh of the gods was thought to be golden. The blue-striped gold head cloth reflects the royal color of truth and noble birth.

▲ ► King
Monarchs were once seen as earthly counterparts of God. The ceremony ascribed to kings still holds power in many countries, and the regalia of crowns, orbs, scepters, and thrones keep the symbolism alive. Coinage and medals also perpetuate the cult of kings, as with this bronze medallion of French "Sun King" Louis XIV (*above*), who claimed to rule by "Divine Right." The Oba ("king") of Benin (*right*) was considered a divine being descended from a god. Like the leopards he held, he was feared and respected.

OBA KING OF BENIN

POWER GAMES

Card games and the ancient game of chess use representations of royalty and the court—including kings, queens, and armies—in a symbolic playing out of the conflict between opposing forces. The object of a game is to build up an unassailable power base to trump (overcome) one's opponents, or to defeat them by destroying their armies.

▲ Chess
Popular since medieval times, chess represents a battle between kings, queens, and their supporting "pieces" and "men." The term "checkmate" comes from the Arabic meaning "the king is dead."

◄ Cards
Playing cards developed with "court" ranks and highly symbolic images of royalty, especially in 16th-century France. Representations of the jack (formerly the knave), queen, and king appear often with full-length ermine robes, orbs, crown, and swords—making them the most iconic "royals."

► Emperor

In China and Japan the emperor was believed to be the son of Heaven, a symbol of moral order who maintained harmony between Heaven and Earth. One of the most famous of these rulers was Qin Shi Huangdi, who became China's First Emperor in 221BCE. At his tomb, outside the city of Xi'an, over 8,000 life-size terracotta soldiers were buried to serve him as symbolic guards in the afterlife.

▲ Empress

An empress represents creation and growth, and carries symbols of royalty. In Ethiopia there was traditionally a king of kings, known to Europeans as an emperor. However, Empress Zewditu of Ethiopia was the "Queen of Kings" and ruled from 1916 to 1930. She was the first woman head of an internationally recognized state in modern Africa, but she held conservative values.

◄ Prince and princess

Both in fable and reality, the prince and princess represent an archetypal hero and heroine. They are often depicted as the young royals-in-waiting, having to overcome obstacles to their alliance and succession. The handsome prince battles fearsome foes and magical obstacles in his quest to rescue his princess. She in her turn endures cruel confinement stoically and embodies beauty with moral courage.

▲ The Fool

Under the guise of entertainer, the fool or jester could joke at his king's expense—and get away with it. The fool was kept at court for luck and to ward off the evil eye. The multicolored and patched costume—motley—symbolized the fool's eccentricity.

KNIGHTS

Warriors on horseback, knights provided troops and tithes for their king. Symbolically, whether a samurai or a Knight of St. George, knights represented chivalry. This embodied extreme courteousness towards women ("courtly love"), but also to their enemies. Attaining to these ideals became formalized in religious and regal ceremonies, including knighting.

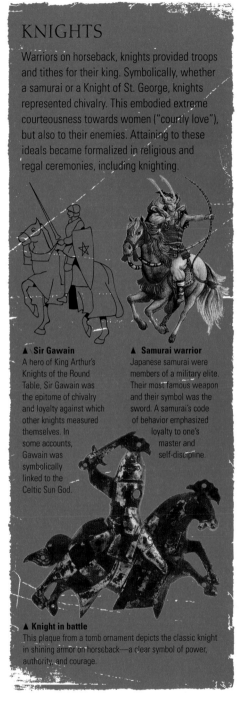

▲ Sir Gawain

A hero of King Arthur's Knights of the Round Table, Sir Gawain was the epitome of chivalry and loyalty against which other knights measured themselves. In some accounts, Gawain was symbolically linked to the Celtic Sun God.

▲ Samurai warrior

Japanese samurai were members of a military elite. Their most famous weapon and their symbol was the sword. A samurai's code of behavior emphasized loyalty to one's master and self-discipline.

▲ Knight in battle

This plaque from a tomb ornament depicts the classic knight in shining armor on horseback—a clear symbol of power, authority, and courage.

SEE ALSO
The Sun *pp.16–17*
Trappings of royalty *pp.218–19*
Tools & weapons *pp.224–25*

TRAPPINGS OF ROYALTY

To affirm their exalted status, rulers have always surrounded themselves with grand accoutrements of office. The symbolic ceremonies of coronations, as well as state functions with processions, banquets, and royal guards, see monarchs draped in finery and jewels as they sit on ornate thrones. These and other trappings of royalty enforce the symbolism of the ruler as a being above ordinary people and in some cases divine or semi-divine.

REGALIA

The emblems and insignia of royalty, known as regalia, are symbolic "props" that lend an "otherworldliness" to a monarch's earthly powers. The crown—be it jewel-encrusted adornment or vibrant plumed headdress—is the quintessential physical and figurative regal symbol.

CROWN OF THE HOLY ROMAN EMPIRE

EGYPTIAN DOUBLE CROWN

► Scepter
The ornamental rod or staff carried by rulers on ceremonial occasions is an emblem of authority and sovereign power. It may have evolved from a lance without the metal point to evoke continued supreme power in peace time. This bejeweled scepter was presented by the French to the 18th-century Chinese Emperor Qianlong.

▲ Fly whisk
Symbols of chiefly ranks, especially in Africa, Asia, and the Pacific, fly whisks were once believed to be held by deities. Tutankhamen had a gold-covered fly whisk with ostrich feathers.

◄ Orb
Representing the cosmos to Ancient Romans, the cross was added in medieval times to symbolize a world under Christian rule. It represents a feminine motif balancing the scepter's male symbolism.

GREAT WHITE UMBRELLA OF STATE

LIBATION VESSEL

▲ Crown
As lords over the "double" land of Upper and Lower Egypt, Egyptian pharaohs were often depicted wearing a double crown (*above*). The Holy Roman Emperor's crown (*top*) was heavy with Christian symbolism, such as the arches representing the vaults of Heaven.

▲ Thai Royal Regalia
Under the Great White Umbrella of State, which symbolizes the king himself, Bhumibol Adulyadej was crowned King of Thailand on June 9, 1946. Regal utensils, including a gold vessel, symbol of both royalty and divinity, were placed by his throne during the ceremony.

ROYAL ARMS AND SEALS

Coats of arms, also called armorial bearings, identified a particular ruler or knight in medieval times. Whether depicted on shields, armor, surcoats, or flags, the various emblems all added up to a status symbol, and the royal arms were the ultimate power signal. Seals and signets bearing the royal arms were embossed in hot wax on documents and letters to authenticate ownership and ensure privacy. Royal seals may also bear a depiction of the monarch. In the days when the majority of people could not read or write, such seals provided an easily understood sign of a king's approval.

Helm

▲ Royal Arms
This coat of arms symbolically represents England, Scotland, Wales, and Ireland with animals, mythical creatures, plants, instruments, and inscriptions. With the helm displayed beneath the crown (*left*), the Royal Arms represent the monarch herself. Without the helm (*right*), they represent the United Kingdom in courtrooms and embassies.

▲ Seal of King Edward III
Royal seals often depict the monarch enthroned, but Edward III's (1327–1377) shows him on horseback to reflect his military successes against the French.

THRONES

The throne is an iconic symbol of the power, stability, and splendor of the ruler sitting on it. Thrones were seats of the gods in Ancient Greek times, and are still often raised on a dais ("platform") for greater impact. The throne is usually placed at the center of the palace, representing the centre of the cosmos. Today it is not just a symbol but part of the language of royalty; the term "Throne" refers to a ruler. The Peacock Throne, for example, refers to the former Persian or Iranian monarchy, while a monarch "dethroned" has lost his or her power.

▲ Lion Throne
The 180-year-old Great Lion Throne of the Burmese kings was raised on a dais to lift the king literally and symbolically above the heads of his subjects.

► Ivory Throne
The Ivory Throne was created for Ivan the Terrible, crowned first Tsar of Russia in 1547. It is shaped as a high-backed chair adorned with ivory and walrus bone. Some of its decorative plaques have biblical themes, including scenes from the life of King David, who symbolized the ideal ruler.

PALACES

As residence of the ruler, a palace symbolizes Heaven and the heart of a realm. Whatever their construction—timber, marble, or stone—palaces reflect the grandest architecture and materials of their time and location, and thereby reflect the grand designs of the patron. The interiors, usually stuffed with royal gifts and purchases, say "look at my unrivalled wealth and taste." However, some of the many rooms of a palace may hold treasures representing spiritual truths.

► The Forbidden City
The symmetry and the relative placing of buildings in Beijing's Forbidden City are in imitation of the Buddhist and Hindu cosmos. Palaces, temples, and homes all face south, the direction of smiling fortune. Some 100,000 symbols of imperial power adorn the walled enclave to ensure Heaven's blessing.

▲ The Palace of Versailles
One of the grandest European palaces was built by Louis XIV, the "Sun King," in the 17th century, at a time of political turmoil. Vastly expensive both to build and maintain, Versailles became the seat of his court and also a symbol of regal opulence.

SEE ALSO
The Sun *pp.16–17*
Coronations *pp.220–21*
Heraldic emblems *pp.318–23*

▲ **Coronation dress**

To symbolize her role as Queen of the Commonwealth, Norman Hartnell's design for Elizabeth II's coronation dress incorporated the emblems of its member countries, including the Tudor rose of England, the Scottish thistle, the Welsh leek, and the shamrock of Ireland, along with the wattle of Australia, the maple leaf of Canada, the New Zealand fern, South Africa's protea, lotus flowers for India and Ceylon (Sri Lanka), and wheat, cotton, and jute for Pakistan. The motifs were embroidered in silks, pearls, diamonds, amethysts, and crystals.

CORONATIONS

In magnificent and solemn coronations, ritual objects, from carriages to crown jewels, become codified signals that symbolically announce the ruler's powers in the land and indeed to a divine power.

The most symbolic ceremony to recognize a new king, queen, or emperor—and so set the seal on the state—is a coronation. They are grand occasions full of pomp and circumstance. Massive symbolism is carried not only in the ritual itself, but clearly in the objects worn, carried, displayed, or sat upon to legitimize the new rule. These objects may be used to anoint or baptize the king, such as sacred shells or horns, or ampullas, or carried, as with the crown, scepter, and orb of Byzantine and western worlds. The throne remains the essential coronation symbol in almost all civilizations. European rituals and objects developed between the 9th and 15th centuries kept the sacred kingship symbolism going, especially through the coronation ceremonies of The Holy Roman Empire and the Papacy.

▲ Gold state coach
Queen Elizabeth II rides to her coronation in the gold state coach, used by British monarchs since 1762. On the roof of the carriage cherubs representing England, Scotland, and Ireland support the royal crown.

QUEEN ELIZABETH II

Queen Elizabeth II's world-televised coronation on June 2, 1953, continued many of the symbols and codes of sacred legitimation of kings and retained the ritual of previous coronations. The Queen was taken from Buckingham Palace to Westminster Abbey in a gold state coach with palm trees at the corners, each rising from a lion's head and loaded with

◀ Crown jewels
The British Crown Jewels are royal ornaments only used in the actual ceremony of coronation as symbols of sacred and temporal authority. Britain is the only European monarchy still using its regalia for the consecration ceremony of crowning the sovereign.

trophies symbolizing the victories of Great Britain in the Seven Years War (1756–1763). Taking place in Westminster Abbey, the coronation is a symbol of the sovereign's earthly and spiritual responsibility, and suggests God's blessing on a reign, an echo of the ancient belief in the divine right of kings.

In an act symbolic of the merging of religious and temporal authority, Elizabeth was then presented by the Archbishop of Canterbury, primate of all England, to the congregation as the legitimate heir to the throne. Having taken the oath of allegiance, the sovereign was dressed in a simple white linen robe, symbolic of purity, and anointed with holy oil poured into an anointing spoon from an eagle-shaped ampulla, the eagle symbolizing royalty. Following the anointing, the monarch was presented with three swords, symbols of mercy, power, and justice, with which she was charged to "distribute justice equally and to protect the Holy Church of God." As well as monarch, Elizabeth was also invested as "Defender of the Faith" and handed the orb, a symbol of the world under Christ. Each item of royal regalia reinforced the sacred nature of her new role.

▲ Royal symbols
Elizabeth II dressed in coronation robes and wearing the Imperial State Crown. The orb and scepter symbolize the Church's authority and the sovereign's duty as Defender of the Faith.

SEE ALSO
Eagles *pp.62–63*
Royalty *pp.216–17*
Trappings of royalty *pp.218–19*

NATIONALITY

Through origin, birth, or naturalization we belong to a specific nation or people. Our national identity is derived from a common culture, language, and history, and outwardly reflected by familiar icons. Whether these icons are statues, dance forms, or folk heroes, we readily latch on to them for their symbolic significance. Fifty years ago there were 82 independent countries, but by the start of the 21st century there were 194. Nationality is important to us and shared symbols reinforce our sense of belonging.

◄ Great Seal of the French Republic
The Seal of France, dating from the fall of the monarchy in 1848, shows the goddess Juno representing liberty. She wears the same crown and robes as America's Statue of Liberty (*see below*). She holds an ancient symbol of civic authority, called a fasces. The figure is surrounded by symbolic objects, including a wheat sheaf (agriculture) and a cog wheel (industry).

▲ Coat of arms
The Norwegian coat of arms depicts a crowned lion holding an axe, symbolizing strength, justic, and royalty. (Norway has a king as head of state.) The orb with cross symbolizes the country's Evangelical Lutheran religion.

▲ Stamps
On British postage stamps a portrait of the reigning monarch represents national identity. Since Britain introduced prepaid postage in 1840, it has remained the only nation in the world that does not identify its stamps by country name.

▲ Monuments
Located in New York Harbor, where transatlantic immigrants first glimpsed their new land, the 151ft (46m) Statue of Liberty holds a torch and tablet representing safety and liberty, and highlighting America as "the light of the world."

▲ Memorials
The General Grant Tree is the only "living" national shrine commemorating the men and women of the United States who have given their lives in service to their country. Each year at Christmas, park rangers place a large wreath at the base of this giant sequoia.

▲ Music and dance
A country's traditional music and dance reflect national character. Flamenco is a classic example, symbolizing through the frenetic and complex footwork, hand clapping, and virtuoso guitar the passion, excitement, and spirit of Spain.

SOCIETY & CULTURE

Bulldog dressed as John Bull, an icon of Britishness since the 1700s

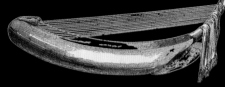

▼ Burmese boat-shaped harp
This highly decorated and arched *saung gauk* ("harp") is regarded as a musical symbol of Burma. The *saung gauk*, which is of very ancient origin, was once referred to as the "voice of the Buddha."

► British bulldog
The bulldog became symbolically linked with British "doggedness" after Winston Churchill and the nation withstood Nazi agression in World War II.

◄ National hero
Nationality is often embodied in its heroes and heroines, real or imagined. Robin Hood "who stole from the rich to give to the poor" became an English icon of freedom for the oppressed, through medieval poetry and minstrel songs, as well as dramatizations in modern-day plays, TV shows, and movies.

BIRDS AND ANIMALS AS NATIONAL SYMBOLS

Most countries have adopted an animal or a bird as an emblem to represent them symbolically, chosen for its strength, beauty, speed, courage, or uniqueness—the Bald Eagle of the United States, for example, or the kangaroo of Australia.

▲ New Zealand kiwi
The kiwi is native only to New Zealand and so has become an emblem of the country. It is emblazoned on the national rugby team's shirts.

▲ Guy Fawkes night
Each November 5, Britain symbolically remembers Guy Fawkes and the 1605 Gunpowder Plot with bonfire and firework displays. Fawkes was part of a Catholic effort to topple the Protestant monarchy. After the plot was foiled, Englishmen were taught "remember remember the 5th of November" to be vigilant in the defence of the realm.

▼ The white elephant of Thailand
In Thailand the white elephant is venerated. The "order of the white elephant" is one of the highest honors bestowed by the king, and a white elephant appears on the flag of the Royal Thai Navy.

◄ Thanksgiving Day
The "turkey and all the trimmings" at the centerpiece of Thanksgiving dinner is today deeply entrenched in American tradition. The meal is symbolically linked to the Pilgrims' desire to celebrate a good harvest in 1621 with a feast, having landed at Plymouth Rock in 1620.

◄ Coat of Arms of the Bahamas
The colorful Bahamian coat of arms has a conch above a shield containing a flamingo, the national bird, and a marlin, symbolizing the island's abundant sealife. The *Santa Maria*, the flagship of Christopher Columbus, appears on the shield.

▲ Russian bear
The Russian bear is a metaphor as well as an anthropomorphic symbol of the nation. It has been used as a caricature since Napoleonic times to depict Russia's size and strength.

SEE ALSO
Mammals *pp.52–55*
Clothing & costume *pp.248–49*
Group affiliation *pp.258–59*
Heraldic emblems *pp.318–23*
Flags *pp.324–29*

TOOLS & WEAPONS

Designed to make or mend, or to kill or maim, tools and weapons have been the ultimate purpose-built objects since the Stone Age. Yet although they are essentially practical objects, both have always had tremendous symbolic significance when linked to religion, folklore, and politics. Weapons and tools can help to identify the gods, in whose hands they may symbolize power, protection, or destruction. Some tools, such as the sickle, represent both death and life.

▲ Hammer and sickle
Workers and peasants were united by the symbol of a hammer and sickle laid across each other—or so the Communists believed when they chose this composite emblem of manual labor in the 1920s.

▲ Ax
Since Neanderthal man could wield an ax, this tool has symbolized power and authority. Axes have always been closely linked to the elements—as conductors of thunderbolts and protectors of crops.

◄ Thor's Hammer
An Ancient Nordic symbol, the hammer of Nordic god Thor holds power over thunder (the repetitive pounding) and lightning. Its Nordic name, *mjolnir*, means lightning. The magical hammer was always on target and always returned after being thrown. Miniature *mjolnirs* were popular Viking amulets, and rivaled the Christian cross.

▲ Scythe
The most recognizable symbol of mortality is the Grim Reaper with his scythe, ready to "harvest" the souls of the dead. The hourglass held in the other hand symbolizes Father Time cut short.

▲ Shield
Both practical and symbolic as a protector, the shield has feminine overtones of chastity as well as power, as with the Greek goddess Athena. A decorated shield can also be an advertisement of status.

▲ Bow and arrow
The bow and arrow together represent hunting and war. The arrow also has a certain phallic quality, and the bow provides sexual tension in its crescent (feminine) shape. The bow has further symbolism in representing spiritual energy and discipline, while the arrow can represent lightning, rain, and power. For Christians, piercing arrows are a symbol of St. Sebastian, who is commonly depicted tied to a post and shot through with arrows.

◄ Spear
Because the spear was regarded as the king of weapons, snapping an enemy's spear was a symbolic act of humiliation, demonstrating superiority. As well as having obvious phallic connotations, spears have religious ties, as with the Spear of Destiny, the lance that pierced Jesus.

◄ Dagger
Used by ancient civilizations for ritual human and animal sacrifice, the dagger is a potent symbol of bloodletting, imminent death, and appeasement of the gods. The *kris* (*left*), a type of dagger used in Southeast Asia, is often decorated with words inscribed from the Koran to represent absolute truth.

▲ Gun
The gun has potent phallic and male aggression symbolism. Its projectile power represents virility and impregnation. The identification of guns with macho males has been frequently reinforced by gangster movies.

▲ Plow
The plow represents penetration and fertilization of the Earth (the female furrow). Plowing also symbolizes the act of creation, as primal matter is broken down into different life forms.

▲ Scales
A set of scales is easily recognizable as a symbol of justice and fairness. Justice is often personified as a blindfolded woman carrying scales. The notion of "balanced judgement" goes back to Ancient Egypt, when the heart of a deceased person was weighed against the feather of truth before Osiris, god of the underworld.

▲ Net
For Christians the net represents harvesting of the faithful: Christ instructed his disciples to become "fishers of men." In older cultures the net is related to the ensnaring powers of the female. To the Chinese the stars at night are the "net of Heaven."

▲ Rope
Symbolically, rope is both restricting and connecting. The Aztecs used rope as a noose but it had trading value, too. As a adder or bridge, it has symbolic links to Heaven. For Hindus rope represents purity because the Hindu god Shiva wore a sacred cord. In Christianity it is a symbol of betrayal, as Christ was bound by his captors.

▲ Hook
For cultures dependent on fishing, such as the Maoris, the fishhook means prosperity. In Polynesia it is associated with strength and leadership. In contemporary culture the hook is both alluring, drawing you in, "hooking" you to an addiction, and painful in its grip and captivity.

SWORDS

With its long blade, the sword's shape lends itself to associations with masculinity. For Crusaders, because it was like the Cross with its straight hilt, a sword justified bloodletting in the name of God. Many Christian saints carry a sword as their emblem. Swords are symbols of royal power, military might, and honor. In Buddhist and Taoist thought swords symbolize discernment cutting through ignorance.

▲ Islamic sword
The Saudi Arabian flag features a sword as a symbol of "strength rooted in faith"—the words in the sacred Islamic text written above it.

▲ Knighting
In the centuries old tradition of knighting, a ruler touches the shoulders of a subject with the flat of a sword as a symbolic raising of rank.

▲ Asante sword
This late 19th-century Ghanaian ceremonial sword has gilded wooden beads on the handle that symbolize wealth and fertility.

▲ Samurai sword
For the samurai the "sword" represented as much a spiritual training as a military one, where Bushido, the "Way of the Warrior," combined Zen with martial arts. The samurai sword is renowned for its beauty and sharpness.

ARCHITECTURE

Throughout history, every culture and society has expressed its aspirations through architecture. From Ancient Greek and Roman buildings representing the power of empire to the celestial symbolism conveyed in the vaulted arches and spires of magnificent Gothic cathedrals, architects have shaped their creations to make a universal visual language. Differently shaped buildings represent differing symbolic ideals: skyscrapers can represent status and achievement, while environmentally aware buildings show our closeness both to nature and natural forms.

BRIDGES

Symbolically, bridges can represent communication between an earthly and divine realm or the transition from one state of being to another. However, depending upon its particular setting, a bridge can attain an iconic quality and become a landmark that defines a place—sometimes a whole country—in our imagination.

▲ **Icon of a city**
Flamboyant yet functional, London's Tower Bridge was a feat of steam-driven Victorian engineering and is now symbolic as a tourist icon of the United Kingdom's capital city.

▲ **Focus of national pride**
Completed in 1932, Sydney Harbour Bridge is an iconic image of Sydney and of Australia itself, representing a modern nation of freedom and opportunity.

REFLECTIONS OF NATURE

Many people make homes from natural materials, from adobe huts in Africa to ice-block igloos in the Arctic. In modern societies, too, the urge to "get back to nature" is increasingly expressed through environmentally aware architecture.

▲ **Earth dwelling**
Zulu homes are always circular. The right-hand side is occupied by the man and the left-hand side by the woman. An area for storing utensils and valuables was believed to belong to the spirits.

▲ **Harmony with nature**
Frank Lloyd Wright's Fallingwater in Pennsylvania demonstrates his concept of organic architecture. Mimicking the pattern of the rock ledges, the house falls in series of cantilevered trays over the falls, embodying the ideal that people can live in harmony with nature.

THE TOWER OF BABEL

A bibilical tower but with real antecedents, the Tower of Babel was an Ancient Babylonian stepped pyramid. The Babylonians were determined to build a tower that would reach the heavens, but according to the Bible, God caused the builders to speak in so many different tongues they could not understand each other, and the tower was never completed. It is thus a symbol of man's arrogance.

▲ **Pride of Man**
The mythical story of this tower is told in the Book of Genesis, and is a symbolic reminder that "pride comes before a fall" when men rebel against God.

FEMININE ARCHITECTURE

Certain shapes used in the design of buildings, whether in their plan or elevation, or the decorations attached to them, immediately signal something to us by association. So low-rise buildings "envelop" and are feminine in form, whereas high-rise structures "rise" in masculine form. Feminine buildings that use curved shapes also symbolize the safety and security of the womb.

▲ Amphitheater
One of the greatest works of Roman architecture, the Colosseum in Rome is a compelling symbol of empire and power and is today an important landmark in Italy's "Eternal City." Its elliptical shape has a feminine, protective symbolism, as well as suggesting a womb-like envelopment.

◄ Castle
Castles, like Bodiam Castle in East Sussex, England, once provided safety for nobles and their serfs in times of war. Surrounded by a moat, the feminine symbolism of protection and nurturing is very strong; however, the castle remains a symbol of strength and power.

MASCULINE ARCHITECTURE

The tower symbolizes power, and in its phallic connotation male supremacy. From medieval spires to the modern skyscraper, humans (and nations) have striven to express their supremacy through sheer, thrusting height. By association, the most symbolic example of affecting a nation's feeling of invincibility was the catastrophic terrorist attack on New York's World Trade Center on September 11, 2001.

◄ Skyscraper
From 1931, New York's Empire State Building was the world's tallest building for over 40 years. Today this Art Deco landmark remains a proud masculine symbol of the United States' unfettered ambition and self-belief.

◄ Lighthouse
Representing a beacon of truth and a symbol of male fertility, the lighthouse also symbolizes Christ's teaching, as it provides light to guide ships to safety just as the soul is drawn to faith.

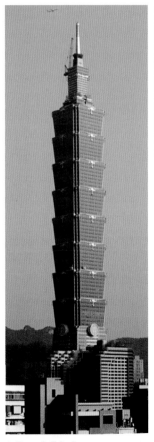

▲ Tower in Taipei
One of the world's tallest structures, Taipei 101's design echoes the Chinese pagoda and a stem of bamboo. The tower thus reflects Taiwan's cultural history, as well as its ambition in the 21st century.

DUAL SYMBOLISM

Many buildings send out both masculine and feminine signals. Tibet's Portala Palace is dedicated to the bodhisattva Avalokiteshvara, who has both male and female forms. A dome can be both masculine and feminine as with London's all-embracing 02 Arena, which suggests a nurturing of knowledge and the arts.

◄ Palace
The Portala Palace in Lhasa (1645–1695) is a symbol of Tibet and also of Tibetan Buddhism (being once the home of Tibet's spiritual leaders, the Dalai Llamas). Rising from a high ridge, the magnificent red, white, and gold palace makes for an imposing sight.

▲ Dome
As with domes in antiquity, London's 02 Arena represents a cosmic canopy. Domes were incorporated from Renaissance times in government buildings to symbolize power.

SEE ALSO
Fertility & childbirth *pp.120–23*
Religious architecture *pp.228–31*
Sacred places *pp.232–33*

RELIGIOUS ARCHITECTURE

Temples, mosques, churches, and shrines are places of worship and as such are filled with reminders of the central belief of the worshipers and their relationship with the deity. Religious architecture is both complex and highly symbolic. Spires, towers, minarets, and domes beckon believers (perhaps summoned by bells or drawn by the muezzin's call to prayer) from afar and point to a celestial, spiritual world.

DECORATION

Religious sites are recognizable by their decorative symbols of faith—such as the cross, star, or crescent Moon—as well as statues of gods, saints, and other sacred shapes and forms carved into the stone, wood, or glass. Symbolism ranges from medieval cathedral gargoyles representing Hell fire and damnation, to beautiful calligraphic representations of the Koran.

▲ **Stained glass**
Traditionally, stained glass windows "illuminated" biblical stories and the saints' lives through a mosaic of colored glass. This example shows St. Beuno (*right*) at St. Winefride's Church, Holywell, Wales.

▲ **Islamic tiles**
Decorative tiles characterize much of Islamic mosque decoration. Human and animal images are avoided, so symbolic geometric designs, passages from the Koran, and plant motifs are favored.

▲ **Lutheran interior**
Mostly found in northwest Europe and North America, Lutheran churches emphasize scripture, so these churches avoid the use of ostentatious art forms and have unadorned interiors—in this case emphasizing the symbol of the cross.

▲ **Interior with saints**
Catholic church interiors are rich in symbolism and decoration. Symbolism is evident in the statues, paintings, and other visual motifs. The dome of the Ocotlan Basilica, Tlaxcala, in Mexico (*above*) has a representation of Mary and the apostles.

▲ **Synagogue**
Jewish law sets only general guidelines for the form of a synagogue, though it does teach that it must contain windows, as there is a world beyond sanctuary in which good works must be done. The Kupa Synagogue in Krakow, Poland (*above*), was founded for the poor in 1643.

◄ **Cao Dai Temple**
The central temple of Cao Dai—a belief system that combines the world's major religions to promote peace—the Cao Dai temple ("high tower or palace") is built on nine levels reflecting the nine steps to Heaven. The ceiling is painted sky blue with white clouds representing the heavens.

▲ Relief sculpture
India is famous for its Hindu relief sculptures in temples and shrines. The sculptures show representations of the many gods and goddesses. Above are relief figures of celestial beings at the Parsvanath Temple in Khajuraho, central India.

▲ Eye of Nepalese stupa
Stupas were originally burial mounds and are a symbol of the Buddha's entry into Nirvana. In this case, the eyes of the Buddha on the Harmika of the Swayambhu stupa in Nepal are a reminder to all of the possibility of enlightenment.

▲ Door guardians
Ancient Chinese Imperial Generals in a martial stance, as well as Imperial guardian lions are popular doorway images in Chinese temples. It is believed that they prevent demons and ghosts from entering.

DIRECTION

The direction in which a religious building is orientated is highly symbolic. East being the direction of sunrise, symbolic of birth, and West being the direction of the sunset, symbolizing death and rebirth. Many ancient cults were Sun-worshiping, and their sacred structures, or shrines, were orientated toward solar activity and cycles.

▲ Mihrab
The Mihrab is a niche in the wall of a mosque, which indicates the *qibla* or direction of Mecca towards which a Muslim should pray. The Mihrab also symbolizes the divine presence on Earth.

▲ Garbha griha
In a Hindu temple there is no large interior space for worship. The principal image is housed in a *garbha griha*, literally "womb-chamber." Other images are located in niches in the cardinal directions.

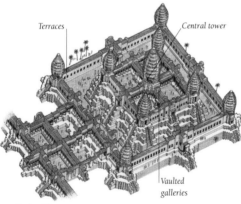

Terraces — Central tower — Vaulted galleries

▲ Angkor Wat
The 12th-century temple complex at Angkor in Cambodia was built for the Khmer ruler, King Suryavarman II. The temple and ascending towers represent Mount Meru, the mountain home of the Hindu gods.

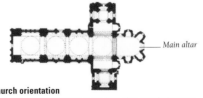

 Main altar

▲ Church orientation
Many churches are constructed in the form of an east-facing cross, symbolic of the Christian faith. They are nearly always oriented so that the main altar is at the east end of the church, facing the Holy Land.

PAGODAS AND STUPAS

Pagodas and stupas are highly symbolic structures. Originally built as burial mounds, they sometimes contained relics of the Buddha or other sacred items. The shape of a pagoda can often be equated with the shape of the Buddha seated in meditation, and as such it can be used as a meditational aid and a symbol of Nirvana.

◄ Chinese pagoda
A Chinese pagoda is distinguished by its roofs, usually seven or nine in number. The separate stories, diminishing in size as they rise upward, symbolize the different levels of Heaven and the stages to enlightenment. Like the ancient Indian stupa, the pagoda was a symbol of the path to enlightenment.

The jewel ("enlightenment"), Sun ("wisdom"), and Moon ("heart").

The parasol represents compassion.

The chest has seven elements of enlightenment, including diligence and joy.

The hall has steps symbolizing the three refuges of the Buddha, dharma, and sangha.

▲ The form of the stupa
The number of terraces and different features of the stupa are based upon the teachings of Buddhism. They are intended to focus awareness, mindful of the steps upward to enlightenment. This example is shaped as the Buddha, crowned and seated in the meditation pose on a throne.

RELIGIOUS ARCHITECTURE

B☉R☉BUDUR

Built in the 8th and 9th centuries, Borobudur on Java is the largest Buddhist monument in the world. Decorated with 504 statues of the Buddha and 1,460 carved stone panels depicting Buddhist stories, Borobudur is a vast book symbolizing enlightenment and the path to attaining it. Devotees ascend both physically and spiritually by walking around the terraces, reading the pictures carved on to the gallery walls as they approach the summit.

1. Base (Kamadhatu)
The reliefs at the base of Borobudur represent *Kamadhatu* (the realm of desire) and symbolize humans still bound by lust.

2. Upper four stories
The reliefs on the upper four stories represent *Rupadhatu* (the realm of form) and symbolize humans that have set themselves free from lust but are still bound by vanity.

3. Upper three terraces
On the circular terraces, statues of the Buddha confined in domes with holes represent *Arupadhatu* (the realm of formlessness) and symbolize people that are free from lust and appearance.

4. Top of the terrace
The structure is erected on a hill in the form of a stepped pyramid of six rectangular stories. The top of the terrace is called *Arupa* and symbolizes Nirvana where the Buddha resides. A statue of the Buddha is located here.

5. Mandala form
When seen from the top Borobudur resembles a mandala, a visual metaphor for the cosmos. Its essential feature is a circle enclosed by a square with four "doors" in the middle of each side, facing the four cardinal points (four main Buddhist elements). Mandalas are used as meditational aids. Although there is no contemporary record of Borobudur being used in this way, it is very likely that it was.

SACRED PLACES

In every culture there are places and spaces that are imbued with a sacredness acquired through hundreds or thousands of years of worship. These may be made by humans, such as temples and pyramids, or natural, as in rivers, rocks, and trees. Whether imbued with religious or folkloric importance, the world is dotted with sacred places that have entered the public consciousness and become, in their own way, symbols of their culture.

▲ Ka'ba
The cubical structure at the Great Mosque in Mecca is called the Ka'ba and is central to Islam. Muslims make the *hajj* ("pilgrimage") there once in their lifetime if they are able. Pilgrims circle the Ka'ba seven times, an act symbolizing Muhammad's seven ascents to Heaven.

▲ Mount Tai
Not merely a mountain home of the gods (like Mount Olympus), Mount Tai was considered a deity itself—the son of the Emperor of Heaven. Chinese emperors have venerated it as their most sacred peak since at least 3000BCE.

▲ Delphi
Home of the mysterious oracle of the Ancient Mediterranean world, Delphi is soaked in legend. Here lay the sacred place of the Earth goddess, Gaia, and the sanctuary of the Greek god Apollo. Nearby, Mount Parnassus is sacred to the Muses in Greek legend.

▲ Chalma
The pre-Columbian sacred cave site of Chalma, Mexico, was used by local American Indian tribes seeking cures. The site and the ritual was adopted and adapted by Spanish settlers who built a pilgrimage church there in the 1530s. Since then the Royal Monastery and Sanctuary has remained a Christian holy place where pilgrims come to seek cures, or give thanks for prayers answered.

▲ Stonehenge
Built around 2000BCE, Stonehenge may have been used as an astronomical clock or cosmic calculator. The site's capacity to determine the dates of the solstices and equinoxes was all-important, since ancient tribes regarded the Sun and Moon as sacred beings. The cycles of the Moon, the seasons, and eclipses could be observed via the configuration of the stones and celebrated in sacred rituals.

▲ Wat Phra Keo
The most revered Buddhist shrine in Thailand is Wat Phra Keo (Temple of the Emerald Buddha) in Bangkok. The Thai king changes the Buddha's clothes three times a year.

▲ **Bodh Gaya**
A symbol of the Buddha's Enlightenment, Bodh Gaya near Bihar in India is a sacred site for Buddhists. Here, the Mahabodhi temple stands beside the Bodhi tree, said to be a descendant of that under which the Buddha achieved Enlightenment.

▲ **St. Peter's, Rome**
In 64ce St. Peter was martyred and 300 years later Constantine, the first Christian emperor of Rome, had a church built on the site. Today St. Peter's Basilica, in the Vatican, is the spiritual center of the Roman Catholic Church.

▲ **Church of the Holy Sepulchre**
One of the most sacred spaces on Earth is on the site of the supposed tomb of Jesus. A tiny chapel in the Church of the Holy Sepulchre in Jerusalem is believed to mark this most sacred of sites to Christians.

▲ **Jasna Góra**
The monastery of Jasna Góra in Poland is one of the largest Catholic pilgrimage sites in the world, and a symbol to Poles of their country and religion. It is home of the icon of Our Lady of Czestochowa.

▲ **The Great Pyramid**
Much more than a giant tomb to protect the Pharaoh, the Great Pyramid may have represented a gigantic portal through which the Ancient Egyptian king would join the Sun god in the sky.

▲ **Varanasi**
Situated by the Ganges, Varanasi is a major pilgrimage site in India and is the most sacred place for Hindus to die and be cremated. The River Ganges symbolizes divine consciousness and thus immortality.

▲ **Teotihuacan**
The Aztec city-complex of Teotihuacan in Mexico houses the Pyramid of the Sun (*above*). It is carved with many symbols, including images of the god of rain and Quetzalcoatl, the plumed serpent god.

▲ **Kelimutu**
A volcano on the Indonesian island of Flore, Kelimutu contains three lakes of varying colors. These are believed to be the abode of the dead, each housing souls according to the lives they led.

ROCK ART

Prehistoric and Australian Aboriginal rock art are the first picture books—storytelling by means of petroglyphs, pictographs, and cave paintings. This highly symbolic sign language predates the pyramids by around 10,000 years. The strong relationship with the landscape and every living creature encountered forms the basis for this art.

◄ **Newspaper Rock, Utah**
Newspaper Rock is a rock-carving etched into a sandstone cliff in the Utah desert in the United States. It records human activity spanning some 2,000 years and includes representations of American Indian cultures, including the Anasazi and the Navajo.

► **Lascaux**
The prehistoric rock paintings of the Lascaux cave complex in France date back to 15000–13000bce. They depict animals, human representations, and signs. The caves were probably used both for hunting rituals and magical rites.

SEE ALSO
Mountains *pp.28–29*
Death & mourning *pp.128–31*
Architecture *pp.226–27*
Religious architecture *pp.228–29*

SACRED PLACES

233

BUILDINGS

For most people the elements that make up a house are purely practical—although architects design buildings with the aim of making them both functional and aesthetically pleasing. In the East the harmony and orientation of a building's interior and exterior is directly linked to a person's spiritual well-being. The Ancient Chinese practice of Feng Shui, also used in many modern western buildings, optimizes the placement of rooms and objects within rooms to ward off evil spirits and bad luck.

▲ **Window**
Just as the eye is likened to the "window of the soul," so symbolically the window has long been considered as the "eye of the soul." Windows let in the light of truth. Stained glass examples do it with overt symbolism, and illuminate the darkness of ignorance.

▲ **Chimney**
Smoke escaping from the hearth through a chimney represents release from an enclosed space, and from an earthbound state to the heavens. Originally, Santa Claus (or Father Christmas) coming down the chimney was as a symbol of divine authority delivering gifts from Heaven. Chimneys, and chimney sweeps, also represent good luck.

▲ **Stairs**
A staircase represents the steps on the spiritual road to enlightenment and knowledge; it can also symbolize the downward descent into darkness and ignorance. A winding staircase, with the upper or lower end unseen, is a symbol of the mysterious.

▲ **Balcony**
Both outside and part of the building, a balcony represents ambivalence and mystery, since it partially conceals and partially reveals. Historically, balconies symbolized "support" and a privileged lifestyle.

▲ **Pillar**
A pillar represents the joining of Heaven and Earth and is often decorated to highlight this link. The Islamic faith has "Five Pillars" representing the five duties incumbent on every Muslim.

◄ **Façade**
The public face of a building represents how one wishes to appear to the world. An open façade with many windows suggests openness and honesty, whereas a windowless façade with enclosed courtyards suggests concealment and secrecy. Ornamental flourishes announce status and power.

SOCIETY & CULTURE

234

▲ Attic
Tucked in beneath the roof, the attic is often the storage place of the home, full of old toys and memorabilia. Symbolically it represents half-remembered or forgotten truths, waiting to be revealed to the seeker.

▲ Basement
Symbolically the basement, cellar, or crypt—often with a vaulted ceiling—represents the underworld. Tombs lie there beneath the world of people and the heavens. In some cultures houses are raised on stilts, and the space beneath (where domestic animals are kept) represents the lower realms.

▲ Arch
An archway symbolizes the passage from one state of being to another. In initiation rites, one who passes through an arch is symbolically reborn. The St. Louis Gateway Arch represents the gateway to the historical American West.

▲ Wall
Symbolic of strength, privacy, and containment, the wall encloses and protects the interior of a building or garden. In some cases, as in the Gaza Strip barrier or the Great Wall of China, it represents division, isolation, and separation.

▲ Floor
The earthly realm between Heaven (the roof) and Hell (the basement or under-floor area) is represented by the floor. Floors are sometimes decorated with symbols and patterns.

▲ Dome
Since antiquity and through diverse cultures and religions, the dome has represented the arc of Heaven and the realm of the gods. That is why many church and temple dome interiors are painted with stars and other celestial objects.

▲ Roof
Representing the feminine, sheltering principle, the roof keeps a building safe from evil forces. It is also a sacred space, symbolizing—and in holy buildings often showing—the heavens, with deities, angels, and gargoyles often added to increase its protective power.

DOORWAY

The entrance to a house or sacred space symbolically marks the divide between the sacred and the profane, the transition from one stage of life to another, the passage from life to death. To ensure an entrance is more secure from evil influences, people carve motifs into the surrounding supports, or add symbolic "totems" to the door itself, such as a horseshoe or door knocker.

► Pilasters
The lintel and pilasters surrounding temple or church entrances are often carved with protective guardian deities. They bear symbols conferring good fortune on those who enter. In eastern countries the lotus is a popular motif.

▲ Door knocker
Although a door knocker can symbolize hospitality, as with a pineapple motif, or good luck, as with a horse shoe or four-leaf clover, the sound of the knocker at the door can be interpreted as a sign of inexorable fate or approaching death.

▲ Hall
Both practically and metaphorically, a hall is a place of transition—leading to other doors and passageways. In this way it symbolizes a moment of choice in life when several "doors" are open to new possibilities, spiritual or otherwise.

▲ **Jacob's Ladder**
Possibly the best-known ladder in western symbolism is Jacob's Ladder. In the Old Testament Jacob, fleeing his brother's anger, lays down to sleep with a stone for a pillow. He dreams of a ladder to the heavens with angels ascending. At the top God gives blessings and promises to protect Jacob on his journey. The ladder thus became a symbol of the comings and goings between Heaven and Earth.

STEPS TO HEAVEN

A ladder or staircase can represent access to the transcendent—each rung or step representing a spiritual stage or new level of awareness on the ascent—or the steep decline to a fiery netherworld.

Like the Tree of Life, ladders and stairs are associated with the knowledge of good and evil. The different levels represent the passage between the earthly and heavenly realms.

THE LADDER

The ladder is a well-known mythological motif most often interpreted as a symbol of achieving personal wholeness. With its two uprights, it is often associated with the two trees of Paradise: the Tree of the Knowledge of Good and Evil and the Tree of Life, the two being joined by the rungs of spiritual knowledge. In Egyptian myth it was linked to Osiris, god of resurrection and the underworld, and since it was usually depicted as being lit by the Sun's rays, it was linked to the Sun god, Re. In Buddhism the Buddha is shown descending a ladder that connects the heavenly sphere with the earthly one, symbolizing the closeness of the enlightened ones to the heavens. The Bible relates the story of Jacob's dream in which angels descend and ascend a ladder, a symbol of communication between the spiritual and physical worlds, or between the conscious and the unconscious self—such symbolism also occurs in Islam, when Muhammad dreamed of a ladder by which the faithful could climb to God.

▲ **The steps of the Buddha**
This stucco relief from the Wat Mahathat temple in Thailand depicts the Buddha descending the steps of a ladder from the Trayastrimsha Heaven, with Brahma and Indra in attendance on ladders on either side.

STEPS ON THE PATH

In many cultures the number of steps on a ladder equates to the number of tests one must pass to attain self-knowledge or enlightenment. Most commonly there are seven steps. In Buddhism, for instance, the seven steps correspond to the seven heavens and seven stages of awareness. From Sumerian cosmology to modern day Freemasonry, the ladder is also depicted with seven steps.

In a church the altar, approached by the priest, is raised several steps above the congregation as a symbol of its sanctity. A throne, too, is raised on steps above floor level, signaling temporal and often spiritual authority.

STAIRS

With a staircase, the different floors represent the different levels of the cosmos, and of attainment in the quest for enlightenment. A spiral staircase indicates a journey perhaps fraught with doubts: its twists are symbolic of the twists of fortune on the spiritual journey. It must be remembered that ladders and stairs do not simply lead upward. The board game Snakes and Ladders is symbolic of the steps upward in one's spiritual life, followed by the many sudden descents of temptation (as symbolized by the snake).

▲ **Spiral staircase**
The spiral staircase symbolizes a gradual elevation to a new kind of consciousness. The end is not in sight as one climbs round and round, physically and symbolically, ascending towards the summit.

◄ **Altar steps**
Altars are often raised on steps, like these at St. John's Co-Cathedral in Valletta, Malta. The steps up to the altar can be seen as a ritual ascent. The raised platform upon which the altar rests suggests being closer to divinity. Stone altars also signify the indestructibility of the divinity.

SEE ALSO
Snakes pp.66–67
Sacred trees pp.96–97
Egyptian deities pp.138–39
Buddhism pp.164–69
Freemasonry pp.260–61

THE HOME

Womb-like and feminine, the home represents both a sanctuary and security from the outside world. Many familiar everyday objects that we take for granted around the home, such as bowls, clocks, brooms, and mirrors, have long had profound symbolic associations with cosmology and religion. There is often more to the mundane than we realize.

▶ Hearth

The home was, until recently, symbolically centered around the hearth, the fireplace where the family gathered for warmth. The hearth embodies the idea of feminine warmth and nurturing. In Ancient Greek times the hearth was dedicated to the goddess Hestia, who tended the sacred fire on Mount Olympus.

▲ Mirror

A highly complex symbol, the mirror has many meanings. It represents truth, clarity, and self-examination, and reflects the soul. To Taoists it is symbolic of the inner calm of the sage. As it reflects light, the mirror is associated with both the Sun and the Moon. To Hindus it symbolizes the illusory nature of reality. When a mirror breaks it symbolizes the loss of beauty or innocence, or is a presage of bad luck.

◀ Thread

This is a symbol of human life spun by the gods. Greek mythology relates how Theseus escaped from the labyrinth after being given a ball of thread to follow. In Hinduism males from the higher castes wear a three-stranded thread symbolizing reality, passion, and stillness.

◀ Table

To Christians a table represents the Last Supper. A round table symbolizes both the circle of the heavens and equality, for there is no "head of the table." Another well-known example is the Round Table of King Arthur.

▲ Broom

A symbol of cleansing, the broom sweeps away problems. In Ancient Rome it symbolized sweeping away evil in the home that might harm a child. The broom became a tool against curses and people hung a broom on their front door to protect their home from evil spirits.

▶ Pen and ink

Like the Chinese brush, the pen is a sign of learning. It marks our destiny on a sheet of paper. The pen is masculine in shape and dips into the feminine-shaped inkwell to draw upon its creativity.

▲ Bowl

Filled with water, a bowl is a symbol of the feminine principle and of fertility. The alms bowl carried by a Buddhist monk symbolizes the renunciation of worldly things.

▶ Chest

Secrets can be hidden in a chest. The Hebrew Tablets of the Law were kept in a chest, and Greek chests held mysteries only revealed to the initiated. To the Romans the chest was a symbol of mysticism.

SOCIETY & CULTURE

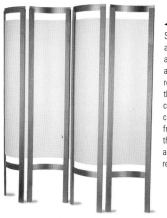

Screen
Symbolic of mystery, a screen half reveals and half conceals. In a Christian church the rood screen separates the nave of the church, where the congregation sits, from the chancel, the area where the altar is and which represents the divine.

Light
Whether in the form of a lamp or a candle, a light symbolizes illumination, knowledge, and the divine. Radiant like the Sun, it is truth, splendor, and the light of Heaven. In Christian art a candle is often used to represent the light of Christ coming into the world.

Knife
Although knives are symbolic of death and sacrifice—the Aztecs used stone and obsidian knives to cut out a victim's heart—they can also represent severance, cutting free. In Buddhism a knife cuts through the bonds of ignorance. It is also the emblem of some Christian martyrs, such as St. Bartholemew.

▲ Timepiece
Like sundials and clocks, the hourglass measures time and is therefore a symbol of mortality. Our lives ebb away like the sand in an hourglass.

▲ Purse
Filled with money, a purse represents worldly vanity and the transience of wealth. In Christian art it is a symbol of St. Matthew, who was a tax collector, and of Judas Iscariot, the apostle who betrayed Jesus Christ for 30 pieces of silver.

Key
Because it provides access to locked rooms, the key is a symbol of wisdom, knowledge, and success. It can also give a person freedom, so it also symbolizes liberation. In Christianity two crossed keys are the emblem of St. Peter, who held the keys to the gates of Heaven.

▲ Box
A symbol of containing, a box represents the feminine. When closed it symbolizes the unconscious, and when opened it can unleash all kinds of evil, as Pandora's Box did, according to Greek mythology.

Loom
An attribute of mother and lunar goddesses, the loom was a symbol of female power and protection. Athena, the Greek goddess of heroic endeavor, was the patroness of crafts and "a weaver of worlds."

Book
An open book is a symbol of learning and wisdom. A closed book signifies an ending, a judgement, or death, as did a snuffed candle or the tolling of a bell (the phrase, "bell, book, and candle" refers to the objects used ceremonially to excommunicate wayward Catholics).

Spinning wheel
Traditionally used to spin yarn, the spinning wheel symbolizes the turning of the universe. Mahatma Gandhi also used it as a symbol of India's struggle for independence.

▲ Fan
A symbol not just of femininity but also of rank, the fan is thought to ward off evil spirits. To Taoists it represents the release of the soul into the realm of the immortals.

SEE ALSO
Greek & Roman deities pp.140–41
Buddhism pp.164–69
Christianity pp.176–79
The Holy Grail pp.208–09
Tools & weapons pp.224–25
Buildings pp.234–35

THE HOME

239

THE ARN⊕LFINI MARRIAGE

Dutch artist van Eyck's most famous work, this painting is thought to commemorate the wedding of wealthy trader Giovanni Arnolfini and Giovanna Cenami. The picture is full of symbolism and hidden meaning and works on many different levels—as a portrait of the two people shown, as a record of a marriage, and as a comment on marriage in the 15th century.

1. The dress
The color of the bride's dress—green—is a strong symbol of fertility. Although she is not pregnant, her pose emphasizes her fertility and the possibility of future pregancies.

2. The candle
The single candle in the chandelier symbolizes the presence of God. Its position next to the bed emphasizes the hoped-for fertility of the wife.

3. & 4. The shoes
The discarded footwear signifies that a religious ceremony is underway. Bare feet touching the ground were believed to symbolize fertility. The positioning of the shoes is also relevant, as the man's lie closer to the door while the bride's red shoes are by the bed, indicating his position in the outside world and her fertility.

5. The dog
A symbol of their loyalty to each other and to God, the dog lying between the couple may also represent earthly love.

6. Crystal prayer beads
The beads that can be seen hanging on the wall are made of crystal, symbolizing purity and the devout nature of the bride.

7. Oranges
These luxury fruits symbolize the wealth of the couple. Also known as "Adam's Apples" they represent the forbidden fruit from the Garden of Eden and symbolize lust, which was sanctified by marriage.

8. Bedstead
A figure with a dragon at her feet is carved on the bedstead. This may be St. Margaret, the patron saint of childbirth.

Convex mirror detail
The mirror is central to the painting, as viewers can see the entire room reflected, including one figure who may be the artist. The small medallions set into the mirror's frame show tiny scenes from the Passion of Christ and represent God's ever-present promise of salvation, a promise that encompasses the figures reflected on the mirror's convex surface. A spotless mirror was also an established symbol of Mary, referring to the Holy Virgin's Immaculate Conception and purity.

Jan van Eyck, *The Arnolfini Marriage*, c1421

SHIPS & BOATS

The ship is a powerful symbol of security, the womb, or a cradling vessel on the cosmic ocean. It also represents exploration of new realms. In Ancient Egypt and Mesopotamia it was a ship that carried the Sun and the Moon across the heavens. The seven Japanese gods of happiness were also borne by ship. To Christians, a ship is a symbol of the Church and also of Noah's ark. A boat can symbolize safety but also death, as it crosses a river to reach the underworld or carries the body of a warrior or nobleman on his final voyage.

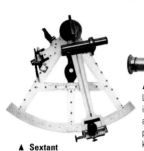

▲ Sextant
An indispensable navigational instrument for mariners in the past, the sextant is symbolic of navigation, adventure, and new horizons. It is also linked to the idea of progress, as it charts new territories and extends the boundaries of knowledge.

▲ Telescope
Like the sextant, the telescope is a symbol of navigation. At a deeper level, its magnifying properties lead to increased knowledge and help to bridge the gap between people and the cosmos. It is also a masculine phallic symbol.

▲ Albatross
To seafarers the albatross is mainly a bird of good omen, symbolizing tireless strength, but it also forewarns of bad weather. Albatrosses were thought to embody the souls of dead sailors, so it is considered unlucky to kill one.

▲ Figurehead
Ships often bore carved wooden figureheads on their prows, which were thought to protect the ship and its crew. The figureheads might represent a god, such as Poseidon, a mermaid, or some other creature of the sea.

▲ Submarine
Primarily associated with warfare, a submarine has mixed symbolism. It has the phallic shape of masculine power and its torpedoes suggest virility, but it also has protective, womblike properties and travels through the creative cosmos of liquid.

▲ Anchor
The anchor symbolizes stability, strength, and hope, as an anchor holds a boat fast in stormy seas. Early Christians used the anchor as a hidden symbol of the cross, and it is often seen on seals, stained glass windows, and tattoos.

▲ Ship's cloth
Some cultures speak of ancestors who came across the sea in ships. The people of Lampang, Sumatra, have ships' cloths that they use in rituals. These depict ships that symbolize their past and their destiny.

▲ Sails
The sails of a ship symbolize the winds and the air, the breath of the soul. Billowing sails suggest pregnancy, but also inconstancy because they change with the wind. To Christians, sails can represent the advent of the Holy Spirit.

◀ Walking the plank
This is a term for death, since it was the ultimate punishment for crimes at sea. The wrong-doer was blindfolded and his wrists bound, and he was made to walk the plank jutting out from the ship's side until he fell into the sea and drowned.

◀ Lifeboat
The lifeboat is a symbol of safety in times of peril. It carries mariners to land, just as the thirst for knowledge bears the soul safely toward ultimate truth.

▲ Compass
The nautical compass, with the points of the star indicating directions, is both a symbol of navigation and exploration, and of safe return to port. It also represents the totality of the Universe and the heavens.

▲ Skull and crossbones
The symbol on the "Jolly Roger," the pirates' flag, the skull and crossbones denoted the bones of pirates' victims. Many pirate ships carried the flag of a neutral country then ran the "Jolly Roger" up the mast just before attacking.

▲ Mast and yardarm
A ship's mast is the focal point of the vessel and symbolizes the *axis mudi* at the center of the cosmos. Its cross shape also symbolizes the Christian cross. A yardarm was a symbol of death to mariners as wrongdoers were hanged from it.

NAUTICAL SYMBOLS

Signalling with flags is centuries old, but the first code of flag signals dates back to the 17th century in England. Pennants and flags carry special meanings and there is now a standard international code of signals by which ships signal to each other.

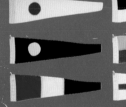

◀ Flags with a message
This flag means "I am on fire. Keep clear of me." At the Battle of Trafalgar Nelson put up pennants saying "England expects that every man will do his duty."

▲ Numbers
Numerical flags were introduced by the British Navy in the 18th century. The three flags on the left above, from the top, represent the numbers one to three, and those on the right the numbers six to eight.

SHIP BURIAL

Traveling across water is often associated with death and the voyage to the afterlife. The Ancient Egyptians built elegant wooden funeral boats to carry their pharoahs across the River Nile to their graves, then buried the boats near the pharoahs. Viking and Anglo-Saxon kings were sometimes buried with a ship laden with household objects, weapons, and treasures that the king might need in the afterlife. A boat burial signified high rank and honor, as well as a journey to the gods.

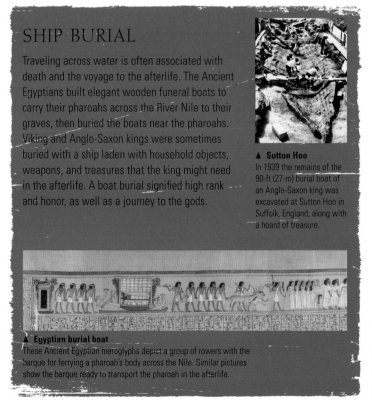

▲ Sutton Hoo
In 1939 the remains of the 90-ft (27-m) burial boat of an Anglo-Saxon king was excavated at Sutton Hoo in Suffolk, England, along with a hoard of treasure.

▲ Egyptian burial boat
These Ancient Egyptian hieroglyphs depict a group of rowers with the barque for ferrying a pharoah's body across the Nile. Similar pictures show the barque ready to transport the pharoah in the afterlife.

GARDENS

Havens, places of inspiration or spiritual nourishment, pleasure grounds, or signs of status—gardens can be all these things. They offer sanctuary from everyday life and balm for the spirit; some gardens serve as a living memorial. As a Paradise on Earth in which the gardener is the creator, the garden symbolizes tamed and ordered nature. From the tranquility of a Zen garden to the restraint of a formal garden, or the exuberance of a wild garden, each has its own symbolic plants, structures, and designs.

▲ **Formal garden**
During the European Renaissance, gardens became increasingly restrained and symmetrical, representing man's mastery over nature, as well as an owner's status. Classical symbolism appears in statuary and garden structures, suggesting a place fit for the gods.

▲ **Wild garden**
In contrast to garden styles that symbolize the bringing of order, the wild garden represents the exuberance of nature and the wildness of the untamed spirit. Nature appears to flourish unrestrained, signifying abundance and the continuing cycle of life.

◄ **Zen garden**
Originally created by Buddhist monks, Zen gardens symbolize the grandeur of nature in miniature. Raked gravel represents water (Yin), while large rocks symbolize mountains (Yang). Together they create an atmosphere of harmony, peace, and remoteness conducive to meditation.

▲ **Islamic garden**
Symbolizing spiritual and sensual nourishment, Islamic gardens are divided into areas based on water and symmetry. These represent the four gardens of Paradise—Heart, Soul, Spirit, and Essence.

◄ **Garden of Eden**
As Heaven on Earth, the Garden of Eden represents a state of "divine innocence" in which humans, God, and nature co-existed in perfect harmony, before Adam and Eve ate the forbidden fruit and were forever banished. It is often depicted in western art and literature. The garden also symbolizes a yearning for lost beauty and innocence.

▲ **Tomb garden**
Some eastern cultures constructed tomb gardens for emperors, such as this one for the Emperor Minh Mang, in Vietnam. These were symbolic earthly Paradises that reflected the deceased's status.

▲ Walled garden
In Persia, walled gardens were traditionally tranquil, inspirational retreats from everyday life. This theme of spiritual refuge continued in medieval Europe; it is also a feminine, protective symbol associated with the Virgin Mary.

▲ Maze
The twists and turns of a maze represent life's pathway. Entering it is equated with death, while emerging is rebirth. Set within a square, the maze represents the four cardinal points and the cosmos.

▲ Knot garden
The formal knot garden, or *parterre*, illustrates human mastery of nature. The square enclosure represents stability and the Earth; the pattern and chosen plants may symbolize love or religion.

▲ Bower
The shaded bower, traditionally constructed from twisted vines or climbing flowers, symbolizes shelter and also the feminine principle; in Christianity it is the Virgin Mary. In literature it is sometimes associated with sensuality and seduction.

▲ Secret garden
Likened to a lost Paradise of love and happiness, the secret garden requires the key of privileged knowledge to unlock its secrets and allow physical and spiritual flowering. This symbolic theme permeates Frances Hodgson Burnett's book of the same name.

◄ Grotto
Originating from the Greek word *kruptos* (meaning "hidden"), grottoes are associated with the underworld, Mother Earth, and the womb; the presence of water represents life, while the grotto itself symbolizes a meeting place between humans and the divine. In ancient times grottoes were often used as shrines.

▲ Fountain
As sparkling jets of water, a fountain represents the feminine principle and the flow of life. The fountain of life is associated with immortality; in Paradise, it spouts from the base of the Tree of Life and forms the Four Rivers.

SEE ALSO

Water *pp.32–33*
Flowers *pp.82–85*
Trees *pp.94–95*
Sacred trees *pp.96–97*
Satan & demons *pp.190–91*
Patterns *pp.290–93*

GARDENS

245

TRIUMPH ⊕F
VIRTUE ⊕VER VICE

This painting by Mantegna shows an enclosed garden with a pond in which the Vices, personified as deformed grotesque beings, thrive. Preceded by a group of cupids, Pallas Athene, the goddess of wisdom and war, strides forward to banish the Vices with the help of two goddesses. By expelling the Vices she seeks to bring about a return to a garden of virtue.

1. The Vices
The Vices depicted include Sloth, Avarice, Ingratitude, Hate, and Ignorance. Sloth, shown as a nightmarish, armless figure being dragged by Minerva, signifies immortal hate, fraud, and malice. The viewer is being warned by Sloth to replace idleness with vigorous intellectual thought on entering the garden. Ignorance (*far right*) is being carried off by Ingratitude and Avarice.

2. The humanized tree
The tree on the left is a humanized laurel tree, which signifies that virtue has been deserted, and that the Mother of Virtue is imprisoned.

3. Diana and the centaur
In the middle of the painting is Diana, goddess of chastity, portrayed according to a Classic model, who is being carried off by a centaur, symbol of lust.

4. & 5. The Cardinal Virtues
Three of the Cardinal Virtues—Temperance, Justice, and Fortitude (or Faith, Hope, and Charity)—having been driven out when the depravities took up residence, return to the garden in a cloud. Another Virtue, Prudence, is walled up inside the stone structure on the far right of the painting, and only a white fluttering banner reflects her cry for help.

6. Distant landscape
Beyond in the distance, a pleasant landscape seen through the tree-lined archways reveals Vices fleeing and new growth rising from old roots. This is a symbol of rebirth and innocence—when the Vices have gone, beauty returns.

Andrea Mantegna, *Triumph of Virtue Over Vice*, c1504

CLOTHING & COSTUME

What people wear is determined by climate, culture, gender, the materials available, and the latest trends. Our clothes send out visual messages about who we are, where we come from, and what our aspirations are. Anyone looking at us can decipher much about our personality and social standing, our ethnic origins, and what we may do for a living. Western styles of dress, particularly for women, are influenced by constantly changing fashions. Many people in other parts of the world dress in traditional styles that reflect their cultural values and are a symbol of their nationality.

► Corset
From the 16th century to the 1950s affluent western women wore rigid, constraining corsets. Victorian corsets in particular created an hourglass figure that cinched at the waist and emphasized the breasts and hips. Symbolically, such corsets reflected the submissive role of women in society.

▲ Jeans
First designed in the US for miners in the Californian gold fields, jeans became ubiquitous as work clothes. Today they are worn everywhere and symbolize social and gender equality.

▲ Tie
Ties often show group affiliation. 1950s Teddy Boys in the UK wore pencil-slim ties, while 1970s dandies favored wide ties. Black ties are worn at funerals, while "white tie and tails" symbolize high society.

▲ Gloves
Gloves were originally a symbol of rank and gentility. Handling someone "with kid gloves" is to treat them gently, and to "throw down the gauntlet" (a 17th-century man's glove) was a challenge to a duel.

BATIK PATTERNS

Batik was the fabric traditionally worn at special ceremonies for Indonesian royal families and is symbolic of Indonesian culture. The intricate patterns produced by wax-resist dyeing are usually geometric but often feature foliage, birds, beasts, or clouds. The colors are usually muted, in keeping with the Indonesian dislike of ostentation.

► Traditional designs
The elaborate designs can express specific greetings, such as "Live long and prosper," "Be happy," or "A man with dignity." Formerly, different patterns signified belonging to a particular family or tribe.

► Bark cloth
For thousands of years the people of the Pacific islands wore clothes made of tapa, decorated bark fabric. Designs included geometric interpretations of plants, fish, and seashells, reflecting the islanders' daily lives and their closeness to nature. Balance and symmetry were important symbolic components of the designs. Today tapas are worn only at important ceremonies, such as a wedding.

▲ Ao dai
The elegant Vietnamese *ao dai* is a long, flowing tunic slit at the sides and worn over silk trousers. It has come to represent womanhood and is also seen as a symbol of Vietnam. The male version of the *ao dai* has a shorter tunic.

▲ Arabian dress
The traditional long, loose robes of Arab men are a symbol of the desert landscape. They allow air to circulate freely, keeping the wearer cool, and are worn with a flowing headdress to protect the head from the heat of the sun.

▲ Masai costume
The Masai of East Africa wear simple draped robes that have become an unofficial symbol of East Africa's cultural heritage. The image of the Masai warrior standing tall and proud, spear in hand, is a symbolic icon of the region.

▲ Hula skirt
These "grass" skirts, originally made from strips of tapa cloth, are symbolic of Hawaiian culture. In the hula dance, danced to chants relating ancient stories of creation and mythology, they are worn with heavy garlands of flowers.

▶ Indian sari
A symbol of India's rich culture and the dignity of its women, the sari is an elaborate garment that can be tied in many different ways, depending on region and the status of the wearer. Occupation, caste, and religion are all expressed in this graceful apparel.

FOOTWEAR

From Roman sandals to luxury high heels, footwear has often been indicative not just of climate, but also of social status and fashion. Until the early 20th century it was common in China to bind girls' feet to keep them small, as tiny feet were a symbol of feminine delicacy and submissiveness.

▲ Sneakers
Originally designed as sports shoes, sneakers quickly evolved into fashion items. They are now worn by men and woman alike as everyday casual shoes.

▲ Platform shoes
Platform shoes have been in and out of fashion for centuries. They embody the human desire to "walk tall" and attract attention. For some they symbolize glamour and sexiness.

▲ Kimono
The traditional T-shaped embroidered kimono is a universal symbol of Japan. The colors and decorative motifs chosen—often drawn from the natural world—have strong symbolic connotations and reveal much to the informed observer about the wearer's age, status, wealth, and taste.

▲ Longyi
This traditional Burmese costume comprises a piece of cloth that is worn round the lower body. Both men and women wear the longyi. Men sometimes tuck up the longyi between their legs for ease of movement. The garment is usually made of cotton, but silk is worn on special occasions.

▲ Kilt
In Scotland the kilt, part of the national costume, is symbolic both of kinship and masculinity. Members of different clans can be identified by the color and pattern of the tartan from which their kilts are made, and they parade them with pride at national sporting and other cultural events.

SEE ALSO
Nationality *pp.222–23*
Headwear *pp.250–51*
Uniforms *pp.252–53*
Jewelry *pp.254–55*
Masks *pp.270–71*

HEADWEAR

Hats and headdresses are redolent with meaning. They can signal, at a glance, whole cultures or religions, or may identify occupation, status, gender, or function. Headwear can represent authority and power: the symbolic "pinnacle" of that power is the crown worn by a monarch. Metaphorically, we "put on different hats" to suggest a change of outlook. Removing a hat in certain social situations can indicate humility (in church, for instance), or be a sign of good manners.

▲ Fez
The tassled, brimless cap was once part of Turkish national dress. The fez was outlawed, along with the veil for women, when Turkey became a republic in 1925.

▲ Mitre
Christian bishops, archbishops, cardinals, abbots, and the Pope wear this tall headdress. The cleft in its crown may symbolize the "cloven tongues" of the day of Pentecost, when the Apostles were filled with the Holy Spirit and spoke in foreign tongues.

▲ American Indian feather headdress
Thought to have originated with the Sioux American Indians, the feather headdress is highly symbolic. Each feather was earned through an act of courage—the most prized feather was the eagle's.

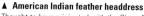

▲ Kippah
The traditional slightly rounded skull cap, called the kippah, is worn as a religious symbol in Judaism. Most Jewish men cover their heads when praying or attending the synagogue.

▲ Pith helmet
Made originally from pith bark, and later cork, the pith helmet was the practical and iconic standard issue headdress for European colonial rulers in Africa and India.

▲ Top hat
Synonymous with 1940s high society, the upstanding top hat suggested raffish male elegance. Today the "topper" is still worn at weddings and other formal occasions.

▲ Turban
In the East the turban represents faith and status. Turbans have been worn by Arabs, Incas, Babylonians, and Egyptians. For Sikhs it is still an essential part of their attire.

▲ Mortarboard
Evolving from a cap worn by Roman Catholic clergy, the mortarboard, when worn by graduates and teachers, symbolizes the knowledge gained through education.

▼ Veil

The veil is a traditional feminine attire denoting modesty and purity. Today a variety of veils, including the *burqa* and *niqab*, are worn by Muslim women as religious dress and a symbol of modesty. In Christianity a woman who becomes a nun is said to "take the veil."

MEDIEVAL NUN'S VEIL, WORN BY THE WIFE OF MARTIN LUTHER

VEILED MOROCCAN WOMEN

▼ Chef's hat

The chef's hat is instantly recognizable in Europe. Worn since the 16th century, the *toque*, as it is known in France, indicates rank in the kitchen. The higher hat is worn by the head chef, whereas ordinary cooks wear a lower version.

KITCHEN ORDERLY

SOUS CHEF

HEAD CHEF

▼ Cap

The baseball cap originated in the 1840s with the New York Knickerbockers. Since then it has become a "social leveler," worn by US presidents (Bush and Clinton) and rappers alike. Symbolically as American as apple pie, it is also worn in countries around the world. The flat cap, which has a long association with the working classes in the United Kingdom and Ireland, is now a symbol of country pursuits.

FLAT CAP

BASEBALL CAP

WIGS

False heads of hair were worn in Ancient Egypt, Ancient Greece, and by the Romans. They became part of fashionable men's attire in 17th-century France and later England. In the 18th century wigs were adopted by both sexes as a symbol of affluence and high status. Wigs were first worn by lawyers during the reign of Charles II. They have become a worldwide symbol of the British legal system and also provide an element of anonymity in the courtroom.

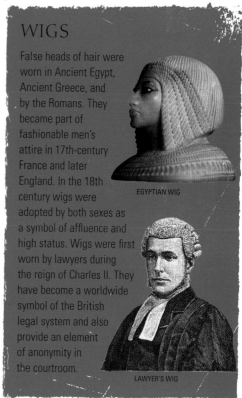

EGYPTIAN WIG

LAWYER'S WIG

▲ Policeman's helmet

The "comb-", "ball-"; or "rose-top" British policeman's helmet evolved from the top hat worn by the original police force from 1829. The helmet's distinctive domed shape is a potent symbol of law and order.

▲ Beret

The circular beret is traditionally associated with the French working man. It is also symbolic of military courage, especially when colored, as in the elite US Army Special Forces, the "Green Berets."

▲ Bearskin

The heavy fur caps worn by Irish, Scots, Grenadier, Coldstream, and Welsh Guards were first adopted in 1815. They symbolize the defeat at Waterloo of the French Imperial Guard, who also wore them.

▲ **Military uniform**
Members of China's elite Honor Guard marching in line during a welcome ceremony at
the Great Hall of the People in Beijing, China, for the prime minister of the Republic of
Korea. The ceremonial nature of the synchronized military marching reinforces the
symbolism of the uniforms—a uniformity of purpose and pride as the nation's defenders.

UNIFORMS

For centuries people have worn uniforms to symbolize occupation, status, or affiliation. Different uniforms create different impressions: of authority, or being part of a group or a caring community.

Uniforms usually bear a badge or emblem denoting the body they represent. Some uniforms identify state authority, symbolizing the day-to-day rule of law, as with the US Marines, while others symbolize a celebratory or ceremonial duty, as with the Vatican's Swiss Guards. For many, a school uniform is the first uniform they will wear. School uniforms need to be practical and comfortable but also distinctive, so that a child's school can be easily identified.

MILITARY DRESS

Military uniforms symbolize courage since it is in these uniforms that men and women fight for their countries. Some are ceremonial, like the scarlet tunics and huge black bearskin hats of the Grenadier Guards. Other uniforms are designed for combat, such as the camouflage khaki used by desert-fighting soldiers. Rank is usually indicated by emblems worn on the upper arm and shoulders. Usually, the more stripes, brocade, or medals, the more senior or honored the officer.

▲ **Nurse**
Nurses' uniforms are often made from blue material as this color is believed to be both soothing and reassuring and a sign of benevolent professionalism.

RELIGIOUS UNIFORMS

Robes worn by members of religious orders act as symbolic uniforms, identifying the wearers' beliefs to an onlooker. Hierarchy can be expressed by the richness of a robe or by its color; for example, in some religions gold represents light and the highest truth. Buddhist monks wear plain saffron or ocher robes to symbolize the falling yellow, orange, or brown leaves as colors of renunciation in the pursuit of enlightenment. Nuns can also be distinguished by the habit they wear. Since they have eschewed all worldly considerations their clothing is simple. Nurses' uniforms evolved from nuns' habits (nuns traditionally tending to the sick). A nurse's uniform symbolizes professional care and cleanliness the world over.

IDEOLOGY

A uniform can also signify ideological allegiance to a group, as with the Italian revolutionary Giuseppe Garibaldi and his band of guerilla "Redshirts" in the 1860s, and Oswald Mosley and his British Union of Fascists, who became known as "Blackshirts" in the Britain of the 1930s. By contrast, the Salvation Army has adopted a uniform that is military in style to reflect the Christian "army" "fighting" for good in society and providing practical care for all in need.

▲ **Canadian Mountie**
The Royal Canadian Mounted Police have red uniforms to mark the connection with Britain and also to differentiate them from the United States military who wear blue.

▲ **School uniforms**
Throughout the world school uniforms help to promote the identity and values of a particular school. Here Japanese schoolgirls gather in their uniforms to celebrate a festival. Japanese junior and senior high school uniforms traditionally consist of a dark military style dress for the boys and a sailor-style outfit for the girls.

SEE ALSO
Clothing & costume *pp.248–49*
Headwear *pp.250–51*
Group affiliation *pp.258–59*

UNIFORMS

JEWELRY

Since prehistoric times, people have adorned themselves with jewelry, using all types of decorative objects from shell and bone to precious stones. Jewelry has always had great significance as a symbol of status and power, or as the identifying mark of a clan or tribe. It is also an age-old token of love or honor, and may be worn simply as a statement of wealth. Some gemstones or motifs are rich in symbolic meaning, representing, for example, faithfulness or fertility, or conferring protection on the wearer.

► Egyptian coin necklace
Jewelry reflects wealth, and this Egyptian necklace has real coins. In traditional ceremonies such necklaces are worn to represent the dowry of the bride. Coin necklaces and other coined jewelry, such as ankle bracelets, are also popular accessories with belly dancers.

▲ Sumba earrings
On the Indonesian island of Sumba the distinctive ornaments known as *mamuli* are given as wedding gifts and worn as earrings or pendants. They symbolize fertility and may bear mythical motifs.

▲ Totem bird
This elaborate pre-Columbian golden eagle head was worn as a lip plug, which was inserted into a slit in the lower lip. It would probably have been worn by a warrior and may have represented a protective beast to ward off evil spirits.

▲ Love ring
Love rings were fashionable in the 19th century. Made of interconnecting hoops, with hands clasped around a heart, the rings symbolized the inseparability of the lovers who wore them.

▲ Signet ring
A sign of power, the signet ring was used by royalty and nobles to literally imprint their authority. They would press the ring into wax to seal and identify letters, contracts, and other documents. Usually worn on the little finger, the ring today often carries a coat of arms or family crest.

► Leg ornament
In parts of Africa and Asia leg ornaments were worn by women in some cultures to signify wealth. They could be very heavy, some weighing as much as 33lb (15kg), and were prized for their bulk and their craftsmanship. Leg ornaments made of silver show Islamic influences—to Muslims silver signifies purity.

▲ Inca necklace
Jewelry found in Inca tombs, including bracelets, necklaces, and earrings, shows great silver- and gold-smithing skills. In Inca society, jewelry symbolized status and power. This necklace, which encircles smaller ornaments, is made with turquoise, shell, and gold.

SOCIETY & CULTURE

► African beads
Throughout the African continent beads serve as money, symbolize power and wealth, and act as spiritual talismans. Masai women are famed for their elaborate beaded collars, and in Zulu culture colors and patterns convey complex coded messages.

▲ Diamond star
This 12-pointed diamond star brooch from about 1870 signifies the radiance of the wearer. A 12-pointed star may be used to represent the 12 Tribes of Israel, the 12 Apostles, or the 12 days of Christmas.

◄ Jade Buddha
In Ancient China jade was considered the noblest of all gems. According to Taoist belief, the stone was formed from dragons' semen. In Buddhism the color green represents harmony and balance, making it appropriate for this pendant.

► Neck rings
Among the Padaung of the eastern Burmese hills, women traditionally wear neck rings as a sign of beauty. Added one at a time, over several years, to the Padaung, they are a symbol of their homeland and are thought to give the women the elegance of wild geese, and to have magical, protective qualities.

FRUIT JEWELRY

Fruit is linked symbolically with fertility and female sexuality. It also signifies good luck, abundant harvests, and evidence of God's bounty. Such positive symbolism makes fruit a natural and popular motif in jewelry. A fruit can have more than one meaning. For example, an apple can signify temptation ("forbidden fruit") and downfall, but also represent a woman's breasts and sexuality.

► Pomegranate
This Ancient Greek pendant, dated from about 1300BCE, was probably worn by a bride in a wedding ceremony. It represents the many-seeded pomegranate, a popular symbol of fertility.

◄ Silverwork jewelry
This woman from the Leigong Shan area of China is wearing intricately embroidered traditional festival costume and a silverwork necklace, headpiece, and breastplate. This extensive silver jewelry is worn as a sign of one's tribe and marriageable status.

▲ Vine leaves
Grapes and vine leaves represent vibrant life, healthy growth, and good fortune. This Victorian gold and cabochon garnet vine brooch may have been given as a symbolic wedding gift.

SEE ALSO
Precious stones *pp.42–43*
Eagle *pp.62–63*
Fruits of the Earth *pp.98–99*
Love & marriage *pp.126–27*
Taoism & Shinto *pp.170–71*
Shapes *pp.284–89*

JEWELRY

BODY ADORNMENT

In modern western societies body adornment is about self-expression or even shock value. However, it has evolved from deeply rooted rituals to symbolically identifying its wearer as a member of a tribal, military, or sacred community. Body art has been practiced for millennia. The 5,300-year-old mummy known as Ötzi the Iceman, found in the Alps, has 59 tattoos.

PHYSICAL ART

Since Stone Age times, people have used the body as a canvas on which to express cultural identity, signify power or status, honor sacred or ancestral connections, or mark rites of passage. In many societies people have adorned their bodies not just with symbolic clothing and jewelry, but also with make-up, paint, tattoos, body piercings, and even with patterns cut into the skin. The symbolism varies from culture to culture, but often signifies the passage to adulthood, protection from the evil eye, or the desire to frighten foes in warfare.

► Kohl
In Ancient Egypt kohl eyeliner was worn not only to look fashionable but to help cut the glare of the Sun and to prevent eye infections. Women colored the upper eyelid black and the lower one green, a color symbolizing youth and rebirth. Kohl was derived from malachite, which symbolized joyfulness.

▲ Stretched earlobes
In many ancient cultures elongated earlobes were symbolic of royalty and spiritual authority. In some cultures today plugs are inserted into the lobes, signifying beauty and cultural identity. This wearer is a Pokot woman from Kenya.

◄ Lip plugs
In several Amazonian and African groups lip plugs (or labrets) are worn for beauty and status. This engraving is of a 19th-century American Indian; young men received the piercings to symbolize their entrance into manhood.

▲ Scarification
Cutting the skin to create decorative scarring is most widely practiced in Africa. It is mainly done to enhance beauty, but the patterns used also symbolize group identity or rites of passage. Scarification is seen here on the abdomen of a girl from the agro-pastoral Toposa people of Sudan.

▲ War paint
Ever since the Stone Age, warriors have decorated themselves with paint, shells, feathers, or animal teeth. In New Guinea symbolic red and yellow-ocher paint is applied, while feathers and other items invoke magical spirits that endow the warriors with courage and invincibility.

► Henna
Obtained from the plant *Lawsonia inermis*, which grows in the arid regions of North Africa, the Middle East, and India, henna symbolizes good luck on festive occasions, such as weddings. It is used here to decorate the hand of a Moroccan Berber woman in preparation for her wedding.

TATTOOS

Tattooing is one of the oldest forms of art and possibly one of the most painful. In some societies, tattoos are indelible marks of tribe or social status, signifying the passage to adulthood, identifying the wearer's rank or skills, and enhancing sexual allure. Traditionally, tattoos were believed to protect the wearer from evil. Symbolic motifs were tattooed on to the skin and acted as talismans throughout life.

◄ US Navy
Here a sailor is being tattooed by a shipmate aboard the USS *New Jersey*. The anchor remains the preeminent symbol of the Navy in both service emblems and tattoos.

▲ Maori mokas
Until the 1870s, Maori men in New Zealand etched deep tattoos, or mokas, over their faces. Indicating a man's status and identity, they were added in stages from puberty onward in a series of initiation rites.

◄ Female facial tattoo
A Koya tribeswoman south of Baliguda in Orissa, India, shows the facial tattoos common among hill tribes of this region. The tattoos signify tribal affiliation and beauty. The Koya practise the art of "face reading" and worship the goddess Vana Durga.

▲ Gang member
The prevalence of tattoos in gangs, such as these tattoos on a deported Honduran member of the 18th Street gang in Los Angeles, has led to the stereotype that people with elaborate tattoos may be troublemakers.

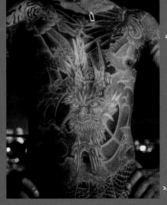

▲ Totally tattooed
The full-body tattoo was traditionally associated with the *yakuza*—the Japanese mafia. This one features the water dragon motif, once regarded by 18th-century firefighters as a protective symbol.

PIERCINGS

Body piercings, also known as body modification, have become popular in modern western culture. Multiple ear piercings and piercing of the navel, nipples, tongue, and labia are commonly found, and bolts are sometimes inserted through the penis. Piercings are mostly undertaken as a fashion statement, to enhance sexual pleasure, and also to symbolize the transition to adulthood.

◄ Multiple piercings
A strikingly adorned woman poses at an international tattoo convention. Extravagant piercings such as these are a way of expressing individuality; they symbolize freedom of choice and the personal allegiances of the wearer.

◄ Nose rings
Throughout India nose rings are often used as adornments. Tradition has it that before her wedding a Hindu girl would perform a *puja* ("act of reverence") to the goddess Parvati to bring her husband-to-be prosperity, health, and a long life. During the *puja* her nose would be pierced and a ring inserted to symbolize her married status. Placing it in the left nostril was believed to make childbirth easier.

BODY ADORNMENT

The need to belong to a group is a powerful urge common to all human societies. Whether by birth or belief, group affiliation gives us a sense of community, of history, of memories, and of aspirations, all of which serve to add to our sense of cultural identity.

Communities are united by shared histories, often of struggle, as well as by customs and traditions. Belonging is often symbolized outwardly by clothing, codified behavior, celebrations, competitions, and cultural icons, allowing instant recognition.

SP⊕RTS

Most sports carry highly visible identifiers, emblems, and "coats of arms" (sports effectively being a substitute for war). Supporters wear the "strip" and other emblems of their team to show their support. One of the world's most iconic symbols is the five linked rings of the Olympics, representing five continents joined in the ideal of competitive sports, while the Olympic ceremony evokes the spirit of sport since antiquity.

▲ **Barcelona FC**
The badges of football teams convey symbolism beyond that of sports. The club badge of FC Barcelona incorporates the flags of Catalonia and St. George (patron saint of Catalonia), combining the sporting and political history of a nation and its capital city.

▲ **All Blacks**
The national New Zealand rugby union team are the All Blacks. Their name is said to derive from a newspaper misprint describing them as "all backs" (that is, no forwards). Their team colors are black, with a native silver fern to symbolize their nationality. They perform a Maori war dance before matches to invoke the spirits of good fortune.

◄ **Three Lions**
The emblem of England's cricket and football teams is three lions, adapted from the royal coat of arms introduced in Norman times to symbolize royal power. The three lions appeared on the first England football shirt in 1872 and their symbolism is now reinforced with a song of the same name.

CLUBS AND GANGS

People are often drawn to join a society for their own age group and gender, whether it is Girl Scouts or Gay Pride. This is sometimes done to gain a stronger social voice to advance a cause but is often simply a desire to socialize with one's own kind. There will frequently be costumes, rituals, and activities to symbolize that belonging, or a shared taste perhaps in fashion and music, such as punk or country and western. Teenagers in particular join "tribes" as a rejection of adult codes of behavior, using slang that is deliberately incomprehensible to outsiders.

▲ **Hells Angels**
The motorcycle groups known collectively as Hells Angels were first seen in the USA after World War II, their name and insignia inspired by an Air Force squadron. At first they symbolized merely rebellion and a rejection of the mainstream norms, but today the name is

▲ **Women's Institute**
The largest voluntary organization for women in England and Wales, the Women's Institute was originally associated with homemade jam and cakes. Since the advent of feminism, the WI has become a powerful voice on local community and

▲ **Punk**
The punk movement in music, fashion, literature, and graphics snowballed in the mid-1970s. The movement represented a reaction against the glamour of progressive rock and the older generation. Punk ethics emphasized personal choice and freedom, symbolized by

WORSHIP AND CELEBRATION

The urge to share sacred rites and rituals, to wear symbolic talismans, and to communally demonstrate one's faith goes back to antiquity. Today regular worship at a religious center is traditional in most cultures, and for believers it symbolizes the practice of their faith. Christians traveling away from home are likely in most places to find a church where they can attend Sunday service. Similarly, no matter where they are, Muslims will use a prayer mat to kneel and face east to Mecca, their action symbolically stating their spiritual submission to God.

◄ Carnival
The origins of carnival (from the Latin *carne vale*, meaning "farewell to flesh") date back to the Ancient Greek Spring festival. The celebrations were adapted by the Christian religions to precede the beginning of Lent—traditionally a time of abstinence from all pleasures. Rio de Janeiro's famous carnival in February has come to symbolize Brazil and its unique samba music and dance.

▲ Semana Santa
During Holy Week in Spain, many participants in the traditional processions wear the *nazareno*, or penitential robe, and drape their heads with cloth held up by a cardboard cone. They carry crosses, and some have chains and shackles. Processional floats bear images and scenes symbolizing the story of the Passion of Christ.

◄ The Russian Orthodox Church
In Russia the Orthodox Church traditionally provided spiritual strength, education, and a unifying force to the common people. In the Soviet era Christian group worship and celebrations were banned as they were regarded as symbolizing the old order of society. Services were held in secret, and Bibles had to be smuggled into the country.

POLITICS

Symbolism is rife in politics, particularly in its signs of affiliation. Every party has its logo and insignia of power, from Gandhi's spinning wheel, symbolizing non-violent opposition, to the US Democrats' donkey, which represents strength and courage. Supporters wear these logos or carry them on banners and flags to show their commitment to a cause. Such symbols can galvanize a crowd, as with the sea of swastikas at Hitler's Nuremburg rallies in the 1930s.

▲ Chairman Mao
The Thoughts of Chairman Mao, or the "Little Red Book," was the most visible icon in China of the Cultural Revolution of the 1960s. In propaganda pictures Red Guards were always seen with a copy.

◄ Mau Mau
In the 1950s a militant African nationalist movement called the Mau Mau began violent resistance to British colonial rule in Kenya. The movement was especially noted for its ritual oaths, used to symbolize unity and independence.

▲ Che Guevara
Born in Argentina, Che Guevara joined Fidel Castro to fight for the Cuban revolution in the 1950s. He was seen as a romantic revolutionary hero and his image became a symbol of resistance for left-wing students in the 1960s.

SEE ALSO
Christianity *pp.176–79*
Islam *pp.180–81*
Shapes *pp.284–89*
Brands & logos *pp.316–17*
Heraldic emblems *pp.318–23*

GROUP AFFILIATION

259

FREEMASONRY

Probably the world's oldest association for men, Freemasonry is a fraternity with millions of members. Its workings are secret and it makes extensive use of signs and allegories. It developed out of groups, or lodges, of stonemasons who built the cathedrals of medieval Europe. Some claim that it goes back to the building of the Temple of Solomon, but documented meetings only date from the 17th century. Freemasonry is certainly the largest "enclosed society" and exists in various forms across the world.

SYMBOLS OF FREEMASONRY

Since Freemasonry emerged from the craftsmen's guilds, many of its symbols were linked to building and stonemasonry. The level and square are clear examples. As cathedral building declined, the lodges accepted non-masons to boost membership and they developed signs more associated with religious orders and crusading brotherhoods.

▼ First Degree Tracing Board
New members are initiated into the secret language of Freemasons through the use of a tracing board on which the many symbols of the organization are displayed.

The Sun is the embodiment of male energy, light, and warmth.

Surrounded by rays of light, the all-seeing eye is sometimes seen as the omnipotent God watching over humanity.

Jacob's Ladder connects the pathway between Heaven and Earth. Its three principle rungs are Faith, Hope, and Charity.

The key represents the key to truth, which only the worthy can turn.

The uncarved block of stone, the ashlar, represents the unformed, whereas the carved block (opposite it) represents the perfected.

INITIATION OF THE NOVICE

Freemasonry teaches lessons of morality through ritual. Members working through the rituals are taught by "degrees." Each degree is a "step" in the process. As with many societies, Freemasonry has its own ceremony that welcomes the candidate into its mysteries.

▲ Initiation ceremony
During the ceremony the novice is blindfolded, symbolizing his ignorance of the truth, then exposed for the first time to the lodge. He promises to do his duty to God and his country.

The Moon symbolizes mystery and creation.

The three pillars are, from left to right, Doric, Ionic, and Corinthian in style. They represent the "rule of three": the strength, wisdom, and beauty once displayed in the building of the Temple of Solomon.

The black-and-white checkered floor symbolizes the forces of dark and light and good and evil, and the struggle between the two.

The four compass points appear on the border of the Tracing Board and denote orientation and earthly strength.

MASONS' TOOLS

While there may well be stone-workers who are Masons, Freemasonry does not set out to teach the skills of stonework. Instead, it uses the work of medieval masons as an allegory for moral development. So the symbols of Freemasonry are the common tools used by medieval stonemasons, such as the apron (originally of lamb skin), gavel, ladder, level, and so on.

▲ Square
An emblem of the Lodge Master, the square "sets" members on the correct path to civic duty and represents a moral code. The square is also an instrument that gathers disparate elements into order.

▲ Level
The level symbolizes equality and justice. The level and plumb are nearly always united in ritual. Masons are said to meet "on the level," meaning that all Masons are brothers, regardless of occupation or income.

▲ Gavel
The hammer, or gavel, is a formative, masculine force and is symbolic of justice and authority. Traditionally, the Freemason's gavel is made of beech, which indicates both prosperity and endurance.

▲ Trowel
The Masonic trowel literally and metaphorically "cements" brotherhood and spreads brotherly love. It remains an important symbol of Freemasonry's unity and brotherhood among men.

◄ Plumb rule and line
Builders use the plumb rule and line to determine the vertical from a given point. For the Masons these tools symbolically indicate moral rectitude and upright behavior. Also, the plumb rule is an emblem of the junior warden of a lodge.

◄ Ladder
The ladder is the link between Heaven and Earth. Some Masons will climb with their eyes fixed on the goal at the very top of the ladder but for most, only one or two rungs are visible before them. As the Mason's character becomes stronger, so more rungs are opened up to him.

◄ Compasses
An important Masonic emblem, a pair of compasses represent God drawing His plans for the world. When seen with the square, the combination of upward- and downward-pointing triangles might indicate a primitive sexual symbolism of combined male-female physicality.

MASONS' MARKS

All Masons have their own identifying mark, following the stonemasons of medieval Europe, who marked stones in buildings and other public structures with symbols or letters. The swastika shape is an ancient and universal symbol of the Sun and the cycle of birth and rebirth. It was especially popular in India (long before the Nazis usurped it).

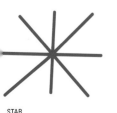

STAR

SWASTIKA

CIRCLE

GRIPS AND HANDSHAKES

Freemasonry is often associated with secret knuckle-to-knuckle handshakes, grips, and passwords. There are different, quite involved, symbolic handshakes by which Freemasons recognize each other. Being secret, the significance is not readily available to the non-initiated. Suffice to say there is a hierarchy of greetings (and welcoming into the community) according to the Mason's degree of initiation.

◄ Handshakes
Among the esoteric grips and handshakes, the "Boaz" (*top*) is recognized as the "Grip of the Entered Apprentice." It is claimed that each Mason presses the thumb against the top of the first knuckle-joint of their fellow Mason. The "Tubulcain" (*middle*) represents the "Pass Grip of the Master Mason," while the "Lion's Paw" (*bottom*) signifies the "Real Grip of a Master Mason."

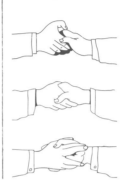

DOLLAR BILL

America's first president, George Washington, was a Mason, as were many signers of the Constitution. American Republican values dovetail with Masonic values: civic duty and a high regard for learning and progress. Freemasonry symbols were absorbed as emblems of the nation, and the all-seeing eye and pyramid both appear on the dollar bill.

All-seeing eye

Pyramid

SEE ALSO
Steps to Heaven *pp.236–37*
The home *pp.238–41*
Shapes *pp.284–89*

ART

Artists have always incorporated symbols into their works. Many paintings deploy a symbolic language so that objects and figures represent not just themselves but also ideas and concepts. By looking at the symbolism present in works of art, we can examine the beliefs and ideologies that determined an artist's thinking. An understanding of the pictorial language of symbolism can also reveal both the beliefs and emotions of the artist's imaginative world.

NATURE

The systematic use of symbols from the natural world has often been used by artists to express allegorical meaning, as in the formalized paintings of China's Ming dynasty (*see right*). While Brueghel's innovative visual language (*see below*) is used to represent a country landscape and the activities of its people in the grip of a cold winter. Gauguin (*see bottom*) uses an individualistic and elemental language to expresses his unique vision of nature and people's place within it.

▲ **Yin Hong, *Birds and Flowers of Early Spring***
This Ming dynasty hanging scroll, dating from c1500, is a fine example of the birds and flowers genre of painting of China's Ming dynasty. The works were hung in imperial halls and served as metaphors for the Emperor and his court by using nature to convey symbolic meaning. Here the subject of the painting is an allusion to imperial allegiance: the pheasants symbolize bravery and steadfastness, while the partridges represent the loyal followers of the Emperor.

◄ **Peter Brueghel, *Hunters in the Snow***
This is one of a cycle of six paintings from 1565 in which Brueghel portrayed the seasons and the country activities associated with them. This scene depicts man (in the foreground) against the vastness of nature as we look down through the bare trees to the physical world of the snow-covered village, frozen lakes, and distant mountains.

◄ **Paul Gauguin, *Where Do We Come From? Who Are We? Where Are We Going?***
Gauguin's 1897 painting shows various figures contemplating the questions of human existence. The painting should be read from right to left. The three women and sleeping child represent the beginning of life; the middle group symbolize young adulthood; and in the final group Gauguin wrote that "an old woman approaching death appears reconciled to her thoughts."

SOCIETY & CULTURE

RELIGION

Artists of all cultures have reflected their religious convictions through their work, and symbolism is an important element in most religious art. Religious iconography has been used to convey religious meanings in art from Ancient Egypt through to the Renaissance and beyond. Christian art uses symbols, such as the crucifix, snakes, and haloes, to convey allegorical meaning. Bosch, one of the finest medieval painters, depicts humanity as fundamentally flawed. Salvation is achievable but only by the greatest effort, whereas Buddhist Burmese miniatures depicting the life of the Buddha show the spiritual path to enlightenment.

▶ **Hieronymus Bosch,**
Death and the Miser
This panel painting from c1490 by the Flemish artist Hieronymus Bosch shows the end of the life of a miser. Symbolic oppositions of good and evil occur throughout the painting. The dying man seems torn between salvation and avarice (one of the seven deadly sins). A demon looking out from under the bed tempts him with a bag of gold, while his guardian angel on his right encourages him to acknowledge the crucifix in the window. Death, in the form of a skeleton holding an arrow, enters at the left. A lantern containing the fire of Hell is carried by a demon on top of the bed.

▲ ***The Future Buddha's Courtly Life***
This 19th-century Burmese manunscript shows Prince Siddhartha carried by his father, the king, on a sacred white elephant and sheltered from the Sun by a parasol, symbolizing royalty. The king performs the Plowing Ceremony, a symbolic act ensuring the fertility of the fields.

▲ Stanley Spencer, ***The Resurrection, Cookham***
In this painting from c1925, Spencer visualizes the resurrection of the dead in a churchyard in Cookham, England, the village where he lived. As a devout Christian, Spencer's faith shaped his art and he sought to symbolize the sacred in the lives of ordinary people.

SEE ALSO
Birds pp.58–61
Buddhism pp.164–69
Christianity pp.176–79
Numbers pp.284–89

POLITICS

The portraiture of the early 16th century, as exemplified by Holbein, has a subtle political dimension. By the careful deployment of objects and symbols surrounding his subjects, Holbein gives us an insight into the political tensions within England in 1533. In contrast, The Italian Futurist movement of the early 20th century showed a more direct engagement in social themes, particularly urban life, and was political in its intent. Alternatively, Socialist Realist art of the 1930s in the Soviet Union was an aspect of Stalin's rule and sought to express the struggles of ordinary people and to educate and inspire the masses. Socialist Realism demanded that an artist show honesty, and support for the revolution.

▶ **Hans Holbein the Younger, *The Ambassadors***
Holbein's painting of 1533 depicts two French ambassadors surrounded by a range of symbolic objects. On the upper shelf is a celestial globe, suggesting Copernicus's view that it was the Sun, not the Earth, that was the center of the solar system. In the foreground is the distorted image of a skull, a symbol of mortality. When seen from a point to the right of the painting, the distortion is corrected.

▲ **Umberto Boccioni, *Street Noises Invade the House***
Boccioni's 1911 work is his attempt to symbolically create a representation of time and movement. Boccioni not only creates the forms of the street, but also incorporates the rhythm and sound of the chaotic street scene into the painting.

▲ **Alexander Deineka, *We Are Mechanize Donbas***
As a Socialist Realist artist, Deineka was interested in creating a true depiction of the life and work of the Soviet people. This poster from 1930 also successfully attempts to symbolize the revolutionary spirit of Communism in Stalin's Soviet Union.

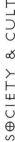

SOUL

The Emperor Jahangir, who commissioned the portrait of the dying courtier Inayat Khan, was especially interested in recording the phenomenon of death, as in the almost objective miniature below. In contrast, in Expressionist art the emphasis is on subjective feeling and painting that symbolizes the state of mind of the artist. Non-naturalistic colors and distorted forms are used to symbolize inner turmoil. Munch's iconic *The Scream* (*right*) deals in particular with the question of existential angst and how in a godless universe we are left with uncertainty and anxiety.

▲ **Edvard Munch, *The Scream***
Munch's *The Scream* is an icon of modern art. This famous Expressionist image, painted in 1893, depicts an agonized figure who cries against a blood red skyline. For many it has come to symbolize modern man in an attack of existential anguish.

◄ **Anonymous, *Inayat Khan Dying***
This example of Mughal Indian miniature art from 1618 depicts a dying courtier at the court of Emperor Jahangir. The Emperor was a great patron of the arts, and under Jahangir painting was an aristocratic pursuit depicting the life of the court. The subject here is diminished by alcohol and opium addiction and his blindness is unsparingly depicted. Because of the work's intimacy we feel like intruders on the scene.

DREAM

Sleep and dream were common subjects for Henry Fuseli, one of the most important figures in the Romantic movement. Indeed, Fuseli was an artist who was ahead of his time in exploring the human psyche through his art. By the 1920s (nearly a century after Fuseli's death) the Surrealists—greatly influenced by Sigmund Freud's theories of the unconscious and dreams—began to explore similar themes. Surrealist artists, such as René Magritte, Paul Delvaux, and Salvador Dalí, all used the concept of the unconscious mind to create individualistic and fantastical symbolic imagery.

▲ **Paul Delvaux, *Les Vestales***
Painted in 1972, this work deals with one of Delvaux's favourite subjects—that of unattainable dream-like female figures located in an architectural setting. In this case, the figures are the Vestal Virgins, consecrated to Vesta, the Roman goddess of hearth and home, and vowed to chastity. The objects and architecture create a dream-like world.

◄ **Henry Fuseli, *The Nightmare***
In this 1781 painting Fuseli depicts a woman in the grip of a disturbing dream. The artist conjures up a terrifying image filled with eroticism and fear. The incubus sitting on the woman's body is symbolic of the darkest fears of nightmares. The painting is viewed by many as anticipating Freudian ideas about the unconscious mind.

SEE ALSO
The night sky *pp.20–23*
Vanitas *pp.132–33*

BIRTH ⊕F LIQUID DESIRES

A flamboyant painter and sometime writer, sculptor, and experimental film-maker, Salvador Dalí was probably the greatest Surrealist artist, using bizarre dream imagery to create unforgettable and unmistakable landscapes of his inner world. Dalí's most surreal work examines his own subconscious and records the fears and fantasies found there through symbolic images. In this painting there are four figures interacting with a strange structure.

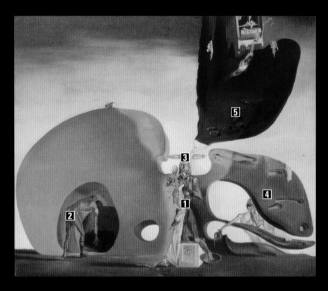

1. & 2. The figures
The people at the center might be father, son, and mother, fused into the nightmarish figure of a hermaphroditic creature. The figure on the left has been interpreted as an image of the artist himself. These figures symbolize Dalí's difficult relationship with his father.

3. Loaf of bread
The problems experienced between father and son were frequently linked by Dalí to the legend of William Tell, the Swiss archer who was compelled to shoot an apple placed on his son's head. For Dalí this myth symbolized the fear of castration of a son by his father. The apple is replaced here by a loaf of bread.

4. The shadow
The dark shadow hanging over the scene comes from an unknown source and may symbolize the threat Dalí felt from his father. More generally it represents a feeling of sadness and death.

5. The cloud
A black cloud emerges from the loaf of bread. Within this cloud there is an inscription in French: *Consigne: gâcher l'ardoise totale?* which can be translated as "Note of Advice: should one spoil the whole bill?," adding to the enigmatic quality of the picture.

Salvador Dali, *Birth of Liquid Desires*, 1931

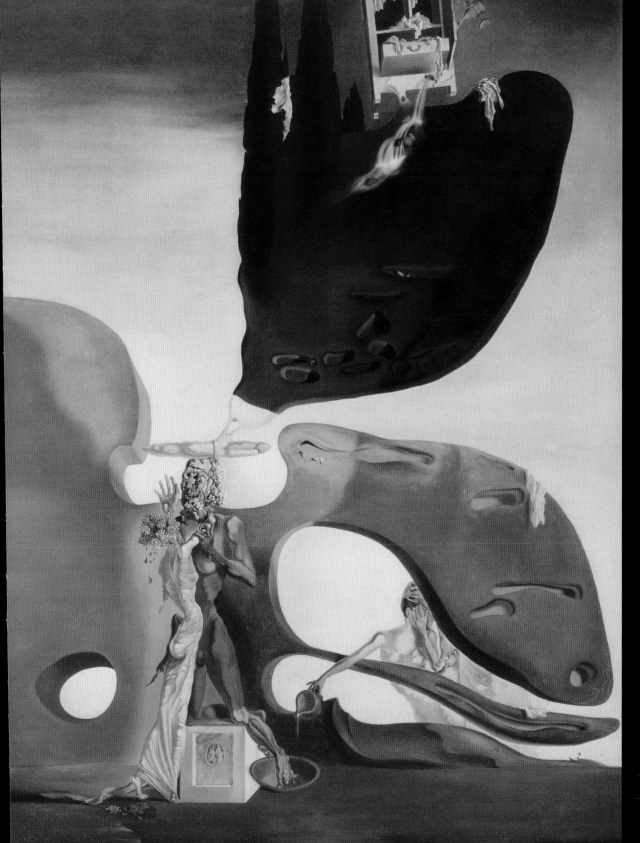

DANCE & THEATER

From war stomps to waltzes, and from break dancing to belly dancing, the movement inspired by dance is totally expressive as a sign of pleasure, athleticism, exuberance, or solemnity. In antiquity dance evoked the sacred spirits or celebrated rituals marking nature's cycles, as well as an initiation, betrothal, or battle. The theater, which often incorporates dance, provides a symbolic representation of the world we live in through the acting, sets, and theme.

▲ Kabuki
A very formalized, traditional Japanese entertainment, *kabuki*—from *ka* ("song"), *bu* ("dance"), and *ki* ("skill")— relies on symbolism, from make-up to props, to convey a story. For example, fans are fluttered to suggest cutting flowers or drinking sake.

▲ Sword dance
Dances involving swords occur all over the world, from Scotland to the Philippines, either to ward off evil spirits or to strengthen the sword in battle. Some end with a motion symbolizing the cutting off of a head. Others recall victory in war or ancient sacrificial rites.

◄ Maypole dance
The dance around the maypole has been performed in Europe since Greek and Roman times in celebration of Spring, a time of new life and abundance. The maypole can be viewed either as a phallic symbol or as a representation of the tree around which people danced in ancient fertility rites.

▲ Thai dancers
The stylized hand movements of Thai dancers enhance their representation as heavenly creatures. Some dances involve the dexterous holding of candles or the wearing of long brass fingernails, and these carry their own symbolism.

▲ Ballet
The precise movements and gestures of a trained Classical ballet dancer can convincingly suggest emotions or tell a story. In early forms of ballet the dancers styled their movements to imitate the deportment and behavior of their patrons, the aristocracy.

◄ Mime
Using gestures, postures, and facial expressions, a mime artist creates a character or story without spoken words. We understand the actor's meaning through coded signs that replace verbal communication.

▲ Whirling dervishes
The original whirling dervishes were the Mawlawiyah, a 13th-century Muslim fraternity. They were so-named by Europeans because they performed prayers spinning on their right foot. Their dance symbolizes a spiritual journey toward perfection.

▲ Classical Indian dance gestures
In India hand gestures in traditional dance convey moods, actions, objects, or creatures. Every hand movement has a symbolic and precise meaning. The body becomes effectively a life-size puppet, as only a restricted set of gestures is used.

▲ Shadow theater of Indonesia
One form of Indonesian shadow theater, *Wayang Kulit*, involves flat leather puppets held behind a white screen so that their shadows are visible to the audience on the other side. The shadow figures symbolize the deeper truths of good and evil.

▲ Chinese opera
Both the singing and acting in Classic Chinese opera are highly stylized to symbolize universal concepts, such as love, bidding farewell, or vengeance. Percussive instruments, including gongs, cymbals, and clappers, control the rhythmic elements of the drama.

◄ Ibsen's symbolic plays
Plays can convey symbolism in the story, set, or dialogue. The 19th-century Norwegian playwright, Henrik Ibsen, created a series of "symbolic plays." In *The Master Builder* the protagonist creates towers—"castles in the air"—that symbolize his ambition "to get to the top."

◄ Sophoclean tragedy
In *Oedipus the King* Sophocles uses blindness and sight as symbols of ignorance and knowledge. Oedipus is ignorant of the truth of his life and the fact that he cannot escape his destiny. When enlightened, he blinds himself, choosing to go on living in darkness.

▲ Shakespeare's drama
In Shakespeare's *Macbeth* blood comes to symbolize the protagonists' guilt. Through words and gestures they show that their crimes have stained their consciences in a way that cannot be washed clean.

SEE ALSO
Hands & feet *pp.116–19*
Masks *pp.270–71*
Musical instruments *pp.274–75*
Sign languages & signals *pp.330–31*
Symbolic gestures *pp.334–37*

MASKS

As well as representing concealment and identification with or transformation into another being, masks can symbolize emotions or aspects of character. Since ancient times, masks have been used in the ritual dances and ceremonies of many cultures to represent deities or ancestral animals. In drama, masks can represent comedy or tragedy; and in western art, a mask can be a symbol of deceit and vice.

RANGDA

BARONG

▲ Rangda and Barong
Performed at Balinese celebrations, the Barong dance-drama relates a Classical myth. A witch figure, Rangda is the "black widow" and her mask personifies evil. The Barong symbolizes health and good fortune. A beard of human hair hangs from his mask, draped with frangipani flowers believed to contain his magic powers. The pair act out a "trance-dance" combat between good and evil.

▲ Indian mask
In India masks are seen as *Maya*, that is, they have the power to make humans believe in illusion. Masks are worn at all types of ritual and performance, during which the living gods are believed to descend into the masks.

▲ Javanese mask
This highly stylized tiger demon mask appears in a Classical epic dance-drama known as *wayang topeng*. This was popular in Javanese courts from about 1000CE, and may be related to ancient masked dances seen throughout the Pacific islands.

▲ Noh theatre mask
In the traditional Noh theater of Japan highly stylized masks represent gods, demons, and men and women both young and old. Their colors can symbolize emotions, such as anger and passion, and traits, such as evil-mindedness.

▲ Kwakiutl mask
American Indian Kwakiutl dancers are able to assume more than one identity by using a "transformation mask." When the dancer pulls levers and strings, the outer mask opens to reveal another within. Kwakiutl masks are used to relate myths. American Indians also adopted the use of bird or animal totem masks to represent the emblem of a family line.

► New Guinea mask
The *jipae* or "basket" mask worn by the Asmat tribe represents a recently deceased member of the community. The *jipae* is lured from the forest at night to join the men in a ritual feast before departing for the world of the dead. The wearer of the mask then assumes that person's worldly responsibilities.

◄ Greek theater mask
The Ancient Greeks devised masks as theatrical devices to represent characters, who might have been hero, villain, or god. The chorus, too, was masked.

▲ Husk mask
The Iroquois American Indians wore corn-husk masks to frighten away evil spirits. Husk faces were regarded as spirits who acted as healers of illness in the home. The Iroquois had a "False Face Society," made up of a group of medicine men who were thought to possess special powers when they put on their masks.

► Venetian mask
Masked balls, or masquerades, first became popular public events in Venice in the 15th century. For wealthy Venetians they provided an escape from everyday formality and an entry into a world of mystery, deceit, and sexual freedom.

▲ Igbo mask
The Igbo of West Africa have a ritualistic "beautiful maiden" mask to represent the feminine spirits. The mask is designed to enchant onlookers and appease the spirits. The face is often white, not black, as the spirit world is believed to be the opposite of the living world.

► Cameroon mask
This Bamileke mask from Cameroon is made up of hundreds of colorful beads, and represents the elephant and the leopard—royal symbols of the king's power and wealth. According to Bamileke legend, the king can transform himself into either one of these animals at will.

► German mask
Harking back to medieval regional folk celebrations and customs, hand-carved wooden masks are worn at certain carnivals in southern Germany and Switzerland. Festival masks can represent "good" and "idealized beauty," or be grotesque versions symbolizing "ugliness" or "beastliness."

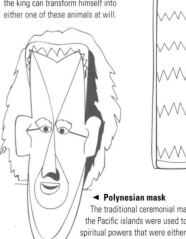

◄ Mardi Gras mask
Masks are worn during the festival of Mardi Gras, a period of carnival and feasting before Lent, the period of fasting and prayer before Easter. Mardi Gras is most elaborately celebrated in New Orleans. The masks are comic or satiric and generally a good-natured excuse for a romp and ribaldry.

▲ Aztec mosaic mask
The mask shown here, dating from the 15th or 16th century, is thought to represent the great sky god of the Aztecs, Tezcatlipoca. The mask was made of alternate bands of turquoise and lignite set on a human skull. The skull was cut away at the back and lined with leather.

◄ Polynesian mask
The traditional ceremonial masks of the Pacific islands were used to symbolize spiritual powers that were either good or evil. Each island had masks that were exclusive to its particular culture.

SEE ALSO
Meso- & South American deities pp.144–45
Nature spirits pp.148–49
Shamanism pp.154–55
Dance & theatre pp.268–69

▲ **Jack and the Beanstalk**
The classic fairy tale of *Jack and the Beanstalk* grew out of an oral tradition, possibly from
Nordic sagas, and is laced with symbolism. The beanstalk represents the tree of "life" or
"wisdom." Each time Jack climbs it he comes back with more worldly goods and wiser ways.

FAIRY TALES

Tales of wonder and imagination, rich in symbolic meaning, fairy tales are folk stories that have been handed down from generation to generation.

▲ Ali Baba
After discovering and taking treasure hidden in a cave by 40 thieves, Ali Baba spends years avoiding retribution and ends up rich and successful.

Fairy tales are folk stories that depict symbolically the death of innocence and the birth of childhood. They also emphasize societies' ideals and teach us to face our fears. Indeed, the psychologists Sigmund Freud and Carl Jung interpreted elements of fairy stories as signaling our deepest anxieties and universal fears and desires.

THE BEAST

In the tale of *Little Red Riding Hood* we see the familiar theme of overcoming the beast. The innocent child is eaten whole by the wolf but the beast's belly is ripped open, revealing the child (and her grandmother) alive inside. Innocence has died but new life has emerged. In *Beauty and the Beast*, Beauty sacrifices herself up to the Beast in order to save her father. When she falls in love with the Beast, finding good in him, Beauty releases him from his enchantment and he is restored to his state as a handsome prince; thus his bestial nature is overcome and good is triumphant.

CULTURE CLASH

Fairy tales can be interpreted in different ways. Some people see a religious or cosmological significance in them, whereas others see a psychological explanation. Alternatively, it is possible to read some stories in terms of a clash of cultures, since so much history involves the merging of cultural

◄ Beauty and the Beast
After meeting the Beast at his castle, Beauty loses her fear of him and starts to fall in love. Because she loves him for his true self, he is transformed and restored to his state as a noble prince.

▲ Little Red Riding Hood
In *Little Red Riding Hood* the evil wolf preys upon the innocent child. However, evil is vanquished and good prevails.

RAGS TO RICHES

Some stories have heroes on a quest. Sometimes they are heroic figures bringing a happy ending to the heroine's plight. In other stories, though, the hero may not be noble or even particularly worthy. In both *Ali Baba*, from *The Thousand and One Nights*, and *Jack and the Beanstalk*, wealth and wisdom are gained after many tribulations. The lesson is that all good things, material and spiritual, need to be earned.

traditions. One interpretation of *Snow White*, for instance, is that this tale represents the overtaking of the old order (the cult of the pre-Christian Mother goddess) by a new order (the Catholic Church). Snow White, a pure maiden at ease with the forest animals and forest people (the seven dwarfs) who care for her when she is cast out by her jealous stepmother, is a metaphor for the old matriarchal nature religions. Her wicked stepmother, who replaces her real mother, Mother Nature, represents the Church that destroyed the ancient faith. Snow White's father represents the ordinary man who wavered between the two faiths.

▲ Snow White
The poisoned apple that the "stepmother queen" (disguised as a kindly old woman) gives to Snow White symbolizes Eve's fall from grace, and with it that of "the Mother Nature cult", which the church condemned.

SEE ALSO
Sacred trees *pp.96–97*
Christianity *pp.176–79*

MUSICAL INSTRUMENTS

The earliest music was probably based on natural sounds and rhythms, such as the beating of a heart, the crash of thunder, or birdsong. Musical instruments symbolize the harmony of nature and the pulse of life. Stringed instruments represent the sounds of Heaven, while drums and other percussion instruments are often associated with revelation, ecstasy, and divine truth. Some instruments have become symbols of nations, while others are identified with war, spiritual well-being, or celebration.

▲ Flute
To Hindus Krishna's flute is the voice of eternity calling to all. In the Pacific the flute is the voice of the spirits, and to Christians it symbolizes the soul's longing for God. In Chinese myth it denotes harmony.

▲ Bagpipes
The national instrument of Scotland, the drone of the bagpipes symbolizes Scottish freedom and strength. Other cultures have long linked it to strength, virility, and freedom from oppression.

▲ Koto
This 13-stringed zither-like instrument is a symbol of music and the national instrument of Japan, where it has been played since the 8th century. The Chinese *ch'in* and Korean *kum* are similar instruments.

ANTHROPOMORPHIC HARP

► Harps
In Judaism and Christianity the harp, an emblem of King David, symbolizes sacred music and is often associated with angels. The Dagda, the father god of the Celts, played a magic harp that put the seasons in the right order, and the harp is the emblem of both Wales and Ireland. The strings of the harp also symbolize the ladder leading to the next life.

IRISH HARP

▲ Trumpet
The trumpet was blown as a call to arms in Roman times and is often linked with battle. Both the Bible and the Koran say that the trumpet shall sound on the last day, when the dead shall be raised.

▲ Drum
Associated with thunder, the drum symbolizes the heart of the universe: Shiva beats out its rhythm in his cosmic dance. A drum beat calls people to prayer and was often used to accompany soldiers into battle.

◄ Bells
The pure chimes of bells symbolize harmony between people and Heaven, wisdom, and the warding off of evil spirits. Bells chime to mark the hours of the day, signal important events, and call people together. "For whom the bell tolls" signifies everyone's death. Finger bells and wind chimes represent the sounds of Heaven. In some cultures bells denote virginity and in others rank and dignity.

▲ Lyre
Orpheus played a lyre that symbolized the harmony of the Universe and he could control men and beasts with his music. Apollo also played the lyre, and it is the emblem of Terpsichore, the muse of dance and song.

◄ Gong

The deep sound of the gong is believed to have magical and protective qualities. In Buddhist temples it marks the stages of the service and wards off evil spirits. It is sacred and often elaborately decorated. In Indonesia gamelan orchestras, including gongs and other percussion instruments, are used to accompany nearly all rituals and ceremonies.

▲ Zither

In Ancient China the zither, or *ch'in*, was the symbol of music and an instrument of worship. When a scholar or sage played the zither, it had the power to reveal to him the essential truth.

◄ Organ

The sounds of the organ have been associated with the Christian faith and Church since the 10th century. Most older churches and cathedrals have an organ, the main purpose of which is to accompany the hymns sung in God's praise, and to encourage a spiritual experience and celestial contemplation.

◄ Didjeridu

A single note "drone" pipe, the didjeridu has been used by Australian Aboriginals to accompany the voice for thousands of years. Its deep, booming tones evoke a powerful spiritual sound that has become a symbol of Australian Aboriginal culture. It vies with the flute as the oldest known wind instrument.

▲ Cymbals

The cymbals represent the two hemispheres. They are an attribute of the Neolithic Mother Goddess, Cybele, and were associated with the wild dances of Bacchus, the Roman god of wine. Tibetan Buddhists play them for both "peaceful" and "wrathful" rituals.

▲ Lute

The lute was very popular in Renaissance and Baroque Europe and was an attribute of the personifications of Music and Hearing. In China it represented harmony, both in marriage and government, and was one of the four symbols of the scholar.

▲ Mu-yu

Mu-yu means "wooden fish" in Chinese and these small percussion instruments are traditionally fish-shaped. They are used as ritual slit drums in Buddhist and Daoist devotions. In Korea and Japan they are also ritual time markers. *Mu-yu* are played in temples, where they are resonant of ceaseless prayer.

▲ Sitar

The Indian stringed instrument, often accompanied by tablas, has been popular for some 700 years and is a symbol of Hindu music. Popularized by the great musician Ravi Shankar, the sitar has become synonymous with Indian culture.

SEE ALSO
Greek & Roman Deities *pp.140–41*
Hinduism *pp.158–63*
Angels *pp.188–89*
Nationality *pp.222–23*
Steps to Heaven *pp.236–67*

MUSICAL INSTRUMENTS

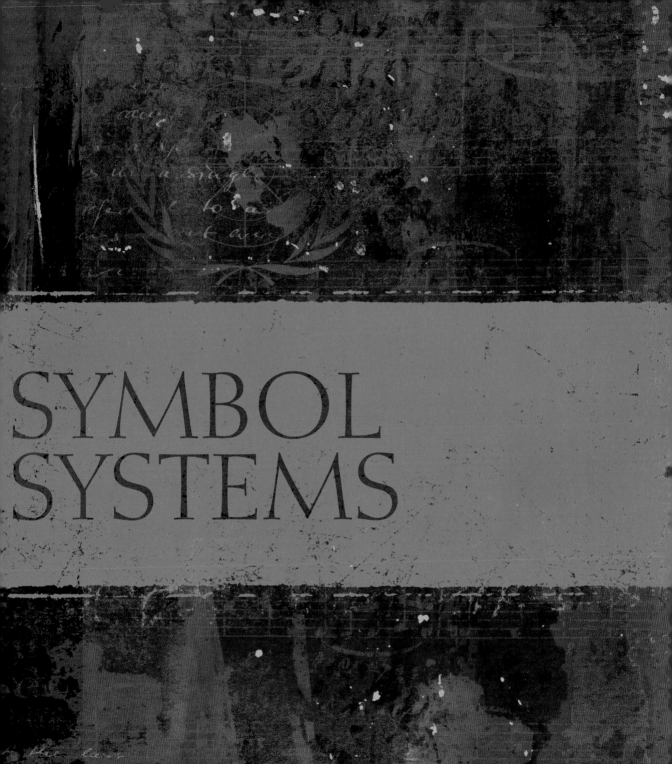

SYMBOL
SYSTEMS

A symbol system is made up of a group of symbols that are interrelated. Such groups range from formally defined systems, like alphabets and numerals, to less formal groups, such as shapes and colors. Some symbol systems evolved over thousands of years and vary between cultures, while others sprang into being relatively quickly and are widespread or even universal. In an ever-shrinking modern world of instant mass communication, affordable international travel, multinational corporations, and global sports, new universal symbol systems are constantly emerging that increasingly transcend language barriers.

The purest example of a symbol system is an alphabet, in that each character is relatively meaningless in isolation. Some letters make sense when used on their own but most only have meaning when used with others. Numerals are more independent and can be used alone at their simplest level—that is, as symbols of the numbers they represent. But the wider symbolism of most numbers relies on their mathematical relationship with the first five numbers; for example, seven symbolizes wholeness because it is the sum of divinity (three) and the material earth (four). With less formal systems, such as shape and color, although the symbolism of each system member can stand alone, it often tells only one side of the story—for instance, the gloomy, evil symbolism of black is far less potent without the contrasting purity and holiness associated with white.

The symbolism of shape and color evolved over such a long time that it almost seems genetically programmed within each culture. The symbolism of heraldry and flags, however, sprang into being much more quickly, and

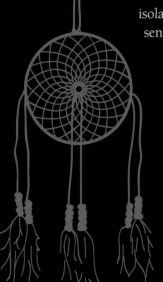

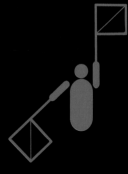

THE PUREST EXAMPLE OF A SYMBOL SYSTEM IS AN ALPHABET, IN WHICH EACH CHARACTER IS RELATIVELY MEANINGLESS IN ISOLATION

both were created consciously and controlled as recognizable systems. Heraldry constitutes one of the most complex and richly resonant symbol systems, and to those involved its symbolism is specific, clear, and unambiguous. The symbolism of national flags is similarly unambiguous. Relatively recent phenomenona, many flags contain universal symbols, such as crosses for Christian nations, crescents for Islamic nations, and literal representations of animals or celestial bodies. The inter-relationship of national flags within the system can be seen in the way that some flags inspire others, for instance, the French tricolor inspired the use of tricolors by other nations born of revolution, while Ethiopia's colors inspired the flags of so many newly independent African countries that red, green, and yellow are known as the "pan-African colors."

Examples of international signs include universal symbol systems, such as musical and mathematical notation, currency symbols, and weather symbols. The shape and color of signs is also highly significant, indicating whether they convey prohibition, warning, instructions, or information.

Equally important for international travelers are professional symbols that enable tourists to find a pharmacist or barber, and brand logos that ensure they can always find their favorite training shoes, soft drinks, or hamburgers. But what about the most important sign of all for international communication? It is, of course, the universal use of a male or female figure to denote lavatories.

COLORS

People in every culture respond emotionally to colors, often without realizing it. For example, psychologists have established that "warm" colors (red, yellow, and orange) stimulate, while "cold" colors (blue, indigo, and violet) soothe and relax. Although interpretations may vary from culture to culture, color symbolism is universal, making it one of the most important human symbol systems.

RED

The warmest of the warm colors, red is the most stimulating but also the most ambiguous color. It is the color of love and passion, but also of aggression and war; of good luck but also of danger; of fertility but also of Hell fire. Red is a warning not to proceed but also a spur to action, both politically (red being the color of revolution) and emotionally ("seeing red").

▲ Fire
In both the East and the West, red is the color of fire, and in many cultures is associated with the flames of Hell. Red also represents spirited behavior, masculine energy, and anger.

▲ War
Red is the color of war. Mars, the red planet, is named after the Roman god of war, but has borne the name of other martial deities in other cultures. The Babylonians called it Nergal, and the Ancient Greeks "star of Ares."

▲ Love and passion
Red roses are a symbol of love. In western culture red represents passion, often illicit ("red-light district," "scarlet woman"). In the East, red symbolizes pure love and is worn by brides in India, China, and Japan.

▲ Fertility and rebirth
Red symbolizes fertility and rebirth due to its association with, among other things, the womb, ripening fruit, and the myth of the phoenix, a bird that destroys itself in fire but rises again from its ashes.

▲ Bloodlust
Through its power to arouse anger and aggression, red symbolizes bravery and virility but also bloodlust. In the Christian Church red represents Christ's sacrifice on the cross and the blood shed by martyrs.

ORANGE

As a combination of red and yellow, orange shares some of the symbolism of these colors. It can represent the point of balance between the passion of red and the spirituality of yellow, or tend toward either extreme. Orange might symbolize luxury and splendor but it can also mean the renunciation of worldly pleasures (as in the orange robes of some Buddhist monks). Brides in Ancient Rome wore orange. The reddish-orange gemstone jacinth symbolizes fidelity.

▲ Renunciation
Buddhist monks wear orange to affirm their adoption of a simple life.

◄ Permanence
Roman brides sometimes wore orange as a symbol of the permanence of marriage.

YELLOW

Yellow is associated with gold, brightness, enlightenment, and the Sun. As many spring flowers are yellow, it is also associated with new life. In many countries yellow symbolizes cowardice; in other countries it represents envy. A yellow flag was once used to symbolize disease and quarantine.

▲ Sun
Yellow symbolizes the Sun (and the Sun God Apollo) and therefore life and warmth. In eastern thought yellow is the color of the solar chakra, which is associated with the element of fire.

▲ Royalty
In China and Southeast Asia yellow symbolizes royalty. It was adopted as the imperial color in China in the 6th century. Only an emperor could wear yellow—a symbol that he was equal to the Sun—and some monks.

▲ Treachery
Renaissance art shows Judas Iscariot wearing a yellow cloak. In 1215 the Lateran Council ordered Jews to wear yellow badges (as would the Nazis, centuries later) on the basis that their race betrayed Christ.

▲ Homecoming
In the United States it is traditional to decorate a person's home town with yellow ribbons when he or she returns from danger, such as war—hence the popular song "Tie a Yellow Ribbon Round the Old Oak Tree."

GREEN

Green is the color of spring and therefore of youth, hope, and joy—but it is also the color of decay, and often symbolizes jealousy. Green is sacred to Muslims. Some say this is because the prophet Muhammad's cloak was green, others say it is because green is the color of new life.

▲ Nature
Chlorophyll gives plants the green color that has been associated with nature since antiquity. Osiris, originally the Ancient Egyptian god of vegetation (later of the underworld), was often colored green.

▲ Youth
Because of its association with spring, green symbolizes youth. There are two aspects to this: the positive associations of vigor and strength, counterbalanced by naïvety or inexperience (greenness).

▲ Ecological movement
As the color of nature, green symbolizes the ecological movement and people's concern with preserving the Earth's resources. It is the name of most environmentalist political parties.

▲ Fertility
The Green Man appears in many cultures as a symbol either of a specific nature god or of fertility in general. The Green Man was adopted by the Christian Church as a symbol of Easter and Christ's resurrection.

BLUE

As the color of the sky, blue symbolizes emptiness, the infinite, and the divine. The deepest color, and the purest apart from white, blue also symbolizes calmness, reflection, and the intellect. In the West, blue has various colloquial connotations, such as depression (the blues), sexual explicitness (blue movies), and class (blue-collar workers, blue-blooded).

▲ Naïvety
In Scandinavia to refer to a person as "blue-eyed" means they are naïve or gullible. Similarly, in Japan "blue" indicates naïvety or inexperience in the same way as "green" does in the West.

▲ Divinity
Blue often symbolizes divinity. The Ancient Egyptian god Amun was often depicted in blue, as are the Hindu gods Rama, Shiva, and Krishna.

▲ Calmness
A cold color, associated with water, blue induces calm and reflection. For Buddhists, blue is the color of Aksobya, the directional Buddha of steadfastness and strength.

▲ Purity
In artistic convention, angels' blue robes symbolize divine wisdom, while the Virgin Mary's blue robe symbolizes purity. In Roman Catholic art, blue represents humility, and in Ancient Egypt blue was the color of truth.

SEE ALSO
Egyptian deities *pp.138–39*
Greek & Roman deities *pp.140–41*
Buddhism *pp.164–69*
Christianity *pp.176–79*

PURPLE AND VIOLET

Due to the cost of the original dye, purple vestments were the preserve of the rich. Therefore, since antiquity, purple has symbolized luxury, wealth, and power in many cultures. Balanced between the passion of red and the reason of blue, purple also symbolizes temperance and considered action.

▲ **Priestly power**
In the Roman Catholic Church, violet is used during Advent and Lent for priests' robes and church drapery, symbolizing Christ's death and resurrection. In Europe violet was once the color of "half mourning."

◄ **Imperial power**
Tyrian purple dye, also known as "imperial" purple, was far more expensive than gold, and came to symbolize the rank of a Roman emperor. In medieval Europe blue dyes were expensive, and the bluer shade of "royal purple" acquired equivalent symbolism.

▲ **Modesty**
The symbolism of the violet flower has changed from excess (it was worn in Dionysian orgies) to modesty (as in "shrinking violet"). White violets symbolize innocence, and blue violets fidelity.

PINK

In western culture pink traditionally symbolizes femininity (hence the pink ribbon, *below right*). Baby girls in the West are traditionally dressed in pink. The association of pink with the gay movement originated during World War II when the Nazis forced gays to wear pink triangles, but pink is now worn as a badge of Gay Pride. The "pink pound" or "pink dollar" refers to gays as a consumer group.

▲ **Gay Pride**
Men at a Gay Pride rally wear pink in a flamboyant display of solidarity.

▲ **Pink ribbon**
Pink has become the color officially identified with the Breast Cancer Awareness campaign.

BLACK AND GRAY

As an absence of color or light, black is sometimes considered neutral but more often symbolizes evil (the powers of "darkness") and secrecy. It also represents the underworld, with its associations of sorrow, misfortune, and death. Gray often symbolizes gloom, anonymity, or uncertainty but, as a balance between black and white, it is also a color of mediation.

▲ **Evil**
Black symbolizes morality (as in a priest's robes) but more often evil (as in the "black arts"). In European culture the raven is a portent of ill fortune, disease, and death.

▲ **Mourning**
Wearing black as a symbol of mourning is a convention dating back thousands of years. Queen Victoria famously wore black throughout the 40 years of her widowhood.

▲ **Age and death**
In astrology black symbolizes the planet Saturn, which is named after the Roman god Saturn (Greek Chronos) who was associated with time, old age, and death.

SYMBOL SYSTEMS

WHITE

In many cultures white symbolizes purity, innocence, and holiness, but in Chinese, Japanese, and Indian traditions white is linked to death and mourning (as it once was in Europe). For Buddhists, white is associated with the lotus flower—a symbol of light and purity—and with knowledge, or "illumination." For American Indians white symbolizes the spirit, and in Sufism it symbolizes wisdom.

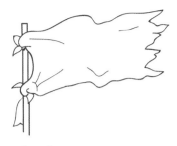

▲ **Surrender**
The use of a white flag as a symbol of surrender dates back as far as the first century CE in Ancient China. Its use is now enshrined in the Geneva Convention, and its misuse constitutes a war crime.

▲ **Cowardice and peace**
In Britain and the former British Empire a white feather symbolizes cowardice—fighting cocks with white tail feathers were said to be poor fighters. Some pacifist organizations have adopted it as a symbol of peace.

▲ **Holiness**
White represents holiness and sanctity in many cultures. For this reason Celtic druids (*above*) wear white robes, sacrificial animals are often white, and in the Roman Catholic Church white is worn at festivals of Christ.

▲ **Innocence and purity**
In the western world, brides wear white as a symbol of innocence and purity, as do those being baptized or taking first communion. By association, the white lily symbolizes purity and the Virgin Mary.

COLOR CODES

Color coding is one of the ways in which color symbolism enters everyday life. Universally, green is used to indicate safety or "go," while red indicates danger or "stop." Yellow or amber indicate potential hazards. Color coding is also used for industrial applications and in sports.

Fire extinguisher codes (in Europe, red = water, yellow = foam, black = carbon dioxide (CO_2), blue = powder)

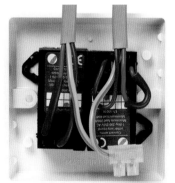

Electrical wiring (in Europe, brown = live, blue = neutral, green + yellow = earth)

Traffic lights: red + amber = prepare to go

Pedestrian crossing: green = safe to cross

Karate: black belt = highest level

SEE ALSO
Birds *pp.58–61*
The lotus *pp.86–87*
Love & marriage *pp.126–27*
Death & mourning *pp.128–31*
Western astrology *pp.200–03*

SHAPES

As the building blocks for everything that is visual, shapes can be highly symbolic. From earliest times they have been used to denote levels of meaning not easily represented in other ways, especially when written language is unknown. The most basic shapes—circles, squares, and triangles—are used symbolically in all cultures, and many other shapes have been devised and allotted symbolic meanings.

CIRCLES AND SPHERES

The circle and the sphere share much of their symbolism, as two- and three-dimensional representations of the same ideas. The circle is a common symbol for God. Most religions equate it with the heavenly sphere and the movements of the stars and planets. To Hindus and Buddhists the circle represents birth, death, and rebirth; to Buddhists it also represents the Wheel of Law.

▲ **Circle**
Having no beginning and no end, the circle is a universal symbol of completeness, eternity, and perfection. It represents male and female principles, and can denote God, the waters encircling the Earth, or the cycles of life.

▲ **Shou**
Shou, the Taoist character for longevity, is often depicted as a circular symbol, as here. In China it is sometimes paired with other symbols of long life, and when coupled with the peach it symbolizes a long and happy marriage.

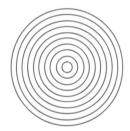

▲ **Concentric circles**
Concentric circles symbolize the orders of creation. Australian Aboriginals use concentric circles in their Dreamings to signify still water or campsites.

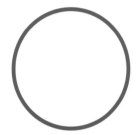

▲ **Zen circles**
For Zen Buddhists, concentric circles symbolize the various steps toward inner perfection, and the harmonization of the spirit as one progresses from one stage to the next.

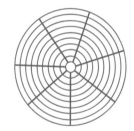

▲ **Dante's circles of Hell**
Italian poet Dante saw the Christian Hell as nine concentric circles. Each circle is assigned to a different category of sinner, from pagans and the unbaptized in the first circle to traitors in the ninth, at the center.

▲ **Round table**
The Round Table of Arthurian legend symbolizes equality, with no knight able to claim precedence from his position at the table. The same symbolism occurs in the 21st-century concept of "round table" conferences.

▲ **Stonehenge**
Stonehenge is evidence that the circle was an important symbol in prehistoric Britain, but its function is uncertain. It may have been a place of worship, an astronomical clock, or a shrine to the Sun God and the Earth Mother.

▲ **Ring**
Rings symbolize the binding nature of a pledge, such as a marriage vow. They are traditionally worn as a symbol of love, and sometimes of power and authority. A ring can also represent protection against destructive forces.

▲ Shield of the Trinity
The three outer circles of the *scutum fidei* (shield of the Trinity) symbolize the Christian Trinity of Father, Son, and Holy Spirit. Each is linked to a fourth circle in the center, which symbolizes God as three-in-one.

▲ Sphere
Sharing its symbolism with the circle, the sphere usually represents Heaven and/or the spiritual universe. Dante describes Heaven as a series of concentric spheres based on a universe with the Earth at its center.

► Dome of St. Paul's Cathedral
Spheres symbolize Heaven and are represented architecturally by the domed roofs of mosques, Byzantine churches, and some Renaissance churches. The base of such buildings is usually a cube, representing Earth.

SPIRALS AND HELICES

The spiral is closely linked to and often confused with the helix, both in shape and symbolism. These shapes have complicated meanings. They are, most importantly, associated with powerful forces such as the rotation of the Earth, whirlwinds, and whirlpools. In most cultures the spiral is regarded as a feminine shape.

▲ Spiral
This is an ancient symbol of energy (which was thought to flow in spirals) and of life's rhythm. For the Mayans it was the symbol of the winter solstice and a new annual cycle, and for Polynesians it symbolizes immortality.

▲ Spiral dances
In their gyratory dances, the Whirling Dervishes symbolically enact a circular ascending journey toward realization of the Divine. Spiral dances such as these also reflect the movement of the planets.

▲ Mother Earth fertility symbol
Found on figures dating from the Stone Age, the spiral has long been a symbol of fertility, both in its own right and through its symbolic links to the cycles of the Moon and to other fertility symbols such as the helical horn.

▲ T'ai Chi circle
This double spiral symbolizes the relationship between Yin and Yang, the interdependent elements of Taoist philosophy, which together create a balanced whole. A symbol of life, it represents the resolution of opposites.

▲ Churning of the Milky Ocean
In this Hindu myth a helix symbolizes the resolution of opposites. The serpent Vasuki twists into a helix around Mount Mandara, then the *devas* (gods) and *asuras* (demons) use the serpent as a rope to spin the mountain and churn the ocean in order to bring forth the elixir of immortality and other wonders.

▲ Double spiral
Similar to the T'ai Chi circle, this symbol represents the interdependence of opposites, such as birth and death (or birth and "rebirth" following an initiation), and male and female.

▲ Triple spiral
The Celtic triskele (triple spiral) is an ancient solar symbol that has been adopted by some Christians to symbolize the Holy Trinity. It is also used by some neo-pagans to symbolize the Triple Goddess.

▲ Helix
The helix shares much symbolism with the spiral, including its significance as a fertility symbol. The double helix (as DNA) is becoming a symbol of the scientific understanding of humanity.

SEE ALSO
Love & marriage pp.126–27
Buddhism pp.164–69
Taoism & Shinto pp.170–71
The Holy Grail pp.208–09
Sacred places pp.232–33

SHAPES

TRIANGLES AND PYRAMIDS

The triangle shares its symbolism with the number three, which represents beginning, middle, and end. In many cultures, from the Ancient Egyptians and Babylonians to modern Christians and Hindus, the triangle relates to trinities of gods. It also symbolizes other threesomes, such as body, soul, and spirit; and man, woman, and child.

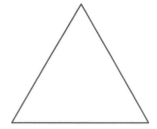

▲ Upward-pointing equilateral triangle
In many ancient cultures this symbolized the male organ and the element of fire. It represented health to the Hittites, the Sun (and by extension, fertility) to the Mayans, and a sacred mountain in Pueblo art.

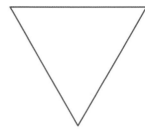

▲ Downward-pointing equilateral triangle
This triangle symbolized woman in most traditional cultures. In Ancient India, Greece, and Rome it represented the female pubic area (which is triangular). It also represents the element of water.

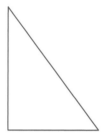

▲ Right-angled triangle
In cultures where an equilateral triangle symbolizes deity, a right-angled triangle, half an equilateral triangle, represents humanity and in some cases the Earth. In Masonic symbolism it represents water.

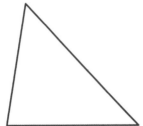

▲ Scalene triangle
In Masonic symbolism a scalene triangle – in which the internal angles and the lengths of the sides all differ – represents the element of air.

▲ Isosceles triangle
An isosceles triangle is one in which two internal angles and the lengths of two sides are equal. In Masonic symbolism this type of triangle represents the element of fire.

▲ Freemasons' triangle
The base of the Masonic triangle symbolizes Duration, and the sides Light and Darkness. The whole triangle symbolizes spiritual development, and ideals such as Faith, Hope, and Charity.

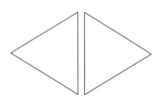

▲ Triangles base to base
In some cultures triangles placed base to base symbolize the waxing and waning of the Moon.

▲ Triangles point to point
Triangles placed point to point represent male and female, and the touching of the Earth and sky. In India they represent Shiva's hourglass drum, or *damaru*, the sound of which initiated the dance of creation.

▲ Pyramid
The pyramid's square base symbolizes Earth, while its apex represents Heaven. As well as being the burial chambers of Egyptian pharoahs, pyramids feature in the religious sites of several other ancient cultures.

In alchemy, the four elements are represented by equilateral triangles. An upward-pointing triangle symbolizes fire; upward-pointing through a horizontal line represents air (because fire rises through air); downward-pointing symbolizes water; and downward-pointing through a line symbolizes earth (water falls through earth). All four symbols are combined in the hexagram, a very powerful alchemical symbol.

FIRE

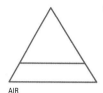

AIR

WATER

EARTH

SQUARES AND CUBES

Like the circle in relation to the sphere, the square and the cube share much of their symbolism as two- and three-dimensional representations of the same ideas. In contrast to the motion implied by the circle and the dynamism of the triangle, the square and the cube symbolize pause or cessation. This is not always a negative quality; it can imply stability and lasting perfection.

▲ **Square**
In the cosmology of many cultures, the square represents Earth and the four directions. In Islamic thought the square represents the heart, open to four influences: divine, angelic, human, and diabolic.

▲ **Square haloes**
Some Christian imagery shows figures with square haloes. This symbolizes the fact that the person was alive and earthbound – the square meaning Earth – when the image was painted.

▲ **Cube**
The cube symbolizes the material universe, representing wisdom, truth, and moral stability. As a symbol of Islam, the Ka'ba, the cube represents the unity of the Muslim people and the oneness of God.

▲ **Hidden cross**
The cube is also a covert Christian symbol, in that it unfolds into the form of a Latin cross, or crucifix. A cross of six equal squares forms the ground plan of many Christian churches.

▲ **Cloistered courtyard**
Since medieval times, the square as a symbol of permanence and stability has been expressed architecturally in the plan of religious buildings, towns, public squares, and cloistered courtyards.

▲ **Architectural cube**
In Islamic architecture the marriage of the cube, symbolizing the material world, and the sphere, symbolizing the spiritual, can be seen in the quadrilateral base and domed roofs of mosques and the tombs of Muslim saints.

SEE ALSO

SHAPES

STARS

Stars in general are symbolic of wisdom and spiritual guidance, starlight being a metaphor for the light of wisdom shining through the darkness of ignorance or the light of morality shining through the darkness of sin. In many cultures stars are strongly linked with destiny. In addition, there are numerous individual star shapes with specific associated symbolism.

▲ Stars in the sky
In many cultures the stars represent mythological figures or deities who may exert influence over those born under their sign. In other cultures stars symbolize the dead. For some, the Morning Star symbolizes the principle of life.

▲ Star of the Order of the British Empire
Every British order of chivalry has a star in its insignia, symbolizing the eminence of its members. Pictured is the star of a Knight Commander (KBE) or Dame Commander (DBE) of the Most Excellent Order of the British Empire.

▲ Saints and stars
Christian art traditionally depicts a number of saints with stars, such as St. Dominic, who appears with a star in drawings, paintings, and statuary. Other starred saints include Humbert and Peter of Alcantara.

▲ Stars of approval
The star has long been a symbol of excellence. In the hotel and restaurant industries "star ratings" from one to three (for "very good", "excellent", and "exceptional") were pioneered by the Michelin Guides from 1900.

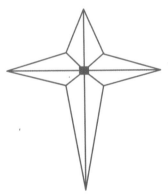

▲ Star of Bethelehem
This four-pointed star symbolizes the birth of Jesus, recalling the New Testament story of the Nativity, in which the star leads the three wise men to Bethlehem to worship the newborn Christ.

▲ Pentagram: 5-pointed star
With the single point upwards, the pentagram symbolizes the universal human, its points representing the head, two arms, and two legs. When inverted, it symbolizes the Devil, the two upper points representing horns.

▲ Hexagram: 6-pointed star
A hexagram comprises two interlocking equilateral triangles. As such, in Hinduism it represents the joining of male and female, and in alchemy the conjunction of the four elements. As the Star of David it is the symbol of Judaism.

▲ Heptagram: 7-pointed star
The seven-pointed star shares much of its symbolism with the number seven. For pagans this star is a magic symbol. To Christians it symbolizes the seven days of creation, and to Buddhists it represents the seven steps to enlightenment.

▲ Star of Lakshmi
In Hinduism an eight-pointed star symbolizes *ashtalakshmi*, a group of eight goddesses who together represent the eight forms of Lakshmi, the goddess of abundance (in terms of health, knowledge, strength, and prosperity).

CR⊕SSES

Though best known in the modern world as a Christian symbol, the cross long predates Christianity. A cross in a circle represented the Sun to neolithic peoples, and later the cross was sacred to the Aztecs and the Ancient Egyptians. In general, crosses share much symbolism with the square or cube, as well as with the number four.

▲ Basic, or Greek, cross
In western thought a cross with equal arms symbolized the four elements; in the East it symbolized the four winds and four cardinal points. A similar shape, the *visra vajra*, symbolizes the power of the Buddha's teachings.

▲ Hot cross bun
The cross is said to symbolize the crucifix. Traditionally eaten by Christians on Good Friday, buns marked with a cross were also eaten by pagan Saxons in honour of the goddess Eostre, who gave her name to Easter.

▲ Maltese cross
Many medals are in the shape of a Maltese cross. These include the Victoria Cross (*above*), Britain's highest military honour. The Maltese cross has been a symbol of bravery and Christian virtues since the Crusades.

▲ Solar cross
Also known as the wheel cross, this ancient symbol appears in prehistoric art worldwide. It symbolizes the return of the Sun and the cycle of the seasons. Over time, the "wheel" lost its rim to become a basic cross.

▲ Ankh
An Ancient Egyptian hieroglyph (possibly combining the *tau* cross of Osiris and the oval of Isis) symbolizing life. The ankh was later adopted by Coptic Christians as the *crux ansate* ("cross with a handle").

▲ Tau cross
Named after the Greek letter T, it is a symbol of salvation. It marked out Israelites who were to be spared from slaughter. It was also the symbol of the Roman god Mithras, the Greek god Attis, and St. Anthony of Egypt.

▲ Latin cross
The Latin cross has come to symbolize Christianity. However, it has been found on artefacts that long predate the Christian era and Christians did not widely adopt the Latin cross until the 3rd century CE.

▲ Swastika
Also known as the fylfot and the gammadion, this has symbolized the Sun, the cardinal points, the four winds, the four elements, lightning, Thor's hammer, the Buddha and, notoriously, Hitler's Nazi party.

CRESCENTS AND P⊕LYG⊕NS

Just as the cross is not an exclusively Christian symbol, so the crescent is not an exclusively Islamic one – it also symbolizes the Roman goddess Diana, the female in general and, paradoxically, both chastity and birth. In astronomy and astrology the crescent is a literal symbol of the Moon, and in alchemy it symbolizes silver, the metal associated with the Moon.

▲ Crescent
As a symbol of power, the crescent dates back to Babylonian and Sumerian times. It was used in Persia and the Ottoman Empire, and adopted by Muslim countries. Later it was identified with Islam itself.

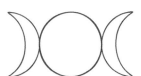

▲ Triple Goddess
Many ancient mythologies describe Triple Goddesses or a goddess with three aspects. Symbols for such Triple Goddesses include the one above: a waxing crescent, a full Moon, and a waning crescent.

▲ Interlaced crescents
Another symbol sometimes used to represent the Triple Goddess (*see left*) is made up of interlaced crescents. This symbol also formed the emblem of 16th-century French courtesan, Diane of Poitiers.

▲ Hexagon
In Christianity the hexagon symbolizes death. In Islam it symbolizes Heaven and also the six positions of matter (over, under, in front, behind, left, and right) and the six directions of movement (up, down, forward, backward, left, and right).

▲ Octagon
In the Christian symbolism of St. Ambrose the octagon is the counterpart of the hexagon (*left*), representing resurrection. Baptismal fonts often have eight pillars, symbolizing eternal life, and a hexagonal basin symbolizing the death of sin.

▲ Mandorla
This almond-shaped symbol sometimes appears in Christian art as a halo surrounding Christ and, rarely, the Virgin Mary. The mandorla symbolizes the interraction of the spiritual and material worlds.

SEE ALSO
The night sky *pp.20–23*
Egyptian deities *pp.138–39*
Hinduism *pp.158–63*
Buddhism *pp.164–69*
Judaism *pp.172–73*
Christianity *pp.176–79*
Alchemy *pp.210–11*

SHAPES

289

PATTERNS

Many patterns are regarded as universal symbols. Such patterns, which may be found on anything from coins to buildings, often symbolize the inner human condition, rather than external phenomena. Yantras and mandalas, for example, represent the search for inner peace. In medieval times labyrinths and mazes symbolized the search for a true path to God, with obstacles to be overcome and moral choices to be resolved on the way.

LABYRINTHS AND MAZES

Technically, a maze contains many pathways, only one of which leads to the center (multicursal), while a labyrinth has only a single path that always leads to the center (unicursal). Ancient labyrinths and mazes were devised as symbolic traps for malevolent spirits, while medieval ones represented symbolic pilgrimages.

▲ **Medieval labyrinth**
Labyrinths are considered to have reached the height of perfection during the medieval period. The pattern of such labyrinths is based on concentric circles.

▲ **Knossos labyrinth**
A silver coin of the 3rd century BCE shows the labyrinth at Knossos in Crete, which, according to myth, imprisoned the Minotaur, who was half-man, half-bull.

▲ **Cretan labyrinth**
One of the earliest known labyrinth patterns is the relatively simple design seen on Cretan coins. This was based on a spiral, which began from a cross shape.

▲ **Ornamental maze**
Today, the religious significance of mazes and labyrinths has largely disappeared. Most, like this hedge maze, serve for amusement or as examples of garden art.

YANTRAS AND MANDALAS

A yantra is a Hindu or Buddhist diagram used for meditation, symbolizing the universe and its divine powers. A mandala can most simply be described as a circular yantra, again representing the universe. At the center of a mandala, a square symbolizing a sacred space is often enclosed. Western artefacts loosely regarded as mandalas include the traditional American Indian woven circles known as dreamcatchers.

Lotus   Triangle   Circle   Square

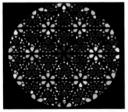

▲ Tibetan mandala
At the center of this mandala, Buddhist deities reside in a palace. Tibetan monks sometimes create healing mandalas made from colored sand.

▲ Yantra
The basic elements of a yantra are triangles (cosmic energy), lotus petals (unfolding consciousness), and a square (the Earth), with gateways at the cardinal points.

◄ Rose window
Rose windows may have been designed to serve a similar purpose to mandalas as objects of contemplation and meditation. Their colored panels are thought to symbolize pathways leading to salvation at the center.

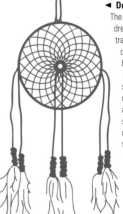

◄ Dreamcatcher
The American Indian dreamcatcher is traditionally hung over a bed to trap bad dreams before they reach the sleeper. This device is regarded as a mandala symbolizing the relationship of the universe to the subconscious.

► Mandala in nature
The basic pattern of the mandala is repeated frequently in nature. The spirals of seeds in a sunflower head, the rings in a tree trunk, a snowflake, a cell with a nucleus at its center—these all reflect the mandala's symbolic representation of the universe.

SUNFLOWER SEEDS

TREE RINGS

SEE ALSO
Fabulous beasts *pp.74–77*
Flowers *pp.82–85*
The lotus *pp.86–87*
Religious architecture *pp.228–31*

PATTERNS

291

TIBETAN MANDALA

The word "mandala" is from the Classical Indian language of Sanskrit. Translated it means "circle," or "completeness." The design of the pattern within a circle symbolizes wholeness and the cosmos. The series of interwoven geometric shapes are intended to direct thoughts, as mandalas are used as a spiritual tool to aid meditation.

1. The inner circle

The inner area of the mandala is the starting point for many mandalas. It is the focus of the energy of the cosmos and the center toward which the viewer's meditation is drawn. Here the deities Hevajra and Nairatma embrace. Together in blissful harmony, they symbolize the state of enlightenment when the two halves are completely merged. They are personifications of the Buddhist belief that all beings are without ego. They are immediately surrounded by eight female figures known as *dakinis*, each representing a cardinal point.

2. The square

Surrounding the circle is a square with four gateways that symbolize boundless thoughts—loving kindness, compassion, sympathy, and equanimity.

3. Concentric circles

The continuing pattern of concentric circles represents cosmic aspects of the Universe, such as energy fields and atmospheric zones.

The circles from the inside out are made up of lotus petals, symbolizing rebirth; eight graveyards, which represent awe-inspiring places where ascetics meditate; a diamond or *vajra* circle symbolizing illumination; and an outer circle of flame, which represents the process of transformation ordinary humans have to undergo to enter the territory within.

4. The figures outside the circle

The figures on the outside of the circle serve as protectors.

5. Colors

The colors used represent different attributes of the Buddha: white represents his purity, blue, the vastness of his teaching and the truth of what he taught, and red represents his warmth and compassion.

NUMBERS

Ancient cultures did not believe in chance, so the existence of a given number of objects or phenomena took on great significance. Thus numbers, which originated as a way of counting, acquired powerful symbolism. As well as expressing quantities they assumed individual qualities and were even imbued with cosmic powers. The study of those powers is known as numerology, which Plato called "the highest level of knowledge".

I One symbolizes the First Cause, the primal beginning, or creation. In monotheistic religions the number represents God the Creator – most overtly in Islamic literature, where one specifically represents One God. One also symbolizes humankind, reflecting our species' unique upright stance. The unicorn's single horn is a symbol of power and purity; the one eye of the Cyclops, a mythological Greek giant, symbolizes the power of unreason over intellect. In modern western culture to be "number one" is to be the best.

2 To Pythagoras two represented diversity, and had the potential for disorder and evil. Thus the second day of the second month was considered evil and dedicated to Pluto, god of the underworld. But two is also a symbol of order and balance in philosophies such as Taoism, where Yin and Yang symbolize the completeness of opposites unified. Two is a lucky number in Chinese culture, on the basis that good things come in pairs.

THREE PETALS ON THE FLEUR DE LYS, FOR GOD, CREATION, AND ROYALTY

3 Three is a sacred number in most religions. The Ancient Egyptians had a powerful trinity of gods (Isis, Osiris, and Horus), as did the Ancient Greeks and Romans. The Greek (Roman) trinity was: Jupiter (Zeus), Neptune (Poseidon), and Pluto (Hades). Jupiter's symbol was three-forked lightning, Neptune's a trident, and Pluto's a three-headed dog. Hindus worship a trinity known as the *Trimurti* ("three forms"), comprising Brahma, the Creator; Vishnu, the Preserver; and Shiva, the Destroyer. Christians believe in a Holy Trinity of Father, Son, and Holy Spirit. In Islam three symbolizes the human soul. To Pythagoras three symbolized perfect harmony, being the sum of unity (one) and diversity (two).

4 A symbol of wholeness and universality, four is often represented by the square and the cross – the numeral "4" is a modified cross. In common with the square, four also symbolizes stability. To Pythagoras four symbolized perfection, being the first square number. Four is taboo in Japan and parts of China because it is a homonym for (sounds like the word for) "death". For American Indians four symbolizes organization: space is divided into four regions, time into four units (day, night, Moon, and year), and human life into four ages (childhood, youth, maturity, and old age).

5 Five symbolizes Man, whose head and four limbs are represented by the five-pointed pentagram. Five was a sacred number to the Mayans, for whom it symbolized the maize god, because maize shoots appear five days after the seed is planted; and for the Aztecs it symbolized completeness and the awakening of consciousness. Five has great significance in Islam, being the number of pillars of piety, hours of prayer, elements of the Hajj, and other religious aspects.

6 In common with the hexagram, a six-pointed star, six can symbolize harmony and perfect balance. In China six symbolizes Heaven; and to Christians it represents completeness, because God created the world in six days. To the Mayans six was an unlucky number, signifying death. In modern western culture six symbolizes luck, being the highest throw of a die.

FOUR CARDINAL POINTS ON A COMPASS

SEVEN COLOURS OF THE RAINBOW

NINE WHITE STONES REPRESENT NINE VIRGINS IN CELTIC MYTH

7 Seven symbolizes wholeness in many cultures, being the union of divinity (three) and the material Earth (four). In Hindu, Muslim, and Judeo-Christian scriptures a seventh aspect confers completeness and perfection on a group of six; the number is auspicious in all those cultures. The menorah, a sacred candelabrum whose seven stems represent the days of creation and the celestial bodies, is a symbol of Judaism. In Ancient Egypt seven symbolized eternal life, and to American Indians it symbolizes the Dream of Life.

8 Eight is an auspicious number in eastern thought. For Buddhists the eight spokes of the *dharmachakra*, or Wheel of Law, symbolize the eight-fold path to enlightenment. In China eight is considered lucky because it is a homonym for "prosper" and resonates with the eight paths of the Way, the eight trigrams of the classic work of divination called the *I Ching*, and the eight immortal Chinese deities. Eight is also a recurring number in Japanese Shinto.

9 Being three times three, nine amplifies the power of the number three, symbolizing eternity, completion, and fulfilment. Nine is considered lucky in China, where it sounds like the word for "longlasting", but unlucky in Japan, where it sounds like "pain". The Aztecs considered it unlucky, symbolizing the gods of the night, but the Mayans thought it lucky. In several cultures the ennead, or nine-pointed star, represents nine deities, and in Judaism nine symbolizes intelligence and truth.

10 Being the number of human digits, ten is the foundation of most counting systems, and symbolizes the return to oneness after the cycle of the digits. For this reason (and because it is the sum of the first four digits), Pythagoras considered ten to be a holy number, symbolizing universal creation. In China, as the double of five (which represents totality), ten symbolizes duality.

11 In the American Indian "earth count" 11 represents the stars and, via the metaphor of travelling there, symbolizes altered states of consciousness. In many African traditions 11 is considered holy, and symbolizes fertility because semen is believed to take 11 days to reach the ovum. In other cultures 11 is a symbol of excess and imbalance because it is an increase on ten, which is the symbol of completeness – for this reason St. Augustine said, "the number eleven is the blazon of sin."

12 As the multiple of divinity (three) and the material Earth (four), 12 symbolizes both spiritual and earthly order. In the American Indian "earth count" 12 represents the 12 planets and the 12 winds. Twelve is important biblically, being the number of the tribes of Israel, the disciples of Christ, the fruits of the Tree of Life, and the gates of Jerusalem.

TEN YEARS REPRESENTS A COMPLETED CYCLE IN CLASSICAL MYTH: HERE ODYSSEUS RETURNS HOME AFTER TEN YEARS ROAMING

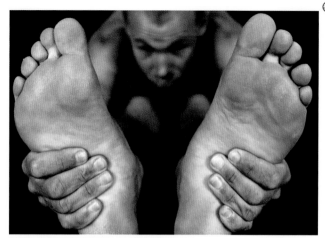
TWENTY SYMBOLIZES THE WHOLE MAN: 20 FINGERS AND TOES

∅ ZER⊕

Zero — from the Arabic *sifr*, meaning "empty" — is a relatively recent invention. For thousands of years mathematicians left a space if there was no number in a given column; then, c876ᴄᴇ in India, the symbol 0 was used to denote the space. Its status as a number was disputed because adding or subtracting it leaves other numbers unchanged, yet placing it after a number increases the number tenfold. Zero symbolizes a person who has no power of their own. In Mayan culture it symbolized the moment between the sacrifice and rebirth of the maize god — echoing its mathematical position between negative and positive numbers.

13 Thirteen symbolizes bad luck in many cultures. It is linked to the 13 people at Christ's Last Supper, one of whom betrayed Him. For Jewish boys 13 symbolizes the age of responsibility, when they become Bar Mitzvah, or "one to whom commandments apply".

20 In the developed world 20:20 means perfect vision, once denoting a person who could read an eye test chart from 20 feet. In many Central and South American cultures 20 symbolizes humans, whose 20 fingers and toes make up a unit.

TWENTY-ONE "KEY OF THE DOOR"

21 Long considered a symbol of perfection (seven times three), in the West 21 is also a symbol of responsibility and adulthood: the symbolic "key of the door" is often bestowed at this age. In many countries people were not eligible to vote before the age of 21 (though this has now generally been reduced to 18).

666, THE NUMBER OF THE BEAST (WHICH IS SEEN SECOND LEFT IN THIS MEDIEVAL TAPESTRY)

40 Recurring frequently in scripture, 40 symbolizes waiting and punishment. Forty days and nights was the length of time Moses spent on Mount Sinai, Elijah was fed by ravens, the rains of the Flood fell, and Jesus fasted in the wilderness. The word "quarantine" derives from this period of time.

50 In modern idiom 50 symbolizes fairness or equality (50:50 split) or ambiguity (50:50 decision). In the US 50 is a symbol of Hawaii, which is the 50th state of the Union. Fiftieth anniversaries of events such as marriage are celebrated as "golden".

666 For Christians 666 symbolizes evil, being the number of the beast referred to in the Bible's Book of Revelation as "six hundred threescore and six". It is thought by many scholars to derive from a numerical code for Emperor Nero's name, and by extension symbolizes false deification of the state. This may date from a time when the early Christians were suffering persecution under Roman rule and could only identify their enemies in a code. There are many other theories about the symbolism of 666 and whether it is a code for another name, but it is still seen by many in the western world as symbol of the Antichrist.

60 The Ancient Babylonians used base 60 for mathematical and astronomical calculations, a system that survives in the modern division of angles and time: 360 degrees in a circle, 60 minutes in an hour, and 60 seconds in a minute.

70 All multiples of seven and ten symbolize perfection to some degree; 70 symbolizes twofold perfection, being ten times seven. In the Bible 70 symbolizes completeness: for example, threescore years and ten is a complete human life cycle.

NUMBER SYSTEMS

The Ancient Babylonian, Egyptian, and Roman numerals all represent the fingers needed to indicate a number. (The Roman V represents a hand with fingers together and thumb outstretched; X is two Vs). Later, symbols were used in a positional notation, in which a numeral's position indicates its power. For instance, in 777 the numeral 7 also represents 700 and 70. In Braille, numbers are created by placing a number sign before a letter (for example, number sign + "a" = 1). Morse numbers are combinations of visual or aural signals.

Babylonian	Egyptian	Greek	Roman	Ancient Chinese	Mayan	Hindu	Arabic	Modern Arabic
𒁹	|	Αα	I	一	•	८	١	1
𒐖	||	Ββ	II	二	••	२	٢	2
𒐗	|||	Γγ	III	三	•••	३	٣	3
𒐘	||/||	Δδ	IV	四	••••	४	٤	4
𒐙	|||/||	Εε	V	五	⎯	५	٥	5
𒐚	|||/|||	Ϛ	VI	六	•/⎯	६	٦	6
𒐛	||||/|||	Ζζ	VII	七	••/⎯	७	٧	7
𒐜	||||/||||	Ηη	VIII	八	•••/⎯	८	٨	8
𒐝	|||/||||	Θθ	IX	九	••••/⎯	९	٩	9
𒌋	∩	Ιι	X	十	=			10

BRAILLE NUMBERS

0, 1, 2, 3, 4, 5, 6, 7, 8, 9, 10, 101

MORSE NUMBERS

0, 1, 2, 3, 4, 5, 6, 7, 8, 9

SEE ALSO
Initiation rites pp.124–25
Love & marriage pp.126–27
Judaism pp.172–73
Christianity pp.176–79

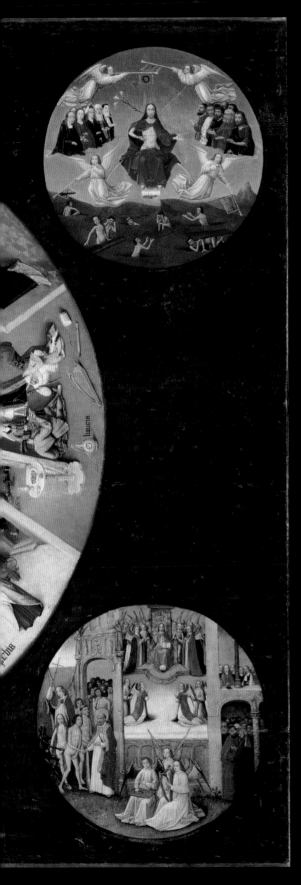

THE SEVEN DEADLY SINS

The 15th and 16th centuries were overshadowed by political upheaval, and the painter Hieronymus Bosch (c1450–1516) produced extraordinary art that echoed the anxiety of his times. In this work he depicts the seven deadly sins, arranged around a wheel with Christ the redeemer at its center.

1. Superbia (Pride/Vanity)
Pride is shown by a wealthy woman staring into a mirror (a symbol of self knowledge). She does not see a devil holding her mirror.

2. Ira (Anger/Wrath)
Ira is depicted by a street fight between two drunk peasants.

3. Invidia (Jealousy/Envy)
In this scene a husband and wife are compared with the dogs below, who ignore the bones within their reach in favor of other bones.

4. Avaritia (Greed/Avarice)
Avaritia is a rich man taking money from a poor man, while at the same time bribing a judge.

5. Gula (Gluttony)
Gluttony is shown by people eating a feast. The food is given by a nun. As they fill themselves, a child defecates in his clothes.

6. Acedia (Sloth/Laziness)
Acedia is shown in a scene in which a woman dressed for church is trying to wake a man deep in slumber, possibly a lazy priest.

7. Luxuria (Lust)
This panel shows two sets of lovers talking, with musical instruments lying on the ground, a symbol of passion.

8. Four last things
In the corners of the image appear the "Four Last Things" showing the viewer what we all ultimately face. Clockwise, from left, they are: death, the Last Judgement, Heaven, and Hell.

9. The circle
At the center of the large circle, which is said to represent the eye of God, is the "pupil" in which Christ can be seen emerging from his tomb. Below is the Latin inscription that translates as "Beware, Beware, God is Watching," implying that no sin goes unnoticed.

Hieronymus Bosch, *The Seven Deadly Sins*, 1485

PICTURE WRITING

Most written languages originated in picture writing, which differs from drawing in that it uses a standard set of symbols known as pictograms or pictographs. From literal representations of objects, pictograms evolved into logograms, which are symbolic, rather than pictorial, representations of words for objects and ideas. Next came syllabaries — symbol systems representing individual syllables — and, finally, alphabets.

CUNEIFORM
3500—650 BCE

Along with Egyptian hieroglyphs, cuneiform is one of the oldest forms of writing. It developed during the 4th millennium BCE in Mesopotamia (present-day Iraq and western Iran), and was used by the Sumerians, Assyrians, Babylonians, and Hittites. The script is made up of wedge-shaped impressions that were scribed into wet clay using sharpened reeds. Cuneiform takes its name from the Latin *cuneus*, meaning wedge-shaped.

SUN

MOUNTAIN

GOD

GRAIN

OX

FISH

▲ **Cuneiform block**
This clay tablet dates from 3000BCE. Later, cuneiform evolved from a purely pictorial system into a script that represented sounds. Cuneiform was first deciphered in 1802 by German philologist Georg Friedrich Grotefend.

EGYPTIAN HIEROGLYPHS

Egyptian hieroglyphs — named from the Greek *hieros* (holy) and *gluphe* (carving) — originated during the 4th millennium BCE. The script developed into a combination of pictograms (literal drawings) and phonograms (symbols representing sounds). It was deciphered in 1819 using text on the Rosetta Stone, carved in about 196BCE in three scripts: hieroglyphic, demotic (the then common script of Egypt), and Greek.

► **Funerary stele, c2250BCE**
The symbols between the two main figures are clues to the meaning of the four lines of inscription on the right of the stele, which describe a king's funeral offering.

EYE OF HORUS

OWL

CROWN

JAR

EAGLE

WATER

ANCIENT CHINESE

Chinese script is the oldest writing system still in use today, dating from c1500BCE. It evolved from pictograms into a combination of pictograms and logograms (symbols representing whole words). In the modern system, older symbols are often combined to form new compound words: for instance, the symbols for "flying" and "machine" are used together for "aeroplane".

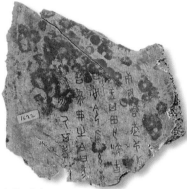

▲ Oracle bone
The earliest examples of Chinese script were carved into shoulder blades of oxen and turtle shells. Cracks made by heating these so-called "oracle bones" were interpreted as divine insights, which were recorded.

HORSE   WINE

MUSIC   JADE

OMEN   PEACEFUL

MAYAN HIEROGLYPHS

Mayan hieroglyphs originated around the 3rd century BCE. They evolved from pictograms into a combination of pictograms, logograms (whole words, as illustrated), and syllabograms (representing syllables). Scripts were usually written in paired columns of glyphs reading from right to left and from top to bottom.

CLOUD

MOUNTAIN

SNAKE

SUN

FIRE

TO SCATTER

WATER

WOMAN

SPIRIT

SKY

▲ Panel from Yaxchilan temple, c725CE
This limestone panel shows a bloodletting ritual in which King Shield Jaguar holds a torch, while his queen, Lady Xoc, draws blood from her tongue. The hieroglyphs at the top and side of the panel record the date and other information.

SEE ALSO
Egyptian deities *pp.138–39*
Divination *pp.196–99*
Meso- and South American *pp.344–45*

ROCK ART

Stone age rock paintings have been found throughout the world, some of them more than 30,000 years old. Another prehistoric form of rock art is the petroglyph, which is a carved, as opposed to a painted image and dates back some 15,000 years. Both of these art forms long predate the evolution of fully fledged pictorial languages.

▲ **Navajo petroglyphs**
Deer, bighorn sheep, buffalo, geometric shapes, and bear footprints appear in these petroglyphs. They were carved over a period of 1,500 years by Anasazi, Fremont, and Navajo people in what is now Newspaper Rock State Historic Monument in Canyonlands National Park, Utah.

TRAIL BLAZES

A blaze is a mark made on a tree by chipping off part of the bark, and is usually done to mark a trail – hence the word "trailblazing". Today, particularly in conservation areas where carved blazes are considered unecological, trails can be "blazed" with paint, fixed markers, flags, or stone cairns. The system of blazes shown below was developed in the 1930s by members of the New York–New Jersey Trail Conference.

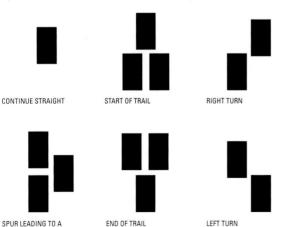

CONTINUE STRAIGHT

START OF TRAIL

RIGHT TURN

SPUR LEADING TO A DIFFERENT TRAIL

END OF TRAIL

LEFT TURN

AMERICAN INDIAN PICTOGRAMS

Like the peoples of Europe and Asia, American Indians developed rock art into a formalized system of pictograms such as those illustrated below. The systemized use of pictograms in the visual language of totem poles is arguably the earliest form of writing in North America.

CAMP FIRE

DISCOVERY

DUCK

EAGLE

FISH

▲ **American Indian pictograms**
Pictograms of handprints, animals, and geometric shapes feature in this ancient example of American Indian rock art in the Willow Springs area of the Red Rock Canyon National Conservation Area near Las Vegas, Nevada.

ENCAMPMENT

FAST HORSE

HORSE

HORSE TRACKS

HOBO SIGNS

A hobo is a travelling worker, not a tramp – who travels but doesn't work – or a bum, who neither travels nor works. Theories about the derivation of the word vary. It may come from "hoe-boy" (farmhand), "Ho, boy" (a greeting), or be an abbreviation of Houston and Bowery in New York, where travelling workers once gathered. Hoboes use symbols to give directions, warnings, and information to other hoboes.

KIND WOMAN

WOMAN

GOOD SPOT FOR A HANDOUT

CAN SLEEP IN BARN

GENTLEMAN

WEALTHY

NO ALCOHOL IN TOWN

TOWN ALLOWS ALCOHOL

GOOD WATER

GO THIS WAY

GET OUT FAST

DON'T GO THIS WAY

WORK AVAILABLE

TELL HARD LUCK STORY HERE

FAKE ILLNESS HERE

HELP IF SICK

DOCTOR

TELEPHONE

MAN WITH GUN

DOG

BAD DOG

OFFICER

POLICE OFFICER LIVES HERE

JUDGE

NOTHING DOING HERE

OWNER HOME

OWNER OUT

NO ONE HOME

SOMEONE HOME

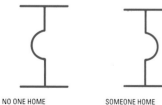
BE READY TO DEFEND YOURSELF

HOLD YOUR TONGUE

SAFE CAMP

SAFE AREA

SEE ALSO
Mammals *pp.52–55*
Birds *pp.58–61*
Aquatic creatures *pp.68–71*
Tribal totems, heroes & tricksters *pp.150–51*

PICTURE WRITING

303

HIER⊕GLYPHS

This band of hieroglyphs decorated the side of an Egyptian jewelry chest that was found in the tomb of Yuya and Tuya, who lived in the 18th Dynasty (1539—1295BCE). They were the parents of Queen Tiye, who was married to Pharoah Amenhotep III. The hieroglyphs on the chest express a wish for good fortune for the couple in the afterlife.

1. Duck
The duck, along with the other birds and animals, faces left, indicating that the hieroglyphs read from left to right.

2. Ankh
"Life" is represented by the ankh, which against the blue background gains a further meaning of "waters," suggesting the cosmic waters from which all life emerges and to which it eventually returns.

3. Hieroglyphic signs combined
The central ankh hieroglyph is flanked by scepters representing the god of discord, Seth, who symbolizes dominion. Below it is the half-moon shape, neb, which means "all." Read together, the hieroglyph symbolizes "all life and dominion."

4. Cartouche
The symbols enclosed in the lozenge shape, known as a "cartouche," show the name of the king. Cartouches were only used to display the name of a ruling monarch, in this case, Amenhotep III.

ALPHABETS

The first alphabet appeared when pictograms evolved into symbols that represented individual sounds. All alphabets derive from the North Semitic, which developed in the Mediterranean c1700BCE. This system paved the way for the Phoenician alphabet – the first major script based on speech sounds. This led to the Hebrew alphabet, European alphabets (via Greek), and Asian alphabets (via Aramaic).

MODERN ROMAN	NORTH SEMITIC	PHOENICIAN	EARLY HEBREW	ARAMAIC	LATE HEBREW
A	alef	'aleph	'alep	aleph	aleph
B	beth	beth	bet	beth	beth
G	gimel	gimmel	gimel	gimel	gimel
D	daleth	daleth	dalet	delath	delath
H	he	he	he	he	heh
W	vav	waw	waw	waw	vav
Z	zayin	zayin	zayin	zayin	zayin
H	cheth	heth	het	heth	cheth
T	teth	teth	tet	teth	teth
Y	yod	yodh	yod	yodh	yod
K	kaf	kaph	kap	kaph	kaph
L	lamed	lamedh	lamed	lamedh	lamed
M	mem	mem	mem	mem	mem
N	nun	nun	nun	nun	nun
S	samekh	samekh	samek	samekh	samekh
O	ayin	'ayin	ayin	'ayin	ayin
P	pe	pe	pe	pe	peh
S	tsade	tsade	tsade	sadhe	tsaddi
Q	quf	qoph	qop	qoph	qoph
R	resh	res	res	resh	resh
S	shin	sin	sin	sin	shin
T	tau	taw	taw	taw	tau

GREEK

The antecedent of all modern European alphabets, the Greek alphabet evolved from the Phoenician one over a period of 200 years, from 1000–800BCE. The word "alphabet" derives from the first and second Greek letters, alpha and beta.

A	B	Γ	Δ	E	Z	H	Θ	I	K	Λ	M
ALPHA	BETA	GAMMA	DELTA	EPSILON	ZETA	ETA	THETA	IOTA	KAPPA	LAMBDA	MU
N	Ξ	O	Π	P	Σ	T	Y	Φ	X	Ψ	Ω
NU	XI	OMICRON	PI	RHO	SIGMA	TAU	UPSILON	PHI	CHI	PSI	OMEGA

ETRUSCAN

This alphabet evolved c700–600BCE in Etruria (now Tuscany and Umbria) from a version of the Greek alphabet taken to Italy by emigrants from the Aegean island of Euboea.

A	B	C	D	E	W	Z	H	TH	I	K	L
M	N	O	P	M	Q	R	S	T	Y	PH	KH

ROMAN

The Roman alphabet evolved c600BCE from the Etruscan. It continued developing until the mid-19th century, when V and J were finally accepted as letters in their own right rather than as variants of I and U. It is now used by some 2 billion people worldwide.

a	B	C	D	e	F	G	H	I	J	K	L	m
A	B	C	D	E	F	G	H	I	J	K	L	M
N	O	P	Q	R	S	T	U	V	W	X	Y	Z
N	O	P	Q	R	S	T	U	V	W	X	Y	Z

ELDER FUTHARK

Elder Futhark, or Old Futhark, is the oldest of the runic alphabets, which developed in northern Europe, possibly from the Etruscan alphabet. Runic alphabets were known as *futhark* from their first six letters.

F	U	TH	A	R	K	G	WV	H	N	I	JY
E	P	Z	S	T	B	E	M	L	NG	O	DW

CYRILLIC

Now used in Russia and eastern Europe, this alphabet is thought to have been developed from the Greek c900CE by St. Cyril and St. Methodius. Originally known as the Glagolitic alphabet, it was later renamed after St. Cyril.

А	Б	В	Г	Д	Е	Ё	Ж	З	И	Й
A	B	V	G	D	E	YO	ZH	Z	I	Y
К	Л	М	П	О	П	Р	С	Т	У	Ф
K	L	M	N	O	P	R	S	T	U	F
Х	Ц	Ч	Ш	Щ	Ъ	Ы	Ь	Э	Ю	Я
KH	TS	CH	SH	SHCH	-	Y	'	E	IO	YA

SEE ALSO
Picture writing *pp.300–03*
Sign languages & signals *pp.330–31*

ARABIC

Evolved from the Nabataean Aramaic alphabet during the 4th century BCE, largely by adding dots to existing letters to accommodate the greater number of consonants used in Arabic. Today it is the world's third most widely used alphabet, after Roman and Chinese.

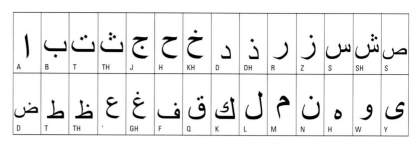

ا	ب	ت	ث	ج	ح	خ	د	ذ	ر	ز	س	ش	ص
A	B	T	TH	J	H	KH	D	DH	R	Z	S	SH	S

ض	ط	ظ	ع	غ	ف	ق	ك	ل	م	ن	ه	و	ی
D	T	TH	'	GH	F	Q	K	L	M	N	H	W	Y

BRAHMI

Evolved in India during the 6th century BCE from an Aramaic or Semitic alphabet. It is the antecedent of many Asian alphabets (mainly Indian), including Devanagari, Bengali, Khmer, Tibetan, and Burmese.

A	Ā	BA	BHA	GA	GHA	DA	DHA	DA	DHA	HA	VA
U	U	O	GA	GHA	GHA	THA	THA	TA	YA		KA
LA	LA	MA	-M	NA	NA	NA	SA,SA	SA		SA	AI	I
Ī	E			PA	PHA	CA	CHA	KHA	RA		SA	TA

DEVANAGARI

A modern Indian alphabet that was developed from Brahmi during the 11th century to write the sacred language Sanskrit. It has since been adapted for Hindi, Sindhi, Marathi, and other languages, and is India's most prevalent script (and the world's fourth most prevalent), with 260 million users.

क	ख	ग	घ	ङ	च	छ	ज	झ	ञ	ट	ठ
KA	KHA	GA	GHA	NA	CA	CHA	CHA	CHA	NA	NA	NA

ड	ढ	ण	त	थ	द	ध	न	प	फ	व	भ
DA	DHA	NA	THA	THA	DA	DHA	NA	PA	PHA	BA	BHA

म	य	र	ल	व	श	ष	स	ह	ळ		
MWA	YA	RA	LA	VA	SA	SA	SA	HA	LA		

KHMER

The Khmer (Cambodian) alphabet evolved from the Brahmi during the 7th century CE. It is the world's longest alphabet, being a syllabic system in which each consonant has two forms (the top form alone and the combination of both forms). There are also a number of vowels that are not illustrated here.

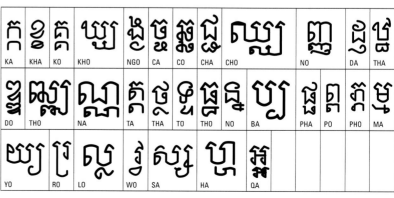

KA	KHA	KO	KHO	NGO	CA	CO	CHA	CHO		NO	DA	THA
DO	THO	NA	TA	THA	TO	THO	NO	BA		PHA	PO	PHO	MA
YO	RO	LO	WO	SA	HA	QA						

CHINESE HAN

Chinese script is the oldest writing system still in use today, dating from c1500BCE. It is not an alphabet but a logography – a combination of pictograms and logograms (abstract symbols representing whole words), some of which are illustrated here.

美	清	英	命	花	恕	朋友	恩	福	和
BEAUTY	CLARITY	COURAGE	DESTINY	FLOWER	FORGIVENESS	FRIEND	GRACE	HAPPINESS	HARMONY

貴	愛	月	平	神	星	日出	安	孚	智
HONOUR	LOVE	MOON	PEACE	SPIRIT	STAR	SUNRISE	TRANQUILLITY	TRUTH	WISDOM

M⊕RSE

During the 1830s and 40s US artist and inventor Samuel Morse developed his famous Morse alphabet of dots and dashes, in which the shortest codes were assigned to the most commonly used letters. The historic first message "What hath God wrought?" was sent on 24 May 1844.

BRAILLE

Developed in 1821 by French educationalist Louis Braille, who was blind from the age of three. Braille was based on a system originally devised by Charles Barbier in an attempt to enable Napoleon's army to communicate silently in the dark. Louis Braille improved it by creating the characteristic cells with six raised dots, which remain the standard form of written communication for the blind.

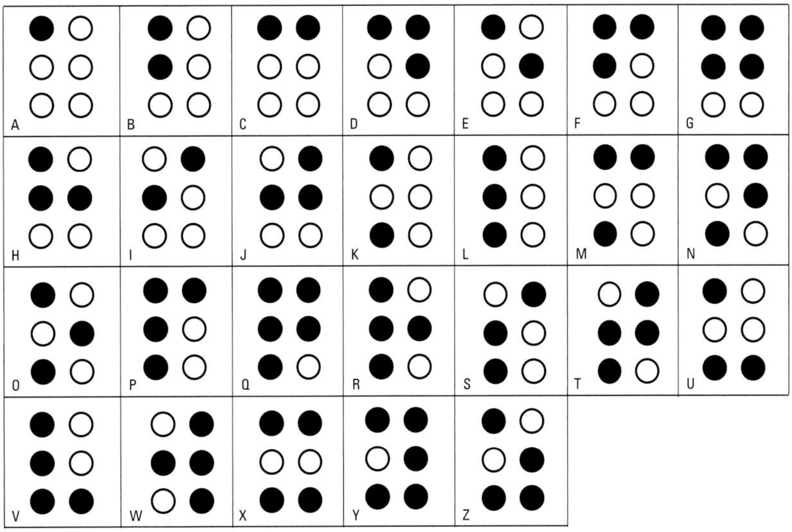

SEE ALSO
Numbers *pp.294–97*
Picture writing *pp.300–03*

INTERNATIONAL SIGNS

Pictures cross language barriers in a way that words cannot. For instance, a cigarette with a red line through it is universally recognizable as a "No Smoking" sign. Like all traffic and other public information signs, it communicates an instruction clearly and without words. More complex ideas can be communicated non-verbally using internationally recognized symbol systems such as musical and mathematical notation.

PUBLIC INFORMATION SIGNS

Designed for maximum visual impact, traffic and public information signs use simple, unambiguous images and an almost subliminal system of shape and color to convey warnings, instructions, and directions.

Warning: diamond with yellow background (here, road narrows)

Warning: triangle with red edge (here, pedestrian crossing)

Prohibitory: circle with red edge (here, no motor vehicles)

Mandatory: circle with blue background (here, ahead only)

Informative: quadrangular (here, restaurant)

Safety information: green quadrangle (here, first aid)

HAZCHEM WARNING SIGNS

HAZCHEM is an acronym for HAZardous CHEMicals. All road and rail vehicles transporting such substances must carry a warning sign identifying the chemical and providing information for emergency services dealing with any incident.

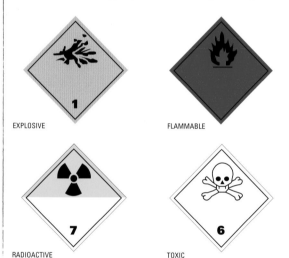

EXPLOSIVE

FLAMMABLE

RADIOACTIVE

TOXIC

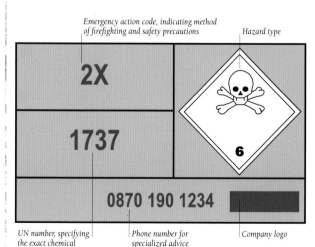

Emergency action code, indicating method of firefighting and safety precautions

Hazard type

UN number, specifying the exact chemical

Phone number for specialized advice

Company logo

WEATHER SYMBOLS

Television weather symbols are self-explanatory (*see bottom of page*). But the World Meteorological Organization has devised a more complex system. This uses symbols for rain, snow, drizzle, and so on, arranged in various permutations to represent the intensity of each type of precipitation.

INTERMITTENT LIGHT RAIN

CONTINUOUS LIGHT RAIN

INTERMITTENT MODERATE RAIN

CONTINUOUS MODERATE RAIN

CONTINUOUS HEAVY RAIN

LIGHT RAIN SHOWER

MODERATE RAIN SHOWER

HEAVY RAIN SHOWER

SNOW

DRIZZLE

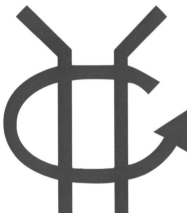

TORNADO

FREEZING RAIN

FREEZING DRIZZLE

THUNDERSTORM

FOG

STATIONARY FRONT

HAZE

COLD FRONT

OCCLUDED FRONT

WARM FRONT

SUNNY

SUNNY INTERVALS

LIGHT RAIN

HEAVY SNOW

THUNDERY SHOWERS

HAIL SHOWERS

PACKING

The packaging of easily damaged goods and freight is labeled with symbols that can be recognized worldwide.

FRAGILE

KEEP DRY

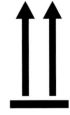

THIS END UP

SEE ALSO
Head trophies *pp.110–11*
Shapes *pp.284–89*

MATHEMATICAL SYMBOLS

Mathematical symbols have evolved over centuries. The signs "+" and "-" first appeared in a 15th-century book by German mathematician Johannes Widman; "=" and "√" appeared in the 16th century, and "x" and "÷" in the 17th.

PLUS

MINUS

MULTIPLY

DIVIDE

EQUALS

DOES NOT EQUAL

IS APPROXIMATELY EQUAL TO

GREATER THAN

GREATER THAN OR EQUAL TO

LESS THAN

LESS THAN OR EQUAL TO

SQUARE ROOT

ONE SQUARED

PARALLEL

PERCENTAGE

ONE DEGREE

SUM

PROPORTIONAL TO

INFINITY

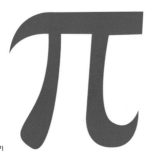
PI

CURRENCY SYMBOLS

These symbols often comprise the initial letter of the currency name, crossed to differentiate it from a standard letter. Exceptions include "£" (from "L," denoting the Latin *libra*) and "$" (possibly from a Spanish coat of arms).

Euro (Europe)

Pound sterling (UK and dependencies; Egypt; Lebanon; Syria)

Dollar (USA; also other countries, preceded by abbreviation of name)

Yen (Japan)

Yuan Renminbi (China)

Rupee (India, Mauritius, Nepal, Sri Lanka)

Pesos (South America)

Rial (Middle East)

Naira (Nigeria)

Ruble (Russia, Belarus)

Kroner (Denmark)

Baht (Thailand)

SPORTS SYMBOLS

As with traffic signs, a clear, simple image says it all in a way that crosses all language barriers. Here are just nine of the many sports played by the iconic figure in black.

BOWLING

GOLF

TENNIS

SWIMMING

WEIGHT LIFTING

SKIING

CYCLING

GYMNASTICS

RUNNING

MUSICAL NOTATION

Pitch is shown by position on the five-line stave (with higher notes on the treble clef and lower on the bass clef). Duration is shown by the appearance of the note or rest. Flats and sharps modify pitch; other symbols indicate volume.

TREBLE CLEF WITH SCALE OF 8 NOTES ON A STAVE

BASS CLEF WITH SCALE OF 8 NOTES ON A STAVE

BREVE

BREVE REST

SEMIBREVE

SEMIBREVE REST

MINIM

MINIM REST

CROTCHET

CROCHET REST

QUAVER

QUAVER REST

BEAMED NOTES

DOTTED NOTE

FLAT

SHARP

DOUBLE FLAT

DOUBLE SHARP

NATURAL

f
FORTE (PLAY LOUDLY)

P
PIANO (PLAY SOFTLY)

ff
FORTISSIMO (VERY LOUD)

CRESCENDO (gradually become louder)

DIMINUENDO (gradually become softer)

EMOTICONS

An emoticon ("emotion" + "icon") is used to convey feeling in a written message. The first symbols were proposed by Scott Fahlman of Carnegie Mellon University in 1982.

:-) OR :)
SMILING

!-(
BLACK EYE

:-{}
BLOWING A KISS

:'(OR :'-(
CRYING

:*)
DRUNK

:-(OR :(
FROWNING/SAD

:-x
KISS

:-D
LAUGHING

:-#
MY LIPS ARE SEALED

@}->--
ROSE

:-/
SCEPTICAL

8-)
SUNGLASSES

;-) OR ;)
WINKING

:-0 OR :0
WOW

SEE ALSO
Picture writing *pp.300–03*

PROFESSIONAL SYMBOLS

Professional and trade symbols fall into three main categories. There are those, ranging from the literal to the lateral, that represent given professions—such as the pretzel for bakers and the caduceus for medicine.

Quality-control symbols indicate that goods meet specified degrees of purity or ethical standards, while marks of compliance indicate that goods meet the safety standards set by the regulating body.

THE PROFESSIONALS

There is no rhyme or reason why some trades and professions are represented by universally recognized symbols and others are not. Here is a selection of some of the symbols that do signify a particular occupation, and the meanings, obscure or otherwise, behind them.

▲ **Red Cross**
A reversal of the Swiss flag, this was adopted in honor of the Swiss founder of the Red Cross to symbolize protection for those engaged in humanitarian work.

▲ **Dentistry**
The triangle and the circle both symbolize health in many cultures. The icon at the center is the staff of Asclepius, the Greek god of healing (Aesculapius to the Romans).

▲ **Barber**
The white spiral represents bandages wrapped round the pole that patients gripped in the days when barbers practiced bloodletting. Bowls for leeches and blood are also represented.

▲ **Pharmacy**
A symbol for pharmacists is the stylized R, the instruction doctors write on a prescription. It is an abbreviation of the Latin *recipe*.

▲ **Legal profession**
Scales symbolizing justice feature in Ancient Egyptian, Greek, Roman, Christian, and Islamic thought. The scales weigh up both evidence and good deeds against bad.

▲ **Medical profession**
On the caduceus—the mythical wand with which the Greek god Hermes (Mercury to the Romans) bestowed sleep—the twin snakes coiled round the rod symbolize healing and poison, as well as illness and health.

▲ **Bakery**
The use of a pretzel as a literal symbol of a bakery originated in Austria and Germany, and has since spread throughout Europe and the US.

▲ **Pawnbroker**
One of several theories about this symbol is that pawnbrokers adopted three golden globes because the chances were two to one that pawned items would be redeemed.

QUALITY CONTROL

Stamping symbols on precious metals as proof of their purity began in the 14th century. In Britain the symbols became known as hallmarks, because the testing was done at Goldsmiths' Hall. Since then the use of symbols to indicate quality has spread to products as varied as leather and eggs.

Platinum: At least 95%

Mark issued by the London assay office

Sterling silver: at least 92.5%, stamped in Lisbon

Silver: French, marked in year 1797

Platinum: stamped at Dublin assay office

International wool secretariat: 100% new wool

Real leather

Sterling silver: at least 92.5%, made in Finland

Silver: stamped at Dublin assay office

Silver: Britannia standard, at least 95.8%

Pure cotton

Goods produced by organic farming

British egg information service logo

Silver: at least 83%, made in Sweden

Silver: 90%, stamped in Italy

Gold: stamped at Dublin assay office

Meets soil association standards of organic farming

Organic produce

Meets ethical trading standards of fairtrade foundation

Swedish state control mark

Sterling silver: at least 92.5%

Gold: 18 carat, at least 75%, made in Lisbon

STANDARDS COMPLIANCE

Many countries have standards associations that set and measure standards of quality, safety, security, environmental impact, and other factors relating to goods and services. Products and services meeting those standards have the right to display the symbol of the appropriate association.

Australian Standards Association

British Standards Institution

Council of the European Union

Dansk Elmateriel Kontrol (Denmark)

Canadian Standards Association

China Compulsory Certification Scheme

SEE ALSO
Snakes pp.66–67
Human body pp.112–15
Shapes pp.284–89

BRANDS & LOGOS

The origins of brand logos date back thousands of years. The Ancient Egyptians, Greeks, Romans, and Chinese all stamped goods such as pottery or bricks with symbols to indicate who had made them; and in Europe the medieval trade guilds extended the practice. In the 19th century, trademarks began to be seen not merely as marks of origin but as badges or signatures. This gave rise to the modern conception that brands reflect the "personality" of products and services or their producers.

Oxfam

▲ **Oxfam International**
The name is a contraction of Oxford Committee for Famine Relief, which was founded in 1942 to provide relief for Nazi-occupied Greece. The logo comprises the letters "O" and "X," stylized to represent a head and shoulders.

▲ **WWF**
The World Wildlife Fund was launched in the UK in 1961, when London Zoo's giant panda, Chi Chi, was world famous. Co-founder Sir Peter Scott designed the original logo, which capitalizes on the panda's cuddly appeal.

▲ **CND**
The Campaign for Nuclear Disarmament logo made its debut in 1958, on the first Aldermaston peace march. The circle symbolizes life, while the lines represent the arm position for signalling "ND" (nuclear disarmament) in semaphore.

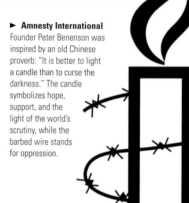

► **Amnesty International**
Founder Peter Benenson was inspired by an old Chinese proverb: "It is better to light a candle than to curse the darkness." The candle symbolizes hope, support, and the light of the world's scrutiny, while the barbed wire stands for oppression.

◄ **European Union**
The official description states: "Against the blue sky of the Western world, the stars represent the peoples of Europe in a circle, a symbol of unity. Their number shall be invariably set at twelve, the symbol of completeness and perfection."

► **Interpol**
The globe symbolizes this police organization's worldwide reach, with olive branches representing peace, a sword for action, and scales for justice. "OIPC" and "ICPO" stand for International Criminal Police Organization in English and French.

◄ **Olympic rings**
The rings symbolize the union in sports of Africa, America, Asia, Europe, and Oceania. The colors (including the white field) symbolize competing nations, being the colors appearing on their national flags in 1913 when the rings were conceived.

▲ United Nations
The UN logo symbolizes the world united in peace. Rendered in the official UN colors, the polar projection of the globe shows much of the world's landmass. The globe is enclosed by olive branches, a universal symbol of peace.

▲ World Health Organization
The WHO logo comprises that of the UN overlaid with the staff of Asclepius, the Greek god of medicine and healing. Asclepius was often depicted holding his physician's staff with a snake entwined round it.

▲ FedEx
The positive-reverse arrow embedded between the "E" and the "X" symbolizes the speed and precision of Federal Express. Remarkable for the designer's restraint in concealing the arrow, the FedEx symbol was ranked as one of the top eight logos in recent design history.

▲ Guinness
The harp was an important part of Celtic culture, and the harp of High King Brian Boru has been a symbol of Ireland since the 13th century. Guinness adopted it in 1862. The orientation of the image is the reverse of that on the national coat of arms.

◄ Microsoft Windows
Windows is so-called because it provides graphic "environments" (windows), which users navigate using a mouse—a revolutionary concept when it was launched in the 1980s. The symbolism is literal, the logo being a stylized window with four colored panes.

▲ BMW
This logo commemorates BMW's origins as an aeronautical engine manufacturer. The checkered roundel is taken from the flag of Bavaria (home of BMW), and represents a white aircraft propeller against a blue sky.

▲ Mercedes Benz
The three-pointed star symbolizes inventor Gottlieb Daimler's dream of building motor vehicles for land, air, and sea. Daimler cars were marketed as Mercedes—the name of a board member's daughter. The star was retained after the Daimler company merged with Benz in 1926.

▲ Ferrari
The black stallion was chosen in honor of Italian WWI flying ace Francesco Baracca, who used it on his plane, and as a good luck symbol intended to guide Ferrari drivers to victory. Yellow is the color of Modena, where Ferraris are built.

▲ Peugeot
The lion, from the coat of arms of Franche-Comté, was first used in 1847 to mark saw blades made by the Peugeot family's hardware business. It symbolized strength, flexibility, and speed of cut.

▲ Citroën
As with Peugeot, Citroën's logo dates back to earlier business. In 1913, André Citroën began manufacturing gearwheels. He pioneered a double-helical design, symbolized by the double chevron.

SEE ALSO
Mammals *pp.52–55*
The home *pp.238–41*
Musical instruments *pp.274–75*
Shapes *pp.284–89*

BRANDS & LOGOS

317

HERALDIC EMBLEMS

One of the most complex and richly resonant uses of symbols is in coats of arms, which originated with those worn by medieval knights for identification in battle. The main element of a coat of arms is the escutcheon, or shield, which is decorated with various colors, shapes ("ordinaries"), and emblems ("charges"). Because creation of coats of arms was regulated by the king's heralds, the art became known as heraldry.

COLORS AND ORDINARIES

The escutcheon (shield) may be divided by "ordinaries." These are often in symbolic colors such as sable (black: prudence; grief), argent (white/silver: innocence; peace), azure (blue: fidelity), gules (red: fortitude), vert (green: love; hope; joy), or (gold/yellow: faith; glory), and purple (royalty; justice).

▲ **Bend**
Often said to represent a baldric (soldier's shoulder sash) or a scaling ladder. When reversed it is known as a bend sinister.

▲ **Chevron**
Symbolizes protection. Variations include chevron couped (not touching the sides of the escutcheon) and chevron in chief (touching the top).

▲ **Cross**
Heraldry recognizes more than a hundred types of cross. A Christian symbol derived from the crucifix and adopted during the Crusades, it is one of the oldest ordinaries.

▲ **Fesse**
Some heralds trace the origin of the fesse to the military girdle; less romantic ones think it simply reflects the physical structure of early shields.

▲ **Pale**
Said to derive from the wooden "pales" used to make palisades, this ordinary symbolizes martial strength and fortitude.

▲ **Pile**
Often said to represent a stake used in the building of a military bridge, the pile (like the fesse, above) may simply reflect the structure of early shields.

▲ **Roundel**
A circular "subordinary" (a symbol considered less important than an ordinary or an "honorable ordinary") symbolizing trustworthiness.

COMMON CHARGES

▲ **Antelope**
The antelope, or agacella, symbolizes a person who is slow to anger but fierce when provoked. It also represents sacrifice and guardianship.

▲ **Leopard**
In heraldry "leopard" and "lion" can mean the same animal. Both symbolize courage, and are common on royal coats of arms.

▲ **Pelican**
Often shown tearing her breast to feed her young on her blood, the pelican symbolizes charity and self-sacrifice.

▲ **Greyhound**
Dogs symbolize faithfulness and loyalty. The greyhound specifically is an emblem of swiftness and nobility.

▲ **Stag**
This symbolizes peace and harmony. In the case of the Hertford coat of arms, the presence of a hart is a visual pun (known in heraldry as "canting").

▲ **Red hand**
This symbol of Ulster is used by barons. It comes from a myth about a king who seized Ulster with his severed hand.

▲ **Anchor**
A Christian emblem of hope, the anchor also symbolizes steadfastness and security. It often appears in the coats of arms of maritime institutions.

▲ **Hunting horn**
The bugle-horn (see above) and the hunting horn represent nobility, hunting being considered a noble pastime.

▲ **Saddle**
Symbol of horsemanship (and thus readiness to serve one's country), the saddle is more literally the emblem of the Company of Saddlers.

▲ **Wheel**
Most commonly seen as the wheel upon which St. Catherine was martyred (see above) or carriage wheels, this emblem represents fortune.

ANIMAL ATTITUDES

▲ Couchant
A beast lying down with its head erect.

▲ Dormant
A beast lying down with its head resting on its forepaws.

▲ Displayed
A bird (usually an eagle) facing the observer with its wings and talons outstretched and head to one side. A displayed eagle appears on the US presidential seal.

▲ Gardant
A beast with its face turned to the observer, to symbolize prudence. This lion sejant gardant (seated and looking, see sejant below), represents prudence and wisdom.

▲ Hauriant
A fish or aquatic mammal (sea mammals were once considered to be fish) shown upright on its tail. Often represented for literal rather than symbolic reasons.

▲ Naiant
A fish, aquatic mammal, or aquatic bird shown swimming. Fish were often chosen as visual puns, for instance, lucie for the Lucy family, eel for Ellis, chub for Chobbe.

▲ Passant
A predator walking with its far forepaw raised and looking ahead (see also trippant, below). This attitude symbolizes resolve.

▲ Passant gardant
A predator walking while looking directly at the observer, symbolizing resolve combined with prudence.

▲ Passant regardant
A predator walking while looking backward over its shoulder, symbolizing resolve and circumspection.

▲ Rampant
A predator rearing on its hind legs while looking ahead. This attitude symbolizes magnanimity.

▲ Rampant gardant
A predator rearing on its hind legs while looking at the observer. It symbolizes magnanimity and prudence.

▲ Rampant regardant
A predator rearing on its hind legs while looking backward over its shoulder, symbolizing magnanimity and circumspection.

▲ Saliant
A beast, such as a lion or a wolf, shown leaping or springing, an attitude symbolizing valor.

▲ Sejant
A beast shown seated, symbolizing justice, wisdom, and good counsel. Two beasts sitting back to back are termed sejant addorsed.

▲ Statant
A beast (or a bird such as a stork or heron) standing still with all four (or both) feet touching the ground. In the case of beasts, the attitude symbolizes readiness for battle.

▲ Trippant
A beast of the chase (such as a stag or deer) shown running, with its far foot raised. The same position as passant, which is applied only to beasts of prey.

▲ Volant
A flying bird, which symbolizes nobility acquired through merit. The attitude also represents readiness for action.

CADENCY MARKS

To differentiate between two or more sons entitled to bear the family arms, the system of cadency marks evolved, with different symbols for each son. Sons of sons added a mark to a mark: for example, the fifth son of a third son would add an annulet to a mullet.

FIRST SON: LABEL OF THREE POINTS

SECOND SON: CRESCENT

THIRD SON: MULLET

FOURTH SON: MARTLET

FIFTH SON: ANNULET

SIXTH SON: FLEUR DE LYS

SEVENTH SON: ROSE

EIGHTH SON: CROSS MOLINE

NINTH SON: OCTOFOIL

SEE ALSO
Mammals *pp.52–55*
Birds *pp.58–61*
Aquatic creatures
   pp.68–71
Christianity *pp.176–79*

HERALDIC EMBLEMS

C⊕ATS ⊕F ARMS

A full coat of arms comprises an escutcheon (decorated shield) together with a helmet, crest, mantling (drapery), and supporters (figures on either side of the shield). Often, but not always, there is a motto. Originally, heraldic emblems were embroidered on the surcoats knights wore to protect their armor from dirt and the heat of the Sun. The heraldic system, dating from the 12th century, is no longer restricted to the aristocracy, and is now used to create coats of arms for institutions, cities, and nations.

Helmet *Crest*

Mantling

Escutcheon

▲ **Arundel**
The UK borough's coat of arms shows three stylized swallows, known in heraldry as martlets. This is a visual pun, common in heraldry—the French for swallow is *hirondelle*, which sounds similar to Arundel.

White rose of Yorkshire

Miner's lamp

▲ **Castleford**
The town is represented by a castle on a ford. Its Roman origins are seen in the crest—a Roman eagle, which wears a miner's lamp symbolizing the local coal industry.

Crest granted by Elizabeth I. The lion wears a crown and holds a Tudor rose

Supporter

▲ **Oxford**
The escutcheon depicts the city's origin as a ford used by oxen. The supporters represent two members of Elizabeth I's court: the black elephant of Sir Francis Knollys and the green beaver of Henry Norreys.

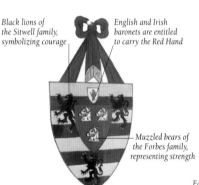

Black lions of the Sitwell family, symbolizing courage

English and Irish baronets are entitled to carry the Red Hand

Muzzled bears of the Forbes family, representing strength

▲ **Sitwell**
The main escutcheon is the original Sitwell coat of arms, while the smaller one is the Forbes coat of arms. Having no brothers, Lady Sitwell (née Forbes) is entitled to use it and Lord Sitwell chose to incorporate it in his own.

Crozier and mitre of the Bishops of Urgell

Three red pales for the Counts of Foix

VIRTVE VNITA FORTIOR

Four pallets for Aragon

Two cows for Foix-Béarn

▲ **Andorra**
The arms represent various co-princes of Andorra: a mitre (for the Bishop of Urgell); three pales (for the Count of Foix); four pallets (for the Crown of Aragon); and two cows (for the House of Foix-Béarn).

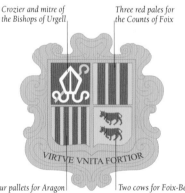

Olive branch supporter

Dominican banners hanging from spears

DIOS PATRIA LIBERTAD

REPUBLICA DOMINICANA

Palm branch supporter

▲ **Dominican Republic**
The red and blue quarters of the escutcheon reflect the national flag. The cross at the centre symbolizes the national religion. A Bible lies open at John 8:32: "And the truth shall set you free."

Picks symbolize the mining industry

ONE ZAMBIA ONE NATION

◄ **Zambia**
The wavy lines symbolize the white water of the Victoria Falls. The crest, a golden eagle, represents liberty and hope for the future. The supporters are the nation's people.

Corn, representing the country's agriculture

◄ **Ecuador**
The arms depict Mount Chimborazo and the Guayas River, a boat (trade), and the Sun (pre-Colombian traditions). The crest is a condor, for power and courage, while the palm and laurel leaves symbolize peace and dignity.

▲ Sorbonne
The seal reflects the Sorbonne's ecclesiastic origins. In medieval times, *universitatis* also meant "guild," so the motto says:"Guild of masters and scholars of Paris."

▲ Sydney University
The open book, symbolizing knowledge, also represents Oxford university, while the royal lion represents Cambridge. The four stars stand for the Southern Cross, a constellation of the southern hemisphere.

▲ Heidelberg University
As with the Sorbonne, the seal reflects the university's medieval architecture and ecclesiastic origins. Originally known as Ruprecht Karls University, Heidelberg is Germany's oldest educational institution.

▲ Cambridge University
Granted in 1573, the arms include a cross (Christianity), four lions passant gardant (resolve and prudence), and a book (knowledge).

▲ Harvard
The escutcheon—in the university's crimson color—shows three open books symbolizing knowledge, their pages spelling out the Latin *veritas* (truth).

⊕RIENTAL BADGES ⊕F H⊕N⊕UR

Japan is the only nation outside Europe to have a traditional system of symbolic crests similar to that of heraldry. Like heraldry, the Japanese system of *mon* ("emblems") originated with medieval aristocracy and the emblems were often worn in battle for identification. *Mon*, which are usually circular, may represent insects, plants, celestial bodies, or objects such as arrows and gongs. Symbolic patterns, including circular badges, were also once used on traditional Chinese court dress to denote rank.

CANOPY

RADISH

FLOWERING TREE: CREST OF AN EMPRESS

PARASOLS

GONG

SEE ALSO
Mammals *pp.52–55*
Birds *pp.58–61*
Plants *pp.80–81*
Flowers *pp.82–85*
Christianity *pp.176–79*

HERALDIC EMBLEMS

321

THE PRINCE ⊕F WALES'S C⊕AT ⊕F ARᴍS

The design of the Prince of Wales's coat of arms dates from the reign of Queen Victoria, but the various elements represent centuries of history. The Prince's sons, Princes William and Harry, were given their own coats of arms on their 18th birthdays. In both of these, the main elements derive from the Royal Arms; additionally, the arms carry emblems of the Spencers, family of the princes' mother, the late Diana, Princess of Wales, as well as cadency marks to distinguish the two sons.

1. & 2. Supporters
The supporters of the shield are a lion (courage) and a unicorn (virtue). Both carry white labels around their necks to show that the arms belong to the eldest son of the Sovereign.

3. Escutcheon
The shield's quarters depict the royal emblems of the United Kingdom: the gold lions represent the sovereigns of England; the red lion belongs to Scotland; and the harp is for Ireland.

4. Prince's badge
The three ostrich feathers are the badge of the Heir Apparent. They are encircled by a jeweled coronet, below which is the Prince of Wales's motto, *Ich dien* ("I serve").

5. Welsh dragon
Opposite the Prince's feathers is the badge of the red dragon, a symbol of Wales.

6. Royal helm
Immediately above the shield is the Royal helm. The Royal family's gold and ermine mantling is draped on either side.

7. Royal crest
Surmounting the coat of arms is a gold lion. It stands on a large coronet, while around its neck it wears the coronet of the Prince of Wales and, again, a white label.

8. Duchy of Cornwall
The Prince of Wales is also the Duke of Cornwall, and the smaller shield depicts 15 bezants (gold coins), the arms of the Duchy of Cornwall. The coins represent the ransom money raised to free a Duke of Cornwall imprisoned during the Crusades.

Prince William's coat of arms
A white cadency mark, a label of three points, shows that the arms belong to a first son. The red escallop derives from the Spencers. Such shells were originally a symbol of pilgrimage.

Prince Harry's coat of arms
The cadency mark is a label of five points, which is used by all grandchildren of a sovereign except the eldest male heir. Prince Harry's arms bear three escallops from the Spencers.

FLAGS

Flags are powerful emblems of identification, and can be symbols either of allegiance or oppression. A flag may be both a rallying point for supporters of a nation or cause, and a target for those who oppose what it signifies. Originally used to identify military units on the battlefield, flags are now most commonly used as symbols of state. The flags of all 194 internationally recognized nation states appear on the next six pages.

AFRICA

MOROCCO

ALGERIA

TUNISIA

LIBYA

EGYPT

SUDAN

ERITREA

DJIBOUTI

SOMALIA

UGANDA

KENYA

RWANDA

CHAD

MAURITANIA

MALI

SENEGAL

BURUNDI

CENTRAL AFRICAN REPUBLIC

DEMOCRATIC REPUBLIC OF CONGO

NIGER

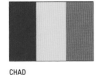

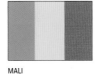

CHAD

MAURITANIA

MALI

SENEGAL

THE GAMBIA

CAPE VERDE

GUINEA-BISSAU

GUINEA

▼ Ethiopia

Green, yellow, and red have been Ethiopia's colors since the repulsion of Italian colonists in 1896. Interpretations of the symbolism vary, but generally red is held to represent the blood that was shed in the struggle for independence, yellow is held to symbolize peace, and green the fertility of the land. These "pan-African colors" have also been adopted by other African nations emulating Ethiopa's independence. The pentagram, derived from the Seal of Solomon, symbolizes hope for the future, while the rays emanating from it symbolize peace and unity for Ethiopia's various ethnic groups.

Green for fertility

The pentagram symbolizes hope, peace, and unity

Red for bloodshed

Yellow for peace

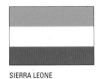

SIERRA LEONE

LIBERIA

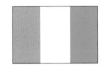

IVORY COAST

BURKINA FASO

COLOMBIA

VENEZUELA

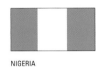

BENIN

NIGERIA

CAMEROON

EQUATORIAL GUINEA

GUYANA

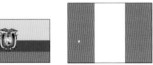

SURINAME

REPUBLIC OF THE CONGO

ANGOLA

ZAMBIA

TANZANIA

ECUADOR

PERU

MOZAMBIQUE

NAMIBIA

BOTSWANA

LESOTHO

BRAZIL

CHILE

SEYCHELLES

COMOROS

MADAGASCAR

MAURITIUS

BOLIVIA

PARAGUAY

GHANA

TOGO

SÃO TOMÉ AND PRINCIPE

GABON

URUGUAY

ARGENTINA

MALAWI

ZIMBABWE

SWAZILAND

SOUTH AFRICA

SEE ALSO
Colors pp.280–83
Shapes pp.284–89

FLAGS

325

CANADA

MEXICO

GUATEMALA

BELIZE

ICELAND

NORWAY

EL SALVADOR

HONDURAS

NICARAGUA

COSTA RICA

DENMARK

SWEDEN

▼ United States

The first US flag (raised in 1776) had 13 stripes, representing the union of 13 rebel colonies, with the British flag in the top corner. The first Stars and Stripes was introduced the following year, when the British flag was replaced by a circle of 13 white stars on a blue background. Since then there have been 26 variations, the first being in 1794 when two more stars and two more stripes were included after the admission of Vermont and Kentucky to the Union. In 1818 it was decided that the number of stripes would revert to 13 (symbolizing the original states) and that stars would be added only for new states.

PANAMA

JAMAICA

FINLAND

⚙

ESTONIA

50 stars representing the current 50 states *13 stripes symbolizing the original 13 states*

CUBA

THE BAHAMAS

LATVIA

LITHUANIA

HAITI

DOMINICAN REPUBLIC

POLAND

GERMANY

ST. KITTS AND NEVIS

ANTIGUA AND BARBUDA

DOMINICA

ST. LUCIA

BELGIUM

IRELAND

ST. VINCENT AND THE GRENADINES

BARBADOS

GRENADA

TRINIDAD AND TOBAGO

FRANCE

LUXEMBOURG

MONACO

ANDORRA

PORTUGAL

SPAIN

ITALY

MALTA

VATICAN CITY

SAN MARINO

SWITZERLAND

LIECHTENSTEIN

AUSTRIA

HUNGARY

CZECH REPUBLIC

SLOVAKIA

SLOVENIA

CROATIA

BOSNIA AND HERZEGOVINA

MONTENEGRO

SERBIA

ALBANIA

MACEDONIA

BULGARIA

GREECE

ROMANIA

MOLDOVA

BELARUS

UKRAINE

RUSSIAN FEDERATION

▼ The Netherlands

Officially adopted in 1572, during the Eighty Years' War against Spanish rule, the Dutch flag is the world's oldest tricolor. It was based on the colors of the then ruling Prince of Orange, whose flag was an orange, white, and blue tricolor known as the "Prince's Flag." For some reason lost to history—perhaps for greater clarity, or because orange dye faded to red – this later mutated into the current red, white, and blue tricolor. In 1972 the Dutch commemorated the 400th anniversary of the new flag with a special postage stamp. Dutch settlers ensured that the original Prince's Flag survived until 1994 in the flag of South Africa, known as the "Prinsenvlag."

The oldest tricolor. The simple, bold idea of using three bands of color has since been adopted by more than fifty nations.

▼ United Kingdom

Popularly called the Union Jack, the flag of the UK is officially known as the Union Flag. It symbolizes the union of the crowns of England, Scotland, and Ireland. In 1603 King James VI of Scotland became King James I of England, and three years later the English and Scottish flags were merged into a new British flag combining the red cross of St. George on a white field (England) and the white saltire of St. Andrew on a blue field (Scotland). On January 1, 1801, after the Act of Union with Ireland, the red saltire of St. Patrick was added to complete the current flag. The Union Flag is a component of the flags of Australia, New Zealand, Fiji, and Tuvalu.

St. George's Cross (England)   *St. Patrick's Saltire (Ireland)*

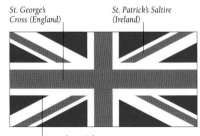

St. Andrew's Saltire (Scotland)

SEE ALSO
Colors pp.280–83
Shapes pp.284–89

FLAGS

327

AUSTRALIA

VANUATU

AZERBAIJAN

ARMENIA

TURKEY

GEORGIA

FIJI

PAPUA NEW GUINEA

LEBANON

SYRIA

CYPRUS

ISRAEL

SOLOMON ISLANDS

PALAU

JORDAN

SAUDI ARABIA

YEMEN

OMAN

MICRONESIA

MARSHALL ISLANDS

UNITED ARAB EMIRATES

QATAR

▼ **Nepal**

Nepal has the only national flag that is neither square nor rectangular. The double triangle combines two pennants from rival Nepalese rulers. The blue border symbolizes peace and harmony, while the crimson field represents bravery. The crescent Moon represents the Royal House, while the Sun is the symbol of the Rana family of Nepal. Interpretations of these symbols vary, but include the hope that Nepal lasts as long as they remain in the sky.

NAURU

KIRIBATI

BAHRAIN

KUWAIT

For centuries a red pennant has been a Hindu symbol of victory.

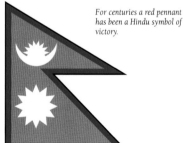

TUVALU

SAMOA

IRAQ

IRAN

TONGA

NEW ZEALAND

TURKMENISTAN

UZBEKISTAN

KAZAKHSTAN

MONGOLIA

KYRGYZSTAN

TAJIKISTAN

AFGHANISTAN

PAKISTAN

BHUTAN

INDIA

MALDIVES

SRI LANKA

BANGLADESH

BURMA

THAILAND

LAOS

CAMBODIA

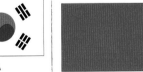

VIETNAM

MALAYSIA

INDONESIA

EAST TIMOR

SINGAPORE

BRUNEI

PHILIPPINES

TAIWAN

CHINA

NORTH KOREA

SOUTH KOREA

JAPAN

⊕THER FLAGS

▲ **White flag**
An internationally
recognized symbol
of truce, ceasefire, or
surrender. Protection for
the bearer is enshrined in
the Geneva Convention.

▲ **Green flag**
"Go"—this flag is used
on roads, railroads, and in
other situations to signal
that all is clear and it is
safe to proceed.

▲ **Blue flag**
Awarded to beaches that meet standards of cleanliness,
safety, services, and environmental management set by
the Foundation for Environmental Education.

▲ **Red flag**
"Stop!"—in most
situations this is
recognized as a sign of
danger and/or as a signal
to stop. The Red Flag is
a symbol of socialism.

▲ **Checkered flag**
Used for over a century
in motor racing to
indicate that the leader
has completed the course,
this flag is now used in
other fields to indicate
successful completion
of a task.

▲ **Buddhist prayer flags**
The five flags represent space (blue), water (white), fire
(red), air (green), and earth (yellow). They embody prayers
carried on the wind to bring luck and promote peace.

SEE ALSO
The Sun *pp.16–17*
The Moon *pp.18–19*
Colors *pp.280–83*
Shapes *pp.284–89*

FLAGS

SIGN LANGUAGES & SIGNALS

Sign languages are distinct from symbolic gestures, although there is some overlap. A gesture can convey a single idea but sign language is a system of gestures and signs that enables users to communicate complex ideas manually rather than verbally. Sign languages for the deaf have been evolving since the 16th century, and there are many other situations where non-verbal communication is desirable or essential.

AMERICAN SIGN LANGUAGE MANUAL ALPHABET

Manual alphabets are a useful starting point for learning a sign language. However, most signing conveys entire words, rather than letter-by-letter spelling—the alphabet is used mainly for proper nouns and specialized or technical terminology.

A

B

C

D

E

F

G

H

I

J

K

L

M

N

O

P

Q

R

S

T

U

V

W

X

Y

Z

SEMAPHORE

Frenchman Claude Chappe invented a semaphore system in 1793, which was later adapted for use with hand flags, as seen here. It was the first system (apart from smoke signals) to enable people to "speak" beyond the range of sound.

"REST" OR "SPACE"

"NUMBERS"

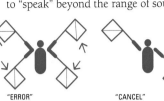

"ERROR"   "CANCEL"

A OR 1

B OR 2

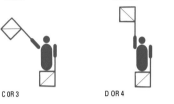

C OR 3   D OR 4   E OR 5   F OR 6

G OR 7   H OR 8   I OR 9   J OR "LETTERS"

K OR ZERO   L   M   N

O   P   Q   R

S   T   U   V

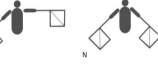

W   X   Y   Z

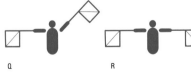
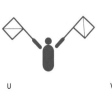

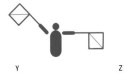
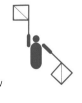

AIRPORT MARSHALLING SIGNALS

The instructions conveyed by these signals are very simple, but vital for organizing pilots and ground crew in an extremely noisy environment. Signalers wear gloves or hold illuminated beacons.

PROCEED   THIS WAY

TURN LEFT   TURN RIGHT

STOP   START ENGINES

INSERT CHOCKS   PULL CHOCKS

CUT ENGINES   SLOW DOWN

SEE ALSO
Alphabets *pp.306–09*
Symbolic gestures *pp.334–37*

SIGN LANGUAGES & SIGNALS

SCUBA DIVING

It is necessary for divers to be able to communicate with their dive buddies underwater. A standard set of signals has evolved to convey vital messages, such as "going up", "going down," or "I've no air left in my tank."

OK/ARE YOU OK?

SOMETHING IS WRONG

UP/LET'S GO UP

DOWN/LET'S GO DOWN

1500 PSI LEFT IN TANK

750 PSI LEFT IN TANK

I AM OUT OF AIR

STOP

SLOW DOWN

STAY/MOVE TOGETHER

STAY AT THIS DEPTH

WATCH/LOOK

I AM COLD

I CAN'T CLEAR MY EARS

FEELING BREATHLESS: 1

FEELING BREATHLESS: 2

CRICKET UMPIRE'S SIGNALS

BYE

WIDE

DEAD BALL

LAST HOUR

OUT!

NO BALL

SIX

LEG BYE

FOUR

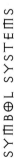

AMERICAN FOOTBALL

TIME OUT

TOUCHDOWN

PERSONAL FOUL

OFFSIDE

HOLDING

ILLEGAL MOTION

FIRST DOWN

PASS INTERFERENCE

PENALTY REFUSED

ASSOCIATION FOOTBALL

DIRECT FREE KICK

INDIRECT FREE KICK

RED CARD SENDING OFF

YELLOW CARD CAUTION

ADVANTAGE

SEE ALSO
Hands & feet *pp.116–19*
Symbolic gestures
pp.334–37

SYMBOLIC GESTURES

The saying "actions speak louder than words" is often true of gestures—although, like words, gestures can be misinterpreted. Conscious gestures such as hand signals often transcend language barriers but sometimes mean different things in different cultures. Subconscious gestures can reveal what a person is really thinking, but the interpretation of body language is less precise and always depends on context.

CONSCIOUS GESTURES

Head and hand signals are useful for reinforcing or replacing the spoken word. But beware—even the most innocent of signals may mean different things to different people. What may seem perfectly friendly to one person may cause deep offense to another.

▲ Wink
A wink can mean any number of things, from an innocent greeting to a sexual suggestion, or from a hint or warning to a signal of collusion between two people.

▲ Raised eyes
Eyes raised upward, often accompanied by an audible "tut," is a common sign expressing condescension, boredom, or exasperation.

▲ Raised eyebrow
Raising one eyebrow is a sign of scepticism or disbelief. In this gesture conflicting thoughts are signaled by the two sides of the face being at odds.

▲ Nod
In most western cultures a nod means "yes" but in some countries, including Sri Lanka, it means "no." It is also often used as a gesture of recognition or greeting.

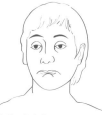

▲ Head-shake
In most cultures this means "no," but in India and Pakistan a front-facing "wobble" from side to side means "yes." In North Africa the shake is a single sharp turn to one side and back.

▲ Protruding tongue
Children the world over stick out their tongues as a rude but relatively playful gesture. This is commonly the first insult that they learn to use.

▲ Cheek kiss
In western cultures a kiss on the cheek is a greeting or farewell gesture between friends. In France most people kiss both cheeks; in Belgium they kiss one cheek, then the other, then the first again.

▲ Hand kiss
A gesture of respect and courtesy, this was once *de rigueur* for a gentleman greeting a lady. It is now rare other than in highly formal situations or when performed with a sense of irony.

▲ Foot kiss
A gesture of humility and respect, this is referred to in various books of the Judeo-Christian Bible, and is performed by the Pope during Holy Week.

▲ Blown kiss
Blowing a kiss is a gesture used to symbolize a kiss from a distance, sometimes instead of a wave to a departing friend, lover, child, or parent.

▲ Bow
In western cultures this often implies a "lesser" person showing humility in front of a "greater" (such as commoners to royalty). In Japan two equals meeting often bow to one another as a sign of mutual respect.

▲ Wave
Often used as a farewell gesture, the wave is also used as a greeting or simply to attract attention. In China a wave with the palm facing downward means "come here."

▲ High five
A gesture of greeting, celebration, or mutual congratulation, often used when a team scores in a sports event.

▲ Handshake
In western culture the handshake is a relatively formal gesture implying mutual respect. It is commonly used on meeting, parting, or reaching an agreement.

▲ Hands up
A gesture of surrender, the raised arms show that the person is not carrying or about to reach for a weapon.

▲ Praying hands
The Christian attitude of prayer is used as a symbol of greeting and respect in India and Southeast Asia, and in the West as a secular gesture of pleading.

▲ Pleading hands
In the West this is a more emphatic gesture of pleading than the praying hands gesture.

▲ Finger on lips
An almost universal gesture symbolizing sealed lips and used as a request for silence. Often accompanied by an audible "shhh!"

▲ Finger to brow
Often done with the finger tapping the brow or circling alongside it, this indicates craziness; that a person is "cuckoo" or has "a loose screw."

▲ Finger to eye
In Saudi Arabia this gesture indicates a person's stupidity, meaning: "I can see clearly that you are a fool.'

◄ Cocking a snook
A jocular or playful gesture of mockery, on a par with sticking out one's tongue.

▲ Teeth flick
This is a common gesture of insult in Mediterranean countries. It precipitates a fight in Shakespeare's *Romeo and Juliet*, in which one of the Capulet servants "bites his thumb" at a Montague servant.

▲ Thinking
Often adopted when a person is deep in thought, this gesture is a modified form of "praying hands," with the fingers touching the lips or chin.

▲ Crossed fingers
This widespread gesture, indicating that a person is wishing for good luck, symbolizes the sign of the Christian cross.

▲ Thumbs up
A sign of approval in the West, it derives from a gesture used to express audience opinion at Roman gladiatorial games. In the Middle East, West Africa, South America, and Russia it is used as an insult.

▲ V for victory
This gesture was popularized in World War II by Winston Churchill as a sign for victory. During the 1960s hippies adopted it as a gesture of peace.

▲ Horns
Often used as a sign of protection against evil or bad luck, or to ward off the evil eye, this gesture is used by Satanists to indicate the Devil.

▲ Query
In Italy a gesture of fingers and thumb together with the hand twitching up and down means: "What do you want?" or "What do you mean?"

▲ OK
In the US and Europe this gesture means "OK," and in Japan it is the symbol for money, but in other countries it can be offensive: in Germany and Brazil it is a vulgar anatomical reference.

SEE ALSO
Hands & feet pp.116–19
Christianity pp.176–79
Sign language & signals pp.330–31

▲ Horns (variation)
In Mediterranean countries this gesture represents the horns of a cuckold; in Japan it has the related meaning of an angry or jealous woman.

▲ "The finger"
Also known as the middle finger salute and flipping the bird, this is an offensive gesture meaning "screw you." The Romans called the gesture *digitus impudicus.*

▲ "The Vs"
In the UK, and in Australia (where it is known as "the forks"), a V-sign with the knuckles outward (the reverse of the victory sign) means "piss off." In the US it is synonymous with the Victory/Peace sign.

▲ Index finger
In western cultures this usually signifies the number one, although it is sometimes used as an imperative "wait." In the Middle East, Turkey, and Greece it has the same meaning as the middle finger does elsewhere: "screw you."

▲ Clinton thumb
Popularized by President Bill Clinton, who may have adopted it from John F. Kennedy, this gesture is used to provide emphasis without pointing a forefinger, which can be interpreted as over-assertive or aggressive.

▲ Time out
In the US this gesture means "time out" in most sports, with the notable exception of basketball, in which it is the signal for a technical foul. In Britain it symbolizes "tea break," and in Japan it means "check, please.'

▲ Beckon
A widespread gesture meaning "come here." Often used in a superior or impolite way, it could also be a sexual invitation, depending on facial expression and circumstance.

▲ Vulcan salute
Used in the TV series *Star Trek* by Mr. Spock, a member of the fictional species of pointy-eared Vulcans, this gesture means "Live long and prosper." It originates in a Jewish gesture of benediction.

▲ Fig
To the Romans this was a good luck gesture, and in some countries it is still used for luck. In Turkey, Indonesia, and Russia it is an obscene gesture meaning "screw you." In the Indian subcontinent it is used as a threat.

▲ Point
This is a universal means of indicating a particular object or direction. In most cultures it is considered rude to point directly at a person—when indicating a person it is more polite to use an open hand.

▲ Bang bang
Depending on context this gesture, miming a pistol shot, can be a playful greeting or a menacing threat. Aimed at one's own temple, it is used to acknowledge an error or indicate the wish to escape from a boring situation.

▲ Blah blah
This sign, which mimics lips moving excessively, is a contemptuous gesture meaning "boring" or "I'm not listening." Also used by referees in some sports to signal that a player is guilty of dissent.

▲ Clenched fist
A universal gesture of aggression when held in front of the body. A clenched fist held high is often used by nationalist, revolutionary, and oppressed groups to indicate defiance, and it is also a military signal requesting heavy weapons.

BODY LANGUAGE

In general, body language is something that people give out and respond to subliminally, although people who understand the signs may use them consciously to reinforce their verbal communication. Posture, orientation, disposition, eye movement, and other factors can reveal a great deal about a person's true feelings and attitudes, even though he or she may not be aware of sending out signals. Body language is often associated with flirting and sexual relationships, but it can also play an important role in interviews and business relationships.

▲ Eye contact
Too much eye contact can appear rude, over-familiar, or aggressive; too little can indicate a lack of interest. Little or no eye contact shows that a person is either very shy or being deliberately deceptive.

▲ Distance
Standing or sitting too far away appears "stand-offish," while standing too close appears pushy, or just plain rude. Distance doesn't have to remain constant—there are moments when it makes sense to lean closer momentarily or to move closer and stay closer.

▲ Orientation
Legs crossed away from a person (as the woman is doing here) or body turned away indicates defensiveness or lack of interest, and vice versa. Gestures with the palms up or outward, as the man is doing, are open and friendly.

▲ Standing up with hands on hips
Hands on hips indicate openness and confidence. Keeping one's head upright, rather than tilted to one side, gives an air of confidence and authority.

▲ Standing up, arms folded, and slouching
Shoulders slouched, arms folded or hugging the body, head tilted, and eyes looking down all indicate nervousness or defensiveness.

▲ Standing with arms close to body
Standing with the arms held close to the sides or behind the back indicates that a person is quietly confident and ready to take what comes.

▲ Sitting with ankle resting on opposite knee
Sitting with one ankle resting on the opposite knee is known as the "figure four." This is often seen as a defensive posture, though here, with the relaxed attitude and open arms, it is probably more about comfort.

▲ Closed leg postures
Generally speaking, sitting or standing with the limbs open implies openness, and having them folded or closed implies defensiveness. However, in the case of short skirts the closed posture is simply a question of decency.

SEE ALSO
Hands & feet *pp.116–19*
Sign language & signals *pp.330–33*

GLOSSARY

A

Allah
The Arabic word for God.

Amulet
This small talisman symbolizes beneficent power; it is traditionally worn for protection and strength.

Ankh
A cross that is shaped like a "T" with a loop at the top, this Ancient Egyptian symbol, meaning "eternal life," is often worn around the neck.

Apostle
A missionary or disciple of the early Christian Church.

Asana
The four poses in which the Buddha appears—seated, standing, walking, or reclining—are referred to as asanas.

Ascetic
This religious devotee renounces material comforts in favor of austere self-discipline.

Assyria
An ancient nation and empire, Assyria covered the northern half of Mesopotamia, now part of Iraq.

Auspicious symbol
In Buddhism there are eight auspicious symbols that each signify some aspect of the Buddha's teaching.

Avatar
This Sanskrit word, meaning "descent," refers to an earthly incarnation of a Hindu deity.

B

Babylonia
The ancient kingdom of Babylonia was in Mesopotamia, set between the Tigris and Euphrates rivers, now Iraq.

Bar/Bat Mitzvah
At 13, a Jewish boy is considered an adult, responsible for his moral and religious duties and is called a Bar Mitzvah, as is the ceremony that initiates and recognizes him as such. Bat Mitzvah is the female equivalent.

Black magic
This is practiced for evil purposes, often in league with evil spirits.

Blaze
This refers to the description of a coat of arms in heraldic terms.

Bodhi tree
In Buddhism this is a fig tree under which the Buddha sat when he attained Enlightenment.

Bodhisattva
A bodhisattva is one destined to attain Buddhahood, who serves as a guide to others on the path to enlightenment.

Brahma
A Hindu creator god, Brahma was a member of the triad, known as the Trimurti, that also included the gods Vishnu and Shiva.

Braille
A system of writing and printing for the blind or visually impaired, it comprises raised dots representing letters and numerals that are identified by touch.

Buddha
An enlightened, omniscient being, Buddha may refer to either the historical, mortal Buddha, Gautama Sakyamuni, or abstract manifestations of the supreme Buddha nature.

Byzantine world
A reference to the Byzantine Empire and its distinctive architecture, art, and culture, which gradually emerged from the Roman Empire after 330CE when the capital of the empire was moved from Rome to Byzantium, now Istanbul.

C

Cadency mark
A heraldic system evolved to differentiate between sons who were also entitled to bear the family arms; each one had his own mark, and sons of sons added their own mark.

Caduceus
In Greek mythology this was a winged rod entwined with two snakes carried by, among others, the god, Hermes; it was later used as a physicians' symbol.

Carnality
A word describing physical, especially sexual, desires.

Chakra
According to yoga philosophy, the body has seven "chakras," or centers of spiritual energy, relating to our physical, mental, and emotional states.

Charge
This is a heraldic image, such as an animal, object, or shape on a shield.

Christ's Passion
The Passion of Christ represents the suffering of Jesus at the Crucifixion.

Chthonic god
This is a god who is of, or relates to, the underworld.

Comet
A celestial body traditionally seen as inauspicious, a comet symbolizes the coming of war or some other calamity.

Cornucopia
A cone-shaped receptacle overflowing with fruit, flowers, and grain, a cornucopia symbolizes prosperity. It is associated with Greek mythology.

Cosmic ocean
This represents the primordial waters from which all life emerged.

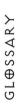

Culture hero
A superhuman, human, or animal figure that is admired or revered, a culture hero is one who has benefited an entire culture through a heroic or compassionate deed; some are traditionally called upon for protection or guidance.

Danse macabre
In this medieval "dance of death," a skeleton symbolizing death leads a procession to the grave.

Darshan
This is a Hindu term meaning "a viewing," especially of a sacred image or holy person.

Dharma Wheel
An important symbol of the Buddha's teachings that is also known as the Wheel of Law.

Dharmachakra mudra
This Buddhist hand gesture signifies the Wheel of Law being set in motion, as the Buddha gave his first sermon after attaining Enlightenment.

Diwali
The Hindu festival of lights, Diwali marks the beginning of winter.

Druid
An Ancient Celtic priest, diviner, magician, and/or teacher.

Dynasty
This represents a succession of rulers from the same family or line.

Emoticon
This symbol uses punctuation marks to convey feelings in a written message.

Enlightenment
In Buddhism and Hinduism enlightenment is a blessed state in which an individual rises above desire and suffering and attains Nirvana.

Ermine
Associated with royalty, white ermine fur is used to trim royal robes; the animals' black tail-tips are incorporated at regular intervals, accenting the white.

Evil eye
Some cultures believe that certain people can curse victims by looking at them. People often wear amulets to avert the effects of the evil eye.

Expressionism
This early 20th-century art movement set out to portray the artist's often intense inner emotions; reality is distorted, color is typically intense, and brushwork is loose, as in the work of Edvard Munch.

Feng Shui
This Ancient Chinese practice of positioning objects or orientating buildings, is based on a belief that a good flow of "chi," or energy, promotes harmony, prosperity, and health.

Five Pillars of Islam
These represent the five duties incumbent on every Muslim: the profession of faith in one God and in Mohammad as his Prophet, praying five times a day, fasting during the month of Ramadan, giving alms, and making *hajj* or pilgrimage to Mecca.

Four elements
In alchemy the four elements (fire, earth, air, and water) are represented by equilateral triangles.

Fraternity
A fraternity represents a group of men who have come together for a common purpose or interest, as in Freemasonry.

Freudian
This describes specific attitudes, beliefs, or behavior that relate or subscribe to the psychoanalytic theories of Sigmund Freud.

Futurism
Originating in Italy in the early 20th century, this art movement set out to express the dynamism of contemporary life, especially in its mechanization.

Granthi
This literally translates as "the keeper and the reader of the Sikh scripture."

Grimoire of Honorius
A manual for black magic, this can be used for invoking demons and spirits.

Grim Reaper
This mythological figure is a personification of death, and is portrayed as a skeleton carrying a scythe, and wearing a black gown, robe, or hooded cape.

Gunpowder Plot
This foiled attempt by English Catholics in 1605 to blow up the Houses of Parliament, is commemorated annually on November 5 in the UK.

Gurdwara
A Sikh temple, the gurdwara is the focal point of religious life for Sikhs and a symbol of worship.

Guru
A term meaning "spiritual teacher," used in Sikhism, Tibetan Buddhism, and Hinduism.

Hazchem
This is an acronym for "Hazardous Chemicals."

Henna
A reddish-brown dye obtained from the leaves of *Lawsonia inermis*, it is used as a body adornment and hair dye and symbolizes good luck on festive occasions such as weddings.

Heptagram
A seven-pointed star believed to have magical properties, this has various associations, ranging from Kabbalah to a symbol for warding off evil.

Heretical
This describes beliefs or behavior that go against established doctrine.

Hexagram
The geometric symmetry of this six-pointed star made it a popular spiritual or magical symbol in many cultures.

Hieroglyph

A character in any of a number of pictorial writing systems; the best known system and one of the oldest is that of Ancient Egypt.

Hobo

A drifter or migrant worker who moves aimlessly from place to place, a hobo has no permanent home or job.

Homonym

A homonym is a word that sounds or looks like a word with another meaning; for example, the word for four in China and Japan also sounds like their word for "death," so it is considered to be unlucky.

I Ching

An Ancient Chinese system of divination based on a book of Taoist philosophy, *I Ching* is expressed in hexagrams chosen at random and then interpreted to answer specific questions and offer guidance. There are 64 hexagrams in total, each composed of two groups of three lines that may be broken or solid.

Iconography

This is the art or representation by pictures or images of a chosen subject; Christian iconography ranges from representations of angels to saints.

Incarnation

This refers to the bodily manifestation of a divine being, an idea common in religions, such as Buddhism and Hinduism.

Inuit

An indigenous word meaning "the people," Inuit is the collective name for a widely scattered group of people living in the Canadian Arctic and Greenland.

Jungian

A devotee of the psychological doctrines of Swiss psychologist and psychiatrist, C.G. Jung, Jungian theory stresses the contribution of cultural and racial inheritance to an individual's psychology, and maintains that there are two basic types of people, introverts and extroverts.

Ka'ba

Islam's most sacred shrine, the Ka'ba, is in the Holy Mosque in Mecca.

Kabuki

A highly stylized, traditional Japanese drama, *kabuki* evolved from Noh theater, in which elaborately costumed male performers play both the male and female roles.

Kachina

The Native American Hopi believe in supernatural beings called Kachinas—rain-bringers and spiritual messengers that also intercede in village life and

mete out punishment. Kachina dolls, called *tithu*, are given to girls and brides on dance days to teach them about the different Hopi Kachinas.

Kami

These are nature spirits that are worshiped in Shintoism.

Labyrinth

A complicated arrangement or structure of interconnecting paths, passageways, or tunnels, also known as a maze, in which it is easy to become confused and lost.

Libation vessel

This is a drinking vessel that is traditionally horn or cup shaped.

Linga

Also called lingam, a linga is a stylized phallus worshiped by Hindus as a symbol of the god Shiva.

Logo

This is a symbol, name, or trademark designed for easy and immediate recognition.

Lutheran

Of or relating to the Protestant movement based on the principles of the German reformer Martin Luther (1483–1546). Lutheran theology was founded in Germany at the start of the Reformation in the 16th century and had as its original goal the reformation of the western Catholic church.

Magic Square

This is a square containing numbers that are arranged in equal rows and columns, such that the sum of each row, column, and sometimes diagonal is the same. Found in many cultures, engraved on metal or stone, or worn as talismans, they are believed to have divinatory and astrological qualities associated with longevity and good health.

Mandala

A symbolic design representing the Universe, the mandala is used in Buddhism and Hinduism as a meditation tool.

Mandorla

This almond-shaped halo surrounds the entire body and signifies holiness or the Holy Spirit. In art it often surrounds the image of Christ or the Virgin Mary.

Mantra

Traditionally, a mantra is a sacred word or phrase repeated in prayer, meditation, or incantation associated with Hinduism and Buddhism.

Martyr

A martyr is an individual who dies for his or her religious principles.

Medieval times

Also known as the Middle Ages, this period of European history is often dated from 479 to 1453CE.

Meditation

This is the practice of focusing on something specific, such as an object, sound, or visualization, to heighten

awareness of the moment, reduce stress, and enhance spiritual growth. It features in many eastern religions.

Meso-America
This describes the geographical and cultural area of Central America that spreads from Mexico to El Salvador.

Mesopotamia
This region between the Tigris and Euphrates rivers is now known as Iraq.

Milky Way
Illuminating the night sky, this galaxy includes the Sun and the Solar system.

Ming Dynasty
This Chinese imperial dynasty lasted from 1368 to 1644ce.

Mon
This traditional Japanese system of symbolic emblems is similar to the western system of heraldry.

Monarchy
This term refers to a state ruled or headed by a monarch (a king or queen).

Monotheistic faith
Based on the belief in one god, such faiths include Christianity and Islam.

Morse
This is a telegraph code in which numbers and letters are represented by strings of dots and dashes.

Mother Goddess
Found in many cultures, the idea of the Mother Goddess goes back to earliest times in which a nurturing female deity represented the Earth, and was associated with creation and fertility.

Mudra
In Buddhism a mudra is any one of a series of ritualistic hand gestures, each with its own specific meaning. Mudras are also used in Hindu iconography.

Mughal Empire
Flourished in India from 1526 to 1857, the Mughal Empire spawned a characteristic Indo-Islamic-Persian style of art and architecture.

Mummification
This is the process of preserving a dead body and wrapping it according to Ancient Egyptian practices. The viscera and brain were removed and preserved in special funerary jars; the body was then dried out with sodium carbonate before being wrapped in bandages.

Mysticism
This philosophy is based on the belief that absolute knowledge of God or the spiritual truth can be reached through spiritual intuition that is believed to transcend ordinary sensory experiences or understanding.

Myth
A traditional story, a myth usually involves gods and heroes and typically sets out to explain the origins of a cultural practice or natural phenomena.

N

Nirvana
The ultimate state of Buddhist bliss and freedom from the cycle of birth, rebirth, and union with the universal, it is only attainable after all attachment and desire has been extinguished.

Noble Eightfold Path
According to Buddhist belief, this pathway to enlightenment involves eight factors, such as right thought, right action, and right livelihood.

Omen
This is a phenomenon or prophetic sign believed to herald good or evil.

Ordinary
In heraldry an ordinary is a basic shape on a shield design, such as a bar.

Original Sin
In Christian doctrine Original Sin is the condition of sin into which every human is born, as a result of Adam and Eve eating the forbidden fruit.

Orthodox Church
A community of Christian Churches that has its roots in the Byzantine Empire and acknowledges the honorary primacy of the Patriarch of Constantinople, rather than the Pope.

P

Pagan god
Any god who is not associated with Christianity, Judaism, or Islam, is viewed by followers of these religions as a pagan god.

Passover
This Jewish festival commemorates the deliverance of the Jews from Egypt.

Pentagram
A five-pointed star, the pentagram has magical associations and was symbolically important in Ancient Greece and Babylonia. In Christianity it represents the five wounds of Christ.

Petroglyph
This is an image carved into rock, and is associated with prehistoric art.

Pictogram
A form of visual language, pictograms use symbols or images to convey information, such as the hieroglyphs on an Ancient Egyptian tomb, or male and female figures on a door to represent a public lavatory.

Pictograph
This is an image drawn or painted on to a rock face.

Portent
Another word for an omen, this is a sign or happening that is interpreted as symbolic of a significant event to come.

Primordial waters/ocean
The primordial waters are the waters from which all life emerged, and refer to the time before creation, when the cosmos was a place of chaos.

Psychic powers
This refers to the ability to use extra-sensory perception to see things that are hidden from the senses (including the past and future); such powers were traditionally used by witches and seers.

Psychopomp
A psychopomp is a guide of souls to the underworld, such as Charon or Hermes.

Ptolemaic universe
The model for the Universe according to the Ancient Greek astronomer, Ptolemy, in which the Earth took center-stage and the Sun, the Moon, planets, and stars revolved around it.

Pythagoras
A Greek philosopher considered to be the first true mathematician, Pythagoras (c580–500bce) theorized that numbers contained the essence of all natural things.

R

Reincarnation
In Asian religions reincarnation is the rebirth of the soul in another body.

Renaissance
A revival of the Classical arts, the Renaissance began in Italy in the 14th century and spread throughout Europe until the end of the 16th century.

River Styx
In Greek mythology the River Styx was a river in Hades across which the dead were ferried to the underworld.

Rudra/Shiva
Meaning "howler," Rudra is the malignant Vedic god of storms and winds. As Hindu beliefs developed, Rudra's name changed to Shiva.

Rune
Used in divination, runes are an ancient set of symbols with their origins in the alphabets of Ancient Germanic tribes.

S

Sadhu
In Hinduism a sadhu is a wandering holy man who has renounced the material comforts and earthly pleasures of the world.

Saint
In Christianity a saint is someone who has been officially recognized by the Church, especially through canonization, as being entitled to public worship, and capable of intervening for people on Earth.

Samsara
In Hindu and Buddhist tradition samsara represents the endless cycle of birth and rebirth dictated by karma (an individual's destiny as determined by their conduct during life). Release from samsara only comes with the attainment of true knowledge.

Samurai
This is the Japanese military feudal aristocracy or a professional warrior belonging to this class.

Sarcophagus
A term describing a stone coffin, a sarcophagus is located above ground and is often elaborately decorated.

Satyr
In Greek mythology a satyr is a woodland deity with the head and trunk of a man, and the pointed ears, horns, and hind legs of a goat. Satyrs have a tendency for lechery and revelry.

Seal of Solomon
Depending on context, the Seal of Solomon is either a six-pointed star, or hexagram, believed to possess magical powers; a Jewish symbol called the "Star of David"; or any one of 25 species of flowering plants from the genus *Polygonatum*.

Sefirotic tree
In Kabbalah, the Sefirotic Tree of Life comprises ten primal numbers and 22 paths representing the forces behind creation. These numbers are shown as circles called Sefirot, which make up a tree form. The Sefirotic Tree is also associated with Tarot cards.

Semaphore
This is a visual system for signaling information using two flags, one in each hand; it employs an alphabetic code based on the position of the signaler's arms.

Semi-god
Part-human, part-god, a semi-god is sometimes also a heroic figure, such as Hercules in Greek mythology.

Shaman
A priest within certain tribal societies, a shaman acts as a medium between the human and spirit worlds, and practises magic for healing or divination purposes, or to control natural events. Both men and women can be shamans.

Shapeshifter
In mythology or fiction, a shapeshifter is someone or something that can change from one form into another; a well-known example is that of a human changing into a werewolf.

Shou
The Taoist character for longevity, *Shou* is often depicted as a circular symbol. In China it is sometimes paired with other symbols of long life.

Socialist Realism
A style of art, literature, and music, established in the Soviet Union in the 1930s, Socialist Realism sought to promote the development of Socialism, and typically portrayed workers and other members of a Communist society in a heroic or idealized manner.

Spirit helper
A spirit acting as an ally or servant of a shaman, a spirit helper is subservient to, rather than the protector or teacher of, the person it assists.

Stupa
Originally an ancient burial mound, a stupa is a dome-shaped monument. After the Buddha's death stupas were erected to house his relics. Important stupas became places of pilgrimage, around which worshipers walk in a clockwise direction.

Sufism
A mystical Islamic movement, Sufism seeks the Truth—divine love and knowledge through the direct experience of God.

Surrealism
A 20th-century art movement that aimed to express the workings of the subconscious mind, Surrealism is typically characterized by dream-like imagery and the unexpected juxtaposition of subject matter. Salvador Dalí was a Surrealist artist.

T

Tabla
This small hand drum originated in northern India.

T'ai Chi circle
This double spiral is a symbol of life and represents the relationship between Yin and Yang, the interdependent elements of Taoist philosophy that combine to create a balanced whole.

Tarot
A means of divination using Tarot cards, these comprise a set of 78 playing cards, including 22 cards portraying vices, virtues, and elemental forces.

Tefillin
One of the two small leather cases containing texts from the Hebrew Scriptures that are traditionally worn by Jewish men during morning prayer.

The Dreaming
In Australian Aboriginal tradition, The Dreaming refers to either the time of creation, or to an individual or group's set of beliefs or spirituality.

The Great Departure
In Buddhism this is the journey made by Prince Siddartha, the future Buddha, when he renounced his princely life in the palace for the life of a wandering ascetic. Buddhist boys entering the monkhood re-enact this scene.

Totem
An animal, plant, or natural object—or a representation of one—a totem is an emblem of a tribe, clan, or family; it is sometimes worshiped as an ancestor, guardian, or creator figure.

Tree of Knowledge
This is the biblical Tree of Knowledge of good and evil in the Garden of Eden; its forbidden fruit was eaten by Adam and Eve, resulting in their Fall from Grace and exile from Eden.

Tree of Life
The mythical Tree of Life grew in Paradise and its fruit, if consumed, bestowed immortality.

Tricolor
A tricolor is a flag comprising three parallel stripes in different colors; these may be vertical, horizontal, diagonal, and of equal or unequal width, and be either defaced (as in bearing an emblem or device) or plain.

Trigram
A figure made up of three solid or broken parallel lines, a trigram is typically used in Chinese philosophy or divination according to the *I Ching*.

Trimurti
Hindus worship the Trimurti, or triad, of the gods Brahma, Vishnu, and Shiva.

Trinity
In Christianity the Holy Trinity symbolizes the Father, the Son, and the Holy Spirit.

Udjat
Depicted as a forward-facing human right eye and eyebrow, the udjat was worn as an amulet. It is also known as the wadjet or the Eye of Horus.

Ushnisha
A sign of the Buddhahood, the ushnisha is usually a knot of hair, a flame-like element, or a bump on the top of the Buddha's head.

Vahana
Hindu gods are portrayed mounted on an animal or bird *vahana*, which represents a specific function associated with the god; for example, Shiva rides a bull, symbolizing strength and potency.

Vanitas
A type of symbol-laden, somber still-life painting, popular in Flanders and the Netherlands in the 16th and 17th centuries, vanitas art serves as a reminder of the brevity of life, the futility of pleasure, and the inevitability of death. Common vanitas symbols include hourglasses and rotten fruit.

Varna
In Hinduism it is any of the four classes that make up the caste system in India.

Veda
A Veda is any of the most ancient and authoritative Hindu sacred texts gathered into four collections.

Vedic
This refers to anything belonging to or relating to the Veda or Vedas (*see above*), the type of Sanskrit in which they are composed, or the Hindu culture from which they came.

Vever
In voodoo each vever is a symbolic design of a specific spirit. It is made on the ground by sprinkling powder, such as cornmeal, prior to or during a ceremony. It serves as a focal point for invocation and as an altar for offerings.

Yang
According to Ancient Chinese philosophy, Yang is one part of two complementary forces or principles that underlie and control all nature. It is masculine and positive.

Yantra
Derived from a Sanskrit word meaning "to sustain," a yantra is a geometric design traditionally used by Hindus to focus on as an aid to concentration during meditation.

Yin
In Ancient Chinese philosophy, Yin is passive, moist, and feminine; it is the opposite of Yang.

Yuga
A yuga is one of the four ages of the Hindu world cycle.

Zen
A school of Mahayana Buddhism that originated in China, Zen Buddhism maintains that enlightenment can be attained only through meditation and the development of mental and spiritual discipline, rather than through worship. It is practiced mainly in China, Japan, Korea, and Vietnam.

Zohar
This Jewish Kabbalistic book is traditionally attributed to Rabbi Simon ben Yochi in the first century CE.

Zoroastrian
A member of a religion founded in Persia by Zoroaster around the early second millennium BCE; modern-day devotees include the Parsees of India.

FURTHER READING

Ayto, J. (ed.) (2007). *Brewer's Dictionary of Phrase and Fable.* Orion: London.

Bacquart, J.B. (1998). *The Tribal Arts of Africa.* Thames & Hudson: New York.

Barbier, J.-P. & Newton, D. (1988). *Islands and Ancestors: Indigenous Styles of Southeast Asia.* Metropolitan Museum: New York.

Baring, A. & Cashform J. (1991). *The Myth of the Goddess. Evolution of an Image.* Penguin: London.

Bechert, H. & Gombridge, R. (1984). *The World of Buddhism.* Thames & Hudson: London.

Becket, Sister W. (1994). *The Story of Painting.* Dorling Kindersley: London.

Belcher, S. (2005). *African Myths of Origin.* Penguin Classics: London.

Black, J. & Green, A. (1992). *Gods, Demons and Symbols of Ancient Mesopotamia.* British Museum Publications: London.

Blurton, T.R. (1992). *Hindu Art.* British Museum Publications: London.

Brown, D. (2003). *The Da Vinci Code.* Corgi: London.

Bruce-Mitford, R. (1972). *The Sutton Hoo Ship Burial.* British Museum Publications: London.

Burr, E. (Trans.) (1994). *The Chiron Dictionary of Greek and Roman Mythology.* Chiron Publications: New York.

Campbell, J. (1992). *The Masks of God: Primitive Mythology, vol. 1.* Arcana: New York.

Campbell, J. (1992). *The Masks of God: Oriental Mythology, vol. 2.* Arcana: New York.

Campbell, J. (1992). *The Masks of God: Occidental Mythology, vol. 3.* Arcana: New York.

Campbell, J. (1992). *The Masks of God: Creative Mythology, vol. 4.* Arcana: New York.

Carr-Gomm, E. (2001). *The Secret Language of Art.* Duncan Baird: London.

Caruana, W. (1987). *Aboriginal Art.* Thames & Hudson: London.

Chetwynd, T. (1982). *Dictionary of Symbols.* Harper Collins: London.

Chevalier, J. & Gheerbrant, A. (1996). *The Penguin Dictionary of Symbols.* Penguin: London.

Christie, A. (1968). *Chinese Mythology.* Hamlyn: London.

Cirlot, J.E. (1971). *A Dictionary of Symbols.* English translation. Routledge & Kegan Paul: London.

Cooper, J.C. (1992). *Symbolic and Mythological Animals.* Harper Collins: London.

Cooper, J.C. (1978). *An Illustrated Encyclopaedia of Traditional Symbols.* Thames & Hudson: London.

Cotterell, A. (ed.) (1999). *The Encyclopedia of World Mythology.* The Foundry: London.

Craze, R. (1997). *Practical Feng Shui.* Anness Publishing: London.

Crossley-Holland, K. (1980). *The Norse Myths: Gods of the Vikings.* Harmondsworth: Penguin.

Dallapiccola, A. (2002). *Dictionary of Hindu Lore and Legend.* Thames & Hudson: London.

Eberhard, W. (1986). *A Dictionary of Chinese Symbols.* Routledge & Kegan Paul: London.

Eiseman, F.B. Jr. (1990). *Bali. Sekala & Niskala Vol. 2: Essays on Society, Tradition, and Craft.* Periplus Editions: Singapore.

Epstein, I. (1959). *Judaism.* Penguin: Harmondsworth.

Feest, C. F. (1992). *Native Arts of North America.* Thames & Hudson: London.

Ferber, M. (2007). *A Dictionary of Literary Symbols.* Cambridge University Press: Cambridge.

Ferguson, G. (1961). *Signs and Symbols in Christian Art.* Oxford University Press: New York.

Findlay-Brown, I. (1998). *Visions from Vietnam. Contemporary Vietnamese Art from British Private Collections.* Asia House: London.

Fisher, R. E. (1993). *Buddhist Art and Architecture.* Thames & Hudson: London.

Fontana, D. (1993). *The Secret Language of Symbols.* Pavilion Books: London.

Foster, R. & Tudor-Craig, P. (1986). *The Secret Life of Paintings.* BBC Press: London.

Glassé, C. (2001). *The Concise Encyclopedia of Islam.* Stacey International: London.

Gombrich, E.H. (1989). *The Story of Art.* Oxford University Press: Oxford.

Gombrich, E.H. (1960). *Art and Illusion. A Study in the Psychology of Pictorial Representation.* Phaidon Press: Oxford.

Govinda, Lama A. (1960). *Foundations of Tibetan Mysticism.* Hutchinson Group: London.

Graham-Campbell, J. & Kidd, D. (1980). *The Vikings.* British Museum Publications: London.

Hall, J. (1974). *Dictionary of Subjects and Symbols in Art.* John Murray: London.

Hall, J. (1994). *Illustrated Dictionary of Symbols in Eastern and Western Art.* John Murray: London.

Hall, J. (2003). *The Crystal Bible: A Definitive Guide to Crystals.* Godsfield Press: London.

Herbert, P. (1992). *The Life of the Buddha.* British Library Publications: London.

Honour, H. & Fleming, J. (1982). *A World History of Art.* Fleming-Honour: London.

Hoult, J. (1987). *Dragons: Their History and Symbolism.* Gothic Images Publication: Glastonbury.

Huntington, S.L. (1985). *The Art of Ancient India.* John Weatherhill: New York.

Hutt, M. (1994). *Nepal: A Guide to the Art and Architecture of the Kathmandu Valley.* Kiskadale: Stirling.

Ibbott, S. (1994). *Folklore, Legends and Spells. Rural Traditions in Lore and Legend, Witchcraft and Spells.* Ashgrove Press: Bath.

James, G. (1912, 1996). *Japanese Fairy Tales.* Senate: London.

Jansen, E.R. (1993). *The Book of Hindu Imagery. Gods, Manifestations and their Meaning.* Binkey Kok Publications: Holland.

Jensen, H. (1970). *Sign, Symbol and Script.* George Allen & Unwin: London.

Jones, D.M. & Molyneaux, B.L. (2002). *The Mythology of the Americas. An Illustrated Encyclopedia of the Gods, Spirits and Sacred Places of North America: Mesoamerica and South America.* Anness Publishing: London.

Jordan, M. (1993). *Encyclopedia of Gods: Over 2500 Deities of the World.* Facts on File: New York.

Kana-Devilee, P. & Uterwijk, R. (1996). *A Divine Gesture: A Hundred Characteristics of Hindu and Buddhist Gods in the Rijksmuseum.* Zuidvleugel Rijksmuseum: Amsterdam.

Knappert, J. (1993). *The Encyclopdaedia of Middle Eastern Mythology and Religion.* Element Books: Longmead, Dorset.

Knappert, J. (1992). *Pacific Mythology.* Harper Collins: London.

Lao Tzu, *Tao Te Ching*, translated by D.C. Lao. (1963). Dover Publications: New York.

Little, B. (1999). *The Illustrated Herbal Encyclopedia.* Abbeydale Press: Leicester.

Lundquist, J.M. (1993). *The Temple: Meeting Place of Heaven and Earth.* Thames & Hudson: London.

Marshall Cavendish (1987). *Dreams and Destiny: Telling Fortunes and Reading Dreams.* Marshall Cavendish: London.

McArthur, M. (2002) *Reading Buddhist Art.* Thames and Hudson: London.

McCloud, W.H. (ed.), (1999). *Sikhs and Sikhism.* Oxford University Press: India.

McNeill, D. (1998). *The Face.* Little Brown & Co.: London.

Megaw, R. & V. (1989). *Celtic Art From Its Beginnings to the Book of Kells.* Thames & Hudson. London.

Meyer, A.J.P. (1995). *Oceanic Art.* Kohnemann: Köln, Germany.

Miksic, J. (1990). *Borobudur, Golden Tales of the Buddha.* Periplus Editions: Singapore.

Miller, M.E. (1986). *The Art of Mesoamerica.* Thames & Hudson: London.

Millman, D. (1993). *The Life You Were Born to Lead: A Guide to Finding your Life Purpose.* H.J. Kramer Inc: Tiburon, California.

Moore, A.C. (1995). *Arts in the Religions of the Pacific: Symbols of Life.* Cassell: London.

Murray, P. & L. (1996) *The Oxford Companion to Christian Art and Architecture.* Oxford University Press: Oxford.

Guirand, F. (ed.). (1968). *New Larousse Encyclopedia of Mythology.* Hamlyn: London.

Orliac, C. & Orliac, M. (1995). *The Silent Gods: Mysteries of Easter Island.* Thames & Hudson English edition: London.

Price, S. & Kearns, E. (eds) (2003). *The Oxford Companion to Classical Myth and Religion.* Oxford University Press: Oxford

Radice, B. (ed.) (1975). *Hindu Myths.* Penguin Classics: Harmondsworth.

Rawson, P. & Legeza, L. (1973). *Tao: The Chinese Philosophy of Time and Change.* Thames & Hudson: London.

Rawson, P. *Tantra.* (1973). Thames and Hudson: London.

Rawson, P. (1978). *The Art of Tantra.* Thames & Hudson: London.

Reid, A. (1988). *Southeast Asia in the Age of Commerce 1450–1680. Volume One: The Land Below the Winds.* Yale University Press: Newhaven and London.

Rogers, S. (1983). *Power and Gold: Jewelry from Indonesia, Malaysia and the Philippines from the Collection of the Barbier-Mueller Museum Geneva.* The Barbier-Mueller Museum: Geneva.

Ryken, L., Wilhoit, J., & Longman, T.(eds.). (1998). *Dictionary of Biblical Imagery.* Inter-varsity Press: Westmont, Illinois.

Sharper Knowlson, T. (ed.) (1994). *The Origins of Popular Superstitions and Customs.* Studio Editions: London.

Shepherd, R., Shepherd, R., & Kennedy, R. (2002). *1000 Symbols: What Shapes Mean in Art and Myth.* Thames & Hudson: London

Stutley, M. & Stutley, J. (1977). *A Dictionary of Hinduism. Its Mythology, Folklore and Development 1500 BC–AD 1500.* Routledge & Kegan Paul: London.

Thomas, N. (1995). *Oceanic Art.* Thames & Hudson: London.

Too, L. (1996). *The Complete Illustrated Guide to Feng Shui.* Harper Collins: London.

Tregear, M. (1980). *Chinese Art.* Thames & Hudson: London.

Tresidder, J. (ed.) (2004). *The Complete Dictionary of Symbols in Myth, Art and Literature.* Duncan Baird: London.

Versluis, A. (1994). *Native American Traditions.* Element Books: Shaftesbury.

Walker, B.G. (1988). *The Woman's Dictionary of Symbols and Sacred Objects.* Harper Collins: San Francisco.

Werner, E.T.C. (1994). *Myths and Legends of China.* Dover Publications: New York.

Werness, H.B. (2000). *The Continuum Encyclopedia of Native Art.* Continuum: New York.

Wheatley, D. (1971). *The Devil and All His Works.* Peerage Books: London.

Willett, F. (Revised ed.). (1993). *African Art: An Introduction.* Thames & Hudson: London.

Wittkower, R. (1977). *Allegory and the Migration of Symbols.* Thames & Hudson: New York.

Yong Y. & Cotterell, A. (1975). *The Early Civilization of China.* Weidenfeld & Nicholson: London.

Zaehner, R.C. (ed.) (1967). *The Concise Encyclopedia of Living Faiths.* Beacon Press: Boston.

Zimmer, H. (1946). *Myths and Symbols in Indian Art and Civilization.* Pantheon Books: New York.

INDEX

ACKNOWLEDGMENTS

Dorling Kindersley would like to thank: Ann Baggaley, David Tombesi-Walton, Diane Vowles, and Angela Wilkes for editorial help; Mandy Earey, Peter Laws, Dean Morris, Simon Murrel, and Adam Walker for design help; Caroline Hunt for proofreading; Dorothy Frame for indexing; Richard Attwood and Jo Walton for picture research assistance; Lucy Claxton, Rose Horridge and Emma Shepherd for picture library assistance; Adam Brackenbury and John Goldsmid for creative technical support; and Lee Ellwood, Tim Lane, Megan Jones, Ella Peters, and Sarah Ruddick for modeling.

Miranda Bruce-Mitford would like to thank: Dr. Martha Black, Curator of Ethnology, Royal British Columbia Museum (for totem pole details); Dr. Laurent Dousset, Centre de Recherche et de Documentation sur l'Océanie (for help on The Dreaming painting); Dr. Heather Elgood, Director, Asian Arts Diploma, School of Oriental and African Studies, (for advice on Islam spread); Dr. Elisabeth O' Connell, Department of the Ancient Near East, The British Museum (for information on ancient Near East); Shaukat Dungarwalla (for advice on Islam spread); John Lewis, formerly of the University of London (for help on Freemasonry); and Robert Greenfield, Kate Bevington, and John Cordingley for their encouragement.

PICTURE CREDITS

Dorling Kindersley would like to thank the following for their kind permission to reproduce their photographs:

Key:
(a=above; b=below/bottom; c=center; f=far; l=left; r=right; t=top)

4Corners Images: Borchi Massimo 29c; **akg-images:** Biblioteca Nacional. Madrid 38; British Library 44; Musée Condé 156; DACS London 2008 265br; Erich Lessing 116cl, 116tr, 202, 203c, 218l, 298-299, 299cra; Musée du Louvre/Erich Lessing 67br, 246-247, 247c; Narodni Galerie, Prague/Erich Lessing 29tl; Jean-Louis Nou 39c, 157tc; Staatsbibl. Preuß.Kulturbesitz. 211bc; **Alamy Images:** 257c; Rex Allen 229tc; Allover Photography/Viennaphoto 335cr; Arco Images/Dolder, W. 256bl; ArkReligion.com 184tc, 185tc; Bill Bachmann 226tr; Graham Bell 79bl; Biju 127cr; Peter Bowater 287crb; Celtic Collection - Homer Sykes 295tr; Chris Stock Photography 334br; Ashley Cooper 285tl; Dennis Cox 255cl; Danita Delimont/Cindy Miller Hopkins 285cra; Danita Delimont/Walter Bibikow 314cb; Detail Nottingham 223cra; Leslie Garland Picture Library 79br; Glenn Harper 74tc; Christoph Henning/Das Fotoarchiv/Black Star 125br; Nigel Hicks 227cr; Holmes Garden Photos/Neil Holmes 258bl; Robert Holmes 227bc; imagebroker/Barbara Boensch 222tl; Images Etc Ltd/Tony Craddock 284c; Images&Stories 125tl; Interfoto Pressebildagentur/Alamy 185br; Jon Arnold Images Ltd 107bl; Jon Arnold Images Ltd/Gavin Hellier 228bl; Jupiterimages/Brand X/Steve Allen 232br; Justin Kase zfourz 314br; K-Photos 284br; Kalpana Kartik 254l; Mathew Lodge 285tr; Melvyn Longhurst 258tc; Craig Lovell/Eagle Visions Photography 111tl, 233cr; J Marshall - Tribaleye Images 242crb; Mary Evans Picture Library 20-21, 21cr, 77br, 96, 116c, 223bc, 223tr; Michael Matthews 335tc; Neil McAllister 233tr; Megapress 244br; Stuart Melvin 284bl; Eric Nathan 197br; Dave Pattison 129tl; Pick and Mix Images 289ftr; Pictorial Press Ltd 237c; Helene Rogers 151cr; Paul Rollins 155br; Steve Allen Travel Photography 281fcla; Stocksearch 235tl, 281ca (ribbon); Gary Stone 249tl; Paul Stuart 296tc; Keren Su/China Span 281cb; tompiodesign.com 115bl; V&A Images 160bc; Visual Arts Library (London) 75c, 242bc; Visual Arts Library (London)/French School, (12th century) 287ca; Marcos Welsh 153bl; wsr 126br; **Amnesty International UK:** 316tr; Ancient **Art & Architecture Collection:** 67c; Ronald Sheridan 57br; **Art Resource, NY:** Kimbell Art Museum, Fort Worth, Texas 262r; **The Art Archive:** 273cr; Bodleian Library Oxford 265tl; Culver Pictures 63tc; Musée du Petit Palais Avignon/Gianni Dagli Orti 236; Museo del Templo Mayor Mexico/Gianni Dagli Orti 63br; National Anthropological Museum Mexico/Gianni Dagli Orti 39bl; National Museum of Art Mexico/Gianni Dagli Orti 108tl; Gianni Dagli Orti 97bl; Victoria and Albert Museum London/Eileen Tweedy 162-163, 163cr; **Arundel Town Council:** 320tl; **The Bridgeman Art Library:** Anthony Crane Collection, UK 273c; Bibliotheque des Arts Decoratifs, Paris, France, Archives Charmet 154tc; Bibliotheque Nationale, Cabinet de Medailles, Paris, Archives Charmet 56; Bibliotheque Nationale, Paris, France 208; British Library, London, UK, © British Library Board. All Rights Reserved 263cl; Chandigarh Museum, Chandigarh, Punjab, India, Ann & Bury Peerless Picture Library 285crb; Czartoryski Museum, Cracow, Poland 67tl; The Detroit Institute of Arts, USA, Founders Society purchase with Mr and Mrs Bert L. Smokler 265bl; Dinodia 291tr; Dorset County Museum, UK 99tr; Galleria dell' Accademia, Venice, Italy 112, 113; Guildhall Library, City of London 321bl; Horniman Museum, London, UK, Photo © Heini Schneebeli 186; Kress Collection, Washington D.C., USA 263r; Kunsthistorisches Museum, Vienna, Austria 218bl, 226br, 262cl; Louvre, Paris, France, Giraudon 111c, 133tc; Mauritshuis, The Hague, The Netherlands 46br; Musee Denon, Chalon-sur-Saone, France, Roger-Viollet, Paris 281cla; Musee des Beaux-Arts, Lyon, France, Peter Willi 36br; Musee des Tapisseries, Angers, France, Lauros/Giraudon 296cr; Museo Archeologico Prenestino, Palestrina, Italy, Roger-Viollet, Paris 39br; Museum of Fine Arts, Boston, Massachusetts, USA, Gift by Subscription 66; Museum of Fine Arts, Boston, Massachusetts, USA, Gift in honour of Edward W. Forbes from his friends 107c; Museum of Fine Arts, Boston, Massachusetts, USA, Gift of John Goelet 292, 293; Museum of Fine Arts, Boston, Massachusetts, USA, Otis Norcross Fund 80cl; Museum of Fine Arts, Boston, Massachusetts, USA, Tompkins Collection 262b; Nasjonalgalleriet, Oslo, Norway/DACS London 2008 265tr; National Gallery, London, UK 240, 241c, 241tl, 264tr; National Museum, Bangkok, Thailand 237c; Nationalmuseum, Stockholm, Sweden 142tr; Niedersachsisches Landesmuseum, Hanover, Germany 264bl; Oriental Museum, Durham University, UK 116br; Paris, France, Peter Willi 133br; Private Collection 203cr; Private Collection, © Look and Learn 225cr; Private Collection, © Michael Graham-Stewart 110; Private Collection, © Philip Mould Ltd, London 40tr; Private Collection, Peter Newark American Pictures 155bl; Private Collection, Photo © Boltin Picture Library/The Bridgeman Art Library 45bl; Private Collection, The Stapleton Collection 256cr; Santa Maria della Grazie, Milan, Italy 209bc; Saqqara, Egypt, Giraudon 124; Sarnath Museum, Uttar Pradesh, India 167cl; St. Bavo Cathedral, Ghent, Belgium, Giraudon 62bl, 62c; Stadelsches Kunstinstitut, Frankfurt-am-Main, Germany 245tl; Stourton Contemporary Art, Australia 152; The Trustees of the Chester Beatty Library, Dublin 78; Tokyo National Museum, Japan 91br; Johnny van Haeften Gallery, London, UK 132; Victoria & Albert Museum, London, UK 216cl; Villa dei Misteri, Pompeii, Italy 280br; **The Trustees of the British Museum:** 118-119, 119cr; Gift of Major Robert Grenville Gayer-Anderson 57tl; **China Tourism Photo Library:** 157bl, 219br; **Christie's Images Ltd:** 182-183, 183cr; **Citroen UK Ltd:** 317br; **CND:** 316tc; **Corbis:** Paul A. Souders 253br; 55bl; Theo Allofs/zefa 87tl; Paul Almasy 130ca; James L. Amos 57c; Archivo Iconografico, S.A. 109bl; The Art Archive/Salvador Dali, Gala-Salvador Dali Foundation/Artists Rights Society (ARS), New York 266, 266-267; Mariana Bazo/Reuters 131tc; Bettmann 111br, 221br, 221tc, 273bl; Stefano Bianchetti 273tl; Blue Lantern Studio 272; BOCOG - HANDOUT/epa 45tr; Tibor Bognar 253bl; Christophe Boisvieux 45c, 87c; Burstein Collection 26-27, 27cr; Christie's Images 170cr; Elio Ciol 194tc; Keith Dannemiller 257bl; Jason Hawkes 245cl; Lindsay Hebberd 74bl; Historical Picture Archive 129fcl; Hulton-Deutsch Collection 130tr, 219c, 259bl; Janet Jarman 257bc; Bob Krist 129br; Frans Lanting 30cr; Charles & Josette Lenars 153; Christian Liewig/Liewig Media Sports 258tr; Philippe Lissac/Godong 172tr; Jeffrey Markowitz/Sygma 336cl; Robert Mulder/Godong 125bl; National Gallery Collection; By kind permission of the Trustees of the National Gallery, London 133bl; Kazuyoshi Nomachi 232tl; Lucy Pemoni/Reuters 131tr; Wolfgang Rattay/Reuters 129cla; Michaela Rehle/Reuters 129tc; Michael Reynolds/epa 252; Günter Rossenbach/zefa 94cl; Bob Sacha 129cra; Albrecht G. Schaefer 111bl; Christine Schneider/Zefa 334fbr; Skyscan 284cb; St James's Palace 232tr; Summerfield Press 70-71, 71cr; Swim Ink 259br; Luca I. Tettoni 97tl; Penny Tweedie 125c; Sandro Vannini 304-305, 305cra; Ron Watts 87bl; Werner Forman 166tl; **DK Images:** American Museum of Natural History 154bc, 154bl, 270bl, 271tr; Anthony Barton Collection 275c; Archaeological Receipts Fund (TAP) 188bc; Ashley Leiman 223bl; Ashmolean Museum, Oxford 42tr; Board of Trustees of the Royal Armouries 225br; Bolton Metro Museum 146tl, 148l; British Library 196tr, 301cla; British Museum 295bl, 301cb; The British Library 181c; The British Museum 73bl, 167tr, 180bl, 243bl; The British Museum/Alan Hills 117tc; The British Museum/Alan Hills and Barbara Winter (c) 120br, 129cl; The British Museum/Chas Howson 59cr, 239cl, 261br; The British Museum/Janet Peckam 171c, 188tr; The British Museum/Nick Nicholls 67bl; The British Museum/Peter Hayman 65c, 107tr, 129tr, 138br, 256tr; Chateau de Saumur 294ca; Conaculta-Inah-Mex/The Instituto Nacional De Antropologia E Historia 145cl; Courtesy of Glasgow Museum 173tc; Courtesy of the Central London Ghurdwara 185bl; Courtesy of the Natural History Museum, London 24br; Crafts Museum, New Delhi 159cl, 161tc; Andy Crawford 239c; Danish National Museum/Peter Anderson 178r; Exeter City Museums and Art Gallery, Royal Albert Memorial Museum 196br; Glasgow Museum 146bl, 149c, 181cl; Golders Green United Synagogue, London 173tr; Alan Hills 249cl; Horniman Museum, London 109tc, 270ca; Ellen Howdon/St Mungo, Glasgow Museums 10tl, 75tl; Sean Hunter 283fbl; Jewish Museum, London 172br; Benu Joshi 233cb; Kelvingrove Art Gallery and Museum, Glasgow Museums 192tr; Barnabas Kindersley 160br; Judith Miller/Anastacias Antiques 190tr; Judith Miller/Arthur Millner 159tc; Judith Miller/Lyon and Turnbull Ltd 127cl; Judith Miller/Potteries Specialist Auctions 223tl; Judith Miller/Sloan's 25tr, 76c, 107tl, 164bl; Judith Miller/Gordon Reece Galleries 271tc; Judith Miller/JYP Tribal Art 270br; Musée National du Moyen-Age Thermes de Cluny 76cr; Museo Internazionale delle Marionette Pasqualino, Palermo 46bl; Museum of Mankind/Peter Anderson 235cl; Museum of the Moving Image, London 269c; NASA 33cl; National Maritime Museum, London/James Stevenson 243tl; National Museum, New Delhi 158tr, 160fbr; National Museums of Scotland 76tl; Natural History Museum 121tr; Pitt Rivers Museum, University of Oxford 154clb, 270cra; Powell-Cotton Museum, Kent 167br; Rough Guides 271bl, 282cra, 283cla; Royal Green Jackets Museum, Winchester 289fcla; Royal Museum of Scotland, Edinburgh 57bl; Royal Ontario Museum Toronto/Francesca Yorke 58tl, 140tr; Scott Polar Research Institute, Cambridge 155tr; St Mungo, Glasgow Museums 173r, 181cr; Statens Historiska Museum, Stockholm 47cl; Kim Taylor 58tc; Steve Teague 164bc; The American Museum of Natural History 150bl; University Museum of Archaeology and Anthropology, Cambridge 155tc; **European Parliament Photo Service:** 316cl; **European Space Agency:** 288cla; **Federal Express:** 317tc; **FLPA:** Frans Lanting 91c; **fotolia:** EyeMark 314cr; James Steidl 314cl; **Freemasons' Hall:** 260bl; **Getty Images:** Bridgeman 128bl; Dave Etheridge-Barnes 257tr; Fox Photos 221bl; Keystone Features 258br; MPI 257tl; National Geographic/Martin Gray 232bl; Antonio Scorza/AFP 259tc; Prakash Singh/AFP 129bc; Stone/Cris Haigh 237bl; Stone/Peter Adams 237br; Stone/Siri Stafford 337br; The Image Bank/Romilly Lockyer 252tc; Pierre Verdy/AFP 282tc; **INTERPOL:** 316br; **IOC/Olympic Museum Collections:** 316bl; **iStockphoto.com:** 131cr, 222bc, 233tc; Androsov Konstantin 126tr; Geir-Olav Lyngfjell 302cla; Stephen Turner 127tr; **David King Collection:** 264br; **Lo Scarabeo:** 198-199; **Mary Evans Picture Library:** 33br, 90, 97c, 107br, 114cr, 130cla, 130tc, 223cr, 282br; **Microsoft:** 317cl; **Oxfam:** 316ftl; **Oxford City Council:** 320tr; **PA Photos:** 220; St James's Palace 323br; **Peugeot:** 317crb; **Photolibrary:** 37cl; Robert Harding Picture Library/Luca Tettoni 230-231, 231cr; **PunchStock:** Comstock Images 268br; **Sir Reresby, Renishaw Hall:** 320cl; **Rex Features:** Mark Baynes 259cl; **Photo Scala, Florence:** Photo Ann Ronan/HIP/Scala 79tc; **Roland Smithies:** 169; **Stapleton Collection:** Victoria & Albert Museum, London, UK 92-93; **SuperStock:** Prisma 219tc; **Tate, London:** DACS London 2008 263bl; **TopFoto.co.uk:** 216r; Ann Ronan Picture Library/HIP 309tl; Art Media/HIP 209c; Fastfoto Picture Library 269cl; Fortean 127clb; Marilyn Kingwill/ArenaPal 269crb; John Richard Stephens 187tl; Charles Walker 157br, 174tr, 180tr, 210bl; Colin Willoughby/Arena Images 269bl; World History Archive 108tc; **TRH The Prince of Wales and The Duchess of Cornwall:** 322-323; **Université Paris-Sorbonne:** 321tl; **University of Heidelberg:** 321clb; **University of Sydney:** 321cl; **V&A Images:** 244bl; **Wakefield Council:** 320tc; **Werner Forman Archive:** Art Gallery of New South Wales, Sydney 147tc; The Palace Museum, Peking 29bl; Private Collection, New York 63bl, 153tl; Spink & Son, London 28; **WWF International:** 316tl

All other images © Dorling Kindersley
For further information see: www.dkimages.com